APPLIED EUROPEAN LAW

APPLIED
EUROPEAN LAW

Editors

Dermot Cahill
T P Kennedy
Vincent Power

BLACKSTONE
PRESS LIMITED

Published by
Blackstone Press Limited
Aldine Place
London
W12 8AA
United Kingdom

Sales enquires and orders
Telephone +44-(0)-20-8740-2277
Facsimile +44-(0)-20-8743-2292
e-mail: sales@blackstone.demon.co.uk
website: www.blackstonepress.com

ISBN 1-84174-175-2
© Law Society of Ireland 2000
First published 2000

British Library Cataloguing in Publication Data
A catalogue record for this book is available from the British Library

Typeset in 10/12pt Meridien by Hewer Text Ltd, Edinburgh
Printed and bound in Great Britain by M & A Thomson Litho Ltd, East Kilbride

EDITORS

Dermot Cahill is a lecturer in European Law with University College Dublin. He was formerly a solicitor with McCann FitzGerald, Solicitors. Dermot lecturers in European Law on the Professional Practice Course and is a visiting professor at the De Paul University Law School, Chicago and the University of Paris X. He writes on issues of European Law and has recently written a book *Corporate Finance Law* (Round Hall/Sweet & Maxwell).

T P Kennedy is Director of Education with the Law Society. He was formerly a lecturer in law with the University of Leeds and a solicitor with McCann FitzGerald, Solicitors. T P lectures in Litigation and European and Business Law on the Professional Practice Course and is a guest lecturer in Trinity College, Dublin. He has written extensively on issues of private international law.

Vincent Power is a partner in A & L Goodbody, Solicitors and Director of its Competition Law Unit. He was formerly a lecturer in law with University College Cork and University College Dublin. Vincent lectures in European and Business Law on the Professional Practice Course and is a visiting professor at the Universiteit Nyenrode in the Netherlands. He has written a number of books on EU law and has recently completed *Competition Law in Ireland* (Butterworths).

PREFACE

The aim of this book is to point out the doctrines, principles and case law of the main areas of EU law of relevance to apprentice solicitors. Where appropriate, it sets out how these principles interface with national legal principles and tenets.

The objective was to describe key EU legal regimes, and then consider how they interface in a practical context with the analogous domestic regimes. For example, the EU Merger Regulation is described, as is its interface with the domestic Irish merger regime under the domestic Competition and Mergers Acts.

We hope that this work will be of assistance to those who seek an understanding of EU law, and also to those who wish to take their understanding beyond the merely theoretical level. It will be of interest to all who find EU law touches upon their practice whether in the public or private sector. Students will also find this book gives them an excellent background in the main areas of EU law.

Every effort has been made to ensure that the text is accurate but the authors would be grateful to learn or any errors or omissions. Any comments or queries on this manual should be sent to the general editors at the Law Society.

While the authors are of course responsible for the contents of the book, we would like to thank Bríd Moriarty for her assistance in reading a draft of this book and making some very helpful comments on it.

Finally special thanks to Yvonne, Jeanne, Edwina and Grace (aged 5 ½) for their unfailing encouragement and support.

Dermot Cahill
T P Kennedy
Vincent Power
October 2000

CONTENTS

CONTENTS

Appendices

CONTENTS

TABLE OF LEGISLATION

EU LEGISLATION

NON-EU LEGISLATION

Ireland

ALPHABETICAL LIST OF CASES

ALPHABETICAL LIST OF CASES

ALPHABETICAL LIST OF CASES

ALPHABETICAL LIST OF CASES

ALPHABETICAL LIST OF CASES

NUMERICAL LIST OF CASES

European Court of Justice

NUMERICAL LIST OF CASES

NUMERICAL LIST OF CASES

NUMERICAL LIST OF CASES

CHAPTER 1

INTRODUCTION

This book describes and discusses a selection of issues relating to European Union and competition law. While the book is designed for those entering practice as solicitors in Ireland, it will be of interest to lawyers generally.

The book examines issues from both the practical and academic perspectives because in EU law, perhaps more than in most areas of the law, it is imperative to understand the theoretical and practical aspects because of the way in which the law evolves. This book is not a treatise on EU and competition law generally; instead, it chooses a selection of areas as illustrations for the benefit of training and educating students of law.

There are many misconceptions associated with EU and competition law. This book aims to dispel some of these misconceptions.

First, there is a misconception that EU and competition law are only relevant for solicitors in large city firms. In fact, solicitors around the country need to be interested in EU and competition law because of such issues as milk quotas and the Common Agricultural Policy. Solicitors in all firms need to be aware of the EU law relating to such issues as the protection of individuals, the recognition and enforcement of judgments, consumer protection, competition, employment and so on.

Secondly, there is a perception that EU law is somewhat 'new' to Ireland. In fact, there is over a quarter of a century of practice in Ireland. The Irish courts are well used to dealing with EU cases; there have been several article 234 preliminary references from the Irish courts (including quite a number from the District Court) to the European Court of Justice; Irish lawyers have pleaded cases before the European institutions, and some Irish judges have had experience of sitting as judges in the European courts in Luxembourg.

Thirdly, there is a perception that EU law is fixed and immutable. In fact, it is evolving and developing at lightning pace. There is no doubt that EU law is changing more rapidly than almost any other area of law. This causes difficulties for lawyers who wish to maintain an up to date knowledge of the area. Nonetheless, the increased availability of information on EU law has helped enormously. In particular, solicitors anywhere in Ireland can have ready access to up-to-date information on EU law via the internet.

Fourthly, there is a perception that EU law is only relevant to big corporate clients. Nothing could be further from the truth. Some of the leading EU cases have been instituted or have involved individuals. Airline stewardesses, art teachers, unemployed workers, students and fishermen have, consciously or unconsciously, made enormous contributions to EU law by virtue of complaints made to the European Commission or cases which they have instituted before the Member State courts.

Penultimately, there is a perception that there must be litigation to solve every case and each case has to involve a case going to 'Luxembourg'. First, many cases may be dealt with by way of complaints without the need to litigate and secondly, the Member State courts may apply entire areas of EU law without the need to have proceedings before the European judicial institutions.

Finally, there is a perception that EU law is for 'experts over there in Brussels'. This is not so. Irish lawyers are very good at understanding and applying EU law. They understand the concept of a written constitution (like the EC Treaty). They equally know how to deal with regulatory mazes. This is not an area solely confined to others – Irish solicitors can advise on, and practise, EU law on an equal footing with the best in the world. This book is designed to help them.

CHAPTER 2

ASSERTING EUROPEAN UNION LAW RIGHTS

2.1 European Union Legislation

This chapter briefly examines various kinds of EU legislation, explores in greater depth the circumstances in which such legislation may be relied on in Irish courts and finally looks at one specific directive and its implementation in Ireland as an example of the rules discussed.

2.1.1 THE TREATY

The EC Treaty itself contains many provisions that are of assistance to citizens of the Union. One example of this is art 141, which calls on states to introduce measures to ensure the equal treatment of men and women in the workforce.

The Treaty defines three kinds of legally-binding acts – regulations, directives and decisions. It also includes recommendations and opinions as two non-legally binding acts. This chapter concerns itself primarily with regulations and directives as the legislative measures which are of most relevance to clients generally.

2.1.2 REGULATIONS

Article 249 of the EC Treaty provides that regulations are of general application. They are to take effect in each Member State simultaneously. They set out specific requirements needing no further implementation by Member States. Regulations ensure uniformity of law throughout the EU. The European Court of Justice (the ECJ) has held that Member States do not need to implement regulations. If Member States make any changes in implementation it could endanger the uniformity of EU law.

2.1.3 DIRECTIVES

Directives contain statements of principles and objectives requiring specific implementation measures by Member States. The directive is the legislative instrument most used by the European Commission and Council and is thus of most relevance to clients.

2.1.4 IRISH IMPLEMENTATION OF EC LEGISLATION

Since Ireland joined the EU, legislation from Brussels has had an increasingly significant impact on the Irish legal system. There have been some difficulties with the incorporation of European law into Irish law. EU law is recognised as part of Irish law. Article 29.4.3 was inserted into the Irish Constitution after a referendum in 1972, which authorised Ireland to join the then EEC. The European Communities Act 1972 was also passed to make the EC Treaties part of Irish law. Article 29.4.3 of the Constitution provides:

> *No provision of this Constitution invalidates laws enacted, acts done or measures adopted by the State which are necessitated by the obligations of membership of the European Union or of the Communities, or prevents laws enacted, acts done or measures adopted by the European Union or by the Communities or by institutions thereof, or by bodies competent under the Treaties establishing the Communities, from having the force of law in the State.*

The effect of this provision is that EU law became part of Irish law. However, the interpretation of this article has given rise to considerable disputes. In *Lawlor v Minister for Agriculture* [1988] ILRM 400, Murphy J held that 'necessitated' included acts consequent upon membership. However, in *Greene v Minister for Agriculture* [1989] 3 CMLR 830 Murphy J held that there are matters 'so far reaching or so detached from the result to be achieved by the directive so as not to be necessitated'.

Section 3(2) of the European Communities (Amendment) Act 1972 allows a Minister to enact Community legislation without the sanction of the Oireachtas. This method of implementation arguably goes beyond art 249 of the Treaty and is thus not 'necessitated' by EU membership. The Supreme Court in *Meagher v Minister for Industry and Commerce* [1994] ILRM 1 held that the timely implementation of directives necessitated the granting to Ministers of these powers. In this case, the Minister had issued regulations in order to implement various directives relating to the use of hormones in livestock. The implementing regulations provided that proceedings could be issued at any time within two years of the commission of an offence under the relevant directives. The High Court initially found that the regulations were unconstitutional, as they were not necessitated by membership. On appeal, the Supreme Court found that this challenged provision was 'necessitated' in order to make prosecutions effective and a certain time period was required to examine specimens under the scheme before summonses could be issued.

2.2 Direct Effect

2.2.1 GENERALLY

Provisions of EU law which give individuals rights or obligations, which may be enforced before their national courts, are termed 'directly effective'. The question of direct effect is of great importance to all Irish lawyers. If a provision of EU law is directly effective, not only must it be applied by Irish courts but it must take priority over any conflicting provisions of Irish law, including the Constitution.

Direct effect may be either vertical or horizontal. 'Vertical direct effect' is where an individual may rely on a provision of EU law to sue the State before his national court. It is known as vertical to reflect the relationship between the State and the individual. Horizontal direct effect is where an individual may rely on a provision of EU law to sue another individual before his national courts.

What provisions of EU law are directly effective? The EC Treaty is silent on this. Article 249 merely provides that regulations are to be binding in their entirety and directly applicable in all Member States. In a series of major decisions, the ECJ has applied the principle of direct effect to Treaty articles, regulations, directives, decisions and even to provisions of international agreements to which the EU is a party. The ECJ has established criteria for invoking direct effect – the provision in question must be clear and precise, unconditional and should not require implementing measures by the State or EU institutions or leave room for the exercise of discretion by the State or EU institutions.

4

2.2.2 TREATY ARTICLES

2.2.2.1 Generally

The question of the direct effect of a Treaty article was first considered by the ECJ in Case 26/62 *Van Gend En Loos v Nederlandse Administratie der Belastingen* [1962] ECR 1. The Dutch Customs Authority transferred a product from one customs class to another. As a result, the product carried a higher import duty than before. Van Gend brought proceedings before the Dutch courts, complaining that the increase in duties was a breach of art 25 (then art 12) of the Treaty. Article 25 requires Member States to refrain from introducing new customs duties between themselves or from increasing existing ones. Van Gend argued that it could benefit from art 25, as this article was directly effective, even though it is addressed to Member States. The Customs Authority argued that art 25 was addressed to States and was intended to govern rights and obligations between States. The Treaty provided enforcement measures at the suit of the Commission or individual States for cases of this nature. Advocate General Roemer suggested that art 25 was too complex for application by national courts and that, if national courts were allowed to apply it, there would be no uniformity of application. The ECJ disagreed, holding that the article was directly effective. The Court said:

> 'The wording of art 12 [now art 25] contains a clear and unconditional prohibition which is not a positive but negative obligation. This obligation, moreover, is not qualified by any reservation on the part of the States that would make its implementation conditional upon a positive legislative measure enacted under national law. The very nature of this prohibition makes it ideally adapted to produce direct effectiveness in the legal relationship between Member States and their subjects.'

Following *Van Gend*, it was thought that only the prohibitions in the Treaty had direct effect. In Case 57/65 *Alfons Lutticke GmbH v Hauptzollamt Saarlouis* [1966] ECR 205, the Court held that this was not the case. It held that art 90(3) (since deleted by the Treaty of Amsterdam), which contained a positive obligation, would become directly effective once the time limit set out in the article expired. Since then a large number of Treaty provisions have been held to have direct effect.

2.2.2.2 Criteria for direct effect

The criteria for a provision to have direct effect may be seen in *Van Gend*. They were more explicitly set out by Advocate General Mayras in Case 2/74 *Reyners v Belgium* [1974] ECR 631, as follows:

- the provision must be clear and unambiguous;

- it must be unconditional; and

- the operation must not be dependent on further action being taken by the EU or national authorities.

The Irish courts have applied these criteria. In *McBride v Galway Corporation* [1998] 1 IR 458, Quirke J looked at the criteria for invoking a directive in a directly effective sense to decide a case. The case concerned an attack by way of judicial review on a proposed location of a sewerage plant for Galway City. The applicant claimed that there had been a failure to comply with the requirements of two directives. Quirke J found that the relevant provisions of the directives were not unconditional and sufficiently precise. Therefore, an individual litigant could not rely upon them before they were transposed into Irish law.

2.2.2.3 Horizontal direct effect of Treaty articles

In *Van Gend* the principle of direct effect operated to confer rights on Van Gend against an organ of the Dutch State. Treaty obligations, even when addressed to States, may fall on individuals also. Can an individual invoke them against another individual? *Van Gend* implies that they can.

Case 43/75 *Defrenne v Sabena (No 2)* [1976] ECR 455 unequivocally established that Treaty articles could have horizontal direct effect. The applicant was a flight attendant employed by Sabena. She brought an action against Sabena based on art 141 of the Treaty. Article 141 provides that:

> *Each Member State shall . . . ensure and subsequently maintain the application of the principle that men and women should receive equal pay for equal work.*

Defrenne claimed that male stewards were being paid more for performing the same tasks as female stewardesses. Sabena argued that Treaty obligations could not be imposed on private persons. The ECJ held that the prohibition on discrimination in art 141 applied to all collective agreements and individual labour contracts. Thus, the ECJ gave direct effect to the article.

The same principle was applied in Case 36/74 *Walrave and Koch v Association Union Cycliste Internationale* [1974] ECR 1405. Motorcyclists who earned their living 'pacing' pedal cyclists sought a declaration that certain rules of the association to which they belonged infringed the Treaty's prohibition on discrimination on grounds of nationality contained in art 12. The ECJ held that:

> 'Prohibition of such discrimination does not apply to the acts of public authorities but extends likewise to rules of any other nature aimed at regulating in the collective manner gainful employment and the provision of services.'

The breadth of the language used closed the issue of whether or not Treaty articles created direct effect between individuals. Thus, it is clear that an individual may rely on a Treaty article as against another individual.

2.2.3 REGULATIONS

Article 249 describes a regulation as of 'general application . . . binding in its entirety and directly applicable in all Member States'. Regulations can produce direct effect, provided that they are unconditional, sufficiently precise and do not require further implementation. (Generally regulations do not require domestic implementation.) Regulations are generally applicable and can obligate other individuals – they are therefore capable of horizontal direct effect. This was seen in Case 93/71 *Leonesio v Ministero dell'Agricolura delle Foreste* [1972] ECR 287. This concerned a regulation that introduced a system of premiums to encourage the slaughter of dairy cows and to dissuade farmers from marketing milk products. The Italian government had failed to put it into effect. Leonesio slaughtered five cows and claimed a premium. The matter was referred to the ECJ as to whether the regulation was directly effective or whether national legislation could postpone payment of the claim. The Court found that the regulation was directly applicable and therefore capable of producing direct effect.

2.2.4 DIRECTIVES

2.2.4.1 Generally

Directives have caused many problems for the ECJ in the context of direct effect. Article 249(3) describes a directive as being: 'binding, as to the result to be achieved, for each Member State to which it is addressed, but shall leave to the national authorities the choice of form and method'. As directives are not described as 'directly applicable', it was thought that they could not produce direct effect. Additionally, as directives are addressed to Member States, who have a certain latitude in how they implement them, their effect would appear to be conditional on implementation by the Member State.

In Case 9/70 *Franz Grad v Finanzamt Traunstein* [1970] ECR 815, the ECJ implicitly accepted that directives were capable of direct effect. A further step was taken in Case 33/70 *SACE v Italian Ministry of Finance* [1970] ECR 1213. In that case, the Court held that a Treaty article should be given direct effect where it was read in conjunction with a directive. The question was whether art 13(2) (deleted by the Treaty of Amsterdam), which called for gradual abolition of taxes having an equivalent effect to customs duties on imports, could be directly effective in the light of a directive setting down time limits for the expiry of such duties, the time limit having passed. In that case the Court did not give direct effect to directives but held that directly effective Treaty articles must be read in the light of directives.

The first case in which a directive was clearly given direct effect was Case 41/74 *Van Duyn v Home Office* [1974] ECR 1337. A Dutch woman wanted to travel to the United Kingdom to take up a job with the Church of Scientology. The UK government believed that scientology was harmful to the mental health of its members and had adopted a policy of discouraging it. Therefore, it normally refused immigration permission to known scientologists. Mrs Van Duyn was refused entry to the UK on this basis. The UK justified its refusal based on public policy reasons in art 39 of the Treaty. Mrs Van Duyn challenged the decision before the UK courts, arguing that art 39(3) and art 3(1) of Directive 61/221 were directly effective. The UK argued that direct effect of directives would undermine the distinction between directives and regulations. The Irish government also put forward similar arguments. The ECJ held that directives were capable of creating direct effect and were capable of conferring rights on individuals, which they could invoke against Member States in actions before the national courts. The Court gave directives direct effect to make them more effective and to estop a Member State from relying on its own wrongdoing. The ECJ feared that if an individual was not enabled to sue the State on foot of an unimplemented directive the State might deliberately delay implementing measures it disliked. This could cause loss to individuals who stand to benefit from the directive. Therefore, it is inequitable to allow a State to put forward its own delay in implementation as a defence.

2.2.4.2 When does a directive become directly effective?

A directive, which has not been implemented, cannot become directly effective before the expiry of the time limit for its implementation has expired. This was established in Case 148/78 *Pubblico Ministero v Ratti* [1979] ECR 1629. Ratti, an Italian solvent manufacturer, sought to defend himself against charges brought under Italian legislation on the labelling of dangerous products. He claimed that the products were labelled in accordance with two directives, which had not been implemented by the Italian government. The deadline for implementation of the first directive had expired though the deadline for the second had not. The Italian court referred the matter to the ECJ, asking whether the directives were directly effective. The Court held that a directive could only become directly effective when the deadline for implementation has expired and therefore, whereas the first directive was directly effective, the second was not.

In Case 51/76 *Verbond van Nederlandse Ondernemingen v Inspecteur der Invoerrechten en Accijnzen* [1977] ECR 113 direct effect was extended to situations where a directive had been implemented but the implementation was not faithful to the requirements of the directive. In that case the Federation of Dutch Manufacturers was allowed to invoke the provisions of the Second VAT Directive, despite its unfaithful implementation by the Dutch government.

Therefore, when advising a client, it is necessary to ensure that the implementation date has passed. However, it may be possible to rely directly on the directive even if the State has purported to implement it. In this case it must be shown that the directive has been implemented incorrectly.

2.2.4.3 Horizontal direct effect of directives

The question of whether directives should give rise to horizontal direct effect is very controversial. For some time, it remained unanswered by the ECJ. Those opposed argued that directives did not have to be published and are addressed to Member States and not individuals and that therefore they should not obligate individuals. Those in favour asserted that Treaty articles are addressed to States but nevertheless obligated individuals and that all EU law should be equally actionable against States to ensure consistency.

In Case 152/84 *Marshall v Southampton and South West Area Health Authority (Teaching) (No 1)* [1986] CMLR 688, the ECJ decided against horizontal direct effect of directives. The plaintiff was a dietician with the Southampton Health Authority. She claimed that her terms of employment, which allowed for the termination of her employment five years before her male counterparts, was in breach of the Equal Treatment Directive 76/207. Such discrimination was permissible under the UK Sex Discrimination Act 1975. The Court of Appeal referred the matter to the ECJ, which held that: 'a directive may not as itself impose obligations on an individual and that a provision of a directive may not be relied upon as such against such a person'. Advocate General Slynn said that directives were addressed to States and not individuals and that this was sufficient to justify limiting direct effect to the State. Ultimately Mrs Marshall succeeded in her claim (on the basis of vertical direct effect), as her employer was a public body and not a private institution.

Though *Marshall* has not been reversed, there were initially some indications that the question of horizontal direct effect would be revisited. In Case C-271/91 *Marshall (No 2)* [1993] ECR I-4367, Advocate General Von Gerven called for the inclusion of horizontal direct effect. In Case C-316/93 *Nicole Vaneetveld v SA Le Foyer* [1994] ECR I-763 Advocate General Jacobs advocated horizontal direct effect. He said that the various doctrines used by the ECJ to circumvent its absence had led to anomalies. He felt that the introduction of horizontal direct effect would be more conducive to legal certainty than indirect effect. In Case C-91/92 *Faccini Dori v Recreb Srl* [1994] ECR 3325, Advocate General Lenz strongly urged the Court to use horizontal direct effect for a directive. In this case, he advocated horizontal direct effect for directives on the basis that this course was justified in the light of the completion of the internal market and the entry into force of the Treaty on European Union.

However, in Case C-192/94 *El Corte Ingles SA v Blazquez Rivero* [1996] ECR I-1281, the ECJ reaffirmed *Marshall (No 1)*. The ECJ refused to allow the terms of a directive to be relied upon directly in litigation between citizens where the directive concerned had not been transposed into national law. The case arose from a dispute between a consumer and a finance company from which she had borrowed money for a holiday. She booked her holiday with a travel agent with which the finance company had a contract giving it the exclusive right to grant loans to the travel agent's customers. When problems arose with the travel agents handling of her contract, she stopped paying under the loan. Article 11(2) of Directive 87/102 on consumer credit provides a remedy against finance companies for consumers in such circumstances, but it had not been implemented into Spanish law in due time. The finance company sued Ms Blanquez Rivera and she was not able to plead the shortcomings of the travel agent as the case turned on her contract with the finance company. The Spanish court referred the question of the direct effect of art 11 of Directive 87/102. It raised the issue of the entry into force of the Treaty of Union and of art 153 of the Treaty which requires the Community to

> *contribute to the attainment of a high level of consumer protection through . . . measures adopted . . . in the context of the completion of the internal market and . . . specific action which supports and supplements the policy pursued by the Member States to protect . . . the economic interests of consumers. . . .*

The ECJ confirmed its earlier ruling and refused to give horizontal direct effect to the directive concerned. It held that art 153 did not change this situation and referred to the possibility of seeking damages from a Member State that has failed to implement a directive.

Thus, one cannot rely on an unimplemented directive to sue a defendant other than the State. Though the ECJ has not yet accepted horizontal direct effect, it has developed a number of alternatives. First, it has developed the doctrine of vertical direct effect to expand the range of bodies against which relief may be sought. Secondly, it has developed a duty of interpretation for national courts (also known as indirect effect). Finally, it has held that individuals may sue a State where that individual has suffered loss because of the failure of a State to implement a directive in certain circumstances. Thus, in a case involving directives, it is necessary to look at a number of different possibilities. We will now examine some of these doctrines.

2.2.4.4 Public bodies

The result of *Marshall* is that the scope of the concept of the State and its reach is crucial. In *Marshall*, the ECJ defined the State as including every aspect of the State and every guise within which the State would be found to exist. In Case C-188/89 *Foster v British Gas plc* [1990] ECR I-3313, the ECJ held that a Member State includes an 'emanation of the State'. This includes every body that is controlled or owned by the State. This is a vague definition and there is some controversy about which organisations may be encompassed by the definition. In *Foster*, six former female employees of British Gas (then owned by the State) claimed that they had been unlawfully discriminated against in that they had to retire at sixty whereas the retirement age for males was sixty-five. The English Court of Appeal held that British Gas was not an emanation of the State, as it was not performing any of the classic duties of the State such as defence or the maintenance of law and order. The ECJ took a different view. It held that art 5 of the Equal Treatment Directive could be relied upon against a body made responsible for providing a public service under State control and which possessed special powers exceeding those normally applicable in relations between individuals.

In Case 224/84 *Johnston v Chief Constable of the Royal Ulster Constabulary* [1986] ECR 1651 it was held that a directive could be relied on against a Chief Constable, as he is responsible for the police service. As a police authority is charged by the State with the maintenance of public order and safety, it does not act as a private individual. On that basis, it could be regarded as an 'organ of the State'. Other institutions, which have been held to be public bodies, include local or regional authorities (Case 103/88 *Fratelli Constanzo v Commune di Milano* [1989] ECR 1839) and tax authorities (Case 8/81 *Becker v Finanzamt Munster-Innenstadt* [1982] ECR 53).

The Irish High Court applied this concept in the context of a personal injuries action in *Coppinger v Waterford County Council* [1996] 2 ILRM 427. The plaintiff suffered serious injuries when he drove his car into the rear of a truck, which was stationary on his side of the road. The car went in some distance under the truck, as it had no rear under run protection. Directive 70/221 requires rear protective devices but, by way of derogation, lifted the requirement for some vehicles, including, 'vehicles for which rear under run protection is incompatible with their use'. The Road Traffic Regulations 1985 required such a protective device. However, art 4(3)(g) provided that 'a vehicle or trailer so constructed that it can be unloaded by part of the vehicle or trailer being tipped rearwards' could be exempt from this requirement. The plaintiff claimed a breach of the directive. Geoghegan J held for the plaintiff. He held that the county council was an emanation of the State. The onus of proving that the protective device was incompatible with the use of the tipper truck fell on the defendant and the defendant had failed to discharge that onus. The court held that the fitting of rear under run protection was not incompatible with the use of the tipper truck. The court found that the obligation in the directive was sufficiently precise to be directly enforceable against the State or an emanation of the State. As Waterford County Council is an emanation of the State, Mr Coppinger was entitled to sue the council on foot of the improperly implemented directive. This case is a striking example of how pervasive direct effect has become in Ireland.

2.2.4.5 **Indirect effect**

Domestic legislation, passed after the publication of a directive dealing with the same subject matter, must be interpreted in the light of the wording and purpose of that directive. The ECJ has even extended this principle to pre-existing legislation. By interpreting legislation in this way a court is giving effect to such directives, albeit indirectly.

This principle was established in Case 14/83 *von Colson v Land Nordrhein-Westfalen* [1984] ECR 1891 and Case 79/83 *Harz v Deutsche Tradax GmbH* [1984] ECR 1921. Both plaintiffs had been rejected after applying for jobs, Ms von Colson with the prison service and Ms Harz with a private company. The German court found that this rejection was based on their gender and awarded damages for travelling expenses. The plaintiffs argued that these limited awards contravened art 6 of the Equal Treatment Directive 76/207, which requires Member States to introduce the necessary measures to pursue their claims through the courts. The ECJ did not address the issue of horizontal/vertical effect and instead concentrated on art 10 of the Treaty, which requires Member States to take all appropriate measures to fulfil their obligations under EU law. The ECJ held that this obligation extends to all authorities, including courts in the Member States. Therefore, national courts are obliged to interpret national law in such a way as to ensure that obligations of a directive are obeyed, regardless of whether the national law was based on any particular directive. The result of this was that a national court was obliged to use national law to ensure an effective remedy – in this case, damages greater than mere travelling expenses. The ECJ emphasised the need for sanctions that would deter any infringement of the directive.

The lack of national law in an area has caused difficulties. In Case 80/86 *Public Prosecutor v Kolpinghuis Nijmegen BF* [1987] ECR 3969, the ECJ held that *von Colson* could not be applied by a Member State to support the prosecution of a Dutch company for stocking adulterated mineral water on the basis of the breach of a directive which had not been specifically implemented. To allow this would have breached the principles of legal certainty and non-retroactivity. This case confirmed the duty of interpretation but was cautious about extending it in a criminal sphere.

However, in Case C-106/89 *Marleasing SA v La Comercial Internacional de Alimentacion SA* [1990] ECR 4135, the ECJ held that national law must be interpreted in accordance with a directive, even if the law in question predates the directive. The plaintiff sought to set aside the memorandum and articles of a company on the basis that it had been established to put certain assets beyond the reach of creditors. The First Company Law Directive sets out the grounds on which a company can be declared void and does not include fraud. The Spanish courts asked whether a directive could be upheld directly against an individual. The ECJ held that directives do not give rise to effects between individuals but it stressed that it was up to the courts to achieve the result required by the directive through the interpretation of the national legislative provision in a manner consistent with the directive. The ECJ held that the Spanish Civil Code, which predated the directive, must be interpreted in the light of it.

More recently, this approach was followed in Case C-91/92 *Faccini Dori v Recreb Srl* [1994] ECR 3325. Signora Faccini Dori entered into a contract for a language correspondence course at Milan railway station. She changed her mind four days later and sought to cancel the contract within the seven-day cooling-off period, provided for by Directive 85/577, a consumer protection measure applying to contracts concluded away from business premises. Italy had not implemented the directive. The ECJ held that the directive could not create horizontal direct effect. However, it did rule that the Italian court had an obligation to interpret its domestic legislation in the light of the directive.

Marleasing was also followed in Case C-334/92 *Wagner Miret v Fondo de Garantía Salaria* [1993] ECR I 6911. The case concerned a claim based on Directive 80/987, a directive guaranteeing employees arrears of pay in the event of their employer's insolvency. The ECJ said that in interpreting national law to conform with the objectives of a directive, national courts must presume that the State intended to comply with EU. They must attempt, 'as far as possible', to interpret national law to achieve the result set out in the directive. If the law cannot be interpreted in such a way, as in this case, the State may be obliged to make good the claimant's loss on foot of the *Francovich* principles (outlined in section 2.3). The case appears to acknowledge that national courts will not always feel able to interpret domestic law to comply with a directive, particularly where the two are at odds and there is no evidence that the legislature intended the national law to comply with the directive's provisions.

This line of authority continued with Case C-63/97 *Bayerische Motorenwereke AG (BMW) v Ronald Karel Deenik* [1999] 1 CMLR 1099. The Trademark Directive should have been implemented in Belgium by 31 December 1992. It was not actually implemented until 1 January 1996. The case arose between those two dates. The implementing legislation provided that any appeal against a decision reached before 1 January 1996 had to be settled in accordance with the rules applicable prior to that date even if the appeal judgment was to be given after that date. The ECJ held that the legislation was valid but was subject to the overriding duty of the national appeal court to interpret domestic law consistently with the Directive, as the Directive should have been implemented at that time.

Indirect effect is sometimes known as 'passive horizontal direct effect' as it allows national courts to give effect to directives in actions between individuals in the guise of interpreting them.

2.3 State Liability

2.3.1 INFRINGEMENT OF THE TREATIES

It is possible for Member States, domestic public bodies, companies or private individuals to infringe EU law in a variety of ways.

A Member State must not apply or disapply national laws which conflict with EU law under the doctrine of supremacy of EU law (*Costa v ENEL*). Failure to do so constitutes an infringement of EU law.

Also, the Treaties impose obligations on Member States, which must be fulfilled. For example, Member States must not impose quantitative restrictions on the free movement of goods between Member States contrary to art 28, or discrimination against migrant workers and their families contrary to art 39. Imposing such restrictions will constitute an infringement of the Member State's Treaty obligations (unless a permitted exception justifying the restriction may be invoked).

However, it is not only Member States which may be responsible for infringing the Treaty. Some Treaty provisions, although addressed to the Member States, may have certain qualities such that they create rights and obligations, not only for the Member States, but also for private individuals. Thus, the ECJ found in cases such as *Defrenne v Sabena* that private citizens may assert rights based on Treaty provisions, which, although addressed to the Member States, are sufficiently clear and precise such that invocable rights may be ascertained from their content.

Not only may private citizens invoke such provisions against the State itself (*Van Gend en Loos*), but also against other private parties (*Walrave and Koch*) where it is alleged that such other parties have infringed Treaty obligations.

Furthermore, some provisions of the Treaties, such as the competition rules (arts 81 and 82), are invocable by private parties against other private parties in domestic litigation in national courts, even though they are not specifically addressed to Member States at all.

Consequently, a private party may be able to invoke such Treaty provisions against another private party in a national court and seek national remedies where it is alleged that one of the parties has infringed a relevant Treaty provision. Of course, the foregoing is not relevant to all Treaty provisions as many, being either vague or merely aspirational in nature, do not give rise to rights that may be asserted by private individuals, either against the State or other private parties. Such provisions will not therefore, on their own, form the basis of a legal action by an individual.

2.3.2 INFRINGEMENT OF SECONDARY LEGISLATION

Article 249 of the EC Treaty makes EC regulations 'directly applicable', which means that they normally may be relied upon in a national court as a cause of action. However, as we have seen with directives, the position is more complicated. Because the Treaty does not state that they are 'directly applicable', they may be relied upon to a far more limited extent. Where a directive has been properly implemented in a Member State, then a party seeking to rely upon it will primarily invoke the relevant domestic implementation measure in the national court (rather than the directive itself) as the basis of their cause of action. However, the problem often arises that the directive has either not been implemented on time (or indeed at all), or perhaps it has been implemented improperly. Either way, the party who attempts to invoke directive-based rights may well be frustrated in their attempts to assert rights that EU law intended them to have. The fault for this lies with the Member State, which has responsibility for implementing directives. Basically, where a directive has not yet been implemented properly, then it can only be relied upon by the individual against the State (so-called 'vertical' direct effect) provided that it meets the criteria for 'direct effect'. However, a non/improperly implemented directive cannot be invoked against non-State parties (ie, parties that are not the State or 'emanations' of the State: *Foster v British Gas*; *Coppinger v Waterford County Council*). This is because the ECJ held in *Marshall* that directives, being addressed to Member States only, are incapable of being invoked in a 'horizontal' fashion. In other words, a non/improperly-implemented directive cannot be relied upon as the source of legally invocable rights against non-State parties even though they may have infringed the directive's principles.

In an effort to prevent Member States escaping the consequences of such an infringement (failure to implement on time/failure to implement properly), the ECJ has attempted to assist EU citizens by equipping them with the action for damages. This action may be invoked against the State, as a cause of action in itself, where it is alleged that the State has infringed EU law by reason of its failure to implement a directive properly, in circumstances which thereby deprive litigants of directive-based rights (rights they would have had, had the directive been implemented properly).

From the cases we are about to discuss, we shall see how the ECJ has delivered a number of key decisions in this area in recent years in order to assist the EU citizen against the defaulting Member State. Not only that, but it shall also be seen how the ECJ has extended the application of the State liability principle, such that a variant of it applies (for liability determining purposes) to a range of situations (other than the mere failure to implement a directive), such as when the State maintains legislation that is contrary to EU law, or poorly implements EU law, or takes an administrative decision that is contrary to EU law.

2.3.3 CONDITIONS FOR STATE LIABILITY FOR MALIMPLEMENTATION OF DIRECTIVES

2.3.3.1 State's liability for damages

In Cases C-6 and 9/90 *Francovich, Bonifaci v Republic of Italy* [1991] ECR I-5357 the ECJ ruled for the first time that a Member State could be sued in damages by individuals in their national courts in the following circumstances. The Italian State had failed to implement a directive, with the result that the applicants, unpaid employees of an insolvent company, were unable to assert rights that the directive had intended them to have. Under Directive 80/397 (1980 OJ L 283/23) Member States were required to ensure that guarantee institutions were set up. The purpose of these institutions would be to ensure that, in the event of employer insolvency, unpaid employee wages would be guaranteed. Italy failed to implement the directive. A group of adversely affected employees, when they found that no such guarantee institution had been set up to guarantee their wages, attempted to invoke the unimplemented directive against the Italian State in the Italian courts. The Italian tribunal hearing the dispute referred to the ECJ under the art 234 referral procedure, the question as to whether the employees' argument was correct in law. The applicants' position appeared hopeless when the ECJ rejected their main argument, which was, that notwithstanding the State's failure to implement the directive by way of a domestic implementation measure, the directive itself could be invoked against the State under the doctrine of 'direct effect'. This argument was rejected because the directive did not satisfy the criteria for direct effect, according to the ECJ. This was because the directive did not impose any obligation on the State to guarantee the unpaid wages, but merely to ensure that institutions that would do so, were established.

However, heralding a dramatic new development, the ECJ proceeded to rule that a Member State could, however, be sued in damages for infringing EU law where the following three criteria were satisfied:

(a)   Did the directive aim to create rights for individuals?

(b)   Could the content of such rights be ascertained from the directive's provisions?

(c)   Was there a causal link between the State's failure to implement the directive and the damage that resulted?

Thus, an individual who could satisfy these conditions now had the right under EU law to sue a Member State in damages in a national court where the State's failure to implement a directive was the cause of the individual's loss. Particularly of significance, was the fact that an individual could assert such a cause of action even in respect of provisions of a directive which were not capable of being directly effective.

In *Tate, Robinson v Minister for Social Welfare* [1995] 1 IR 418 Ireland was held liable to compensate a large group of litigants prejudiced by the State's failure to implement an equal treatment directive. It is estimated that the cost to the State of this single action eventually amounted to more than £250 million.

2.3.3.2   Uncertainties after *Francovich*

At paragraph 38 of *Francovich* the ECJ had stated:

'Although State liability is thus required by Community law, the considerations under which that liability gives rise to a right to compensation depend on the nature of the breach of Community law giving rise to the harm.'

After *Francovich* it was unclear whether the *Francovich* criteria would be used solely as the criteria to determine Member State liability where there was a complete failure to implement a directive in a State's domestic legal regime or, whether these criteria would also be used for determining liability in other situations, such as, for example, where a Member State had improperly implemented a directive, thereby causing an individual to suffer loss.

Several art 234 reference judgments delivered by the ECJ in the last few years have considerably clarified this issue for the national courts. The *Francovich* criteria do not appear to apply where the State, rather than failing to implement a particular directive at all, instead has improperly implemented the directive. Instead, other criteria are used.

However, in order to understand the ECJ's reasoning on this issue, first it is necessary to examine the ECJ's case law on the issue of State liability where the State has legislated contrary to EU law.

2.3.3.3   **Where the Member State has legislated contrary to EU law**

In order to understand why the ECJ has so ruled, consideration must first be given to the Court's case law on a separate issue, ie, what criteria apply to determine Member State liability in damages where there has been national legislation that is contrary to EU law. This issue arose in Joined Cases C-46 & 48/93 *Brasserie du Pêcheur SA v Federal Republic of Germany* and *R v Secretary of State for Transport, ex parte Factortame Ltd* [1996] ECR I-1029 ('*Brasserie du Pêcheur/Factortame 3*'). In *Brasserie du Pêcheur*, the relevant issue was whether Germany had acted contrary to EU law in enacting beer purity legislation which had the spin-off effect of preventing the applicants from exporting French beer into Germany for two reasons. First, German beer purity law only allowed the sale of alcohol as 'beer' on German territory if it was produced in a certain manner. Second, German law prohibited the import of beer containing additives. The applicants claimed that such laws were contrary to art 28 on the free movement of goods under the EC Treaty, and therefore they claimed that under EU law they should be afforded the right to seek damages from Germany in the German courts for alleged loss thereby arising. (Under German law the applicants had no cause of action.)

The background to *Factortame 3* was that it had been held earlier by the ECJ in Case C-221/89 '*Factortame 2*' [1991] ECR 3905 that the UK Merchant Shipping Act 1988 was contrary to art 43 of the Treaty because it prevented Spanish fishing vessels being registered to fish from British ports. Inter alia, art 43 prohibits EU Member States from unfairly discriminating on grounds of nationality or domicile against other EU Member State nationals who wish to set up in business. Accordingly, the applicants were now seeking to ascertain whether EU law would provide an action in damages actionable in the UK courts to compensate them for alleged loss arising from the UK's maintenance of laws that were clearly contrary to the Treaty. British law did not provide any such remedy in damages.

As the essential issue in both cases was so similar, the ECJ joined both actions together. Referring to *Francovich*, the ECJ indicated that that case had concerned a 'reduced' discretion-type situation: the Community had adopted a directive which set out Member State obligations and therefore the discretion of the Member States to adopt legislative or economic choices in implementing the directive was severely restricted. Hence, the criteria for determining State liability in damages in a national court under EU law where the State had failed to exercise its reduced discretion, had to be necessarily favourable to an aggrieved litigant who was alleging loss as a result of the State's failure to act.

However, crucially, the ECJ also recognised that different criteria must apply where the State was acting in a 'wide' discretion situation. Pointing out that the Member States must not always be living in fear of damages actions when acting in a field that falls within the scope of the EC Treaty, the Court held that in *Brasserie du Pêcheur* the Member States had a wide discretion to legislate as there had been no Community harmonisation in the beer sector at the time of the enactment of the German beer legislation. Similarly, in *Factortame 3*, the ECJ pointed out that the EU fisheries policy left it up to the Member States to set out a registration regime for fishing vessels. Therefore, according to the ECJ both of these cases presented wide discretion-type situations, and so the criteria to be used to determine Member State liability would be necessarily different from the *Francovich* criteria:

(a)   EU law must have conferred rights on individuals;

(b)   the breach of that law must be 'sufficiently serious', and

(c)   there must be a direct causal link between the individual's loss and the damage sustained.

It is the second criterion that appears markedly different from the *Francovich* criteria. Elaborating on what it could mean, the ECJ held that in a wide discretion-type situation, a breach was 'sufficiently serious' where the State had 'manifestly and gravely' disregarded the limits of its discretion to legislate in conformity with EU law. Furthermore the ECJ helpfully elaborated a number of criteria, which may assist in deciding this issue:

(i) the degree of clarity and precision of the rule breached;

(ii) the measure of discretion left by that rule for the Member State/EU authorities when called upon to implement it;

(iii) whether the infringement and the damage caused was intentional or involuntary;

(iv) whether any error of law was excusable or not;

(v) whether an EU institution's actions may have contributed to the breach, and

(vi) whether the Member State had adopted or retained national measures contrary to EU law.

The ECJ continued to elaborate that a breach would be 'sufficiently serious' where, for example, a previous ruling of the ECJ had ruled that the point in issue in a dispute infringed EU law; or where an art 234 preliminary ruling delivered by the ECJ already existed on the point at issue; or where the settled case-law of the ECJ has previously taken a different view.

Applying such criteria to the two cases before it, the ECJ held in *Brasserie du Pêcheur* that Germany's beer marketing requirements constituted a breach of art 28 which would be difficult to regard as 'excusable error' as similar measures had been condemned previously in the landmark '*Cassis de Dijon*' judgment (Case 120/78 *Rewe-Zentral AG v Bundesmonopolverwalthung fur Branntwein* [1979] ECR 649) and the incompatibility of such a requirement was 'manifest'. On the other hand, the ECJ pointed out that the German law prohibiting the importation of beers made with additives was 'less conclusive' until the ECJ held it was illegal in Case 178/84 *Commission v Germany* [1987] ECR 1227 in 1987. Clearly therefore, the ECJ was attempting to assist the national court in indicating to it that while the 'beer' description law was definitely not an excusable legislative error, the national court would have to consider more carefully whether the additives prohibition was a breach of 'sufficiently serious' proportions.

In *Factortame 3*, the ECJ pointed out that the requirement of the UK Merchant Shipping Act 1988 that registration of vessels was dependent on the owner's domicile was prima facie contrary to art 43 of the EC Treaty ('*Factortame 2*'). The guidance that the ECJ gave here to the national court in order to assist it in deciding if the breach was 'sufficiently serious' would be the examination of factors such as:

(a) legal disputes relating to certain features of the Common Fisheries Policy;

(b) the attitude of the Commission, which had made its attitude known to the UK in good time;

(c) the views of the national court in the national proceedings as to the state of certainty of EU law, and

(d) whether the Member State complied diligently with any interim relief ordered by the ECJ.

Therefore, it appears that where the State has legislated contrary to EU law, the criteria that will be used to determine the State's liability in damages will be the *Brasserie du Pêcheur/ Factortame 3* criteria – which lean more in favour of the Member State – rather than the *Francovich* criteria which lean much more in an aggrieved applicant's favour.

2.3.3.4   Where the State has made an administrative decision contrary to EU law

In Case C-5/94 *R v Ministry of Agriculture, Fisheries and Food, ex parte Hedley Lomas (Ireland) Ltd* [1996] ECR I-2553 the ECJ held in an art 234 referral that the UK Ministry of Agriculture's refusal to issue an export licence to the applicant to export sheep for slaughter to Spain was contrary to art 29 of the Treaty. The Court found that the UK's refusal to issue the licence was groundless and that the refusal constituted a quantitative restriction contrary to art 29, which was not justifiable under art 30. Accordingly, the Court found that the *Brasserie du Pêcheur/Factortame 3* liability-determining criteria should apply. It further found that the breach was a 'sufficiently serious' breach and left it up to the national court to consider whether the third element of the *Brasserie du Pêcheur/Factortame 3* test (ie, causation) was satisfied.

2.3.3.5   Where the Member State has improperly implemented a directive

The issue of where a State has improperly implemented a directive is given consideration in the section on EU Law: Implementation Problems. However, for the sake of completeness it is relevant to briefly consider the issue here also. In 1996, the ECJ elaborated on this issue in Case C-392/93 *R v HM Treasury, ex parte British Telecom* [1996] ECR I-1631, ie, as to which of the two sets of liability-determining criteria should apply where a Member State poorly implements a directive: the *Francovich* criteria or the *Brasserie du Pêcheur/Factortame 3* criteria?

In this case, the ECJ had to consider whether the UK was liable in damages to British Telecom where it was alleged that the UK had transposed a public procurement directive incorrectly, thereby allegedly causing loss to British Telecom. (Directive 90/531 concerns public procurement in the water, energy, telecommunications and transport sectors.) The facts briefly were that the directive required certain contracts to be publicly tendered but permitted certain operators such as British Telecom to decide which contracts in its sector should be so designated and which should not. However, the UK had implemented the directive by actually designating the relevant contracts without affording British Telecom the opportunity to do so. The ECJ held that the UK had breached the directive because the directive intended British Telecom to have the right to designate the relevant contracts. However, the Court went on to elaborate that the *Brasserie du Pêcheur/Factortame 3* criteria (not *Francovich* criteria) would be the criteria that would apply to determine whether or not the UK was liable in damages for loss thereby allegedly caused to British Telecom.

The ECJ opted for the *Brasserie du Pêcheur/Factortame 3* criteria as the relevant liability-determining criteria. Justifying its decision, the ECJ stated that it was concerned to ensure that the exercise of legislative functions by the State in a field governed by EU law should not be hindered by the prospect of actions for damages whenever the general interest required the State to adopt measures that may affect individual interests. As a result, it opted for the *Brasserie du Pêcheur/Factortame 3* liability criteria rather than the *Francovich* criteria. Thus, the ECJ had to consider whether the UK's breach – incorrect implementation of a directive – was 'sufficiently serious' or not.

In making this assessment, of relevance was the clarity and precision of the rule breached. In the case before it, the ECJ concluded that the relevant article of the directive was imprecisely worded and reasonably capable of bearing the interpretation given to it by the UK, which the ECJ found had acted in good faith. Furthermore, there was no guidance available to the UK as to the correctness or otherwise of its interpretation of the directive either from the case law of the ECJ or from the Commission, which at no time had indicated to the UK that it was unhappy with the way in which the directive had been implemented. Accordingly, the ECJ concluded that there had been a breach, but not a 'sufficiently serious' one.

This judgment is helpful in several respects. On one hand it illustrates in a practical sense the kind of analysis the ECJ is likely to carry out when requested to consider whether a

State's poor implementation of a directive constitutes a 'sufficiently serious' breach of EU law. This is particularly evident in the weight that the ECJ gives to relevant considerations which demonstrate whether or not the Member State had acted in good faith, such as the imprecision of the directive's phrasing; the background to the legal dispute; whether the Commission had ever indicated to the Member State that it was unhappy with the national implementation measure, etc. Also the ECJ appears to place emphasis on whether previous judgments of the ECJ had any bearing on the legal issues raised in the dispute. On the other hand, it is not good news for parties who are adversely affected by a State's failure to implement a directive properly because the ECJ applied the less favourable *Brasserie du Pêcheur/Factortame 3* liability criteria rather than the *Francovich* criteria.

The *Francovich* criteria therefore appear confined to determining State liability in damages where there has been a complete failure to implement a directive, rather than also applying to the poor implementation situation. This is not such good news for litigants against the State who are affected by poor implementation – they will have to satisfy the *Brasserie du Pêcheur/Factortame 3* liability criteria instead. The potency of the *Francovich* criteria for errant States is demonstrated by Cases C-178,179,188-190/94 *Dillenkofer v Federal Republic of Germany* [1996] ECR I-4845. In this judgment, the ECJ was called upon to consider which set of criteria would apply to determine liability where a Member State, Germany, had failed to implement a directive by the due deadline for implementation. The directive in question, Council Directive 90/314, was intended to protect holidaymakers in the event of tour operator insolvency. Germany had particular difficulties implementing the directive on time, had failed to do so, and therefore in its defence argued that the 'sufficiently serious' test should apply (such that Germany's failure should not be deemed 'sufficiently serious' in light of its particular difficulties). The ECJ held that where a Member State fails to take any measures to implement a directive, then the *Francovich*, as opposed to the *Brasserie du Pêcheur/Factortame 3*, criteria apply to determine liability. No doubt there will be many other examples of this arising, thereby giving rise to Member State, and ultimately taxpayer, liability where Member States fail to implement directives on time.

2.3.4 CONCLUSION

Clearly the ECJ has recognised that Member States will be liable in damages under EU law to aggrieved parties who suffer loss as a result of the State's:

(a) failure to implement EU law at all, or

(b) improper implementation of EU law, or

(c) taking of administrative action that is contrary to EU law, or

(d) adoption of legislation that is contrary to EU law

However, crucially, depending on which situation it is, either the *Francovich* or the *Brasserie du Pêcheur/Factortame 3* criteria will be applied. Undoubtedly, the *Francovich* threshold for the litigant is much easier to satisfy, ie, the fact of non-implementation constitutes an actionable breach as per scenario (a) above. However, in all of the other situations, (b) – (d), the *Brasserie du Pêcheur/Factortame 3* criteria appear to apply.

In this situation, the evidential burden both on aggrieved litigants and their legal advisers requires a much greater effort in order to demonstrate successfully that a poorly implemented directive constitutes a 'sufficiently serious' breach such that it constitutes an actionable cause of action in damages against the State in the national courts.

2.4 National Limitation Periods

2.4.1 THE EMMOTT DOCTRINE

In the preceding sections we have examined various doctrines, which may be of assistance to clients asserting rights based on EU law before national courts. However, in advising clients one is always aware of limitation periods. Such a limitation period may well have expired before an individual is aware of the cause of action. Limitation periods in Ireland or other Member States of the EU may operate to deprive a client of a cause of action based on EU law.

In Case C-208/90 *Emmott v Minister for Social Welfare* [1991] ECR I-4269, the ECJ held that limitation periods under national law do not begin to run until full implementation of the relevant directive. Mrs Emmott, a married woman, had been receiving disability benefits between December 1983 and May 1986 at a lesser rate than married men or single men and women. A directive provided that such discrimination was to be ended and national rules were to be adjusted accordingly by 23 December 1984. The implementing legislation did not come into effect until May 1986. Mrs Emmott brought judicial review proceedings in July 1988. The State claimed that she was barred from bringing proceedings as the time limit for judicial review had expired. The ECJ rejected that argument. It held that, until a directive had been properly implemented, any domestic limitation period could not be said to begin to run.

The ruling in *Emmott* was modified by subsequent judgments. In Case C-338/91 *Steenhorst-Neerings v Bedrijfsvereniging voor Detailhandel, Ambachten en Huisvrouwen* [1993] ECR I-5475 the ECJ differentiated a rule restricting the retroactive effect of claims for benefits for incapacity for work-based rights conferred by an improperly implemented directive from a mandatory time limit for the bringing of proceedings. In Case C-410/92 *Johnson v Chief Adjudication Officer* [1994] ECR I-5483 the ECJ held that a rule which limited the period prior to the bringing of a claim in respect of which arrears of benefit were payable, was compatible with EU law since it did not constitute a bar to proceedings.

2.4.2 RESTRICTION OF THE DOCTRINE

A further restriction of the doctrine laid down in *Emmott* was advocated in Case C-2/94 *Denkavit International v Kamer von Koophandel en Fabrieken voor Midden-Gederland* [1996] ECR I-5063. The case concerned the purported implementation of a directive on capital duty by the Netherlands. The issue came before the ECJ as to whether a national limitation period could bar the exercise of a legal remedy where a directive was improperly implemented. In his opinion, Advocate General Jacobs advocated a restriction of the *Emmott* principle. He said that *Emmott* had to be read in a qualified sense and should not be taken as establishing that improper implementation of a directive did not, in the absence of other circumstances, preclude a Member State from relying on a limitation period. Notwithstanding its general language, the judgment in *Emmott* was to be read

> 'as establishing the principle that a Member State could not rely on a limitation period where a Member State was in default both in failing to implement a directive and in obstructing the exercise of a judicial remedy in reliance upon it, or where the delay in exercising the remedy and hence the failure to meet the time-limit was in some other way due to the conduct of the national authorities'.

The ECJ decided the case on one of the other questions referred to it and did not address this point. Advocate General Jacobs repeated his invitation to the ECJ in Case C-188/95 *Fantask v Industrimisteriet* [1998] 1 CMLR 473. The ECJ agreed with him and distinguished its decision in *Emmott*. The ECJ said that *Emmott* was a case decided on its own specific facts. It held that the Danish Government could rely on a five-year limitation period for actions for recovery of debts even where a directive had not been properly implemented.

2.4.3 LIMITED APPLICATION OF THE EMMOTT DOCTRINE

However, at much the same time in Case C-246/96 *Magorrian and Cunningham v Eastern Health and Social Services Board* [1998] All ER (EC) 38, the ECJ examined the application of national limitation periods in direct effect cases. The applicants were nurses who had been the victims of indirect discrimination and were entitled to rely directly on art 141 of the Treaty. The ECJ had to decide for what time period they were entitled to recover the additional benefits that they should have received. It held that the direct effect of art 141 could be relied upon from 8 April 1976, the date of the judgment in *Defrenne v Sabena*, when art 141 was held to be directly effective. The UK authorities had sought to invoke a rule restricting claims of such benefits to two years before the date of a successful claim. The ECJ held that such a rule would prevent them claiming benefits from 1976 to 1990 and thus effectively denied them a remedy. Thus, the ECJ held that such a rule was contrary to Community law. The ECJ distinguished its earlier rulings in *Steenhorst-Neerings* and *Johnson*. The ECJ appears to be recognising that some limitation periods are reasonable, but not those which deprive an applicant of any opportunity to assert an EU law right.

This is consistent with more recent decisions of the ECJ. In Case C-231/96 *Edilizia Industriale Siderguica Srl (Edis) v Ministero delle Finanze*, 15 September 1998 (unreported) an Italian charge on registration of companies, payable annually, had been held by the ECJ to be contrary to EU law. Edis had paid the charge between 1986 and 1992. The charge was reduced by Italian law in 1993 and ceased to be annual. Edis sought a refund. Italian law provided that any claim for a repayment of charges wrongly paid must be brought within a period of three years from the date of payment. The ECJ distinguished between national limitation rules, which would deprive an applicant of a remedy, and domestic procedural rules to deal with a situation of this nature. The Court held that it is compatible with EU law to lay down reasonable limitation periods for bringing proceedings. The limitation period must be equivalent to similar limitation periods for domestic actions. The ECJ appears to be distinguishing between situations where national limitation periods which would deprive an applicant of a remedy or limit it to such an extent that it is meaningless (and there is some evidence of male fides on the part of the State) and situations where national limitation periods merely have a procedural impact.

In Case C-228/96 *Aprile Srl, en liquidation v Amministrazione delle Finanze dello Stato*, 17 November 1998 (unreported) the Italian State Finance Administration had collected certain customs charges from Aprile, a company in liquidation. In two cases in 1989 and 1991, the ECJ held that these customs charges were contrary to EU law. Italy abolished these charges from 13 June 1991 and 1 November 1992. However, these measures did not have retrospective effect. There was no provision made for repayment of amounts collected in breach of EU law. Aprile sued, seeking to have the amounts reimbursed. The case was defended on the basis that the relevant limitation period barred the action being taken. The Italian court asked the ECJ whether national rules providing for a limitation period of three years for reimbursement of customs charges rather than the ordinary limitation period of ten years for actions for the recovery of sums paid but not due was compatible with EU law. The ECJ emphasised that national laws safeguarding rights derived from EU law must be as favourable as those governing equivalent domestic actions and must not render virtually impossible or excessively difficult the exercise of those rights. Reasonable time limits, which meet these requirements, are permissible. The ECJ held that a time limit of three years appeared reasonable. It pointed out the actions for reimbursement of charges levied in breach of EU law should be governed by limitation rules, which are equivalent to limitation rules applying to the reimbursement of such charges under national law. The limitation period need not match the most favourable period available under national law. The ECJ went on to consider its earlier ruling in *Emmott*. It held that the *Emmott* principle applied only in its particular circumstances – where a time bar deprived the plaintiff of any opportunity to rely on her right to equal treatment under a directive. It now has to be read in the light of subsequent judgments in *Steenhorst-Neerings* and *Fantask*.

Case C-326/96 *Belinda Levez v TH Jennings (Harlow Pools) Ltd* [1999] 2 CMLR 363 once again concerned limitation periods in the context of gender discrimination. In February 1991, Ms Levez had been recruited as manager of a betting shop owned by the defendant at an annual salary of £10,000. In December 1991, she was appointed manager of another shop belonging to the same employer, replacing a man who had received an annual salary of £11,400 since September 1990. The work performed and the conditions of employment for managers in the betting shops run by Jennings Ltd were the same. However, the salary of Ms Levez did not reach £11,400 until April 1992. Ms Levez left the employment of Jennings in March 1993. She then discovered that, until April 1992, she had been paid less than her male predecessor. She brought a claim under the Equal Pay Act 1970 in September 1993. However, the Act provides that arrears of pay can only be paid in respect of a two-year period before the proceedings commenced. Thus, she was not entitled to arrears of pay before 17 September 1991. The Employment Appeal Tribunal referred two questions to the ECJ.

The ECJ emphasised that it is for national law to establish the procedural rules for the safeguard of rights individuals derive from EU law. Such rules may not be less favourable than those governing similar domestic claims. These rules also must not make virtually impossible or excessively difficult the exercise of rights conferred by EU law. In this sense, a national rule limiting arrears of pay to two years before the initiation of proceedings was not open to criticism. However, in the circumstances of the case, Ms Levez had been inaccurately informed or deliberately misled. She was not in a position to realise the extent of the discrimination against her until April 1993. The ECJ held that to allow an employer to rely on a national rule imposing such a time limit in these circumstances would be incompatible with the principle of effectiveness of EU law. Enforcement of the rule would make it virtually impossible or excessively difficult to obtain arrears of remuneration in respect of gender discrimination and would facilitate the breach of EU law by an employer whose deceit caused the employee to delay in bringing proceedings.

2.5   EU Law: Implementation Problems

2.5.1   DIRECTIVES AND THEIR IMPLEMENTATION

Much of our domestic legislation results from the State's obligation to implement European Community directives. Between 60–70 per cent of Irish legislation in the decade 1990-2000 has been taken up with implementing directives. As legal instruments, directives by their very nature set out objectives to be achieved on an EU-wide basis, leaving it up to the individual Member States to choose the means by which to give effect to the directives' provisions. While enacting an Act of the Oireachtas is one way to achieve implementation, the more usual method is for the relevant Minister to adopt a statutory instrument. In practice, this gives rise to many difficulties of a practical nature for legal advisers, because frequently the implementing statutory instruments may be either insufficiently detailed or their wording may be obtuse and unduly technical. This may leave the client and the legal adviser uncertain as to the correct interpretation of the directive concerned and, furthermore, unsure of whether the directive has in fact been correctly implemented in the first place. In the earlier section on Direct Effect we saw how the ECJ has developed several techniques for getting around this difficulty.

2.5.2   GOOD PRACTICE CHECKLIST: FOUR STEPS

When a legal issue arises which involves consideration for the very first time of an unfamiliar directive, four good practice checks should be carried out as a matter of course before the specific content of such a directive is considered in detail. It is essential that a solicitor carry out such checks. Not only do they ensure that the solicitor is familiar with the directive's background, but also they ensure, vitally, that the solicitor is aware of whether the time limit for the implementation of the directive has actually expired.

Detailed consideration will be given below to these four good practice steps, which are:

(1) What do the preamble paragraphs of the directive under consideration reveal about the directive's objectives?

(2) Does the directive under consideration follow on from a previous directive in either the same or a related field?

(3) Has the time limit for implementation of the directive under consideration expired?

(4) Has any domestic implementation measure (ie, an Act or statutory instrument) come into force?

Assuming that the answer to good practice steps (3) and (4) is 'yes', the substantive provisions of both the directive and the domestic implementation measure will require examination in detail.

2.5.3 EXAMINATION OF DIRECTIVE AND DOMESTIC IMPLEMENTATION MEASURE

A substantive examination of the operative provisions of the directive and of the domestic implementation measure will indicate:

(a) what obligations the directive imposes on the Member State or individuals, and

(b) whether the directive has been properly implemented by the domestic implementation measure.

However, should the answer to good practice step (3) be 'yes' (ie, the directive's implementation deadline has expired) but answer to good practice step (4) be 'no' (ie, either no domestic implementation measure has been adopted, or one has, but it is deficient in that it has failed to implement a relevant provision of the directive properly) then the issue will arise as to whether the directive's provisions are nevertheless directly effective notwithstanding improper implementation of the directive. In this situation, a key issue will be whether the directive's provisions are sought to be implemented by 'vertical' direct effect or by 'horizontal' direct effect. (The difficulty facing 'horizontal' attempts to invoke otherwise unimplemented directives was considered at length at **2.2** above in the section on Direct Effect.)

Furthermore (or alternatively), the particular circumstances may give rise to consideration being given to whether a remedy in damages should be pursued against the State for loss arising out of improper implementation of the directive. This issue is considered at the end of this Chapter, and in more detail in the section on State Liability at **2.3** above).

2.5.4 CASE STUDY

2.5.4.1 Commercial Agents Directive

A case study of a particular directive's implementation history is perhaps the most effective way to demonstrate how the good practice steps should be used. Also, it allows us to assess the effectiveness of the various legal tools available in the event of a failure to implement a directive, either at all, or incompletely. Council Directive 86/653 of 18 December 1986 on the Coordination of the laws of the Member States relating to Self-Employed Commercial

Agents, otherwise known as the Commercial Agents Directive, has been chosen for this exercise.

2.5.4.2 Summary of changes required by directive

A brief summary of the changes heralded for the commercial agent/principal relationship by the case study directive is useful in order to demonstrate, in broad terms, some of the important changes that the directive brought about to Irish law governing the legal relationship between commercial agents and their principals for the sale of goods.

Information (art 12)

The principal is obliged to provide the agent with information concerning anticipated volumes of business, the acceptance by customers of orders procured by the agent, and information showing how the agent's commission is calculated and paid. The agent also has the right to inspect the records and books of the principal in respect of these matters. These changes enhance the rights of commercial agents, amending the previous common law position where the agent had no such rights unless expressly granted by the principal in the agency agreement.

Notice periods (art 15)

Where an agency contract for a fixed-term agency appointment continues to be performed after the expiry of the fixed term, art 14 of the directive deems the appointment to be converted into an agency appointment of indefinite duration. This heralds a significant change in the legal relationship between agent and principal, because art 15 stipulates prescribed minimum notice periods that must be observed in respect of termination of appointments of infinite duration. In a major departure from the traditional common law position, the directive further stipulates that parties may not agree to shorter notice periods.

Commission (arts 10 and 8)

Where the agent is to be paid by way of commission, the principal must pay the agent within certain defined periods. For example, under art 10 the commission is due once either the principal has executed his side of the transaction, or the principal should have executed his side of the transaction, or the third party has executed its side of the transaction. Article 10 further elaborates by stipulating that the commission shall be paid not later than the last day of the month following the quarter in which it became due. The directive expressly forbids derogation from this regime, thereby preventing the parties attempting to derogate at common law.

Article 8 provides that where an agent is paid by way of commission, the agent, even after the agency appointment is terminated, is entitled to commission where the transaction was entered into within a reasonable time after the agency appointment was terminated, provided that the transaction in question was mainly attributable to the agent's efforts during the period of the agency appointment. This right to post-termination commission is a major advance on the agent's previous common law position, which was that there was no such entitlement, unless expressly agreed between the parties. The directive does, however, impose some restriction on the entitlement of the agent to avail of this right, and indeed the right to commission generally. First, art 11 provides for two grounds, which, if they apply, are grounds of extinguishment of right to commission. Secondly, art 9 provides that the agent may have to share commission with other agents in certain circumstances.

Right to indemnity or compensation (art 17)

The common law did not afford the agent a right to compensation or indemnity upon termination of appointment. By contrast, some Member States have afforded a very high level of protection to commercial agents under their domestic laws, such that agents operating in those jurisdictions have many of the directive's rights already guaranteed by their domestic law. This was not the position, however, in Ireland or the United Kingdom.

The right to indemnity or compensation is a very valuable entitlement for the agent. Article 17 of the directive provides that Member States are obliged, where they do not already so provide, to adopt measures to ensure that agents within the meaning of the directive have the right to seek an indemnity from the principal for the value of commissions lost due to termination of appointment, or, that the agent is provided with the right to seek compensation from the principal for damage suffered by the agent due to termination of appointment by the principal. This directive therefore heralds a major change in the common law because the directive envisages that Member States who do not already so provide for these measures in their domestic law must take measures to ensure that the agent will have a non-derogable right to either indemnity or compensation as a matter of law.

2.5.4.3 Good practice four-step checklist (as illustrated by the Commercial Agents Directive case study)

What we are attempting to do here is to ascertain, quickly and in broad terms, what are the objectives of the directive. The appropriate place to begin this enquiry is with the directive's preamble paragraphs because the preamble will always be drafted in general terms, which will be easy to read and understand. This will permit the reader, with little effort, to gain a basic understanding of what the directive is trying to achieve. Indeed it may be readily apparent in some cases from a perusal of the preamble that the directive will not be relevant to a client's legal problem, thus ruling out wastage of the practitioner's valuable time consulting an irrelevant directive. For example, a perusal of the preamble to this directive would quickly alert one to the fact that the directive is not concerned with agents who deal in services, as opposed to goods. Therefore, it is always a sensible idea, when examining an unfamiliar directive for the very first time, to read the preamble paragraphs first. Perusal of the preamble to the Commercial Agents Directive reveals much valuable information.

Step 1: objective of the directive

Whereas trade in goods between Member States should be carried on under conditions which are similar to those of a single market, and this necessitates approximation of the legal systems of the Member States to the extent required for the proper functioning of the common market; whereas in this regard the rules concerning conflicts of laws do not, in the matter of commercial representation, remove the inconsistencies referred to above, nor would they even if they were made uniform, and accordingly the proposed harmonization is necessary notwithstanding the existence of those rules;

A cursory reading of the preamble reveals that the object of the directive is to harmonise the laws of the different Member States between principals and self-employed commercial agents in the case of those agents who have authority to conclude contracts for the sale of goods on behalf of a principal. This is confirmed by art 1(2), which expressly provides that a 'commercial agent' is one who has continuing authority to negotiate the sale or purchase of goods on behalf of, and in the name of, a principal. As there is no mention of services we may infer that sale or purchase of services by an agent are excluded from the directive's scope.

Step 2: does the directive follow on from a previously enacted directive?

A directive's preamble will normally reveal whether other directives have preceded the current directive, thus saving much time, as well as alerting the reader at an early stage to the fact that there are existing directives in the relevant area. Where there are such directives, they should immediately be located and consulted along with any relevant domestic implementation measures in order to permit appreciation of whether the new directive amends, replaces, or adds to the pre-existing directives' regime.

Whereas the restrictions on the freedom of establishment and the freedom to provide services in respect of activities of intermediaries in commerce, industry and small craft industries were abolished by Directive 64/224/EEC;

In the instant case, we note from the relevant preamble paragraph that reference is made to Directive 64/224. It is most unclear, from the brief reference to it here in the Preamble, what precisely that directive achieved, so it will be necessary to locate and consult that directive to see what bearing, if any, it may have on matters at the present time.

Step 3: has the time limit for implementation passed?

Indication of a directive's implementation time limits varies from directive to directive. Usually, time limits will be set out at the end of the directive in a substantive article. However, to comprehensively cover this aspect, one should examine:

(a) the preamble paragraphs of the directive;

(b) the articles near the end of the directive, and

(c) whether there are different time limits indicated in different 'Chapters' of the directive.

The first two fields of enquiry listed above are relevant to the case study directive, but the third is not.

The preamble

Whereas additional transitional periods should be allowed for certain Member States which have to make a particular effort to adapt their regulations, especially those concerning indemnity for termination of contract between the principal and the commercial agent, to the requirements of this Directive,

While no specific dates are mentioned, we are told that certain Member States require additional time to adjust their laws in order to comply with the directive. This should alert the reader to the fact that Member States are sometimes allowed extra time to comply with a directive where major changes to a particular State's national law are required. As it happens, Ireland is in such a position with the Commercial Agents Directive because art 22 provides extra time for Ireland (and the United Kingdom) to comply.

The articles near the end of the directive

Usually, an article near the end of the directive will detail the general implementation deadline for the directive. However, with some directives, there will be different deadlines for the implementation of specific articles of the particular directive concerned; or there may be different deadlines for implementation in different Member States.

Article 22 (general implementation deadline) of the Commercial Agents Directive provides:

1. Member States shall bring into force the provisions necessary to comply with this Directive before 1 January 1990. They shall forthwith inform the Commission thereof. Such provisions shall apply at least to contracts concluded after their entry into force. They shall apply to contracts in operation by 1 January 1994 at the latest.

The general deadline for implementation of the directive by Member States was 1 January 1990. However, art 22(3) further provided that:

However, with regard to Ireland and the United Kingdom, 1 January 1990 referred to in paragraph 1 shall be replaced by 1 January 1994.

Thus, it appears that a specific derogation was granted to Ireland and the United Kingdom. These Member States had extra time (until 1 January 1994) to comply. Where such extra time is permitted to a Member State, it is a general indicator that the particular directive heralds major changes for domestic law in that Member State.

Different time limits in different directive 'chapters'

Sometimes, very lengthy and complicated directives may indicate in the body of the directive that certain articles shall only need to be implemented at a later date than the other parts of the directive. This may not be indicated clearly or specifically at the end of the directive. While not relevant in the case of the directive under discussion, it is something to be vigilant about in longer more complicated directives.

2.5.4.4   Where no domestic implementation measure has come into force by latest date permitted by directive

As directives require an act of domestic implementation in order to be properly effective in the domestic legal regime, the question arises whether a domestic implementation measure such as an Act or a statutory instrument was adopted.

It appears that SI 1994/33 (European Communities (Commercial Agents) Regulations 1994) was adopted near the end of February 1994, although reg 2(3) purports to implement from 1 January 1994:

> *(3) The Directive shall, subject to these Regulations, apply to the relations between commercial agents and their principals from 1 January 1994.*

> *GIVEN under my Official Seal, this 21st day of February 1994.*

> *RUAIRÍ QUINN,*
> *Minister for Enterprise and Employment.*

It is apparent that this statutory instrument, because the Minister only adopted it on 21 February 1994, was not in force by the latest possible due date set by the directive, ie, 1 January 1994 (see art 22(3), reg 2(3) which purports to implement the directive retro-actively as and from 1 January 1994).

At this point, several key issues arise. For example, on 1 January 1994:

(a)   Was the directive actually 'directly effective' notwithstanding the failure to im-plement it on time by the State?

(b)   Could an applicant claim damages against the State for loss occasioned by the State's failure to implement the directive on time?

In other words, notwithstanding the failure to adopt the implementing statutory instru-ment by the date for latest implementation as required by the directive itself (1 January 1994), was the directive nevertheless capable of being directly effective once that date had arrived, or alternatively, could damages have been claimed for loss occasioned due to non-implementation?

(a) Direct effect

In order to see whether any particular provision of the directive satisfies the legal test for direct effect, one must consider whether:

(a)   the provision is clear and unambiguous;

(b)   the provision is unconditional, and

(c)   the provision's operation is dependent on further action being taken by either EU or national authorities in order to give the provision meaning.

In legal terms, what is at issue is whether it is possible from the provisions of the directive to ascertain with certainty:

(i)   the content of the right(s) being alleged to emanate from the directive;

(ii) the identity of the intended beneficiary of the right, and

(iii) the identity of the party against whom the right can be asserted.

An examination of the directive reveals that several provisions are capable of satisfying the direct effect test criteria whereas others are not. While this will be considered in more specific detail below, for now the relevant point to note is that a further question must first be considered, ie, will direct effect be of any practical use in the instant case.

From our discussions in the section on direct effect at **2.2** above, it is clear that a directive may be directly effective against either (i) the State ('vertical direct effect'), or (ii) 'emanations' of the State ('vertical direct effect') but not against private individuals or companies ('horizontal' direct effect not possible: *Marshall v Southampton and South West Hampshire Area Health Authority*). In the case study directive under consideration, vertical direct effect is of no utility unless the agent is dealing with a principal in the form of the State or an emanation of the State (eg, a semi-State body or county council). However, principally what the directive is attempting to achieve is to alter rights and obligations as between private individuals, ie, principals and their agents. Consequently, where the State fails to duly implement the directive then individuals who would otherwise have assumed rights or obligations pursuant to the directive may find that the directive has no such effect, because horizontal direct effect of directives is not permitted by the ECJ.

Thus we see how, even though several provisions of the directive may be capable of satisfying the direct effect test criteria simpliciter, nevertheless they are not capable of being effective, apart from in the 'vertical' sense.

Before considering the other main ground for action (ie, the claim for damages against the State for loss arising out of its failure to implement the directive) brief consideration should be given to the question of whether indirect direct effect may be possible. In other words, could a court interpret the common law on the principal/agent relationship in such a way as to give effect to the terms of the directive along the lines discussed in either the *von Colson* or *Marleasing* judgments? In those judgments the ECJ held that Member State courts were obliged to interpret national law in a manner consistent with EU law in so far as this is possible.

Once again, the ECJ's reluctance to permit horizontal direct effect would pose an obstacle because, in effect, an applicant would be attempting to ask a national court to give direct effect to a provision of an unimplemented directive against another private individual (whether principal or agent). Furthermore, given that the common law (before the directive came along) did not make any provision for many of the rights and obligations which the directive envisages, it is difficult to see how a national court could use the indirect direct effect interpretation technique to read the common law in a manner consistent with the directive because, rather than asking the national court to disapply inconsistent common law, what would be involved would be a request to the court to 'read into' the common law, rights and obligations which had not been present in the common law prior to the directive's enactment.

(b) Damages

An alternative remedy that may be pursued in the event of late implementation of a directive causing an applicant loss is the action for damages against the State for failure to implement the directive on time.

The legal test for award of damages where the State has failed to implement a directive on time is set out in *Francovich*. Damages are awardable against the Member State for loss caused to an applicant who is adversely affected by the State's failure to implement the directive by the due date, where:

(i) the aim of the directive was to create rights for individuals, and

(ii) the content of such rights is ascertainable from the directive, and

(iii) there is a causal link between the Member State's failure to implement and the damage that resulted to the injured party.

2.5.4.5   Where the implementation measure appears to have come into force

As and from 21 February 1994, the directive has been purportedly implemented since this date by SI 1994/33. However, we shall note further below how many aspects of its implementation are less than satisfactory, and so again, the issues raised above arise, namely:

(a) Could the directive be directly effective? (We now know that this is of limited usefulness because horizontal direct effect is not permitted.)

(b) Could a 'Francovich' action for damages arise?

An action in damages may well be possible (as will be demonstrated below when we look at the 'implementation' of art 17), although ultimately this may not be the most satisfactory remedy from a result-perspective as the applicant may have preferred to have obtained the rights the directive intended them to have, rather than having to be merely content with an award of damages.

2.5.4.6   Good practice checklist conclusion

Thus, it will be appreciated how even a summary perusal of the directive's preamble and the implementation deadline (usually found at the end of the directive), can yield so much vital and necessary information on the relevancy and applicability (or not), of the directive to the client's problem that one has been consulted about.

2.5.5   SUBSTANTIVE PROVISIONS OF THE DIRECTIVE

While the preamble is very useful for giving a quick overview of the directive and is referred to when attempting to interpret the articles of the directives, the paragraphs of the preamble are, of course, not the legally operative part of the directive. It is the articles that are the legally operative provisions, ie, the provisions that are legally binding on the Member States.

2.5.5.1   How to begin

A useful way to proceed when engaging in an examination of the substantive articles of any directive is to begin by reading the first few articles, which will often outline, in more specific detail than the directive's preamble, important matters such as who it is intended the directive will affect, what types of arrangements will the directive concern, etc.

For example.

2. For the purposes of this Directive, 'commercial agent' shall mean a self-employed intermediary who has continuing authority to negotiate the sale or the purchase of goods on behalf of another person, hereinafter called 'the principal' or to negotiate and conclude such transactions on behalf of and in the name of that principal.

'Commercial agent' is defined in art 1(2) to mean a self-employed intermediary who has continuing authority to negotiate the sale or purchase of goods on behalf of another person (the principal). This is a typical directive definition which is drafted in wide and somewhat vague terminology, but yet which conveys a certain level or indication of meaning in a general sense. Article 1(3) and art 2 indicate general categories of persons who fall outside the definition of 'commercial agent'. Article 1(3) provides:

A commercial agent shall be understood within the meaning of this Directive as not including in particular:

– a person who, in his capacity as an officer, is empowered to enter into commitments binding on a company or association,

– a partner who is lawfully authorized to enter into commitments binding on his partners,

– a receiver, a receiver and manager, a liquidator or a trustee in bankruptcy.

Article 2 provides:

1. This directive shall not apply to:

– commercial agents whose activities are unpaid,

– commercial agents when they operate on commodity exchanges or in the commodity market, or

– the body known as the Crown Agents for Overseas Governments and Administrations, as set up under the Crown Agents Act 1979 in the United Kingdom, or its subsidiaries.

2. Each of the Member States shall have the right to provide that the Directive shall not apply to those persons whose activities as commercial agents are considered secondary by the law of that Member State.

Particularly noteworthy is art 2(2). Although vague in definition, the statutory instrument has implemented this option with more specificity than is present in the directive, as reg 2(2) of SI 1994/33 provides that:

(1) In these Regulations:

'commercial agent' means a self-employed intermediary who has continuing authority to negotiate the sale or purchase of goods on behalf of another person, hereinafter called 'the principal', or to negotiate and conclude such transactions on behalf of and in the name of the principal;

the term 'commercial agent' does not include-

(a) a person who, in the capacity of an officer of a company or association, is empowered to enter into commitments binding on that company or association;

(b) a partner who is lawfully authorised to enter into commitments binding on the partners;

(c) a receiver, a receiver and manager, a liquidator or an examiner, as defined in the Companies Acts, 1963 to 1990, or a trustee in bankruptcy;

(d) a commercial agent whose activities are unpaid;

(e) a commercial agent operating of commodity exchanges or in the commodity market; or

(f) a consumer credit agent or a mail order catalogue agent for consumer goods, whose activities, pursuant to paragraph (2) of this Regulation, are considered secondary;

(2) The activities of an agent of a category described in paragraph (1)(f) of this Regulation shall be presumed, unless the contrary is established, to be secondary for the purposes of these Regulations.

2.5.5.2 Identify easily applicable provisions

A quick read through the substantive articles of the directive may reveal provisions such as art 6(3). This article renders arts 7-12 of the directive inapplicable in certain circumstances (where the agent is not paid wholly or partly by way of commission). Early location of a provision such as art 6(3) may result in a saving of much relevant time if it turns out to be relevant to the client's situation.

2.5.5.3 Has the directive been properly implemented by domestic implementation measure?

Where a directive has been properly implemented by a domestic implementation measure, then it is moot to consider the question of direct effect or an action in damages against the State, as clearly the State will have fulfilled its duty.

However, notwithstanding the implementation of the directive by a domestic implementation measure, these two questions will arise for consideration in the event that the directive appears not to have been correctly implemented in some key respect.

In order to illustrate this point, consideration is now given to whether SI 1994/33 properly implemented the directive into Irish Law. For this purpose, four sample provisions of the directive are considered.

It shall be seen that, because SI 1994/33 is inadequate as an implementation measure in several respects, a mastery of the techniques of interpretation is essential in order to appreciate whether the directive is, notwithstanding, invocable in any meaningful practical sense.

(a) Example 1: Implementation irrelevant

Article 3 of the directive provides :

1. In performing his activities a commercial agent must look after his principal's interests and act dutifully and in good faith.

2. In particular, a commercial agent must:

(a) make proper efforts to negotiate and, where appropriate, conclude the transactions he is instructed to take care of:

(b) communicate to this principal all the necessary information available to him;

(c) comply with reasonable instructions given by his principal.

Whether or not the directive is correctly implemented or not, the agent has always been under a common law duty to look after the principal's interests. Hence, whether or not the directive has been effectively implemented or not is irrelevant because common law agency principles already reflect the principles contained in art 3.

(b) Example 2 : 'Simple' implementation relevant

Article 13(1) provides:

Each party shall be entitled to receive from the other on request a signed written document setting out the terms of the agency contract including any terms subsequently agreed. Waiver of this right shall not be permitted.

This is an example of a provision, which the implementing measure can be said to have implemented merely by referring to the title of the directive itself. It is clear that both principal and agent are entitled under art 13(1) to receive a written statement from the other of the terms and conditions of the agency arrangement. It is also clear that this cannot be waived. While art 13(1) has not been referred to specifically in the implementation measure, it requires no further action by either the EC institutions or the Member State in order to be legally complete and meaningful: it is clear, unambiguous and unconditional. Hence, it may be said to have been correctly implemented by virtue of SI 1994/33, reg 2(3) of which states:

The Directive shall, subject to these Regulations, apply to the relations between commercial agents and their principals from 1 January 1994.

By virtue of this simple formula, art 13(1) is now effective in law. It is not strictly necessary for an implementation measure to recite the terms of a provision, which is as clear as this is in order for it to be said to be 'implemented'. Because art 13(1) is legally complete in itself, it is not necessary for it to be elaborated upon in the statutory instrument in order for it to be said to be correctly implemented.

Article 13 has therefore been adequately implemented by a domestic measure and thus is now part of the law of the State. Consequently, such a measure has the force of law as between all commercial agents so defined and their principals. It is important to emphasise that had SI 1994/33 never been adopted, then art 13(1), although satisfying the direct effect criteria, would nevertheless only be invocable in a limited sense, ie, in a vertical as opposed to horizontal situation. For this reason, the very existence of the implementation measure is of the utmost importance in order to ensure that art 13(1) is fully effective.

(c) Example 3: 'Complex' implementation relevant because obvious choice is required

Article 7 provides:

1. A commercial agent shall be entitled to commission on commercial transactions concluded during the period covered by the agency contract:

(a) where the transaction has been concluded as a result of his action; or

(b) where the transaction is concluded with a third party whom he has previously acquired as a customer for transactions of the same kind.

2. A commercial agent shall also be entitled to commission on transactions concluded during the period covered by the agency contract:

– either where he is entrusted with a specific geographical area or group of customers,

– or where he has an exclusive right to a specific geographical area or group of customers,

and where the transaction has been entered into with a customer belonging to that area or group.

Member States shall include in their legislation one of the possibilities referred to in the above two indents.

Article 7(1) entitles the commercial agent to be remunerated by way of commission. Article 7(2) demands that Member States choose whether to opt for the first or second indented paragraph in art 7(2). This has been done in the Irish implementing regulations because, in reg 4 of SI 1994/33, the Minister opted for the second indented choice:

In the application of Article 7(2) of the Directive, a commercial agent shall be entitled to commission on commercial transactions concluded during the period covered by the agency contract only where the agent has an exclusive right to a specific geographical area or group of customers and where the transaction has been entered into with a customer belonging to that area or group.

Had reg 4 not been implemented, then a provision such as art 7(2) would remain legally incomplete because the State would have failed to make a legislative choice required of it. Such a provision would be incapable of being invoked by way of direct effect, because its operation would remain dependent on State action in order to render it legally operative.

(d) Example 4: 'Complex' implementation relevant (because oblique choice required)

Article 17(1) provides that:

Member States shall take the measures necessary to ensure that the commercial agent is, after termination of the agency contract, indemnified in accordance with paragraph 2 or compensated for damage in accordance with paragraph 3.

While it is not clearly indicated, a close reading of the entirety of art 17 indicates that Member States had to choose whether to allow for agents to be indemnified under art 17(2) or compensated under art 17(3). Unfortunately, SI 1994/33 does not make any reference to art 17. Therefore, the question arises as to whether art 17 is adequately implemented notwithstanding, or whether at the very least, it is capable of being invoked by way of direct effect notwithstanding the insufficiency of the statutory instrument.

Regrettably, it is submitted that the answer is in the negative because art 17(1) is not sufficiently clear and precise. It requires that the State should opt in the domestic implementing measure for the indemnity or the compensation route for commercial agents upon termination of their appointments. In the event, neither has been chosen as required by the directive, and so the provision is not legally complete. It is dependent on some further action (ie, a choice by the State) before it can have definite legal meaning. Such action (the choosing of either indemnity or compensation) has not been taken by the State in the domestic implementation measure: SI 1994/33.

This is a classic example of a key provision of a directive that is not capable of being legally effective until the Member State renders it so by exercising a choice (ie, indemnity or compensation) in order to give the provision complete meaning in the legal sense.

At this point an interesting question arises. Assume for a moment that art 17 had not suffered from a lack of precision in the first place. For example, assume that art 17 specified a right to indemnity only, with no mention made of compensation. Could art 17 then be relied upon as against a non-State (ie, private) principal by an agent? It could not because, while it would now satisfy the criteria of the direct effect test, the fact remains that provisions that are amenable to the direct effect criteria are only invocable against the State or its emanations, and not horizontally against other private individuals in the absence of effective domestic implementation. The only way therefore that the hypothetical art 17 could be relied upon as a basis for enforceable rights against other private individuals would be if it could be deemed to have been properly implemented by virtue of the fact that SI 1994/33 had been adopted, reg 2(3) of which states that:

> The Directive shall, subject to these Regulations, apply to the relations between commercial agents and their principals from 1 January 1994.

Ultimately, Ireland had to adopt a second statutory instrument (the European Communities (Commercial Agents) Regulations 1997, SI 1997/31) expressly opting for the compensation option in art 17. Only then did the Commission regard art 17 as being effectively implemented in Irish law.

2.5.5.4 Will aggrieved party have remedy in damages against the State for improper implementation of directive?

The next question that must arise therefore is whether an action in damages would lie against the State by an agent who could demonstrate that, but for the State's failure to exercise the option presented in art 17(1), they would now have a right to either compensation or indemnity, under the terms of the directive. Such an action might well lie given that the statutory instrument's implementation of the directive was deficient. However, choice of an appropriate legal test for determining liability in damages presents a different set of problems. This issue is now considered.

Francovich

The legal test for an award of damages where the State has failed to implement a directive is set out in *Francovich*:

(a)   Was the aim of the directive to create rights for individuals?

(b)   Is the content of those rights ascertainable from the directive?

(c)   Is there a causal link between the Member State's failure to implement and the damage that resulted to the injured party?

It could be submitted that art 17(1) might well satisfy all three 'Francovich' criteria because:

(i)   One of the aims of the directive was to require Member States to provide in their domestic laws for the availability of the right to either indemnity or compensation for commercial agents who negotiate sale of goods contracts on behalf of principals on a continuous basis.

(ii)   The content of the right is indemnity as described in art 17(2), or compensation levels as described in art 17(3).

(iii) It could be argued that, because of the State's failure to adequately implement art

31

17(1), the commercial agent has suffered loss of the entitlement to an indemnity or compensation.

However, as we shall see immediately below, the criteria for determining State liability for failure to implement and, on the other hand, improper implementation, appear to vary.

Recent developments

The ECJ has delivered a series of judgments in the last few years which have further refined the principles concerning conditions required in order for there to be an award of damages against a Member State for failure to implement EU law correctly.

From *Francovich* it is quite clear that where a Member State has breached EU law by a total failure to implement a directive into domestic law in circumstances where that directive did intend to confer rights on identifiable beneficiaries, then the Member State could be sued in the domestic courts for damages by parties who suffer loss as a result.

In joined cases *Brasserie du Pêcheur* and *Factortame* the ECJ held that Member States will be liable in damages to EU citizens where Member State laws were clearly, on the basis of previous judgments of the Court, contrary to the Treaty. The case is significant because the Court set out a different liability-determining test to the one set out in the *Francovich*-type situation (ie, complete failure to implement a directive).

In *Brasserie du Pêcheur*, the applicants claimed that they had suffered loss when they had to discontinue beer exports to Germany, as their beer did not comply with the product designation requirements of a German beer purity law. Such laws had in a previous case been held to be contrary to art 28 of the Treaty by the ECJ.

In *Factortame*, the applicants were owners of United Kingdom registered Spanish fishing vessels which were prevented from fishing British fish quotas by the Merchant Shipping Act 1988. The 1988 Act had been found in a previous case to be contrary to EU law as it discriminated on grounds of nationality contrary to the Treaty.

Clearly therefore, in both cases the Member States were maintaining measures in force despite earlier rulings of the ECJ which called into question the validity of such measures.

The ECJ elaborated a set of criteria which must be satisfied in order for an award of damages to lie against a Member State in circumstances where the Member States have a 'wide discretion' to adopt legislation in order to implement a particular EU policy. These appear to be somewhat different from the *Francovich* criteria. The ECJ went on to state that where, as in the two cases before it, the Member State had a wide discretion to adopt legislation in order to implement particular EU policies, then the right to damages will arise provided the following conditions are met:

(a) The particular provision of EU law infringed must have conferred rights. Undoubtedly this was satisfied in the two cases before the ECJ as art 28 (*Brasserie du Pêcheur*: free movement of goods) and art 43 (*Factortame*: freedom of establishment) were applicable respectively, and

(b) The breach must be sufficiently serious. In other words, according to the ECJ, did the Member State unreasonably disregard the limits of its discretion? To assist in deciding this question, the ECJ elaborated a number of criteria, which may assist in deciding this issue, such as:

(i) degree of clarity and precision of the rule breached;

(ii) measure of discretion left by that rule for Member State/EU authorities;

(iii) whether the infringement and the damage caused was intentional or involuntary;

(iv) whether any error of law was excusable or not;

(v)   whether a Community institution's actions may have contributed to the breach, and

(vi) whether there is a direct causal link between the breach by the State and the loss or damage sustained by the parties claiming relief.

Thus, we now have two different sets of liability-determining criteria. The *Francovich* criteria apply where there has been a complete failure to implement a directive into national law. The mere failure to implement constitutes an actionable breach. On the other hand, in so-called 'wide discretion' situations, the less strict *Brasserie du Pêcheur/Factortame* test applies whereby the breach will be actionable provided it is 'sufficiently serious'. This is because the ECJ takes the view that such circumstances are different from the case where a Member State fails to attempt to implement a directive at all. The liability-determining criteria are therefore more generous to the Member States as otherwise they would live in constant fear of litigation. However, what must not be overlooked is that the ECJ did make it clear that Member States will be liable where the breach is 'sufficiently serious'.

Which test will apply to the situation where a State improperly implements a directive – the *Francovich* test or the *Brasserie du Pêcheur/Factortame* test? This is an important question because under the *Francovich* test, breach (mere failure to implement a directive) occasioned an actionable case, whereas under the *Brasserie du Pêcheur/Factortame* test, breach of EU law (maintaining national laws contrary to EU law) was only actionable in damages where the breach was adjudged to be 'sufficiently serious'.

Given that the *Francovich* test was applied where a State had made no attempt whatsoever to implement a directive into national law, it might be thought that *Francovich* might normally be assumed to be authority for permitting one to sue the State in damages where a Member State had implemented a directive, albeit improperly.

However, the ECJ took a different view in *British Telecom*. The United Kingdom had transposed EC directive 90/531 concerning public procurement in the water, energy and transport and telecommunications sectors incorrectly. British Telecom claimed that it had suffered loss as a result of the poor implementation of art 8 of the directive, and it made a *Francovich* claim for damages against the United Kingdom.

The ECJ held that British Telecom was correct in asserting that the United Kingdom had not implemented the relevant article of the directive properly. Therefore the United Kingdom was in breach of the directive in defectively implementing it. Nonetheless, an action in damages could not lie against the United Kingdom because, according to the ECJ, the relevant article of the directive at issue was, '. . . imprecisely worded and was reasonably capable of bearing, as well as the construction applied to it by the Court in its judgment, the interpretation given to it by the United Kingdom in good faith'.

The ECJ continued to state that the United Kingdom had 'no guidance from the case law of the ECJ as to the interpretation of the provision at issue, nor did the Commission raise the matter when the United Kingdom implemented the directive in 1992'.

Thus, concluded the Court, the United Kingdom had not committed a 'sufficiently serious' breach of EU law and thus damages would not lie against the Member State in this circumstance notwithstanding its failure to implement the directive properly.

2.5.5.5   Present position

Where a Member State fails to implement a directive, the *Francovich* test shall apply in actions for damages against the Member State. This has been confirmed by the more recent judgment in *Dillenkofer v Germany*.

On the other hand, where a Member State improperly implements a directive, the *British Telecom* test shall apply. Where the particular directive is vague and ambiguous in meaning, then provided that the State acted in good faith in its attempt to implement, the breach (improper implementation) will not be 'sufficiently serious' and hence not be actionable in damages. However, if the State misimplemented an otherwise clearly-worded provision of a directive, the breach may well be deemed 'sufficiently serious', and thus prima facie actionable in damages.

2.5.5.6   Application of State liability principle to Irish implementation of Commercial Agents Directive, art 17

On the strength of the *Brasserie/Factortame* and *British Telecom* case law, it would appear that until the adoption of SI 1997/31 the test propounded in those cases was the appropriate test to apply rather than the *Francovich* test, because SI 1994/33 presents an improper implementation attempt (ie, SI 1994/33 made no choice between compensation or indemnity although required to do so under art 17 of the directive) rather than a complete failure to implement.

2.5.6   EUROPEAN COMMUNITIES (COMMERCIAL AGENTS) REGULATIONS 1997

In the mid-1990s, the European Commission opened proceedings against Ireland in respect of the failure to properly implement art 17. The proceedings were dropped after the Minister adopted European Communities (Commercial Agents) Regulations 1997 (SI 1997/31). Regulations 1 and 2 of that statutory instrument expressly provide that:

I, Richard Bruton, Minister for Enterprise and Employment, in exercise of the powers conferred on me by section 3 of the European Communities Act, 1972 (No. 27 of 1972), for the purpose of giving effect to Council Directive No. 86/653/EEC of 18 December 1986, on the co-ordination of the laws of the Member States relating to self-employed commercial agents, hereby make the following Regulations:

1. (1) These Regulations may be cited as the European Communities (Commercial Agents) Regulations, 1997.

(2) The European Communities (Commercial Agents) Regulations, 1994 (S.I. No. 33 of 1994) and these Regulations shall be construed as one and may be cited together as the European Communities (Commercial Agents) Regulations, 1994 and 1997.

2. It is hereby confirmed that, pursuant to Regulation 3 of the European Communities (Commercial Agents) Regulations, 1994, a commercial agent shall, after termination of the agency agreement, be entitled to be compensated for damage in accordance with Article 17(3) of the Directive subject, insofar as they are relevant to such compensation, to the provisions of that Article and of Articles 18, 19 and 20 of the Directive.

CHAPTER 3

COMPETITION LAW

3.1   INTRODUCTION

The objective of this chapter is to describe EU and Irish competition law in the context of the practice of solicitors in Ireland.

Competition is the rivalry that naturally exists in a market. Competition law is designed to promote and protect, by use of the law, that rivalry or competition in the market.

EU competition law is embodied in various rules in the EU's Foundation Treaties as well as regulations, decisions and case law adopted by various EU institutions. In practice, while European Coal and Steel Community (ECSC) competition law may be relevant in Ireland (eg the sale of Irish Steel OJ 1996 L121/16), it is EU competition law that is the more relevant.

Irish competition law is embodied in statute law (such as the Mergers and Take-overs (Control) Acts 1978–1996 and the Competition Acts 1991–1996) and case law (such as High Court judgments which constitute, in part, the common law which applies in the absence of statute law).

Despite popular misconceptions, EU competition law is important for Irish solicitors because the practice of EU competition law is of growing importance in Ireland given the increase in cross-border trade between Ireland and the rest of the EU, and EU competition law influences the interpretation and administration of Irish competition law (eg, *Mantruck Services Ltd v Ballinlough Electrical Refrigeration Co Ltd* [1992] 1 IR 351 and *HB Ice Cream v Masterfoods* [1993] ILRM 145).

EU competition law is not confined to those cases involving clients in different jurisdictions engaged in international transactions (eg *Patrick Dunlea & Sons v Nissan (Ireland) Ltd* [1993] IJEL 146). EU competition law may apply to arrangements and practices between clients based entirely in Ireland where there is an effect on trade between Member States.

Irish competition law applies whenever there is an effect on trade in Ireland (Competition Authority Decision No 137 *General Electric Capitol/GPA* 20 October 1993). It is therefore almost inevitable that virtually every solicitor in Ireland will at some stage have to consider the application of Irish competition law and, increasingly so, many solicitors have to consider the application of EU competition law.

3.1.1   CONCEPT OF COMPETITION LAW

Competition law is a set of legal rules designed to ensure freedom or fairness in the marketplace by promoting or protecting rivalry and competition in the marketplace. Both EU and Irish competition law embody rules, which

(a)   usually (but not always) prohibit anti-competitive arrangements between economic operators (these operators are known as 'undertakings');

(b)   always prohibits the abuse of dominance by any undertaking having a dominant position; and

(c)   control many merger and acquisition agreements.

EU (but not Irish) competition law also controls the granting of State aid by Member States (arts 87–89 of the EC Treaty).

Competition law has historically been known in Irish law as restrictive practices law. It is known in US law as anti-trust law because the rules were originally enacted to curb the anti-competitive practices of trusts in the oil and railway sectors.

3.1.2   PURPOSES OF COMPETITION LAW

Competition law is designed to ensure efficiency in the marketplace. It is designed to ensure allocative and productive efficiency. However, there are often several other purposes such as curbing abuses of dominance (eg, predatory pricing, discriminatory pricing and unreasonable refusals to supply goods or services), ensuring easier entry to and exit from the market, and controlling price inflation. Competition law is designed to protect *competition* and not just *competitors* in the market so that sometimes even apparently *unfair* conduct may be legitimate under competition law. The purposes of competition law may evolve and change over time.

3.1.3   RELATIONSHIP BETWEEN EU AND IRISH COMPETITION LAW

As a general principle, both EU and Irish competition law may apply to the same arrangement or practice (*HB Ice Cream v Masterfoods* [1993] ILRM 145). For example, a distribution agreement may be subject to both EU and Irish competition law.

If there is a conflict between EU and Irish competition law then EU competition law prevails. Irish competition law may not permit any arrangement or practice that is prohibited by EU law. However, Irish competition law may be more restrictive than EU competition law provided it does not undermine the purposes and aims of EU competition law.

There are some situations where Irish competition law will not apply. First, if the competition law of the European Coal and Steel Community (ECSC) applies then Irish competition law does not apply (eg Decision No 458 *BnM Fuels Ltd/Fuel Distributors Ltd*, 26 February 1998). For example, in the case of an acquisition in the 'coal' or 'steel' industries (as those terms are defined in the ECSC Treaty) then neither the Irish Competition Acts 1991–1996 nor the Irish Mergers and Take-overs (Control) Acts 1978–1996 apply. Secondly, if the transaction is a 'concentration' (eg, a merger or acquisition) with a 'Community dimension' (eg, financially very large) then only EU competition law applies and Irish competition law does not apply.

It is important that solicitors ensure that arrangements and practices comply with Irish competition law and, where it applies, EU competition law also.

3.1.4   UNDERTAKINGS

Competition law primarily controls the conduct of 'undertakings'. If one is not an undertaking then one is immune from challenge in competition law. (Competition law also controls EU Member States accused of granting unlawful State aid and 'enterprises' which are subject to the Mergers and Take-overs (Control) Acts 1978–1996). If a defendant can demonstrate that it is not an undertaking then it is immune from challenge under EU competition law or the Competition Acts 1991–1996 – for example, the Voluntary Health Insurance Board sought to escape liability under the Competition Act 1991 by claiming that it was not an undertaking (*Deane v Voluntary Health Insurance Board* [1992] 2 IR 319).

Articles 81, 82 and 86 of the EC Treaty control the behaviour of only those entities, which are described as 'undertakings'. There is no definition of 'undertakings' in EC legislation. However, the term is understood as referring to any entity engaged in economic activities such as companies, joint ventures, partnerships, professionals and consultants (eg *Nutricia* OJ 1983 L376/22). Employees are not undertakings. Anyone sued for breaching EU competition law has an absolute defence where it is able to prove that it is not an undertaking (eg, European Parliament written Question No 2391/83 OJ 1984 C222/21, 23.8.84).

Section 3(1) of the Competition Act 1991 defines undertakings as being various entities, which are engaged for 'gain' in the production or provision of goods or services. The term 'gain' implies that the entity is charging in connection with its activities (*Deane v Voluntary Health Insurance Board* and *Greally v Minister for Education* [1995] ILRM 481). Examples include companies, partnerships, joint venture companies, consultants, farmers, co-operatives, universities and semi-State bodies (Decision No 288 *University College Dublin/Bank of Ireland*, 10 March 1994). Examples of entities which are not undertakings, include employees or government Ministers performing regulatory functions (*Greally v Minister for Education*).

3.1.5 PROCEDURAL ISSUES

Procedural issues are examined later in this chapter. However, in the interim, it is useful to note that:

(a) there may be *litigation* on both EU and Irish competition law before the EU and Irish courts;

(b) there may be a *notification* of some arrangements to the European Commission and the Irish Competition Authority so as to ensure that the arrangement is enforceable;

(c) anyone affected by potentially anti-competitive behaviour is able to *complain* to both the Commission and the Competition Authority; and

(d) the Commission and Competition Authority may conduct *investigations* to determine the existence of a breach of competition law. Solicitors must be able to advise on any of these procedures.

Solicitors should also bear in mind that it is often difficult to give precise advice on competition law because of the ambiguous legal rules, developing doctrines, difficult economic issues and absence of precise information in some situations.

3.1.6 PRACTICAL PERSPECTIVE

Solicitors need to be conscious of competition law in such situations as reviewing commercial arrangements, considering how best to defend litigation, as well as advising on acquisitions and joint ventures. Solicitors can use competition law for the benefit of their clients in terms of being able, in certain circumstances, to obtain supplies which are refused, reduce the prices at which goods are supplied or defend litigation. In other words, competition law may be used both as a sword and as a shield.

3.2 Anti-Competitive Agreements: EC Treaty, art 81

3.2.1 INTRODUCTION

This section examines the EU competition law controlling anti-competitive arrangements between undertakings. It therefore examines art 81 of the EC Treaty.

Article 81 is very relevant for solicitors practising in Ireland. It is relevant in the context of various contractual agreements (eg, exclusive distribution agreements, exclusive purchase agreements and solus agreements), commercial arrangements (eg, price-fixing arrangements) and commercial practices (eg, boycotts; *Mantruck Services Ltd v Ballinlough Electrical Refrigeration Ltd* and *Patrick Dunlea & Sons v Nissan (Ireland) Ltd*).

Article 81 provides:

1. The following shall be prohibited as incompatible with the common market: all agreements between undertakings, decisions by associations of undertakings and concerted practices which may affect trade between Member States and which have as their object or effect the prevention, restriction or distortion of competition within the common market, and in particular those which:

(a) directly or indirectly fix purchase or selling prices or any other trading conditions;

(b) limit or control production, markets, technical development, or investment;

(c) share markets or sources of supply;

(d) apply dissimilar conditions to equivalent transactions with other trading parties, thereby placing them at a competitive disadvantage;

(e) make the conclusion of contracts subject to acceptance by the other parties of supplementary obligations which, by their nature or according to commercial usage, have no connection with the subject of such contracts.

2. Any agreements or decisions prohibited pursuant to this Article shall be automatically void.

3. The provisions of paragraph 1 may, however be declared inapplicable in the case of:

– any agreement or category of agreement between undertakings;

– any decision or category of decisions by associations of undertakings;

– any concerted practice or category of concerted practices;

which contributes to improving the production or distribution of goods or to promoting technical or economic progress, while allowing consumers a fair share of the resulting benefit, and which does not:

(a) impose on the undertakings concerned restrictions which are not indispensable to the attainment of these objectives;

(b) afford such undertakings the possibility of eliminating competition in respect of a substantial part of the products in question.

Article 81(1) is a general prohibition on anti-competitive arrangements between undertakings, which have the object or effect of preventing, restricting or distorting competition in the common market or any part of the common market.

Article 81(2) provides that any arrangement prohibited by art 81(1) is prohibited and void. This means that such an arrangement is legally unenforceable in EU law or in the law of any Member State. An arrangement is void and not just voidable so it is legally unenforceable without the need for a court decision. However, art 81(2) does not render the arrangement a criminal offence.

Article 81(3) permits the Commission to exempt an arrangement, which breaches art 81(1) where the arrangement is, on balance, beneficial to the economy. The criteria for exemption are examined below.

Arrangements must comply with art 81 or otherwise they would be unenforceable in whole or in part. A solicitor who fails to advise on the application of art 81 may be negligent.

Why is there an art 81? It is widely accepted throughout the world that anti-competitive arrangements between undertakings are often harmful to the economy because they lead to inefficiency and damage free competition in the marketplace. For example, arrangements between undertakings that involve price-fixing lead to an absence of choice for customers in terms of competition.

3.2.2 ELEMENTS OF ARTICLE 81(1)

A solicitor advising on whether there is a breach of art 81 needs to establish the following elements:

(a) Is there an agreement between undertakings, a decision by an association of undertakings or a concerted practice involving undertakings?

(b) Does the arrangement have the object or effect of preventing, restricting or distorting competition in the common market or any part of the common market?

(c) There is no exemption under art 81(3) permitting the arrangement.

3.2.2.1 Arrangements between undertakings

Article 81 only applies where there is (a) an agreement between undertakings, or (b) a decision by an association of undertakings, or (c) a concerted practice involving undertakings. However, it is relatively easy to establish the existence of such an arrangement. The arrangement need not be legally binding, in writing, governed by the law of an EU Member State, concluded within the EU or concluded for the purpose of breaching competition law. It could be, for example, a contract, a set of terms and conditions, a joint venture agreement or an arrangement between members of a trade association. An oral arrangement would suffice. Similarly, the arrangement may be constructed from a chain of correspondence or conversations (Case T-7/89 *Hercules Chemicals NV v Commission* [1991] ECR-II 1711). A concerted practice is quite a flexible concept and refers to any form of co-operation between undertakings which knowingly substitutes practical co-operation between the parties for the risks of competition (Case 48/69 *ICI v Commission (Dyestuffs)* [1972] ECR 619). Decisions by trade associations may be formal or informal decisions such as codes of conduct, collective boycotts or the conclusions of a meeting that are not reduced to writing.

3.2.2.2 Object or effect

In order to fall within the scope of art 81, the arrangement must have the *object or effect* of preventing, restricting or distorting competition in the common market or any part of the common market. It is important to stress that the term 'object or effect' is disjunctive and not conjunctive (Cases 56 & 58/64 *Consten and Grundig v Commission* [1966] ECR 299). This means that if the parties have the object of distorting competition then that is sufficient to found a breach of art 81. There is no need for the arrangement to have the effect of distorting competition – for example, it is sufficient that there is a cartel to fix prices; there is no need for the cartel to succeed in its objective. Equally, even if the parties do not have the object of distorting competition, it is sufficient that the arrangement has the effect of distorting competition.

There must be an appreciable effect on trade in the common market or any part of the common market (Case 5/69 *Volk v Vervaecke* [1969] ECR 295). The Commission has issued a notice on what it considers as being appreciable (OJ 1997 C372/13) where the Commission has stated that the market share of the participating undertakings must not exceed 5 per cent where the arrangement is horizontal or 10 per cent where the arrangement is vertical in nature. This distinction between horizontal and vertical arrangements is indicative of the fact that competition regulators are more suspicious of horizontal arrangements.

3.2.2.3 Preventing, restricting or distorting competition

The arrangement must have the object or effect of *preventing, restricting or distorting competition*. These three terms are largely synonymous and little turns on which of the three applies in any case. In practice, a distortion of competition will suffice. There is no need to show that the distortion was dramatic or at a particular level.

3.2.2.4 'In the common market or any part of the common market'

The arrangement must distort competition *in the common market or in any part of the common market*. There does not have to be a distortion of competition in a substantial part of the common market. So, for example, the distortion might take place in a town or region but there must nonetheless be an effect on trade between Member States. It is irrelevant that the arrangement has been concluded outside the EU where there is an effect on trade in the common market (Case 114/85 *Ahlstrom Oy v Commission* [1988] ECR 5193).

3.2.2.5 Provided there is an effect on trade between Member States

Article 81 applies only where there is an effect on trade between Member States. This 'effect' is easily achieved in practice. For example, the fact that goods could move across borders would be sufficient. It is sufficient that there is a potential (and not just an actual) effect on trade.

3.2.3 ARTICLE 81(2): PROHIBITED AND VOID

An arrangement that falls within the scope of art 81(1) is prohibited and rendered void by reason of art 81(2). It remains prohibited and void unless it is exempted under art 81(3). If an arrangement is prohibited and void then it is unenforceable as a matter of EU law without any need for a decision of the Commission or a Member State court/institution to that effect. Article 81(2) renders the arrangement *void* and not just *voidable*. This means, for example, that a 'contract', which breaches art 81(1) (and is not exempted under art 81(3)) may not be enforced in the courts of any EU Member State.

If a client is sued for a breach of contract then it may be possible to defend the claim on the basis that the contract is void under art 81(2). Invoking this defence, often known as the 'Euro-Defence', can be troublesome because it may expose the client to actions by others who have suffered because of the arrangement and may also expose the client to an allegation that it has breached Irish competition law which is a criminal offence and a civil wrong.

3.2.4 ARTICLE 81(3)

On occasion, arrangements, which are technically anti-competitive and thus contrary to art 81(1), may still be beneficial to the economy and therefore deserve to be *exempted* so as to permit their lawful operation. Article 81(3) sets out the tests for the granting of an exemption:

> – *any agreement or category of agreements between undertakings;*
> – *any decision or category of decisions by associations of undertakings;*
> – *any concerted practice or category of concerted practices;*

which contributes to improving the production or distribution of goods or to promoting technical or economic progress, while allowing consumers a fair share of the resulting benefit, and which does not:

(a) impose on the undertakings concerned restrictions which are not indispensable to the attainment of these objectives;

(b) afford such undertakings the possibility of eliminating competition in respect of a substantial part of the products in question.

Only the Commission may grant an exemption. The only exception is that historically, in very limited circumstances, the Council of Ministers may grant an exemption. The ECJ and the CFI may not grant an exemption or modify one granted by the Commission. Equally, Member State institutions may not grant exemptions. However, the Commission is considering the possibility of allowing Member States' competition authorities to grant such exemptions but it may take several years before this proposal is implemented. In any event, the jurisprudence developed in regard to exemptions under art 81(3) is very useful in the Irish context because this jurisprudence would be useful in the context of understanding section 4(2) of the Competition Act 1991.

3.2.5   CONSIDERATION OF ARRANGEMENTS

In reviewing arrangements under art 81, a solicitor needs to examine not only the arrangement itself but also the market in which the arrangement operates. This is because there must be a prevention, restriction or distortion of competition in the particular market. For example, if the product market were defined narrowly (eg remould tyres) then an arrangement between two remould tyre sellers who had a combined market share of 70 per cent would be anti-competitive. Conversely, if the market were defined very broadly (eg all tyres) then the arrangement between the two undertakings might not be anti-competitive because they might have a tiny market share of such a market.

In reviewing an arrangement under art 81, one should also have regard to the possible application of Member State's competition law (eg the UK's Competition Act 1998) because the arrangement could also breach Member State law.

3.2.6   NOTIFICATION

If there is an arrangement, which breaches art 81(1), then the parties should consider notifying the arrangement to the Commission under art 81(3) so as to obtain an exemption. An exemption would permit the arrangement to operate legitimately under art 81. The notification is made by way of Form A/B, which is a list of headings that the parties must address rather than a conventional form, which they must fill out. The form addresses such issues as the parties, the market, the arrangement, the reasons why a negative clearance should be issued, the reasons why an exemption should be granted and whether the parties are willing to accept an exemption.

In practice, the Commission rarely grants exemptions but the Commission may issue a so-called comfort letter. This is an administrative letter issued by an official of the Commission indicating that the Commission would be inclined towards granting an exemption or negative clearance but it is not an exemption or negative clearance. This letter is not legally binding in itself.

3.2.7   LITIGATION

It is possible to sue in any Irish court in respect of an anti-competitive arrangement, which the plaintiff believes to be contrary to art 81. Neither the EU nor the Member State has to be involved in the proceedings and it may be entirely between private parties.

If there is a doubt on the law on art 81 then the Irish court may make a preliminary reference under art 234 of the EC Treaty to the ECJ. However, many aspects of the law on art 81 are now very clear and such references are relatively rare.

3.2.8 COMPLAINTS

A solicitor may decide to make a complaint to the Commission about an alleged breach of art 81. The advantages include the complainant does not have to pay the Commission's costs or the respondent's costs; the involvement of the Commission often strengthens the complainant's position; the Commission has various investigative powers (eg to conduct dawn-raids) not available to ordinary litigants; and the Commission has built up jurisprudence on a variety of projects. Complaints have their limitations in terms that the Commission might be unwilling to take up the complaint and the Commission may not award damages to cover the loss suffered by the complainant. This is discussed in greater detail at **3.6** on competition enforcement.

3.2.9 RELATIONSHIP BETWEEN ARTICLE 81 AND ARTICLE 82

Articles 81 and 82 may apply to the same arrangement or practice. This means that even if the arrangement is compatible with art 81 (such as by virtue of a block exemption under art 81(3)), the arrangement may be illegal under art 82 such as where there is an abuse of dominance (Case T-51/89 *Tetra Pak Rausing v Commission* [1990] ECR-II 309).

3.2.10 CONCLUSIONS

Article 81 is a very flexible provision to control anti-competitive arrangements. It controls almost every type of arrangement between undertakings, which could distort competition. Article 81 arises in the practice of solicitors in several contexts such as:

(a) review of arrangements such as contracts and decisions by trade associations;

(b) litigation over contracts and other arrangements; and

(c) complaints to regulators.

Solicitors need to be aware of the jurisprudence on art 81 not only in the context of the provision itself but also as a means of understanding the Competition Act 1991, s 4 which is based on art 81.

3.3 Abuse of a Dominant Position: art 82

Article 82 EC provides as follows

Any abuse by one or more undertakings of a dominant position within the common market or in a substantial part of it shall be prohibited as incompatible with the common market in so far as it may affect trade between Member States. Such abuse may, in particular, consist in:

(a) directly or indirectly imposing unfair purchase or selling prices or other unfair trading conditions;

(b) limiting production, markets or technical development to the prejudice of consumers;

(c) applying dissimilar conditions to equivalent transactions with other parties, thereby placing them at a competitive disadvantage;

(d) making the conclusion of contracts subject to acceptance by the other parties of supplementary obligations which by their nature or according to commercial usage, have no connection with the subject of such contracts.

3.3.1 ARTICLE 82 COMPARED WITH ARTICLE 81

3.3.1.1 Differences

From the text of art 82, it is apparent that art 82 is designed to deal with very different behaviour to that proscribed by art 81. Article 81 prohibits anti-competitive arrangements entered into between at least two undertakings, whereas art 82 proscribes a very different type of behaviour, the abuse of a dominant position.

The implications of this distinction are best illustrated in three respects.

First, art 82 requires that the accused undertaking must not only occupy a 'dominant position' in the relevant market, but furthermore the undertaking must have abused that position. Article 81, on the other hand, does not require that a 'dominant position' be established or that an 'abuse' be established.

Secondly, art 82 does not contain an analogous version of art 81(3). Article 81(3) allows for arrangements that appear to be anti-competitive contrary to art 81(1) to nevertheless be exempted from the application of art 81(1)'s prohibition, where it can be demonstrated that the beneficial aspects flowing from the undertakings' arrangements outweigh the anti-competitive aspects. Article 82 has no such equivalent exemption provision: where an abuse of a dominant position is established, it is prohibited, with no possibility of exemption.

Thirdly, a single undertaking's unilateral behaviour is sufficient to attract the attention of art 82's prohibition (indeed this is almost invariably the position), whereas at least two undertakings are required to be involved before art 81 can be applicable. In this regard however, it is noteworthy that art 82 does refer to the behaviour of 'one or more undertakings'. In Cases T-68, 77 & 78 /89 *Societa Italiana Vetro v Commission* [1992] ECR II-1403 the CFI accepted in principle the argument that the phrase 'one or more undertakings' in art 82 implied that there could be more than one undertaking occupying a collective dominant position. The CFI indicated that in order for this to be established, it would have to be demonstrated that there were links existing between the accused undertakings, which allowed the undertakings to act independently of their competitors, customers or consumers. As an example the ECJ indicated that links could be constituted by economic links (eg, such as agreements or licences), which gave the undertakings involved a technological lead over their other competitors. However, this was not actually found in the case itself because the CFI found that the facts presented before it did not merit a finding of collective dominance. In this regard, the CFI made it clear that the Commission cannot use its findings in a Commission art 81 investigation of the undertakings in order to support a conclusion that collective dominance exists also. The CFI requires the Commission to carry out a full art 82 analysis in order for collective dominance to be established. To date, the notion of collective dominance has arisen on only a handful of occasions.

3.3.1.2 Similarities

There are some similarities between the two articles.

First, both art 81(1) and art 82 are capable of being invoked in national courts, as they are capable of being directly effective.

Secondly, the legal consequences of breaching either article are similar: the proscribed behaviour is prohibited and void (save where an art 81(3) exemption is obtained in respect of art 81(1) breaches).

Thirdly, both articles attach to the behaviour of 'undertakings', which the ECJ has defined to mean any entity, human or corporate, that is commercially active.

Fourthly, the non-exhaustive lists of different types of anti-competitive behaviour listed in both provisions are remarkably similar (although the circumstances in which they will occur will be very different). For example, before an art 81 action may be pursued against two (or more) undertakings accused of colluding to raise their product prices, it must first be shown that they agreed to collude in price-fixing, whereas, under art 82, the accused undertaking will have raised its prices of its own accord without colluding with any other party. Both types of behaviour have the same end result (prices rise), but the circumstances in which the price rises occur are very different. In the art 81 situation there has been collusion between at least two undertakings, whereas in the art 82 situation there has only been unilateral action by a sole undertaking (unless of course a collective dominance scenario exists). Nevertheless, both types of behaviour can be very detrimental to the market for the products or services in question.

3.3.2 ESSENTIAL ELEMENTS OF ARTICLE 82

The critical elements of art 82 therefore are:

(a) that the accused undertaking has been found to occupy a dominant position (in rare circumstances the dominant position can be occupied by two or more undertakings, but this is not common), and

(b) the accused undertaking has been found to have abused its dominant position

(c) in a market that has been defined as including certain products or services in a defined geographical area

(d) where such geographical area constitutes all of, or at least a substantial part of, the common market, and

(e) the abuse has an adverse effect on trade between EU Member States.

3.3.3 RELEVANT MARKETS

In order for an undertaking to fall foul of art 82's prohibition it must first be demonstrated that the undertaking occupies a dominant position in a defined product and geographic market. According to the ECJ in Case 27/76 *United Brands v Commission* [1978] ECR 207, a dominant undertaking is an undertaking that can (because of its large market power in the relevant market) determine its course of action in the market for long periods of time largely free from any constraints that its competitors, customers or consumers might place on its freedom of action.

In order to determine whether an undertaking occupies a position of dominance, relevant markets must be correctly defined. Once the results of this analysis are known, those investigating (or resisting) the alleged art 82 breach will have a fair idea of what is the extent of the market power of the accused undertaking. The two principal relevant markets that have to be assessed are: (a) the relevant product market, and (b) the relevant geographical market.

3.3.4 RELEVANT PRODUCT MARKET

3.3.4.1 Contrasting approaches

In defining the relevant product market, at issue is the ascertaining of what other products may be said to be substitutable with the accused undertaking's product. In other words, do customers or consumers regard any other undertakings' products as competing with the accused undertaking's? Once this analysis is complete, a view will be formed on whether the accused undertaking dominates the market for a particular product, or alternatively whether the accused undertaking has substantial competitors whose products compete with the accused undertaking's products

In attempting to establish the relevant product market definition, the strategy of the Commission (or a private complainant taking an art 82 action in a national court) and that of the accused undertaking will be diametrically opposed. The Commission will be attempting to exclude as many other products from the defined market as possible. The fewer other products that form the relevant product market, the greater the likelihood that the accused undertaking will be deemed dominant. Conversely, the accused undertaking will be seeking to have as many other products as possible included in the relevant product market definition, as that will reduce the likelihood that the accused undertaking will be found to be dominant.

The Commission's traditional general approach in defining relevant product markets appears to be based on primarily assessing demand-side factors in order to assess what products customers or consumers of the accused undertaking regard as being interchangeable with the accused undertaking's products. In general, the Commission does not focus on assessing supply-side factors as part of this analysis, though we will consider below one or two notable situations where this was remarked upon by the ECJ.

In late 1997 the Commission published a Notice on Market Definition (1997) OJ C 372/5 which heralds a change in its approach to relevant product market. In the Notice, the Commission indicated that, when called upon to define relevant product markets, it will no longer regard as being definitive considerations such as whether a product has similar objective characteristics or could be put to the same intended use as the dominant undertaking's. The Commission has indicated that it regards such an approach as no longer sufficient by itself, and it has indicated that it will additionally look to see if there is harder evidence to identify or exclude possible demand substitutes. For example, it intends to assess items such as consumer surveys, barriers to substitution, evidence of demand switching in response to price changes in the recent past etc. However, while this is all very commendable, it remains to be seen whether the Commission will be able to adopt such an approach as such evidence may neither exist nor be easy to gather or quantify in many cases. In an attempt to further demonstrate that its approach is becoming more evidence based than principle driven, the Commission is striving to introduce a more economics-based approach when assessing demand and supply-side factors. Particularly, it intends to use the 'small but significant non-transitory increase in prices' test in order to see if a hypothetical dominant player would find it profitable or unprofitable to increase prices slightly. If the answer is that the dominant player would not find a permanent price rise of between 5 to 10 per cent profitable because it would result in a loss of sales to competitors, then other substitutable products will have to be included in the relevant market definition.

Whether the Commission succeeds in changing its methodology for defining relevant product markets remains to be seen, particularly as the Commission Notice is not a legally-binding document. Furthermore, the Commission cannot overturn the principles laid down by the ECJ over the years. Only time will tell whether the approach to defining relevant markets will change significantly or not.

3.3.4.2   Primarily a demand-side analysis

Michelin (Netherlands) v Commission

According to the ECJ in Case 6/72 *Europemballage Corporation & the Continental Can Company v Commission* [1973] ECR 215, if products are only interchangeable to a limited extent, then they are not part of the relevant product market. In Case 322/81 *Michelin (Netherlands) v Commission* [1983] ECR 3461 (para 48), the ECJ noted that a particular product is not to be included in the relevant product market just because a particular product is partially interchangeable with the accused undertaking's product (such that there is some competitive interaction between them). Here the ECJ was indicating that, merely because there is a limited measure of competition between a product and the accused undertaking's product, this is not sufficient to merit the inclusion of that product in the relevant product market definition. It must further be satisfied that the product's presence appreciably influences the accused undertaking in the way that it behaves. In practice, the ECJ and Commission require a high degree of interchangability before they will admit another undertaking's product into the relevant product market. Reference to the ECJ's judgments will bear out this conclusion.

In *Michelin* the ECJ had to consider whether the Commission was correct in excluding three types of tyre product from the defined relevant product market: the market for heavy vehicle replacement tyres. First it had to be determined whether original equipment tyres (tyres Michelin sold to vehicle manufacturers to put on new cars on the factory assembly line) formed part of the relevant product market. The ECJ found that the Commission had correctly excluded the original equipment car tyres from the relevant product market definition as it found that 'the structure of demand for such tyres characterised by distinct orders from car manufacturers' meant that 'competition in this sphere is in fact governed by completely different factors and rules'. Secondly, the ECJ had to consider whether replacement car tyres formed part of the relevant product market. It held that such tyres were excluded from the relevant market, as interchangeability between car tyres and truck tyres was non-existent, as obviously they cannot be put to the same use. Furthermore, the ECJ pointed out that the 'structure of demand' for each of these groups of products was different. Purchasers of heavy vehicle tyres are trade users who have an ongoing and specialised relationship with the tyre dealer, whereas car tyre users purchase tyres only infrequently and do not require a specialised dedicated service from their dealer. Thirdly, the ECJ had to consider whether retreaded tyres (repaired tyres) formed part of the relevant product market. While the ECJ found that they present 'partial competition' as they were 'partially interchangeable' with replacement tyres, nevertheless it excluded them from the relevant product market definition because users and manufacturers do not regard retreads as interchangeable as they do not regard them as an equivalent product to a new replacement tyre which is regarded as a superior and safer product, and the presence of retreads on the market did not affect the ability of the dominant undertaking (Michelin) to exercise its substantial market power in the new replacement tyre market.

Michelin is an interesting example of how a product may be excluded from the relevant product market definition either because the product has different objective characteristics, or because the requirements of the category of consumers who use the product are different from other consumer categories, or because the product (although similar) is not regarded by consumers as sufficiently interchangeable and therefore its presence on the market does not constrain the accused undertaking exercising its market power vis à vis its product.

United Brands

Another leading decision is *United Brands*. Under consideration in this case was whether the relevant product market was the banana market or the wider fresh fruit market. In attempting to define the market as the wider fresh fruit market, United Brands argued that the price of bananas fell somewhat in the second half of the year when other fruits became seasonally available. According to United Brands, this indicated that there was a competitive market in operation between the banana and other fruits. However, both the ECJ and the Commission rejected this argument as they found that the price of bananas fell only marginally in response to the availability of seasonal fruits. The ECJ found that while banana sales did fall somewhat, this was 'only for a limited period of time and to a very limited extent from the point of view of substitutability'. While significant cross-price-elasticity is a classic indicator of whether a product forms part of the relevant product market or not (in other words will the price of the accused undertaking's product be significantly affected should the price of another product on the market rise or fall), the ECJ was not prepared to make such a finding in *United Brands* on the facts presented. Also the ECJ pointed out that when the other fruits became seasonally available, volumes of banana imports could be adjusted by the accused undertaking, meaning that 'the conditions of competition are extremely limited and that its price adapts without any serious difficulties to the situation where supplies of fruit are plentiful'. Furthermore, the ECJ and Commission found that there were distinct categories of consumer for whom the banana was the only fruit they could consume, and that consequently the presence of these captive consumer categories eliminated other fruits from the relevant product market. In this regard, it was found that very old, very young, and very ill consumers did not readily accept other fruits as a substitute for the banana. Consequently, even though other fruits might be present on the market at all times, for such consumer groups interchangeability was not an option.

Hoffman La Roche v Commission

Another leading case on the issue of relevant product market definition is Case 85/76 *Hoffman La Roche v Commission* [1979] ECR 461 where the Commission defined the relevant product market as being composed of several different separate relevant product markets. Each vitamin produced by Roche fell into a separate individual relevant product market. This was because each vitamin is put to different uses, and therefore different vitamins were not to any significant extent capable of interchangeable use amongst each other. Another issue that arose was whether any of the distinct separate vitamin product markets could have non-vitamins included in them, such as anti-toxidising agents. As well as being used to improve health, vitamins may also be used as additives in food products as anti-toxidants. The Commission excluded synthetically produced anti-toxidants from inclusion in the individual separate vitamin product markets even though in some instances some of the vitamins (eg, vitamins C and E) were capable of being interchangeable with certain synthetic anti-toxidants or food product additives. The ECJ found the Commission was correct to exclude these synthetic agents from the relevant separate vitamin product markets as the ECJ found that while the vitamins were interchangeable with these agents for some uses, they were not for others, and hence they 'belong to separate markets which may present specific features' and this 'does not justify a finding . . . that such a product along with all others . . . which can replace it regarding various uses and with which it may compete, forms one single market'. The ECJ concluded by stating that the 'concept of relevant market implies there must be a sufficient degree of interchangeability . . .'. Consequently, the synthetic agents were not deemed to be part of the relevant separate vitamin product markets as they were only substitutable with certain vitamins, and even then, only to a limited degree.

3.3.4.3   Supply-side analysis

As noted above at the commencement of this section, the Commission, when determining relevant product markets usually only carries out a demand-side analysis (what do consumers regard as sufficiently interchangeable or substitutable with the accused undertaking's product) and does not usually assess relevant product markets from a supply-side perspective. However, two instances where this did arise were in the *Michelin* investigation and the *Continental Can* investigation.

In *Michelin* the Commission had considered whether a truck tyre manufacturer could become an entrant (and therefore a competitor) in the car tyre market. In other words, could a car tyre manufacturer be reasonably expected to adapt an existing plant to produce a truck tyre product and hence become a competitor against Michelin? The Commission found that this was not a possibility as totally different production techniques and plant requirements were involved in truck tyre production as well as considerable investment to modify an existing car tyre plant in order to use it for truck tyre production (or vice versa).

Consequently, no supply-side substitution was likely from any tyre plant not already engaged in truck tyre production.

In *Continental Can* the failure of the Commission to carry out a proper supply-side analysis was deemed fatal to the Commission's investigation. The ECJ annulled the Commission's definition of the relevant product market (defined as the market for manufacturing light metal containers for fish or meat products) because the Commission did not consider whether a meat or fish product producer could commence producing their own containers (and hence become a competitor in the market). Furthermore, the ECJ reprimanded the Commission for failing to consider whether manufacturers of tin containers for vegetable or fruit products could easily and inexpensively adapt their production processes in order to produce metal containers suitable for holding meat or fish products.

However, in general, the Commission does not engage in a supply-side analysis when defining relevant product markets in art 82 investigations. The ECJ is prepared to overlook this provided that the Commission does consider the possibility of substitutes at some point in its overall analysis. In this regard, the ECJ will normally be satisfied as long as the Commission adverts to the possibility of substitutes at the later stage of its investigation when assessing the issue of dominance and market power. Economists, on the other hand, take a very different approach, arguing that it is impossible to define relevant product markets without first defining both demand and supply-side elements.

3.3.5 RELEVANT GEOGRAPHIC MARKET

3.3.5.1 Generally

The second of the relevant markets, which has to be assessed, is the relevant geographical market.

In *United Brands* the ECJ elaborated upon the concept of the relevant geographic market, stating that it is the area where the dominant undertaking, 'may be able to engage in abuses which hinder effective competition and this is an area where the objective conditions of competition applying to the product in question must be the same for all traders'.

Applying this somewhat theoretical explanation to the facts of the case before it, the ECJ determined that the Commission was correct in defining the relevant geographic market as including Germany, Denmark, Ireland and the three Benelux countries. The remaining three Member States, France, Italy and Britain were excluded even though United Brands had substantial operations in these three latter jurisdictions. (There were only nine Member States at the time and United Brands operated in all of them.) The ECJ agreed with the Commission's assessment that the objective conditions of competition were not the same for all traders in those three States because those jurisdictions operated preferential tariff regimes for banana imports originating in their respective former colonies. Consequently, it could not be said that the objective conditions of competition were the same for all importers into those three countries. As for the remaining six Member States where United Brands operated, United Brands attempted to argue that because some of them operated different banana import tariff regimes (eg, zero tariff on imports into Germany compared to 20 per cent tariff in Benelux countries) consequently the relevant geographic market could not include all six remaining States. However, this was rejected by the ECJ, which stated that the objective conditions of competition in each respective State were the same for all traders, and hence there was no valid reason to exclude any of them from the relevant geographic market definition.

It is not necessary that the relevant geographic market extend beyond the territory of a single Member State. *Michelin* presents an example of a situation where the relevant geographic market was confined to the territory of just one State. Michelin had argued that as it operated on a global basis, the relevant geographic market should include more than just the Netherlands territory where its Dutch subsidiary, the subject of the art 82 investigation, operated. Rejecting Michelin's argument, the Commission and ECJ found that the relevant geographic market was confined to the Netherlands as the Dutch subsidiary only sold tyres to customers in the Netherlands and the customers did not seek supplies outside the Netherlands. Michelin's competitors operated on a similar basis.

3.3.5.2 Substantial part of the common market

The relevant geographic market must also constitute either the common market or at least a 'substantial part' of it. This jurisdictional requirement of art 82 is based on the rationale that if the accused undertaking's behaviour affects no more than a purely local market with no inter-State consequences or effects, then it should not properly be the concern of art 82. Article 82 is concerned only with abuses of dominance that affect trade in, at least, a substantial part of the common market. Abuses of dominance that merely affect a non-substantial part of the common market are best regulated by the application of local national competition laws.

Neither the ECJ nor the Commission have elucidated an elaborate test for defining what is a substantial part of the common market. This is probably due to the fact that there is a reluctance to elaborate a definitive test, which might have the unintended consequence of excluding from the jurisdiction of art 82 the activities of an undertaking, which, although affecting a relatively small geographical area, might nevertheless have tremendous implications for inter-State trade. An analysis of the case law would tend to support this view.

For example, in *Michelin*, the Commission found that the Netherlands constituted a substantial part of the common market, and in Case 40/73 *Suiker-Unie v Commission* [1975] ECR 1663 the Commission found that the southern regions of Germany constituted a substantial part of the common market. In Case C-179/90 *Merci Convenzionali Porto di Genova v Siderurgica Gabrielli* [1991] ECR 5889, the ECJ held that the port of Genoa, even though a small area by itself, nevertheless constituted a substantial part of the common market as it was the only main seaport serving the north of Italy and the Austrian and south of Germany regions. In *B&I Line plc /Sealink* [1992] 5 CMLR 255 the Commission found the port of Holyhead to be a substantial part of the common market because it provides the main sealink between the capital city of one Member State (Ireland) and Great Britain.

3.3.6 AFFECT TRADE BETWEEN MEMBER STATES

Before art 82 may apply, the activities of the accused undertaking must affect trade between Member States. It is clear from the case law that such an effect need not be proven as a matter of fact – merely that the behaviour complained of has the potential to affect inter-State trade will cause this criterion to be satisfied. In Cases C-241 & 242/91 *Radio Telifis Eireann & Independent Television Publications v Commission* [1995] ECR I-743, the ECJ stated that:

> 'In order to satisfy the condition that trade between Member States must be affected, it is not necessary that the conduct in question should in fact have substantially affected that trade. It is sufficient to establish that the conduct is capable of having such an effect'.

From analysing the art 82 case law of the ECJ and the Commission, it can be observed that where the relevant geographic market extends to the territory of at least two Member States, then an effect on trade between Member States will be assumed without further analysis. However, in those cases where the relevant geographic market is confined to either the whole or part of the territory of a single Member State, then whether there is an effect on trade between Member States will deserve closer analysis. For example, in *Michelin*, the ECJ indicated that although the relevant geographic market was merely the Netherlands (as the trade in tyres was purely national only), nevertheless there was an effect on trade between Member States. Michelin's Dutch subsidiary's behaviour had the effect of partitioning the Netherlands off from penetration by tyre suppliers based in other

Member States. Cases 6 & 7/73 *Istituto Chemicoterapico Italia SpA and Commercial Solvents v Commission* [1974] ECR 223 is another example of the ECJ's approach. In this judgment, Commercial Solvents was accused of abusing its dominant position in refusing to supply a customer, Zoja, with raw materials essential for the production of Zoja's end product. Commercial Solvents argued that because Zoja exported most of its product to markets outside the common market area, there was no effect on trade between Member States. The ECJ did not accede to this argument because once the elimination of a competitor may result from the dominant undertaking's abuse, the ECJ takes the view that the structure of competition in the common market will be affected and so it will not disclaim jurisdiction merely because there does not seem to be an effect on trade between Member States.

A rare example of where the ECJ disclaimed jurisdiction on the basis that the behaviour complained of did not affect trade between Member States is Case 22/78 *Hugin Kassaregister v Commission* [1979] ECR 1869. The ECJ held that although Hugin's termination of supplies of essential spare parts to its customer Liptons might otherwise be abusive, art 82 jurisdiction was not established, as there was no effect on trade between Member States because Liptons only operated in the London area. This is an interesting decision, because while the Commission had held that London could constitute a 'substantial part' of the common market, the ECJ nevertheless annulled the Commission's findings against Hugin, as the ECJ was not satisfied that there was any effect on trade between Member States.

3.3.7 DOMINANCE

3.3.7.1 Definition

The classic definition of dominance was given in *United Brands* where the ECJ stated that a dominant position is:

> 'a position of economic strength enjoyed by an undertaking which enables it to prevent effective competition being maintained on the relevant market by giving it the power to behave to an appreciable extent independently of its competitors, customers and ultimately of its consumers. In general a dominant position derives from a combination of several factors which, taken separately, are not necessarily determinative'.

Thus, it is clear that the central hallmark of dominance is that the accused undertaking has the ability to act in a manner whereby its freedom of action is largely unrestrained by the activities of its competitors.

3.3.7.2 Dominance does not preclude some competition

It is also clear that it is not required that all competition be eliminated from the particular market before the accused undertaking will be deemed 'dominant'. In *Hoffman La Roche* the ECJ indicated that dominance does not preclude some competition. The notion of dominance implies that the dominant undertaking either has the ability to determine, or at least have an appreciable influence over, the conditions under which the relevant market will develop. This had also been adverted to by the ECJ in *United Brands* where the ECJ stated that 'an undertaking does not have to have eliminated all opportunity for competition in order to be in a dominant position'.

3.3.7.3 Importance of ascertaining market share

The market share attributed to the accused undertaking will be a key component of any art 82 investigation. Once the relevant product market is defined, this assessment will be possible. Traditionally in art 82 investigations, market share has assumed a key role in determining whether the accused entity will be found to be dominant or not. A few general observations may be helpful before the authorities are reviewed below.

In general, where an undertaking has a market share of 50 per cent or more, and its nearest rivals have significantly smaller market shares, that fact on its own will normally deem the accused undertaking to be dominant unless the undertaking can point to other factors which (when cumulatively assessed) de-accentuate rather than amplify, the significance of its large market share. While the ECJ in its judgments seems to indicate that each case will be looked at on its own merits, the practice has been to find as dominant undertakings with market shares of 50 per cent or more, unless other factors can be put forward which reduce the significance of the large market share.

Where an undertaking has a market share in the 40–50 per cent range, market share on its own will generally be insufficient to warrant a finding of dominance. Other factors must be present which, when cumulatively combined with the undertaking's market share, indicate that the accused undertaking is in a superior position overall when compared to its nearest competitors (ie, that the undertaking's large market share allied to additional factors give the undertaking a significant measure of freedom from competitor-constraint).

Finally, an undertaking with a market share of below 40 per cent is unlikely to be found to occupy a dominant position.

An analysis of some of the leading case law will usefully illustrate the foregoing observations. In *Hoffman La Roche* the ECJ stated that:

> 'The existence of a dominant position may derive from a variety of factors which, taken separately, are not necessarily determinative but among these factors a highly important one is the existence of very large market shares.'

Consequently, Hoffman La Roche was found to have a dominant position in several separate vitamin markets purely on the basis of its high market shares, which often were in the 65 per cent or greater range. Although the ECJ did concede at paragraph 40 that each market must be looked at on its own merits, stating that: 'A substantial market share . . . is not a constant factor and its importance varies from market to market according to the structure of markets . . .', nevertheless the ECJ continued to add in paragraph 41 that 'very large market shares are in themselves, and save in exceptional circumstances, evidence of the existence of a dominant position'. The ECJ then continued to make a classic statement, which is worthy of full reproduction as it clearly espouses the ECJ's view of market share and its importance in art 82 cases:

> 'An undertaking which has a very large market share and holds it for some time, by means of volume of production and the scale of the supply which it stands for – without those having much smaller market shares being able to meet rapidly the demand from those who would like to break away from the undertaking which has the largest market share – is by virtue of that share in a position of strength which makes it an unavoidable trading partner, and which has already, because of what this secures for it, at the very least during relatively long periods, that freedom of action which is the special feature of a dominant position.'

However, the ECJ did not indicate what minimum level of market share would be required before market share, purely on its own, would lead to a finding of dominance. In the more recent Case 62/82 *AKZO Chemie v Commission* [1991] ECR I-3359 the ECJ gave such guidance by stipulating that where an undertaking holds a 50 per cent market share or above, then it will be presumed to occupy a dominant position unless the accused undertaking can indicate other factors which reduce the significance of the market power attaching to its significant share of the market.

3.3.7.4   Importance of other cumulative factors

United Brands is a prime example of how the ECJ approaches the issue when a cumulative analysis of various factors has to be undertaken in order to assess the accused undertaking's market power. In *United Brands*, the Commission ascertained that United Brand's share of the market was 45 per cent. Although it did fall to 41 per cent at certain times of the year, nevertheless it had a significantly larger market share than its nearest competitors. Consequently, the issue to be determined was whether there were other factors present in the structure of the banana market which, when cumulatively considered in conjunction with the significant market share, would accentuate, or alternatively diminish, the suspicion that United Brands was dominant in the banana market. The ECJ found United Brands to be dominant for the following reasons:

Vertical integration

United Brands was structurally a superior corporate animal to its competitors in that it was more highly vertically integrated. In this regard, the ECJ adverted to the fact that United Brands owned its own banana plantations, its own research and development facilities, and its own fleet of banana ships. Its competitors, on the other hand, were not as highly vertically integrated. Their ability to develop similar structures was inhibited by huge exit-cost risks. Indeed, the ECJ stated that were a competitor to attempt to so invest, they would 'come up against almost insuperable practical and financial difficulties'. Implicit in the foregoing reasoning is the notion that where an accused undertaking is a more highly developed company than its competitors, then this will amplify, rather than diminish, the suspicion that it may be dominant.

Fragmented competitors

The ECJ also found that United Brand's market share was significantly larger than that of its nearest competitor. This advantage, allied to the fragmented market shares of its competitors, was evidence of United Brands 'preponderant strength' according to the ECJ. What the ECJ was demonstrating here was that as United Brands did not have any competitor who had similar market power, the presence of several smaller competitors was insufficient to act as a counter-balancing competitive force in the marketplace. Implicit in such reasoning is the converse notion that where an accused undertaking (the leading player) has another competitor of equivalent market share and size in the relevant market, it is less likely that the accused undertaking will be found dominant.

Ability to preserve market share despite aggressive competition

The ECJ also pointed out that the Commission had ascertained that United Brands was largely immune from competitive pressures. During the mid-1970s, United Brand's smaller competitors had launched aggressive advertising and price-cutting campaigns with only minimal adverse effect on United Brand's market share. United Brands was able to adopt a flexible strategy by adapting its prices and putting pressure on intermediaries in order to maintain its significant market share (which at no time fell below 40 per cent). Significantly, United Brands continued to be able to sell its bananas at dearer prices than its competitors. The ECJ's reasoning may be criticised on this point as United Brands undoubtedly was operating in a competitive market, and it did lose some market share due to competition. However, on the other hand, it may be pointed out that the competitors did not take significant market share away from United Brands. United Brands was still able to maintain its prime position in the market and prevent its smaller competitors from substantially increasing their 'slice of the cake'. The rationale underlying this approach in the ECJ's reasoning can best be explained by the views of the ECJ put forward in *Hoffman La Roche* where the ECJ would not accept the Commission's argument that Hoffman La Roche's dominance was established merely because it was able to retain its significant market shares in the respective vitamin product markets notwithstanding aggressive competition from its competitors. The ECJ indicated that the successful defence of market share could also occur where there was effective competition. Consequently, the ECJ explained that other factors would require to be identified in order to demonstrate that the retention of market share was due to the existence of a dominant position. Thus the ECJ pointed to other factors identified by the Commission as supporting this conclusion, such as the fact that Hoffman La Roche produced a much wider range of vitamins than did its competitors; it had a huge technological lead over them and had massive resources at its disposal. All of these factors enabled it to defend its market share against attack from its competitors.

Homogenous or innovational product market

The ECJ also alluded to the fact that the product in question (bananas) was a mature product. In other words, the banana is a product, which is unlikely to be dramatically improved in quality or capability because it has reached its developmental potential. Consequently, smaller competitors could not hope to snatch away large amounts of market share through product innovation, as such a prospect appeared unlikely. Implicit in this reasoning is the notion that if a product is not mature in the sense that new technological developments are continuously likely to improve the capabilities of the product, then a more benign view may be taken of the leading player's position in the market. Particularly, this may be so where it seems that the leading undertaking will only be dominant for a relatively short period. For example, the computer industry provides a prime example of where this might occur. There are numerous examples of where an undertaking with high market share for a particular technology loses its leading player position after only a relatively short time. This may be because its competitors quickly developed the ability to develop superior or vastly improved technology and have eclipsed it.

Accused undertaking has strength to absorb losses competitors cannot sustain

United Brands had also argued that it had actually been loss making for a number of years, and hence argued that it could not be dominant. The ECJ's response was typically curt. It stated that:

> 'An undertaking's economic strength is not measured by its profitability: a reduced profit margin or even losses for a time are not incompatible with a dominant position, just as large profits may be comparable with a situation where there is effective competition'.

What the ECJ was indicating here is that a dominant undertaking has the financial muscle to absorb losses, even for long periods, in its bid to outdo its smaller competitors. Consequently, that freedom of action may well be an accurate indicator of dominance.

3.3.7.5   Miscellaneous other factors which indicate dominance

As the facts of each art 82 complaint are unique, it is not possible to exhaustively indicate each and every factor that will contribute to a finding of dominance. Nevertheless, it is worthwhile indicating a few additional factors, other than those outlined above, which deserve attention.

Intellectual property rights

Intellectual property rights are one such example. In Case 238/87 *Volvo AB v Erik Veng (UK) Ltd* [1988] ECR 6211 a national court requested the ECJ in an art 234 reference to consider the following two issues. First, whether ownership of an intellectual property right confers a dominant position on the holder. Secondly, whether it is an abuse of such dominant position if the holder of the intellectual property right refuses to license others to reproduce the subject of the intellectual property right.

It is interesting to note how the ECJ avoided dealing with the first question, instead preferring to adopt the view that the existence of intellectual property right protection in national law is not in itself incompatible with art 82. From this it may be inferred that the existence of such rights does not confer a dominant position status on the holder. In *Radio Telifis Eireann & Independent Television Publications v Commission* the ECJ confirmed this by specifically stating that: 'So far as dominant position is concerned, it is to be remembered at the outset that mere ownership of an intellectual property right cannot confer such a position'.

However, as we shall see when 'Abuses of Dominance' are considered at **3.3.8** below (this involves the second question addressed to the ECJ), there will be some circumstances when the refusal of the intellectual property right owner to allow others have a licence to reproduce the subject of the right will amount to abusive behaviour. Consequently, in such circumstances, the ECJ has no difficulty in finding that the intellectual property owner occupies a dominant position (as a prerequisite to finding that that position has been abused).

Monopsony

Monopsony is another example of where an entity will be found dominant though it is somewhat unusual. Normally, an art 82 investigation will concern complaints against an allegedly dominant supplier. However, sometimes the undertaking allegedly dominant is not a supplier, but rather, a purchaser of products. Such an entity may be the sole, or major, purchaser of the relevant products such that it occupies a dominant position by virtue of the fact that it dictates how the relevant market develops due to its size and influence as the sole or major buyer in the market.

Ownership or control of an essential facility

Ownership or control of an essential infrastructural facility can confer dominance and hence the undertaking operating the facility may be open to claims of abuse of dominance if it does not share the facility with its competitors in a fair fashion. The *B&I Line plc/Sealink* Commission Decision [1992] 5 CMLR 255 is a prime example of the application of the essential facilities doctrine. B&I complained that Sealink, its direct competitor on the Dublin/Holyhead sea route, had put B&I Line at a disadvantage by allocating sailing times to Sealink ferries that interfered unduly with the loading and unloading of B&I Line's ferry while in the port. (Sealink also happened to own and operate the Holyhead port.) The Commission found against Sealink on the basis that it held a dominant position as owner of the port facility, and that in reallocating its own ferries' sailing times, it placed its competitor B&I at a disadvantage thereby abusing its dominant position on the grounds that it was using its dominance in one sector (port operation) to hinder competition in a related market (ferry operations). The Commission stated that:

> 'A dominant undertaking which both owns or controls and itself uses an essential facility, ie a facility or infrastructure without access to which competitors cannot provide services to their customers, and which refuses its competitors access to that facility or grants access to competitors only on terms less favourable than those which it gives its own services, thereby placing the competitors at a competitive disadvantage, infringes article 82 if the other conditions of that article are met.'

A company in a dominant position may not discriminate in favour of its own activities in a related market. The owner of an essential facility which uses its power in one market in order to strengthen its position in another related market, in particular by granting its competitor access to that related market on less favourable terms than those of its own services, infringes art 82 where a competitive disadvantage is imposed upon its competitor without objective justification.

It would appear that wherever use of an essential infrastructural facility is being hindered by the owner of the facility, the owner may well risk being found dominant by virtue of ownership and consequently an art 82 complaint may well follow. However, this new development cannot be regarded as a carte blanche for competitors of undertakings who own their own facilities to be free to take advantage of infrastructural investments made by the competitor/owner (ie take a 'free-ride') in all cases. Clearly, owners of key facilities such as ports or airports are in a difficult position as often there would be no competition against their carriers if they were not required to share their facilities, and share them fairly. Smaller competitors cannot be expected to build their own airport or port as the financial costs are simply too massive. However, owners of non-essential facilities may well be able to resist essential facility-type complaints as they may well be able to argue that the competitors should be required to obtain their own facilities for enabling them access the relevant markets rather than forcing the owners of existing facilities to share them on favourable terms.

3.3.8   ABUSES OF DOMINANCE

Merely because an undertaking is found to be dominant, it does not constitute a breach of art 82. It must further be demonstrated that there has been an abuse of that dominant position. In other words, it must be demonstrated that the dominant undertaking has taken unfair advantage of its market power in a way which is regarded as objectionable by the ECJ or the Commission. While art 82 itself lists four examples of abusive behaviour, this is not an exhaustive list as dominant entities will always be willing to try novel ways of abusing their market power. It is instructive to examine some of these possibilities.

3.3.8.1   Refusal to supply

There may be many reasons why a dominant undertaking will either threaten or effect a refusal or reduction in supplies to a customer. Some of the most common circumstances likely to motivate such behaviour are now examined. What is common in each case is that all indicate how difficult it is for the dominant undertaking to demonstrate that its reason for refusing to supply is an objective one. Furthermore, it will be seen how the ECJ and the Commission have signalled that, while a dominant undertaking is entitled to take steps to protect its commercial interests, it must ensure that it acts in a manner that is proportionate to the threat presented.

As refusing to supply is a drastic response, it will normally be regarded as a disproportionate response and hence an abuse contrary to art 82. While the principles developed by the ECJ and the Commission have for the most part concerned the refusal to supply in the context of the dominant supplier/existing customer relationship, we shall also see how the refusal to supply jurisprudence has been expanded to also cover the relationship between a dominant undertaking who has never had a previous commercial relationship with a customer where it is refusing to supply that customer with a product the new customer wants (see *RTE and ITP v Commission* discussed below).

Refusal to supply and attempted objective justification

To achieve vertical integration. Cases 6 & 7/73 *Istitutio Chemioterapico Italiano & Commercial Solvents v Commission* [1974] ECR 223 is a classic example of refusal to supply. Commercial Solvents produced key ingredients, which were purchased by another undertaking, Zoja, which used the ingredients to make ethambutol, a tuberculosis treatment. Commercial Solvents wished to make the end product itself. Consequently, it decided to end its relationship with Zoja. Zoja was unable to obtain satisfactory levels of supply of the ingredients required for ethambutol production from any other source. The survival of its ethambutol business was threatened by Commercial Solvents' action. The ECJ held that where an undertaking is dominant in the production of a raw material, it cannot, merely because it wishes to enter a downstream market as a competitor itself, cut off supplies to an existing customer who operates in that downstream market in order to eliminate competition in that market from that customer. It will be an abuse of its dominant position where it cuts off supplies to its former customer in such circumstances, unless there is an objective justification. From this decision it is quite clear that a dominant undertaking in one market cannot cut off supplies to its former customer merely because it wishes to compete in the customer's market. A desire by the dominant undertaking to vertically integrate its business would not be regarded as an objective justification in such circumstances.

However, *Commercial Solvents* should not be interpreted over-widely. It is not authority for the proposition that a dominant undertaking, which wishes to integrate vertically, can never cease supplying its downstream customers. If the customer could easily obtain sufficient supplies from another independent source, then the dominant undertaking might well be in a position to cut off supplies to the customer provided that it was done in an orderly fashion to allow the customer to obtain supplies from another source, and provided that the other source could guarantee sufficient supplies. In such circumstances, the customer would not be at risk of being eliminated as a competitor because it could obtain the supplies from another independent source.

To strengthen presence in ancillary markets. *Eurofix-Bauco v Hilti* (1988) OJ L 65/19 provides another prime example of refusal to supply issues. Hilti manufactured a leading product, the Hilti nail gun. It also supplied nails and cartridges for the nails, to be used in the gun. However, Hilti would refuse to supply retailers with cartridges unless they also agreed to purchase Hilti nails for use in the cartridges. Furthermore, Hilti would refuse to honour nail gun consumer warranties if any other type of nail was used in the Hilti nail gun. The Commission condemned Hilti's actions as being an abuse of its dominant position. Its refusal to supply retailers who would not agree to its terms was an attempt by Hilti to corner the replacement nail market and its refusal to honour product guarantees was similarly motivated. The Commission rejected Hilti's objective justification plea, finding that non-Hilti nails neither posed a risk to the nail gun user nor to the operational integrity of the nail gun itself.

Intimidate intermediaries not to co-operate with competitors. *United Brands* demonstrates how difficult it is for the dominant undertaking to reduce or cut off supplies to a customer even where the dominant entity has no desire to compete in the customer's market. Olesen was United Brands' banana distributor in Denmark. United Brands reduced supplies of the product after Olesen had started acting as a distributor for one of United Brands' competitors. According to United Brands, its reason for so doing was that Olesen was devoting a lot of its advertising budget to promoting the rival competitor's product; also, Olesen had been appointed as the sole Danish agent by the competitor and so therefore might be expected to give that competitor's product more attention than United Brands'; and furthermore, United Brands alleged that Olesen was not ripening the product properly, thereby affecting its brand image.

The ECJ rejected all of these attempted justifications. It held that while a dominant undertaking may take steps to protect its legitimate commercial interests, that does not include reducing or cutting off supplies to longstanding customers who abide by regular commercial practice and whose orders are in no way out of the ordinary. In other words, the ECJ was taking the view that it is not abnormal commercial practice for a distributor to act for more than one supplier and yet do a competent job. Furthermore, there was no evidence that Olesen had downgraded its relationship with United Brands by placing significantly lower orders for United Brands' product. Finally, the ECJ found that there was no evidence to suggest that Olesen was not looking after the product properly so far as ripening was concerned. Having therefore rejected United Brands' attempts at objective justification, the ECJ found that the real aim of United Brands' behaviour was abusive: its aim was to dissuade Olesen, or indeed any other intermediaries, from acting on behalf of United Brands' competitors.

Parameters on legitimate dominant undertaking response

The question therefore arises as to what parameters govern the behaviour of a dominant undertaking, which finds it has a problem with a customer? In *United Brands* the ECJ elaborated by indicating that where a dominant undertaking acts to protect its commercial interests, it must take 'reasonable steps' which are proportionate to the threat. It also indicated that refusing to supply a product will normally be regarded as a disproportionate response when the economic power of the dominant undertaking and the affected undertaking is taken into account. Presumably therefore, a more proportionate way to defend commercial interests would be for the dominant undertaking to bring to the attention of the customer the concerns of the dominant undertaking, in an attempt to reach an orderly resolution of the dispute. Where the threat to the dominant undertaking's interests is more severe, then legal action and a remedy in damages might be a proportionate response. However, actually refusing to continue supplies should be seen as a measure only to be adopted in extreme circumstances, such as where irreparable damage would be done to the dominant undertaking's product's brand image and where it could be demonstrated that the customer was making no bona fide attempt to rectify the situation.

The Commission has also elaborated upon the issue of proportionate response in the decision of *Boosey and Hawkes*(1987) OJ L 282/36. Boosey and Hawkes cut off supplies to a good customer who had become associated with a competitor of Boosey and Hawkes. The Commission held that while a dominant undertaking is entitled to take reasonable steps to protect its legitimate commercial interests, such steps must be fair and proportionate to the threat. Furthermore, the Commission indicated that merely because an undertaking becomes associated with a competitor of the dominant undertaking that does not normally entitle the dominant undertaking to withdraw supplies immediately or take reprisals against the customer. The relationship could be terminated in an orderly fashion over a reasonable period, but not abruptly (para 19). This would constitute a proportionate response.

Refusal to supply intellectual property rights

This issue has presented itself in an area fraught with tension between national law and EU law. In *Volvo v Veng* the ECJ had indicated that a refusal to grant a licence by the owner of an intellectual property right (a registered design for Volvo car door panels) to a third party who was willing to pay reasonable royalties, was not an abusive exercise of the intellectual property right. However, the ECJ also continued to hold that such refusal might become abusive where the holder of the right engaged in conduct such as arbitrarily refusing to supply spare parts to independent repairers; or where prices for the parts were fixed at an unfair level; or where a decision was taken to no longer produce spare parts for a particular model even though vehicles of that model were still in circulation. The clear implication of the ECJ's decision was that while on one hand, a refusal to grant licences to others to exploit an intellectual property right is compatible with art 82 (because it merely protects the substance of the intellectual property right), nevertheless where that refusal might affect the structure of competition in markets affected by the refusal (such as the car repair market) then the refusal might become abusive.

Refusal to supply where no prior commercial relationship

In *Radio Telifis Eireann & Independent Television Publications v Commission*, the ECJ held (affirming the CFI) that it is an abuse of a dominant position where the owners of copyright in television programme listings refused to make the copyright information available to a third party who wished to compile that information in a new innovative format which would constitute a competing product to the existing format exploited by the copyright owner. Magill was a publishing company which was willing to pay the copyright owners reasonable royalties in return for granting it the right to publish the listings information in a combined weekly television viewing guide containing all of the schedules of the TV stations broadcasting in the Republic of Ireland and Northern Ireland. This was an entirely new product because the respective TV stations of whom the request was made only published their own respective channels' schedules in their own respective weekly guides. While the ECJ affirmed *Volvo v Veng*, holding that it is only in exceptional situations that the exercise of (or refusal to exercise) an intellectual property right will be abusive, nevertheless it went on to add a further example of abuse to the list of three examples already given in affirmed *Volvo v Veng*. The ECJ held that an abuse of a dominant position will occur where the holder of copyright refuses to allow a third party to exploit the subject of the copyright in circumstances where the third party wishes to make a new innovational product which will compete with and be superior to the dominant undertaking's existing product. The implications of this judgment are far-reaching because clearly an undertaking dominant over the supply of a subject protected by national intellectual property right law may no longer rely on such law to refuse to make a licence available to a third party who wishes to use the subject of the right to create a superior product. A refusal to supply the intellectual property right licence may well constitute an abuse according to the ECJ's reasoning in this judgment.

What is also interesting is that the ECJ indicated that intellectual property rights will be used abusively contrary to art 82 where the holder attempts to extend its monopoly given it by the intellectual property right (monopoly of the television schedules) to an ancillary market (market for television listings guide) without objective justification. As no objective justification existed, the ECJ held that the refusal to supply the listing information to Magill was abusive. In this context, the judgment of the ECJ is not that surprising as it reflects themes seen in earlier judgments. Indeed, it can be said to be similar to *Commercial Solvents v Commission* where the ECJ held that a desire on the part of an undertaking dominant in one market to extend its dominance to a downstream market did not constitute an objective justification, particularly where the dominant undertaking sought to achieve that objective by its refusal to supply.

However, where Magill goes further is that it makes abusive a refusal to supply to a party who has never had a commercial relationship with the dominant entity. In this respect the judgment represents a novel development. The issue therefore arises whether it is also authority for the proposition that a dominant undertaking is now effectively obliged to contract with any party who wishes to do business with it? This would be an over-wide interpretation of the judgment. Magill presented very specific facts: Magill was going to produce an entirely new product not seen before in the market. This constrains the breadth of application of the judgment only to those situations where this element of innovation is present.

This view is borne out by the ECJ's decision in Case C-7/97 *Oscar Bronner GmbH v Mediaprint Zetiungsund Zeitschriftenverlag GmbH* [1998] ECR I-7791 where the ECJ was invited by the Austrian cartel tribunal, the Kartellgericht, to consider whether a newspaper undertaking could rely on the Magill judgment principles in order to require a competitor to provide access to a facility desired by the undertaking. Bronner, a publisher of an Austrian daily newspaper, sought access to Mediaprint's unique home delivery system in return for a reasonable fee. This system ensures that Mediaprint's newspapers are delivered to Austrian homes early each day, such that over 70 per cent of the Austrian newspaper reading population receive a Mediaprint newspaper each day.

Mediaprint would only agree to the Bronner request if Bronner agreed in return to avail of Mediaprint's printing and other services. Bronner refused, and issued proceedings against Mediaprint, the dominant newspaper publisher in the Austrian newspaper market, alleging that Mediaprint's refusal to allow Bronner's newspaper access to Mediaprint's early morning newspaper delivery system constituted an abuse of its dominant position contrary to Austrian competition law principles. The Kartellgericht made a reference to the ECJ requesting a preliminary ruling on whether Mediaprint's refusal constituted an abuse of a dominant position contrary to art 82.

Bronner claimed that the Magill principles applied such that Mediaprint was obliged to grant it access to its unique home delivery system, which Bronner submitted was akin to an 'essential facility'. Mediaprint, in defence, submitted that Magill did not impose any such obligation and that a dominant player should only be forced to contract with other competitors in extreme or exceptional circumstances, and that save in such circumstances, it was not under any duty to subsidise its competitors.

The ECJ held that Magill was a very different situation from that of *Bronner*. In Magill the owners of a copyright were abusing their dominance by refusing to make the subject of the copyright available in circumstances where such refusal prevented the emergence of a new product for which there was potential consumer demand. Such behaviour was not objectively justifiable, and eliminated all competition in the television guide listings market in Ireland. However, in *Bronner*, it was quite different. It could not be suggested that if Mediaprint did not allow Bronner access, Bronner would be eliminated as a competitor. Furthermore, Bronner could set up its own distribution scheme, either alone, or in conjunction with others. According to the Court, Bronner's argument could only succeed if all competition would otherwise be eliminated if Mediaprint refused access, and if the Mediaprint delivery service was indispensable for Bronner to carry on its business.

3.3.8.2 Abusive pricing

Article 82(a) lists as an abuse the setting of unfair purchase or selling prices. This may occur in a number of ways such as unfairly high pricing or unfairly low pricing.

Unfairly high pricing

In *United Brands* the ECJ held that prices set by a dominant undertaking are excessively high where they bear no reasonable relation to the economic value of the product. In order to determine whether there is such a reasonable relationship between costs and price, the ECJ indicated that the production costs of the dominant undertaking must be established. However, there are several difficulties with applying such a test. First, the ECJ did not indicate precisely what costs are allowable as production costs. Second the ECJ did not indicate what level of profit margin constitutes an unreasonable (and hence abusive price). In any event, the ECJ annulled the Commission's finding that United Brands had charged excessive prices for its banana products as the Commission had failed to ascertain United Brands' production costs. Interestingly, about the only concrete point that the ECJ did make was that the fact that United Brands' banana was selling for about 10 per cent more than its nearest branded rival did not indicate an excessive premium was being levied.

The ECJ has also suggested another way by which to assess whether a dominant undertaking's prices are excessive: a comparison of its prices and prices charged by equivalent undertakings in other Member States. This issue arose in Case 110/88 *Lucazeau v Sacem* [1989] ECR 2521 where the national music royalty collection body in France was accused by French disco owners of charging excessive prices when compared to royalties charged in other Member States by equivalent bodies. In an art 234 ruling, the ECJ held that where an undertaking consistently charges higher prices than those charged by similar operators in other Member States, then the price difference must be regarded as indicative of abuse of dominance unless it can be objectively justified. Sacem had argued that it charged higher prices than comparable bodies in other Member States because it had higher administration costs, as its staffing levels were higher. However, the ECJ, while not explicitly pronouncing on the issue, appeared to take a dim view of this attempt at 'objective justification' and the tenor of the judgment appears to suggest that if the accused undertaking's costs are out of line with similar operators in other Member States, then higher operating costs may not be a sufficient objective justification for charging higher prices or fees. Thus, the inefficient dominant undertaking may find its higher operating costs do not afford it protection from an allegation that its prices are excessive.

Unfairly low pricing

A dominant entity must take care to ensure that it does not charge unfairly low prices. While keen price competition may be welcomed by the consumer, often it may have a deleterious effect on the competitive structure of the market in the longer term if a dominant undertaking is allowed to abuse its market power by selling product at an unfairly low price, ie, a predatory price. This is a price, which does not allow an undertaking to recover its full costs. The danger from a competition point of view is that the dominant undertaking may be able to sustain losses on sales for a significant period. At the very least, such a course of action may significantly increase the dominant undertaking's market share because its smaller competitors will be unable to sustain similar below-cost selling for very long. At worst, such a strategy may succeed in driving smaller competitors from the market altogether. Inevitably, once the dominant company has outlasted its competitors, it will be free to raise prices in a market with weakened or non-existent competitive restraints on its behaviour.

Dominant undertakings may also engage in predatory pricing for other reasons, eg, as a means of preventing a potential competitor entering the market in the first instance. An example of this kind of reprehensible behaviour was seen in *AKZO Chemie v Commission*. AKZO supplied peroxides to the plastics manufacturing sector and ECS supplied peroxides to the flour-milling sector. When ECS began offering peroxides to plastics producers, AKZO threatened it with retaliatory action and indicated it would target ECS's flour-milling customer base and offer them peroxides at lower prices. ECS refused to withdraw. AKZO went ahead and sold peroxides to ECS customers at very low prices. A complaint was made to the Commission and the Commission found that AKZO had breached art 82 by engaging in predatory pricing. The Commission decision was appealed by AKZO to the ECJ where the ECJ largely confirmed the findings of the Commission. The ECJ used the opportunity to set out its views on predatory pricing. It provided that art 82 prohibits a dominant undertaking from eliminating a competitor and thereby achieve a strengthening of its position by recourse to means other than those arising from competition based on merit. The ECJ went on to provide that, viewed from such a perspective, not all price competition may be considered to be legitimate competition. It continued:

> 'It follows that Article 82 prohibits a dominant undertaking from eliminating a competitor and thereby strengthening its position by using methods other than those which come within the scope of competition on the basis of quality. From that point of view, however, not all competition by means of price can be regarded as legitimate'.

The ECJ then went on to elaborate how a dominant undertaking will be guilty of abusing its dominant position if it sells its product at a price that does not allow it to recover its costs. It drew a distinction between below-cost selling, where most, though not all, of the costs are recovered (ie, sales below average total cost) and even lower selling prices where even less of the costs are recovered (ie sales below average variable cost). Sales below average total costs ('ATC') indicate a selling price whereby the dominant undertaking recovers a significant proportion (though not all) of its costs via the selling price. As sometimes it may be difficult to know whether a keenly priced product is being sold just above or a little below the level at which ATC are completely recovered, the ECJ will not automatically deem such a level of pricing to be abusive unless it can be shown it was part of a wider plan to eliminate a competitor. In *AKZO*, as the Commission discovered such evidence, sales by AKZO below the ATC level were therefore deemed abusive.

However, where selling price is at such a low level that the dominant undertaking does not even succeed in recovering all of its average variable costs ('AVC'), then such a price is deemed to be abusive automatically. There is no need for evidence to be adduced that such a level of pricing formed part of a plan to eliminate a competitor. As the ECJ explained:

> 'Prices below average variable costs (that is to say, those which vary depending on the quantities produced) by means of which a dominant undertaking seeks to eliminate a competitor must be regarded as abusive. A dominant undertaking has no interest in applying such prices except that of eliminating competitors so as to enable it to subsequently raise prices by taking advantage of its monopolistic position, since each sale generates a loss, namely the total amount of the fixed costs (that is to say, those which remain constant regardless of the quantities produced) and, at least, part of the variable costs relating to the unit produced'.

Again, the ECJ found that in certain instances, AKZO had indeed priced its products below AVC recovery level and so it was automatically deemed to have abused its dominant position.

Discriminatory pricing

A dominant undertaking cannot engage in discriminatory pricing without objective justification. In other words, a dominant undertaking cannot legally sell the same product to two separate customers, charging each a different price, unless it can objectively justify the price difference. The dominant undertaking may well be able to demonstrate such justification, for example, by proving that it costs more to deliver the product to customer A than to customer B. Such an objective difference permits the undertaking to charge one customer more than the other. However, often the dominant undertaking will be charging discriminatory prices without objective justification. For example, in *AKZO Chemie* the ECJ found that AKZO had no objective justification for charging flour millers who purchased peroxides a far lower price than the price it charged plastics producers. AKZO's motivation was far from objective. Its real aim in charging flour millers lower prices was to coerce a competitor, who had begun selling peroxides to the plastics market, to leave the plastics market and remain in the flour-milling market where that competitor had heretofore operated.

United Brands presents an even more infamous example. On this occasion the price discrimination was based on geographical location. United Brands would land its bananas at either Rotterdam or Bremerhaven ports. National buyers would come to the ports from each Member State and purchase the product from United Brands. Although the buyer was responsible for transporting the bananas back to the respective Member States, nevertheless United Brands sold the product to different buyers at different prices. United Brands' explanation for this behaviour was that the price set for each national buyer was determined by the price United Brands calculated the bananas would be sold at in retail outlets in the following weeks in the respective buyers' State. In order to make such a calculation, United Brands would place emphasis on whether in any given Member State a number of factors were likely to affect future retail sales, such as bank holidays, weather forecasts, availability of other seasonal fruits etc. The ECJ held that these factors could not provide an objective justification to justify the charging of different prices to the national buyers because the factors alluded to were relevant only at the retail level and were not relevant to the United Brands/national buyer relationship. Consequently, the ECJ upheld the Commission's finding that United Brands had engaged in discriminatory pricing because it had sold the same product at varying prices, at the same point of sale, and under otherwise similar terms of sale in circumstances where it could not present an objective justification for the varying prices charged.

Clearly therefore, a dominant undertaking must exercise caution when selling a product to customers at different prices. It must be in a position to demonstrate that objectively justifiable reasons exist for the price disparity; otherwise it may fall foul of art 82. The reasoning of the ECJ may be criticised on the basis that dominant undertakings will no longer be able to price products according to what they think they can extract from the market in any one particular Member State, with the result that prices may rise in poorer Member States. As against this, it may also be argued that as the single market process intensifies, the ease with which products may be moved from one Member State to the next, may act as a countervailing force.

3.3.8.3 Illegal rebates

Introduction

When considering whether a rebate (ie discount) system offered by a dominant undertaking offends art 82 or not, a clear distinction must be drawn between a rebate that is predicated upon passing on benefits of economies of scale and volume of business transacted between dominant supplier and customer, and a rebate that has other designs. Rebates are a perfectly acceptable and legitimate means of rewarding customers who do business with the dominant undertaking. Rebates are compatible with art 82 provided they are transparent and genuinely linked to the particular transactions entered into between the parties.

However, if a rebate system is predicated upon other motivations, then it may well violate art 82. Principally, there are two ways in which this abuse may be achieved by the dominant undertaking.

First, the rebate may be so structured that it removes the customer's freedom of action to source product from another competing source. Such a rebate is said to effect market foreclosure because the customer will effectively be prevented by the rebate's terms from sourcing product from the dominant company's competitors. Were the customer to do so, it might risk losing substantial amounts of rebate on its purchases already made from the dominant undertaking. Hence, the customer's freedom to contract with the dominant undertaking's competitors, even for some of the customer's product requirement, may effectively have been eliminated by the rebate system's terms. In this regard it should be noted that the rebate's terms may not be abusive at first sight because the rebate may not expressly prohibit the customer from sourcing product elsewhere. However, the manner in which the rebate is structured may well achieve that effect because, if the customer fails to satisfy the rebate scheme's terms, the customer will fail to earn maximum rebate.

The second way in which the rebate system may offend art 82 would be if the rebate is structured such that customers who purchase similar amounts of the dominant under-taking's product may be effectively charged different prices for the very same product, depending on whether they agree to deal exclusively with (or perhaps, alternatively, obtain most of their requirements from) the dominant undertaking. This may constitute a breach of art 82(c) as it may amount to setting discriminatory prices without objective justification.

Fidelity rebates

A rebate which is predicated upon the customer buying either all or a substantial amount of their requirements from the dominant supplier is known as a fidelity (or loyalty) rebate. Such a rebate becomes problematic from an art 82 perspective if it has the effect of promoting market foreclosure. Typically, under the rebate's terms, the customer will only be able to obtain the most generous rebate on offer if they continue to obtain all (or a certain substantial percentage, eg, 80 per cent) of their requirements for a particular product from the dominant undertaking only. This will breach art 82 in possibly two ways.

First, the customer will be effectively prevented from switching to another competitor of the dominant undertaking for supplies of substantial amounts of product. Should the customer do so, the customer risks losing rebate calculated on all purchases made from the dominant undertaking since the beginning of the rebate calculation period. Such a disincentive will remove the customer's freedom of action and effectively force it to stay loyal to the dominant undertaking.

Secondly, the arrangements may also breach art 82 in that the arrangements may amount to discriminatory pricing because customers who adhere to the rebate system are purchasing the product more cheaply than customers who do not adhere to the rebate system's loyalty terms. (Effectively the customer who adheres to the rebate scheme's terms gets a larger discount than the customer who does not.) It may be difficult for the dominant undertaking to objectively justify such a difference in treatment when its real objective is to prevent the customer switching to its competitors for supplies of product.

Suiker-Unie v Commission is an example of an ECJ decision where both of these fears were realised. Dominant sugar producers in the south of Germany offered a relatively modest discount of 0.3 DM per every 100 kilos of sugar purchased, provided that the customer purchased exclusively from Suiker-Unie. The ECJ upheld the Commission's finding that this amounted to discriminatory pricing without objective justification. Also the ECJ found that the rebate effected market foreclosure because the overall value of the rebate on a customer's entire purchases from Suiker-Unie was sufficiently attractive to prevent them switching to a smaller competitor for even a fraction of their requirements. Put simply, the loss of 0.3 DM on every 100 kilos purchased was a loss that customers could not afford to bear.

Dominant undertakings may also employ a number of techniques to exacerbate the market foreclosing effect of their fidelity rebate schemes. One such example is the device of the 'English clause' used in *Hoffman La Roche* in customers' contracts. At first glance such a clause appeared to ameliorate the effects of a 'substantial requirements' fidelity rebate scheme. The clause provided that if the customer found cheaper supplies elsewhere from another source, they were free to purchase from that alternative supplier without risking losing their rebate on their purchases already made from Hoffman La Roche. The only pre-condition attaching to this arrangement was that the customer would first have to inform Hoffman La Roche to give it the option of bettering the competing supplier's cheaper price. However, upon closer examination, the ECJ found the clause to be objectionable as it in fact aggravated the abuse already effected by the substantial requirements fidelity rebate. The ECJ took the view that the real effect of the clause was to allow Hoffman La Roche to further undermine the structure of competition in the market as it was using its customers as an army of spies to bring information to it regarding competitors' price lists, thereby enabling it to be in a position to react quickly to competitive price cuts by competitors and hence further strengthen its dominance in the market.

Another example of a device employed to further the market foreclosing impact brought about by a fidelity rebate may be seen in *Napier Brown/British Sugar* (1988) OJ L 284/41 where British Sugar imposed a fidelity scheme as follows. Customers who agreed to buy their sugar requirements exclusively from British Sugar earned a generous rebate. However, if any company in the Napier Brown corporate group of sister companies decided to buy sugar from any other supplier, then all of the 'offending' company's sister companies would lose rebate on their purchases from British Sugar even though they had not breached the rebate scheme's terms!

Target rebates

The fidelity rebate is based on whether the customer buys all or most of its requirements from the dominant supplier. The target rebate is based on whether the customer meets sales targets of the dominant supplier's product. Notwithstanding the difference in structure, the target rebate may be incompatible with art 82 for very similar reasons as the fidelity rebate. In other words, the target rebate may promote the objective of market foreclosure and/or effect discriminatory pricing between customers without objective justification. The reason why target rebates will invariably be different from legitimate simple volume discounts is because they achieve either, or both, of the foregoing illegal objectives.

The classic judgment on this area is *Michelin (Netherlands) v Commission* where the ECJ condemned a target rebate scheme put in place by Michelin for its retail customers. Each January, Michelin would impose a slightly higher sales target for the garage dealer. The sales target had to be achieved by the following December. A dealer who met the annual sales target would obtain the most generous rebate on offer. The ECJ found the rebate scheme incompatible with art 82 on several grounds. First, the rebate terms were often not committed to writing. Consequently, the garage dealer was often forced to surpass the target agreed orally with Michelin in order that the dealer could be sure of staying in favour when it came to the awarding of rebate at year-end. As a consequence, dealers were inclined to abandon selling competing tyres in the latter half of the year in order to ensure they surpassed their Michelin sales targets. This effected market foreclosure on Michelin's competitors. Furthermore, the Court found the reference period for rebate calculation (sales of Michelin tyres over an entire calendar year) was abusive. It exacerbated the foreclosing effects of the rebate scheme because the dealer who failed to reach the sales target would lose the right to earn the most generous rebate on offer, which was calculated over an entire year's sales. Consequently, as the sums involved would be substantial, dealers were effectively being 'forced' to abandon selling competitors' tyres for much of the trading year (even though offered on more favourable trade terms) as they could not risk failing to meet the sales target set by Michelin.

Other types of objectionable rebates

Dominant undertakings may also use other devices to further weaken the structure of competition in the market they already dominate. For example, the undertaking might attempt to use the rebate in conjunction with a 'tie'. Article 82(d) prohibits making the conclusion of a contract subject to the acceptance of other obligations that have nothing to do with the subject matter of the contract. An example may be seen in *Hoffman La Roche* where Hoffman La Roche offered a more generous rebate to customers if they agreed to purchase several different types of vitamin from it. This was found to be abusive because the Commission, having first defined each vitamin market as being a separate distinct relevant product market, then went on to find that Hoffman La Roche, in offering more generous rebates to those who bought several types of vitamin from it, was using the rebate scheme's terms to effectively tie sales of one vitamin to sales of another. Given that the vitamins were found to occupy distinct relevant product markets, this effectively meant that Hoffman La Roche was using a rebate scheme to try to effect market foreclosure as it would be attractive to a customer to obtain all of their vitamins from Hoffman La Roche rather than, say, obtaining vitamin A from Hoffman La Roche and vitamin B from a competitor.

Hilti presents yet another example. In that Commission decision, Hilti was found to have abused its dominant position because it offered more generous rebates to retailers who agreed to fit only Hilti nails in Hilti nail guns at point of sale, rather than non-Hilti nails. The Commission condemned this as an abusive rebate. First, there was no objective justification for offering those who fitted non-Hilti nails into the Hilti nail gun a lesser rebate. Non-Hilti nails would not damage the gun, nor were they a danger to consumers. Consequently, Hilti was engaging in discriminatory pricing without objective justification. Secondly, Hilti was attempting to effect market foreclosure because it was using the rebate scheme to tie sales of the nail gun to sales of its own nails. Consequently, Hilti was tying sales of one product to another, without objective justification.

3.3.8.4   Structural abuse

Even a cursory glance at the text of art 82 will reveal that primarily it is intended to prohibit behavioural abuses – market practice abuses. However, in *Continental Can*, the ECJ conceded that art 82 could also be used to prohibit, as an abuse of dominance, behaviour which effected a permanent change in the structure of the market. In *Continental Can*, the ECJ held that where a dominant undertaking acquired control over a competitor, thereby eliminating the competitor as an independent player in the market and strengthening its own dominance in the process, such structural behaviour would constitute an abuse of dominance contrary to art 82. However, art 82 is not the most suitable legal tool for merger control. For example, it cannot be used to prohibit the creation of dominance flowing from a merger between two non-dominant competitors as its jurisdiction is predicated upon at least one player being dominant before the merger takes place. In 1989 the EC adopted the Merger Regulation 4064/89, effectively disapplying art 82 from being invoked by the EC Commission against mergers above a certain financial threshold. However, it would seem that it may still be open to private parties to invoke art 82 in national courts against a merger brought about by an already dominant undertaking because art 82's direct effectiveness capability would not appear to be disabled by the enactment of the Merger Regulation.

3.4   Irish Competition Law Overview

3.4.1   INTRODUCTION

The objective of this section is to provide an overview of the competition law enacted by Ireland. It concentrates on the substantive rules with the next section examining many of the procedural issues.

It is important to stress that competition law in Ireland is comprised not only of the competition law enacted by Ireland but also EU competition law. If there is a conflict between EU and Irish competition law in any specific case, then the former system prevails because EU law is superior to Irish law when there is a conflict by virtue of the doctrine of supremacy of EU law. Solicitors need to be aware of both systems and the EU regime is particularly instructive in trying to understand the Irish regime.

The purpose of Irish competition law is to ensure a competitive and well-run marketplace by:

(a) normally prohibiting anti-competitive arrangements between undertakings except where such arrangements are, on balance, beneficial to the economy;

(b) always prohibiting the abuse of dominance;

(c) (i) prohibiting mergers and acquisitions between financially large-scale enterprises which are contrary to the public interest; and

(ii) prohibiting any merger or acquisition (irrespective of the financial scale of the parties) which is anti-competitive; and

(d) regulating some practices in specific sectors (eg groceries and telecommunications).

3.4.2 SOURCES OF IRISH COMPETITION LAW

Irish competition law is derived from two sources: the common law and statute law.

The common law continues to apply in so far as statute law does not apply. For example, the common law has the 'doctrine of restraint of trade' that prohibits unreasonable restraints on commercial freedom. It remains relevant only in limited contexts such as that of employment agreements or in some sale of business agreements in so far as the statute law does not apply. (It usually only applies when there are not two or more undertakings party to an agreement such as where it is an employment agreement.)

The more important source of Irish competition law is statute law. The statute law comprises primarily the Competition Acts 1991–1996 and the Mergers and Take-overs (Control) Acts 1978–1996.

3.4.3 COMPETITION ACTS

3.4.3.1 Introduction

The Competition Acts 1991-1996 comprise the Competition Act 1991 (the '1991 Act') and the Competition (Amendment) Act 1996 (the '1996 Act'). The former statute is the principal Act and sets out the broad framework of substantive and institutional rules. The latter statute introduced, for example, criminal liability for some breaches of the 1991 Act and conferred on the Competition Authority an enforcement role in regard to the Competition Acts.

3.4.3.2 Application of the Competition Acts

It is useful to examine some aspects of the application of the Competition Acts.

First, the Competition Acts apply to the behaviour of undertakings only. Section 3(1) of the 1991 Act defines an undertaking, for the purposes of the Act, as meaning:

a person being an individual, a body corporate or an unincorporated body of persons engaged for gain in the production, supply or distribution of goods or in the provision of a service.

Competition law only applies to control the behaviour of undertakings and examples include companies, consultants, partnerships, joint ventures, universities and pension trusts. By contrast, employees and Government Ministers acting in a purely regulatory role would not be undertakings. Any defendant, which can demonstrate that it is not an undertaking, is free from liability under the Competition Acts (*Deane v Voluntary Health Insurance Board* [1992] 2 IR 319).

Secondly, the Competition Acts apply to behaviour affecting trade in Ireland. However, the behaviour need not occur in Ireland so long as there is an effect on competition in Ireland – for example, an arrangement concluded in the USA, which fixes prices in, among other locations, Ireland would be prohibited by the Irish Competition Acts. Arrangements which are governed by foreign laws or have clauses which involve the submission of disputes to foreign courts may still be subject to Irish competition law where they have an effect on behaviour in Ireland – for example, it is not possible to circumvent the application of the Irish Competition Acts merely by subjecting an agreement to a foreign legal system.

Thirdly, the 1991 Act entered into force (for the most part) on 1 October 1991 and it is now entirely in force. The 1996 Act entered into force on 3 July 1996. It may be possible to challenge anti-competitive arrangements and abuses of dominance, which predate 1 October 1991 on the basis of EC competition law, which entered into force, in respect of Ireland, on 1 January 1973.

3.4.3.3 Institutional framework

The administration of Irish competition law lies primarily with the Competition Authority. The Authority comprises up to and including five members including one who acts as chairperson. One of the members is the Director of Competition Enforcement who has the responsibility of investigating possible anti-competitive behaviour but is subject to the directions of the Authority. A staff of about twenty-five people including administrators, economists and lawyers supports the Authority. The Authority does not ordinarily institute criminal proceedings itself (except for certain summary prosecutions) but rather recommends to the Director of Public Prosecutions to institute such proceedings. On the civil side, the Authority may institute proceedings seeking an injunction or a declaration in respect of alleged breaches of sections 4 and 5 of the 1991 Act.

The courts also have a role in the institutional structure. Claims under section 6 of the 1991 Act for breaches of sections 4 and 5 of the 1991 Act may be instituted only in the High Court with the exception of claims for a breach of section 5 which may also be instituted in the Circuit Court. Appeals from the Circuit Court lie to the High Court and from the High Court to the Supreme Court. Some summary proceedings may be heard by the District Court. It is possible to plead Irish competition law in defending claims before any Irish court.

The Minister for Enterprise, Trade and Employment has a role to play in terms of developing policy, seeking injunctions and declarations from the courts in respect of alleged breaches of sections 4 and 5 of the 1991 Act, calling for studies and investigations of dominance under sections 11 and 14, respectively, of the 1991 Act.

Aggrieved persons also have a role to play because they bring complaints to the attention of the Competition Authority and institute proceedings in the courts. This means that they play an important role in the administration of competition law in Ireland.

3.4.3.4 Anti-competitive arrangements

Section 4 of the 1991 Act controls arrangements between undertakings which have the object or effect of preventing, restricting or distorting competition in Ireland or any part of the State. It is analogous to art 81 of the EC Treaty. The case law on art 81 is instructive in terms of understanding section 4.

Section 4 provides:

(1) Subject to the provisions of this section, all agreements between undertakings, decisions by associations of undertakings and concerted practices which have as their object or effect the prevention, restriction or distortion of competition in trade in any goods or services in the State or in any part of the State are prohibited and void, including in particular, without prejudice to the generality of this subsection, those which–

(a) directly or indirectly fix purchase or selling prices or any other trading conditions;

(b) limit or control production, markets, technical development or investment;

(c) share markets or sources of supply;

(d) apply dissimilar conditions to equivalent transactions with other trading parties thereby placing them at a competitive disadvantage;

(e) make the conclusion of contracts subject to acceptance by the other parties of supplementary obligations which by their nature or according to commercial usage have no connection with the subject of such contracts.

(2) The Competition Authority established by this Act ('the Authority') may in accordance with section 8 grant a licence for the purposes of this section in the case of—

(a) any agreement or category of agreements,

(b) any decision or category of decisions,

(c) any concerted practice or category of concerted practices, which in the opinion of the Authority, having regard to all relevant market conditions, contributes to improving the production or distribution of goods or provision of services or to promoting technical or economic progress, while allowing consumers a fair share of the resulting benefit and which does not—

(i) impose on the undertakings concerned terms which are not indispensable to the attainment of those objectives;

(ii) afford undertakings the possibility of eliminating competition in respect of a substantial part of the products or services in question.

(3) (a) A licence under subsection (2) shall, while it is in force, and in accordance with its terms, permit the doing of acts which would otherwise be prohibited and void under subsection (1).

(b) Where a licence under subsection (2) covers a category of agreements, decisions or concerted practices, any agreements, decisions or concerted practices (as the case may be) within that category which comply with the terms of the licence need not be notified under section 7 to benefit from the licence while it is in force.

(4) The Authority may certify that in its opinion, on the basis of the facts in its possession, an agreement, decision or concerted practice notified under section 7 does not offend against subsection (1).

(5) Before granting a licence or issuing a certificate under this section, the Authority may invite any Minister of the Government concerned with the matter to make such observations as he may wish to make.

(6) On granting a licence or issuing a certificate under this section, the Authority shall forthwith give notice in the prescribed manner to every body to which it relates stating the terms and the date thereof and the reasons thereof and cause the notice to be published in Iris Oifigiúil and cause notice of the grant of the licence or issue of the certificate, as the case may be, to be published in one daily newspaper published in the State.

(7) The prohibition in subsection (1) shall not prevent the Court, in exercising any jurisdiction conferred on it by this Act, concerning an agreement, decision or concerted practice which contravenes that prohibition and which creates or, but for this Act, would have created legal relations between the parties thereto, from applying, where appropriate, any relevant rules of law as to the severance of those terms of that agreement, decision or concerted practice which contravene that prohibition from those which do not.

(8) In respect of an agreement, decision or concerted practice such as is referred to in subsection (7) a court of competent jurisdiction may make such order as to recovery, restitution or otherwise between the parties to such agreement, decision or concerted practice as may in all the circumstances seem just, having regard in particular to any consideration or benefit given or received by such parties on foot thereof.

Section 4(1) provides that (a) agreements between undertakings; (b) decisions by associations of undertakings, and (c) decisions by associations of undertakings which have as their object or effect the prevention, restriction or distortion of competition in trade in goods or services in Ireland or any part of Ireland are prohibited and void. For an arrangement to fall within the scope of section 4, the arrangement does not have to be in writing, legally binding or embodied in a single document. Examples of arrangements within the scope of section 4 include contracts, decisions of meetings of trade associations, boycotts, non-compete covenants, share purchase agreements, distribution agreements and terms and conditions. Nor does the arrangement have to be concluded in Ireland; it is sufficient that there is an effect on competition in Ireland or any part of Ireland.

One must examine whether the arrangement has the object or effect of distorting competition in Ireland or any part of Ireland. This needs careful examination. First, the arrangement need only have the object *or* effect of distorting (etc) competition. If the parties have the objective of distorting competition, then this is sufficient – for example, a cartel arrangement may not succeed.

Equally, if the parties do not have the objective of distorting competition, but the arrangement has such an effect then that is sufficient. Secondly, there must be a distortion of 'competition'. Mere exclusivity does not mean that there is a distortion of competition. This must be a market specific examination of whether the arrangement distorts (etc) competition in that particular market. This may involve retaining the services of an economist. Thirdly, the effect on competition need only be on 'any part' of Ireland and need not be (unlike section 5) on a substantial part of Ireland.

Section 4(2) provides an escape mechanism from the harshness of section 4(1). Section 4(2) allows the Competition Authority to grant a licence to permit the lawful operation of an arrangement that breaches section 4(1) where certain conditions are met. A licence is comparable to an exemption under art 81(3) of the EC Treaty. It is a permission to lawfully operate, in terms of section 4 (but not section 5) of the 1991 Act, an arrangement which otherwise breaches section 4(1). Only the Competition Authority may license an arrangement – not even a court may license an arrangement even where it would appear that the arrangement deserves a licence. (A court may review whether an arrangement benefits from an existing licence (eg a category licence) but a court may not grant a licence to an unlicensed arrangement.) A licence may be granted to any arrangement falling within the scope of section 4(1) provided the Authority is 'of the opinion', having regard to all relevant market conditions 'that the arrangement contributes to improving the production or distribution of goods or services or to promoting technical or economic progress', but the arrangement must allow consumers (including all commercial purchasers) 'a fair share of the resulting benefit' but the arrangement must not '(i) impose on the undertaking concerned terms which are not indispensable to the attainment of those objectives; [and] (ii) afford undertakings the possibility of eliminating competition in respect of a substantial part of the products or services in question'. The licence may be an individual licence where the arrangement is individually notified to the Competition Authority by the parties or it may be a category licence which covers a category or type of agreement (eg a franchise or distribution agreement). An individual licence may only be granted where the specific arrangement (between Mr Black and Mr White) has been notified to the Competition Authority. However, an arrangement may benefit from a category licence even though the arrangement has not been individually notified to the Competition Authority. Solicitors often draft arrangements to fit within the scope of a category licence so as to avoid the need to notify the arrangement to the Competition Authority.

Section 4(4) provides for the Competition Authority to issue a certificate where the Competition Authority is of the opinion that the arrangement does not have the object or effect of preventing, restricting or distorting competition in Ireland or any part of Ireland in a manner contrary to section 4(1). Again, a certificate may be either individual (following an individual notification of the arrangement to the Competition Authority) or category in nature. Solicitors often try to fit their clients' arrangements within the scope of a category certificate so as to avoid the need for notification. In practice, solicitors who notify arrangements request the Authority to issue a certificate or, in default of the issuance of a certificate, to grant a licence. Section 4 ought to be read in conjunction with section 5 because an arrangement which breaches section 5 ought not to be certified or licensed.

3.4.3.5 Abuse of dominance

Section 5 of the Competition Act 1991 prohibits, without exception, the abuse by an undertaking of the undertaking's dominant position in Ireland or in any substantial part of Ireland. The section provides:

> *(1) Any abuse by one or more undertakings of a dominant position in trade for any goods or services in the State or in a substantial part of the State is prohibited.*
>
> *(2) Without prejudice to the generality of subsection (1), such abuse may, in particular, consist in –*
>
> *(a) directly or indirectly imposing unfair purchase or selling prices or other unfair trading conditions;*
>
> *(b) limiting production, markets or technical development to the prejudice of consumers;*
>
> *(c) applying dissimilar conditions to equivalent transactions with other trading parties, thereby placing them at a competitive disadvantage;*
>
> *(d) making the conclusion of contracts subject to the acceptance by other parties of supplementary obligations which by their nature of according to commercial usage have no connection with the subject of such contracts.*

Neither the term 'dominant position' nor 'abuse' is defined in the legislation. However, the term 'dominant position' is generally taken as meaning having a position of economic strength such that one may act to an appreciable extent (albeit not entirely) independently of the undertaking's competitors, customers and consumers. The term 'abuse' is often construed as meaning the unfair exploitation of one's dominance and examples would include predatory pricing, objectively unjustifiable refusals to supply, discriminatory pricing and unjustifiable tying.

3.4.3.6 Civil litigation

An aggrieved person may institute proceedings under section 6 of the 1991 Act for breaches of section 4 (anti-competitive arrangements) or section 5 (abuse of dominance) of the 1991 Act. Section 4-type claims may be instituted only in the High Court. Section 5-type claims may be instituted in the Circuit Court or the High Court but the Circuit Court has various jurisdictional limitations (geographical and monetary). The aggrieved person (who need not be an undertaking) may obtain a combination of damages, exemplary damages, injunctions and/or declarations. A potential plaintiff should also bear in mind the possibility of complaining to the Competition Authority but a complaint is not always a suitable substitute for litigation.

A defendant in any claim before any Irish court may seek to invoke the Competition Acts as part of its defence. For example, a defendant may defend a contractual claim by arguing that the contract is unlawful under the Competition Acts and the court should do nothing to enforce the contract.

3.4.3.7   Criminal enforcement

If any undertaking is party to an arrangement contrary to the Competition Act 1991, section 4 or an abuse of dominance contrary to section 5 of the same Act then the undertaking could be guilty of a criminal offence under sections 2 and 3 of the Competition (Amendment) Act 1996. Various executives of the undertaking (for example, directors, managers and company secretaries) may also be guilty of criminal offences as well as being civilly liable for the loss which they have caused. The Competition Authority (acting through its Director of Competition Enforcement) would ordinarily investigate such alleged crimes. The Authority may prosecute summarily but all prosecutions on indictment would have to be instituted by the Director of Public Prosecutions and the DPP would normally only act after the Competition Authority had referred the matter to the DPP.

3.4.4   MERGERS ACTS

Many jurisdictions worldwide control the merger or acquisition of companies. In Ireland, the primary means of control is through the Mergers and Take-overs (Control) Acts 1978–1996. These Acts involve prior clearance by the Minister for Enterprise, Trade and Employment of certain types of mergers or acquisitions.

The Mergers Acts apply to the merger or take-over of enterprises where at least one of the enterprises carry on business in Ireland and each of two of the enterprises has assets greater than IR£10,000,000 or turnover greater than IR£20,000,000 in the previous financial year. If there is any doubt on the application of the Mergers Acts then it is wiser to take the prudent approach and notify.

The proposal must be notified within one month of an offer capable of acceptance. The notification must be made by all the enterprises involved in the transaction. The notification is normally made by way of a letter or memorandum. It outlines information on the parties, the transaction, the market, the consideration and a consideration of certain criteria laid down in the Mergers Acts – these criteria relate to such matters as competition, continuity of supplies, employment, regional development and so on.

The Minister has one month in which to consider the notification and to ask any questions. If no question is asked within the month then the transaction is effectively cleared. Otherwise, the Minister has thirty days to refer the proposed transaction to the Competition Authority from (a) the time that the transaction was notified, or (b) when the parties satisfactorily answered the Minister's questions. The Competition Authority prepares a report for the Minister, normally within about thirty days, advising the Minister on whether to permit or prohibit (absolutely or conditionally) the proposed transaction. The test, which the Minister uses, is whether the proposed transaction is in the public interest or common good. The Minister may not prohibit a transaction (whether personally or absolutely) without having a report from the Competition Authority but the Minister may depart from the recommendations of the Authority's report. In practice, very few transactions are prohibited (whether absolutely or conditionally) and the vast majority are permitted unconditionally.

3.4.5   GROCERIES ORDER

Solicitors advising clients who are suppliers to, or retailers in, the grocery trade ought to be aware of the possible application of the Restrictive Practices (Groceries) Order 1987 (SI 1987/142). This is more of a fair trade than competition law measure as it seeks to deal with issues such as payment terms and a ban on below-invoice price selling (not, as is popularly assumed, below-cost selling). The Director of Consumer Affairs rather than the Competition Authority administers it. Various commentators have been very critical of the Order because it interferes with the natural functioning of the market and does not adopt the approach of the Competition Acts to introducing competition in the marketplace. Solicitors have to review the Order in the context of reviewing terms and conditions in the grocery sector, dealing with pricing issues and advising on refusals to supply.

3.5 Mergers

3.5.1 INTRODUCTION

Mergers may be regulated under one legal regime, or a number of legal regimes simultaneously, depending on the nature of the transaction. For example, mergers which exceed a certain financial size will fall under the jurisdiction of the Minister for Trade, Enterprise and Employment pursuant to the Mergers, Take-Overs and Monopolies (Control) Act 1978. Should the merger additionally pose potential competition problems, then the Competition Authority will be involved in regulating the competition aspects of the merger, either because the Minister makes a decision to refer the merger to the Authority to examine competition issues specifically, or because the merging parties may themselves have separately notified the merger to the Authority under the Competition Acts 1991–1996. Other legal rules may also apply to the merger, depending on the particular merger's aspects. For example, some industries have specific merger regulation rules, such as the banking and newspaper sectors.

EU law may also apply to a merger. Where a merger involves one or more Irish-based companies (which often take place as part of a much larger international merger of their massive international parent companies), neither the Minister nor the Competition Authority will have jurisdiction because the EC Merger Regulation 4064/89 transfers exclusive regulatory competence over the entire transaction to the EC Commission's Merger Task Force. Furthermore, although the European Commission will not apply arts 81 and 82 to mergers which fall into this regime, the possibility remains that, at least in the case of art 82, private parties may still be in a position to attempt to invoke art 82 in the national courts to prohibit a merger which strengthens an existing dominant position of an incumbent in a particular market.

Finally, in the case of mergers involving publicly listed companies, the Take-Over Panel Act 1997 Takeover Rules may apply to the merger.

3.5.2 MERGERS, TAKE-OVERS AND MONOPOLIES (CONTROL) ACT 1978

3.5.2.1 'Merger' or 'take-over'

Neither 'merger' nor 'take-over' is defined in the Mergers, Take-Overs and Monopolies (Control) Act 1978 ('the 1978 Act'). Instead, section 1 of the Act deems a merger or take-over to have occurred where two or more enterprises come under 'common control'. Essentially, this occurs where one enterprise acquires the right to manage another enterprise, or acquires more than 25 per cent of the voting rights, or acquires the right to appoint the board of the other enterprise. This control may be acquired solely or in conjunction with other parties. The section further elaborates by providing that control will also be deemed to have been acquired where an enterprise acquires the assets and goodwill of another enterprise such that it effectively replaces the latter enterprise in the particular line of business concerned.

The section also defines a number of situations where a merger or take-over will not be deemed to have occurred, such as where a receiver or liquidator takes control of a business. Similarly, a merger is not deemed to have taken place where companies, which are wholly-owned subsidiaries of the same company merge.

3.5.2.2 'Enterprises'

Section 1(1) of the 1978 Act defines an 'enterprise' for the purposes of the Act as constituting a person or partnership engaged for profit in the supply or distribution of goods or services. There are also a number of exclusions whereby certain activities fall outside the meaning of 'services'. For example, service shall not include the owning and transfer of land where this is the sole activity of the enterprise in which control is acquired. Furthermore, service does not include, inter alia, any service provided by the holder of a licence under the Central Bank Act 1971, s 9.

3.5.3 NOTIFIABLE EVENT

In order for a merger to be notifiable to the Minister, SI 1993/135 provides that the value of the gross assets of each of two or more of the enterprises involved must be at least £10 million in the most recent financial year, or alternatively the turnover of each of at least two or more of the enterprises involved must be not less than £20 million. Section 2 of the Act provides that the Minister may by order bring a merger that does not reach these minimum thresholds within the Act's regime. 'Turnover' does not include payments made in respect of VAT or excise duty obligations. At least one of the enterprises must conduct business in the State.

3.5.4 TIME OF NOTIFICATION

According to section 5 of the 1978 Act, notification must be made within one month of an offer capable of acceptance having been made. Consequently, the moment this one month clock starts to run (and hence the time from when the obligation to notify arises), is not the moment the acquisition of control is legally finalised between the parties but rather is a moment in time far earlier than that, ie, the moment an offer capable of acceptance was put.

SI 1996/381 specifies that a notification fee of £4,000 must accompany the notification.

Normally, where the Commission is notified of a large merger pursuant to the EC Merger Regulation, the Commission has exclusive jurisdiction over the merger such that the national authorities have no jurisdiction. However, in certain instances, the Commission may, at the request of the Member State concerned, decide to remit part of the merger that affects that Member State back to the national merger control authorities so that that part of the merger may be regulated under national merger law. Where this occurs, then the Competition Act 1991, s 19 provides that the one-month clock shall not commence until the Commission makes the decision to remit. In this event, the notification made to the Commission constitutes a notification to the Minister for the purposes of section 5 of the 1978 Act.

3.5.5 FAILURE TO NOTIFY

First, section 3 of the 1978 Act provides that failure to notify a merger or take-over prevents title to shares or assets from passing from one enterprise to another.

Secondly, criminal penalties may be imposed on the person controlling the enterprise(s) that failed to notify. On summary conviction, the penalties are fines of up to £1,000, plus £100 for every day of continued contravention. Conviction on indictment attracts significantly heavier penalties of up to £200,000, and £20,000 for every day of continued contravention. The determinant of liability is whether the person knowingly and wilfully authorised or permitted the contravention.

3.5.6 CONTENTS OF NOTIFICATION

No pro forma notification form exists. However, in practice a notification will be expected to contain the following information:

(a) the identify of the parties and their parent companies or controllers;

(b) up-to-date audited accounts;

(c) full details of the proposed transaction;

(d) full details of future acquisition plans;

(e) identity of other competitors;

(f) market shares of the merging parties before/after the acquisition;

(g) how the proposed acquisition will benefit consumers and market sector;

(h) how employment will be affected in the merging enterprises;

(i) how the enterprises' products or services will be affected;

(j) whether any of the enterprises have been the subject of competition proceedings in other jurisdictions, and

(k) any other relevant factors.

Where a merger or take-over raises potential competition concerns, then the notifying enterprises should also address such concerns in the notification. This is due to the amendment of the 1978 Act brought about by the Competition Act 1991 which amended the 1978 Act such that where the Minister, to whom the merger or take-over is notified under the 1978 Act, has competition concerns about the notified transaction, the Minister may refer the notified transaction to the Competition Authority for its view and opinion before taking a final decision on the notified transaction. Where the Minister continues to have such concerns, the Minister can ask the Authority to examine the transaction and

(a) give its 'opinion' on whether the transaction would be likely to restrict competition contrary to the common good, and

(b) give its 'view' on the likely effect of the notified transaction on the common good under the heads of:

(i) continuity of supplies,

(ii) employment,

(iii) regional development,

(iv) rationalisation and efficiency,

(v) increased production,

(vi) access to markets,

(vii) shareholders,

(viii) employees, and

(ix) consumers.

Where the Minister requests a report from the Authority, the Minister must give the Authority not less than thirty days to make its report.

3.5.7 POSSIBLE MINISTERIAL DECISIONS

Under section 6 of the 1978 Act, the Minister has three months from the time of the notification to deliver a decision. Where the Minister deems notified information to be incomplete, the three-month time limit does not commence until such information is furnished to the Minister.

Where the Minister fails to make any decision within the three-month time limit, the merger or take-over is deemed to have been cleared by the Minister.

Where the Minister decides to involve the Competition Authority, the decision to involve the Authority must be made within thirty days of the notification being made to the Minister. As discussed earlier, the Authority must be given at least thirty days to make its report on a range of matters. Upon delivery of its report, the Minister decides, taking the Authority's report into account, whether to prohibit the merger or take-over by way of

(a)   an 'absolute prohibition order', or

(b)   to permit it, subject to conditions by way of a 'conditional prohibition order'.

It is clear from section 9 of the 1978 Act that the Minister bases the ultimate decision on the exigencies of the common good, and thus is clearly not bound to follow the Authority's report as the common good may involve matters not within the ambit of the Authority's brief.

Whichever order the Minister makes, it must be laid before the Houses of the Oireachtas, stating the reasons on which it is based. The Oireachtas may annul the order within twenty-one days of the order being laid before the Houses. In such event, this is without prejudice to any act entered into in the intervening period by the parties.

An appeal to the High Court may be made against a Minister's order provided it is made within one month of the relevant order coming into effect.

The Minister also has a third option:

(c)   make no order following the submission of the Authority's report.

In this situation, the Minister decides not to make any order, in which event the transaction is deemed cleared without the making of an order once the Minister notifies the parties of this fact.

3.5.8   LEGAL POSITION OF PARTIES UNTIL MINISTER MAKES ORDER

Until the Minister makes an order (or indicates no order will be made), section 3 of the 1978 Act provides that title to shares or assets may not pass between the parties. Of course, if the Minister fails to take either step, section 6 provides that the merger will be deemed to have been cleared unconditionally once the three-month period (which commenced from the time notification was deemed to be complete) has elapsed.

Where a purported sale of shares is rendered invalid by virtue of a breach of section 3, this entitles the vendor of shares to recover damages from the purchaser of the shares.

3.5.9   CONSEQUENCES OF FAILURE TO COMPLY WITH MINISTERIAL ORDER

Failure to comply with a Ministerial order (ie, either an absolute prohibition or conditional prohibition order) is a criminal offence. Conviction summarily may lead to a maximum fine of £500 and/or six months in jail and continued daily penalties of £100 per day in the event of continuing non-compliance. Conviction on indictment attracts maximum penalties in the nature of £5,000 and/or up to two years in jail, again with a daily penalty of £500 in the event of continuing non-compliance. It is also an offence to aid or abet the commission of such offence.

The Minister or any other interested person may also seek to have the order complied with by way of injunction.

3.5.10 COMPETITION ACTS 1991–1996

3.5.10.1 Legal basis of Competition Authority jurisdiction over mergers

Section 4 of the Competition Act 1991 provides that anti-competitive agreements that affect trade within the State are prohibited and void. However, notwithstanding this prohibition, such agreements may nevertheless be permitted provided they are granted a certificate or licence by the Competition Authority. Section 5 of the Competition Act 1991 prohibits the abuse of a dominant position. An undertaking found to be violating section 5 does not merit either a certificate or a licence.

The Authority may be involved in considering a merger where requested to do so by the Minister under the Mergers, Take-overs and Monopolies (Control) Act 1978 (considered above). However, neither the Competition Act 1991 nor the Competition (Amendment) Act 1996 specifically indicate that the Authority has any jurisdiction over mergers under the Competition Acts. Nevertheless, the Authority, invoking the analogy of the ECJ judgment in Cases 142 & 156/84 *BAT & Reynolds v European Commission* [1987] ECR 4487 (which applied the analogous EC provision, art 81 EC, to mergers at EC level), has held that mergers affecting trade within the State do fall within the ambit of section 4 of the 1991 Act. In *Woodchester Bank/UDT Bank* (Decision 6, 1992) the Authority held that the prohibition of anti-competitive 'agreements' in the Competition Act 1991 section 4 includes mergers if the merger has an anti-competitive effect within the State. Consequently, mergers which have either anti-competitive effects intrinsically (such as where a merger will result in a diminution of competition in the relevant market) or which have ancillary elements of an anti-competitive nature (such as non-compete restraints imposed on the vendor of a merged business), fall within the jurisdiction of section 4's prohibition.

3.5.10.2 Dual regulation of mergers with anti-competitive aspects

In practice, the impact of the *Woodchester Bank/UDT Bank* Decision has meant that mergers with anti-competitive aspects, have been regulated by both the Minister (under the Mergers, Take-overs and Monopolies (Control) Act 1978) and simultaneously by the Authority under the Competition Act 1991. Until 1997, when a category certificate was adopted for mergers, this meant that mergers with anti-competitive aspects required separate notification to the Authority in order to be considered eligible for the award of a certificate or licence. (In practice, parties will hope to be awarded a certificate rather than a licence as a licence, unlike a certificate, is only granted for a finite period of time.) However, with the adoption of the category certificate in 1997, mergers whose anti-competitive aspects remain within certain permissible parameters are eligible for the award of a certificate without the need to be individually notified to the Authority. This regime is considered further below.

However, for purposes of distinction, it may be useful at this point to indicate the key differences that remain between the Mergers, Take-overs and Monopolies (Control) Act 1978 and the Competition Act 1991 regimes from a procedural point of view:

(a) Although mergers which meet the financial thresholds of the 1978 Act (ie, notifiable mergers) must be notified to the Minister, all mergers which have an anti-competitive effect must be notified to the Authority irrespective of their financial size, in order to qualify for a certificate or licence (although the obligation to notify will no longer arise if the merger satisfies the terms of the category certificate, considered further below).

(b) The obligation to notify notifiable mergers to the Minister is mandatory under the 1978 Act (notification must be made within one month of an offer capable of acceptance having been made), whereas notification to the Authority under the 1991 Act is not mandatory. However, parties who fail to notify and thereby secure a certificate or licence (or who fail to satisfy the terms of the category certificate) run the risk that the merger will be void under the 1991 Act for want of a certificate or licence.

(c) Not all mergers are notifiable to the Authority: only those with anti-competitive aspects (and which fall outside the category certificate) require individual notification in order to be considered for the grant of a certificate or licence.

3.5.11 THE CATEGORY CERTIFICATE FOR MERGERS

On 2 December 1997 the Competition Authority published Decision 489 setting out its category certificate for mergers and the sale of a business. The Authority indicated that the purpose of the category certificate was to allow parties to a merger with anti-competitive aspects to proceed with the merger without the need to make individual notification to the Authority, on the basis that the anti-competitive aspects did not substantively affect competition adversely. The Authority also emphasised that mergers without anti-competitive aspects did not fall within the Authority's jurisdiction and hence are not affected by the Competition Acts.

3.5.11.1 'Merger'

The Authority uses a similar criterion to that used by the Minister under the 1978 (Mergers and Take-Overs) Act for defining when a merger has occurred, ie, the criterion of 'common control'. Usefully, the category certificate illustrates largely similar examples of situations to those used in the 1978 Act where a business is deemed to have come under 'common control', as well as largely similar examples of situations where common control is deemed not to have occurred (eg, where a receiver or liquidator assumes control of a business).

3.5.11.2 Models for assessing whether competition is threatened by merger

The Authority will only have seisin over a merger where either intrinsically the merger weakens competition in the relevant market, or where its ancillary aspects are anti-competitive. The latter is considered later below.

Whether a merger is intrinsically anti-competitive depends on the state of the relevant market before and after the merger. In order to assess the state of the market in light of the merger, the Authority principally uses two economic models to inform its decision-making process.

The Hirfindahl Hirschman Index ('HHI')

Under the HHI test, a merger is deemed not to be anti-competitive where the level of market concentration is:

(a) below 1,000 points ('market not concentrated'), or

(b) between 1,000 and 1,800 points, and has increased by less than 100 points as a result of the merger ('market moderately concentrated': however, if the merger increases the points level by more than 100 points then the merger may be objectionable from a competition perspective, depending on other factors), or

(c) above 1,800 points, but has increased by less than 50 points as a result of the merger ('market highly concentrated but no adverse effect on competition': however, if increase is by more than 50 points, the merger may be objectionable from a competition perspective).

The points level is arrived at by adding together all the squares of the market shares of all firms who are taken to occupy the relevant market.

Where the Authority is satisfied that there is a significant degree of competition from imports, the Authority will permit the merger to proceed even though the HHI thresholds otherwise indicate a problematic level of concentration after the merger. The Authority has adopted this position on the basis that significant competition from imports will counter any attempts by the merged entities to raise prices.

Furthermore, the Authority will permit a merger of potential competitors to proceed even though HHI concerns are evident, provided that it is satisfied that there are no significant barriers to entry or where there is a realistic prospect of competition from imports. Decisions of the Authority in both the pre- and post- category certificate periods indicate that the Authority is applying the HHI index on a consistent basis (eg, see *Scully Tyrrell/Edberg Ltd* (Decision 12, 1992) and *TDI Worldwide/Metro Poster Advertising Ltd* (Decision 501, 1998). For a negative decision of the Authority, see *David Allen Holdings Ltd/Adsites Ltd* (Decision 378, 1996) where the Authority refused both a certificate and a licence on the basis that a highly concentrated market was further concentrated by the proposed merger in circumstances where there was no prospect of a new competitor entering the market. In such circumstances, the Authority refused to grant either a certificate or a licence. A decision going in the opposite direction was delivered by the Authority in *TDI Worldwide/Metro Poster Advertising Ltd* (Decision 501, 1998) where the Authority found that after the merger the market would be highly concentrated, in circumstances where there was no significant competition from imports and significant barriers to entry existed in the market. Nevertheless, the Authority granted a certificate to the arrangements on the basis that the merged entity would increase competition because it would act as a more effective competitor to the existing larger incumbents in the market.

The Four Firm Concentration ratio ('FFC')

Another guide used by the Authority is the Four Firm Concentration ratio. Under this test, a merger between competitors is not deemed anti-competitive where the combined market shares of the four largest firms is less than 40 per cent in the relevant market.

Even where the 40 per cent threshold is exceeded, the Authority will not refuse to grant a certificate to the arrangements where significant competition from imports exists or, in the case of a merger between potential competitors, where neither significant barriers to entry and the possibility of competition exist. In its decision in *IDG/Cooley* (Decision 285, 1994) the Authority refused to grant a certificate to the take-over of Cooley by Irish Distillers, as the FFC ratio in the Irish whiskey market was exceeded in circumstances where there was no possibility of competition being maintained in the market once Cooley was eliminated as a competitor.

3.5.11.3 Ancillary restraints accompanying a merger

Often, where a company or business is taken over by another, the acquiring party may wish to restrain the former controller of the acquired business from competing. This is necessary to ensure that the goodwill attaching to the acquired business does transfer completely without interference from the vendor. The category certificate deals with such restraints under two distinct headings, depending on whether the vendor retains a link with the business, or not.

Where vendor retains no link with the business sold

Where non-compete restraint imposed.   In this situation, the category certificate provides that the purchaser may restrain the vendor from competing for a period of up to two years from the completion of the sale, in any territory where the vendor operated at the time of the merger, in respect of any goods or services purchased or sold by the vendor at the time of the merger. Any non-compete clause that exceeds any element of these parameters will not be eligible for the category certificate and will require individual notification to the Authority seeking the grant of a certificate or licence. In practice the Authority has often granted certificates to three-year restraints on the basis that the particular circumstances so warrant (eg, *Nallen/O'Toole* (Decision 1, 1992) where the Authority accepted that a three-year restraint was necessary to transfer goodwill in a video shop in a rural area; *ACT/Kindle* (Decision 8, 1992) where the Authority accepted a three-year non-compete restraint because vendors possessed specialised know-how).

Where non-solicitation of either customers or employees imposed. Where non-solicitation restraints are imposed on the vendor vis à vis customers or employees of the sold business, such restraints will qualify for the category certificate provided no more than two years in duration and provided they only concern customers or employees who were such either at the time of the merger or in the two years prior to it. Where a restraint exceeds such parameters, then the parties may notify seeking an individual certificate, which in practice the Authority will grant where the circumstances so warrant (eg, in *Woodchester Bank/UDT Bank* (Decision 6, 1992) the Authority granted a certificate in respect of a three-year non-solicitation of employees clause on the grounds that it did not prevent employees offering themselves to their former employer unsolicited; although in *Phil Fortune/Budget Travel Ltd* (Decision 9, 1992) the Authority refused to grant a certificate to a four-year non-solicitation of employees' restraint on the grounds that it was more than was necessary to ensure the transfer of the goodwill attaching to the sold business).

Where non-disclosure of technical know-how or confidential information imposed. Where a non-disclosure of 'technical know-how' restraint is imposed, then the Authority will, according to the category certificate, permit restraints of up to five years, although such restraint must not be enforced should the know-how enter the public domain before the expiry of the restraint period. In order to qualify as technical know-how, information must be 'secret, substantial and identified in appropriate form'. On the other hand, where information is 'confidential information', meaning information which the vendor is restrained from divulging because it constitutes part of the business sold or merged, then the restraint may be of unlimited duration. However, the category certificate will not permit such restraint to be used to prevent the vendor re-entering the market once the period of a genuine non-compete restraint has expired.

Where vendor retains link with the business sold

The extent to which a vendor who retains a link with the business post-merger, may be restrained, varies according to the nature of the link. The category certificate allows restraints provided they are used to genuinely ensure the transfer of the goodwill, and are not used as a disguised means of protecting the purchaser from competition for a period longer than would otherwise be permissible. Several distinct situations are identified in the category certificate.

Where vendor sells all interest in the business but retains a shareholding

The category certificate will not be available where non-compete or non-solicitation restraints are imposed to run, not from the date of the merger, but from the date of the sale of the shareholding. However, where the vendor retains a shareholding of 10 per cent or more, then two year non-compete or non-solicitation restraints operable from the date of sale of the shareholding may be permissible under the category certificate, presumably (as the category certificate does not elaborate) on the basis that a vendor shareholder who retains a minimum 10 per cent shareholding may be involved in the business in more than just a passive sense, and hence this period of restraint is necessary to ensure that the goodwill passes effectively.

Where vendor retains link by remaining as employee or director

Where the vendor remains as a mere employee or director, then restraints other than general non-compete or non-solicitation restraints operating from the date of the merger are not permitted under the category certificate. Hence, restraints which operate from the date of termination of the vendor's link with the business will not qualify under the category certificate, and will be most unlikely (according to the Authority) to be granted either a certificate or a licence (eg *Apex Fire Protection/Murtagh*, 1993 where the Authority refused to grant a certificate or licence in respect of a one-year non-compete restraint on an employee who left to set up his own business).

However, the Authority has made it quite clear that the prohibition on imposing restraints on the vendor-employee (or director) who remains linked to the business beyond the date of their link terminating does not prevent the purchaser restraining the vendor from divulging confidential information about the business or from soliciting customers or employees who were such at the time of the vendor's departure.

3.5.12 SITUATIONS WHERE THE CATEGORY CERTIFICATE CANNOT APPLY

The category certificate does not apply where:

(a) a party to a merger had a 35 per cent market share before the merger, or

(b) a merger between competitors would lead to either the creation or strengthening of a dominant position, or

(c) the merger takes place in oligopolistic markets (because often competition in such a market is normally weak and a merger of players in it would be likely to further weaken competition).

In any of the foregoing situations, the category certificate cannot apply and the merger will require individual notification to the Authority for consideration by the Authority.

The category certificate states that the Authority will not regard a vertical merger in a particular market as being objectionable unless foreclosure of a relevant market would be likely to result.

3.5.13 EC MERGER REGULATION 4064/89 (1989)

EC Council Regulation 4064/89 ([1989] OJ L 395/1) as amended by Council Regulation 1301/97 ([1997] OJ L 180/1), commonly known as the Merger Regulation, was adopted in 1989 with a view to establishing a single EC-wide regulatory regime for the regulation of large mergers known as 'concentrations' with a 'Community Dimension'. Where such a concentration exists, then it falls to be regulated exclusively by the Commission's Merger Task Force, a dedicated merger control body. National merger control and competition regulators have no competence to deal with the merger, unless either:

(a) the Commission decides that part of the merger would best be regulated by leaving it to the relevant national authorities, or

(b) where a Member State is seeking to protect so-called 'legitimate interests'.

When dealing with a notified concentration, the Merger Task Force commences a Phase I investigation, which must be completed within four weeks. If the Task Force continues to have serious concerns about the concentration at the end of Phase I, it may open a Phase II investigation. Phase II must be concluded within four months.

Concentrations that do not have a Community dimension remain under the jurisdiction of the national authorities, which remain free to apply national merger or competition laws to the concentration.

The Commission cannot apply arts 81 or 82 EC to concentrations with a Community dimension because art 22 of the Merger Regulation disapplies Regulation 17/62 (the enabling legislation permitting the Commission to act under arts 81 and 82) in respect of such concentrations. Although the Commission has reserved its right to apply arts 81 and 82 to non-Community dimension concentrations, in practice it has not done so.

3.5.14 CONCENTRATIONS

3.5.14.1 Acquisition of decisive influence

Article 3 of the Merger Regulation bases the definition of what constitutes a concentration on the notion of whether one undertaking has acquired decisive influence over another undertaking, either solely or in conjunction with other undertakings.

This decisive influence may be acquired in a variety of ways ranging from a simple merger, to the acquisition by either direct or indirect means of the control over the strategic management of another undertaking whether by way of purchase of shares, assets, contractual rights, or a combination of any means which permit the acquisition of decisive influence. Therefore, given that this is a substantive test, it is not strictly necessary that undertakings (for example) cease to exist as separate legal entities before a concentration can be deemed to have occurred. As Commission Notice 98/C 66/02 ([1998] OJ C 66/5) makes clear, what is essential is that the transaction allows an undertaking(s) to, in the words of art 3(3) of Merger Regulation, exercise either actual or even potential control over another undertaking(s) 'having regard to considerations of law or fact'.

3.5.14.2 When is a joint venture a concentration

A difficult issue that caused problems in the early days of the Merger Regulation's operation was how to classify joint ventures for the purposes of the regulation. Should they be regarded as vehicles for anti-competitive co-operation between the parent undertakings of the venture, or should they be regarded as concentrations if they effected structural change in the marketplace?

By their very nature, joint ventures may contain anti-competitive restrictions which may attract the jurisdiction of arts 81 and 82 EC. Joint ventures, which do not bring about a structural change in the marketplace, are properly subject to the application of arts 81 and 82. However, it was felt desirable in the mid-1990s that other types of joint venture (ie, those which seem to effect structural change in market) should have the benefit of the Merger Regulation's regulatory regime, even though they may contain anti-competitive restrictions. The benefit for such joint ventures from a regulatory point of view would be that the strict time limits which apply to the Commission's operations under Phase I and Phase II of the Merger Regulation, would equally apply to consideration of a structural joint venture (whereas, by contrast, under arts 81 and 82 EC, no strict time limits are imposed on the Commission's operations under those articles when considering a joint venture).

Full-function joint ventures

As amended by the amending Regulation 1301/97, art 3(2) of the Merger Regulation now provides that where a joint venture performs all of the functions of an autonomous economic entity, then it shall constitute a concentration within the meaning of the Merger Regulation. This is known as a 'full-function joint venture'. Commission Notice 98/ C 66/1 ([1998] OJ C 66/1) elaborates on this concept, emphasising that a joint venture is full-function where it is able to operate on a daily basis largely autonomously of its parents by having sufficient resources, financial and human, allocated to it. Such a joint venture is more akin to a concentration than a mere joint venture simpliciter because its existence in full-function form creates permanent structural change in the marketplace (just as any other kind of concentration would).

Where a full-function joint venture has anti-competitive restrictions they will continue to be subject to the jurisdiction of art 81 EC but with the important caveat (as per newly introduced art 2(4) Merger Regulation, as amended) that such scrutiny must be conducted within the strict time limits set by the Merger Regulation for the examination of concentrations. However, any restrictions that are neither ancillary to, nor a direct consequence of, the joint venture, will continue to fall outside the Merger Regulation's regime and shall be subject to art 81's jurisdiction in the normal way pursuant to Regulation 17/62.

Where a concentration is not full-function in nature, then it is not a concentration and hence continues to be subject to art 81's jurisdiction in the normal way pursuant to Regulation 17/62.

3.5.15 COMMUNITY DIMENSION

3.5.15.1 Original thresholds

A concentration has a Community dimension where the undertakings involved are of significant financial size. However, as will be seen, it is not necessary that there are significantly large undertakings involved on both sides of the concentration: as long as there are two such undertakings, it is sufficient.

Article 1 provides that a concentration has a Community dimension where:

Scope

1. Without prejudice to Article 22, this Regulation shall apply to all concentrations with a Community dimension as defined in paragraphs 2 and 3.

2. For the purposes of this Regulation, a concentration has a Community dimension where:

(a) the combined aggregate world-wide turnover of all the undertakings concerned is more than euro 5,000 million; and

(b) the aggregate Community-wide turnover of each of at least two of the undertakings concerned is more than euro 250 million,

unless each of the undertakings concerned achieves more than two thirds of its aggregate Community-wide turnover within one and the same Member State.

In Decision IV/ M. 053 *Aerospatiale-Alenia/De Havilland* ([1991] OJ L 334/42) the Commission found that although the target undertaking, De Havilland, was not significantly large to meet the Community dimension thresholds, nevertheless the Community dimension requirement that at least two undertakings do, was satisfied, because the two predator undertakings, Alenia and Aerospatiale, did meet the financial thresholds.

3.5.15.2 Additional thresholds

Article 1(3) was inserted into the Merger Regulation by amending Regulation 1301/97. It provides for additional Community dimension thresholds whereby concentrations involving smaller undertakings may yet be deemed to have a Community dimension. These additional thresholds were added to the Merger Regulation (in order to bring a wider range of concentrations within the Merger Regulation's regime) because it was perceived in the mid-1990s that the original thresholds were too high, thereby depriving cross-border concentrations involving undertakings of significant, albeit not massive, size, of the opportunity to qualify for inclusion under the Merger Regulation's single regulatory regime. Article 1(3) provides:

3. For the purposes of this Regulation, a concentration that does not meet the thresholds laid down in paragraph 2 has a Community dimension where:

(a) the combined aggregate world-wide turnover of all the undertakings concerned is more than euro 2,500 million;

(b) in each of at least three Member States, the combined aggregate turnover of all the undertakings concerned is more than euro 100 million;

(c) in each of at least three Member States included for the purpose of point (b), the aggregate turnover of each of at least two of the undertakings concerned is more than euro 25 million; and

(d) the aggregate Community-wide turnover of each of at least two of the undertakings concerned is more than euro 100 million;

unless each of the undertakings concerned achieves more than two-thirds of its aggregate Community-wide turnover within one and the same Member State.

3.5.15.3 Reckonable turnover items

Article 5 of the Merger Regulation provides that items reckonable as turnover include amounts derived by the undertakings concerned from the sale of products and services in the preceding financial year after deduction of sales rebates, VAT and other direct turnover related taxes. Intra-group sales are not reckonable.

3.5.15.4 Aggregation of turnover

Article 5 also provides that for the purposes of turnover aggregation, turnover of any undertakings controlled by the undertakings concerned must be included, in addition to any turnover of subsidiary undertakings, sister undertakings, parent undertakings or any joint ventures in which any of the aforementioned undertakings are involved as joint controllers.

3.5.15.5 Special turnover rules for some sectors

Special rules are provided for calculation of turnover of banking and insurance undertakings, and the reader is advised to consult art 5 of the Merger Regulation (as amended) for further elaboration.

3.5.16 NATIONAL MERGER AND COMPETITION LAW DOES NOT APPLY

3.5.16.1 Generally

Where a concentration has a Community dimension, then art 21(2) Merger Regulation provides that no Member State shall apply its national competition legislation to such concentration. In Ireland, this means that neither the Mergers, Take-Overs and Monopolies (Control) Act 1978 nor the Competition Acts 1991–1996 may apply to any aspects of such transaction, which take place, or concern trade, in the State.

However, in the event that a concentration is found upon examination by the Commission not to have a Community dimension, then the Commission has no jurisdiction over the concentration under the Merger Regulation. In this circumstance, the Minister will have jurisdiction over any part of the concentration that satisfies the jurisdiction criteria of the 1978 Act (as will the Competition Authority if any part of the concentration, regardless of its financial size, affects competition in the Irish market). Other national merger control or competition authorities will have jurisdiction over any parts of the concentration affecting their respective territories.

Notwithstanding that the Commission finds that a concentration has a Community dimension, there are two situations recognised in the Merger Regulation whereby Member State authorities may acquire jurisdiction over the part of the concentration that affects the State's territory. To these we shall now turn.

3.5.16.2 Article 9: referral to the Member State

Under art 9 of the Merger Regulation, the Commission may, at the request of a Member State, refer a Community dimension concentration to the Member State's authorities for regulation under domestic merger control and competition law regimes where

    (i)   the State can demonstrate to the satisfaction of the Commission that a distinct market exists in that State, and

(ii) the part of the concentration taking place in that State would therefore be best left to the State's own authorities to regulate.

Should the Commission accede to this request, then it may refer either the entire concentration (where the undertakings concentrating both do business and are based in the one State), or the part of the concentration that particularly affects the State (where the undertakings concentrating are based in different States).

However, in practice the Commission is not likely to share jurisdiction readily. The following are the conditions that determine whether the Commission 'may refer' or whether it 'shall refer'. As will be seen, the Commission retains a large measure of control in this area.

'Shall refer'

Article 9 provides that the Commission 'shall refer' to the Member State provided that the State can demonstrate that

(i) a distinct market exists in the State, and

(ii) the concentration will impede effective competition in the State, and

(iii) the distinct market alleged is not a substantial part of the common market.

While this appears to give substantial grounds to the Member State to request jurisdiction over the whole or part of the concentration, nevertheless the Commission retains the ultimate say over whether the alleged 'distinct market' in fact exists.

'May refer'

Article 9 provides that the Commission 'may refer' where the State claims that the concentration will:

(i) either strengthen or create a dominant position,

(ii) which will impede effective competition in the State, and

(iii) affect a market in the State, which is a distinct market.

Although the Commission has generally been reluctant to accede to art 9 requests, in 1998 and 1999 it acceded to several, in some cases referring the entire concentration (eg *Fritz Homann Lebensmittelwerke GmBH/Beeck Feinhost GmBH* (IP/99/220, April 1999), referral of entire concentration by two German undertakings in delicatessen products market to the Bundeskartellamt); and partial referrals in others (eg, concentration in Holland between retail operators KBB and Vendex in the non-food sector (IP/ 98/ 494, June 1998) whereby the Commission regulated the parties' concentration in some sectors but referred the non-food aspects of the concentration to the Dutch authorities for regulation).

Time limits and procedure

Article 9 provides that a Member State must make an art 9 request to the Commission within three weeks of being informed of the notification by the Commission. This is facilitated by the requirement under the Merger Regulation which obliges the Commission to furnish a copy of every notification made to it to the Member States within three working days. The Commission is then obliged to consider and make a decision on the Member State's request within the following time limits:

(a) Where the Commission is still considering a notified concentration under its Phase I investigation at the time the Member State request is made, the Commission is obliged to take a decision on whether to refer within six weeks from the date the original notification was made to it.

(b) However, should the Commission be in the course of a Phase II investigation at the time it received the Member State request, then it is obliged to take a decision on whether to refer within three months from the date the original notification was made to it, unless the Commission has decided within this period to take preparatory steps to either:

(i) attach conditions or obligations to the concentration, or

(ii) prohibit the concentration, or

(iii) take measures to restore effective competition.

(c) Should the Commission have neither adopted preparatory steps nor taken a decision on the referral issue within the three-month period referred to in (b), then it is deemed to have taken a decision to refer at the end of that period, provided the Member State has reminded it of its request during the period.

In the event that the Commission decides to remit the Irish part of the concentration to the Minister for Enterprise, Trade and Employment for review under domestic law, then section 19 of the Competition Act 1991 provides that notification made to the Commission under the Merger Regulation (which the Commission is obliged to transmit to the Minister within three working days of initial receipt) shall constitute a notification to the Minister as if it were originally made to the Minister under the Mergers, Take-Overs and Monopolies (Control) Act 1978. Section 19 further provides that in this circumstance, the time limits under the 1978 Act (under which the Minister is obliged to consider a merger or take-over) shall run from the date on which the Commission decides to remit the Irish part of the concentration to the Minister.

Member State action when a referral request is granted

Article 9(8) of the Merger Regulation provides that the State may only take such measures as are strictly necessary to safeguard or restore effective competition in the market concerned.

3.5.16.3 Article 21: protection of legitimate interests

Notwithstanding that the Member States are precluded by art 21(2) of the Merger Regulation from applying their national competition law to Community dimension concentrations, art 21(3) does permit the Member States to take steps to protect 'legitimate interests' provided that such steps are otherwise compatible with Community law.

Article 21(3) gives three examples of when a Member State may take steps to protect a legitimate interest: to preserve plurality of the media, public security or prudential rules. Where a State wishes to take steps in order to protect any other claimed legitimate interests, the State must first notify the Commission seeking approval before it may act. The Commission has one month in which to take a decision on such a matter. In recognition of this mechanism, section 19 of the Competition Act 1991 amended the 1978 Act such that if the Minister prepares to act under the 1978 Act in order to protect the common good in respect of a Community dimension concentration, then the clock under the 1978 Act will not begin to run until the Commission has made its decision allowing the legitimate interest to be invoked under art 21(3). In such circumstances, there is no need for the merging parties to make a fresh notification to the Minister as the notification originally made to the Commission is treated as such for this purpose.

3.5.17 COMPATIBILITY OF CONCENTRATIONS: DOMINANCE

Article 2(2) of the Merger Regulation provides that a concentration shall be declared compatible with the common market where it neither creates nor strengthens a dominant position in the common market, or a substantial part of it. Article 2(3) provides that a concentration will be incompatible (and therefore, prohibited) where it will strengthen or create a dominant position in a substantial part of the common market in circumstances where competition will be seriously impeded.

Whether a concentration creates a dominant position depends on how the relevant product and geographic market is defined. In this regard the Commission takes similar factors into account in assessing relevant product markets as it does in its general arts 81 and 82 EC practice. To avoid duplication this will not be repeated in this section and the reader is referred to the sections on arts 81 and 82 for relevant market definition methodology.

Once the relevant market is defined, art 2 of the Merger Regulation provides that the Commission must take into account factors such as the need to maintain effective competition in the common market in view of the structure of markets and also to have regard to actual or potential competition from undertakings inside or outside the common market. Other factors to be taken into account include the market position of the undertakings concerned, their economic and financial power, whether there are alternatives available to the market suppliers and users, barriers to entry to markets, the interests of consumers, and the development of technical or economic progress.

In practice, the Commission only infrequently prohibits concentrations as being incompatible, chiefly because the Commission tends to extract modifications from the notifying undertakings such that they alter the structure or terms of the notified concentration, thereby satisfying the Commission that the concentration, as altered, will not affect adversely effective competition in the relevant market. For example, in *Nestle/Perrier* (Decision 190 [1992] OJ L 356/1) the Commission cleared the concentration after Nestle agreed to divest itself of several brands. Furthermore, Nestle agreed to modify its future behaviour by not, for example, making trade statistics available to its other main competitors via a trade association until the figures were of historical interest only.

Only eleven concentrations have been prohibited between 1990 and 1999.

In 1998, in its judgment in Cases C-68/94 and 30/95 *France v Commission* [1998] ECR I-1375 the ECJ accepted that where a company takes over a competitor in circumstances where dominance will be created or strengthened and competition adversely affected, nevertheless the concentration may be declared compatible if it can be demonstrated that the competitor was a failing firm whose market share was going to be subsumed by the stronger undertaking in any event over time.

3.5.17.1 Collective dominance

The Commission has accepted that the notion of collective dominance falls within the scope of art 2. In its decision in *Nestle/Perrier* (Decision 190, [1992] OJ L 356/1) in 1992, the Commission found that dominance can be exercised collectively by two or more firms acting collectively in an oligopolistic market. Due to the structure of the mineral water market in France, the Commission took the view that after the merger the number of major players would be reduced from three to two, and that given that the market was a 'mature' market where future competition was unlikely between the two remaining players in the post-concentration era, the Commission concluded that they would be likely to act as duopolists, ie in a collectively dominant fashion, particularly in view of their past behaviour which they engaged in together before the concentration occurred.

3.5.18 NOTIFICATIONS

3.5.18.1 Obligation to notify

The obligation to notify a concentration arises when either of the earlier of the following events occur, and notification must be made within seven days:

   (a)   the acceptance of an offer, or

   (b)   the announcement of a public bid, or

   (c)   the acquisition of a controlling interest.

3.5.18.2 Suspension

Article 7(1) of the Merger Regulation provides that no concentration may come into legal effect until the Commission has delivered a compatibility decision under art 2, or has failed to make such decision within the strict time limits set by the regulation for Commission decision-making. However, notwithstanding that art 7(1) provides that the concentration is suspended as a matter of law, this is heavily qualified as art 7 provides that even if a transaction is carried out in violation of art 7, its validity ultimately will depend on whether the Commission clears or prohibits the concentration. Furthermore, suspensive effect is further qualified by the remaining paragraphs of art 7 which provide as follows:

(a) article 7 does not prevent a notified public bid from being implemented provided that no voting rights are exercised until the Commission clears the concentration;

(b) article 7 shall not affect the validity of any transaction carried out on the Stock Exchange unless the buyer and seller knew or ought to have known that the transaction was carried out in contravention of art 7(1), and

(c) a derogation can be sought from art 7 by making an application to the Commission for a derogation, pleading that suspensive effect is injurious to the interests of either an undertaking involved in the concentration or a third party.

3.5.18.3 Investigation time limits and legal bases

(a) Phase I

Once it receives a notification, the Commission Merger Task Force has one month in which to consider either that the concentration:

– *is compatible with the common market, or*

– *raises serious doubts as to its compatibility with the common market and hence warrants the opening of a Phase II, four-month investigation, or*

– *falls outside the jurisdiction of the Merger Regulation (in which event national laws apply to the concentration, such as where it does not have a 'Community Dimension')*

The one-month period does not commence however, if the Commission is not satisfied that it has received complete notification information.

Where a Member State makes a referral request under art 9 of the regulation, then art 10 provides that the one-month period is extended to six weeks.

(b) Phase II

Where a concentration raises serious doubts regarding its compatibility with the common market, then a Phase II investigation is opened by the Commission. This means that the concentration will be scrutinised much more thoroughly than was the case under Phase I. Article 10 provides that this Phase II investigation must be concluded within four months and a decision delivered within that time by the Commission.

In adopting its decision closing a Phase II investigation, art 8 of the Merger Regulation provides that the Commission may:

(i) approve the concentration as being compatible with art 2(2) subject to it being modified by the parties, or subject to the parties having given commitments as to future behaviour, or

(ii) prohibit the concentration as being incompatible with the common market, ie, that it either creates or strengthens an existing dominant position which would adversely affect competition in the common market, or a substantial part of it.

In practice, the Commission much prefers the parties to modify the structure of the concentration rather than merely offer post-concentration behavioural commitments, because the former are a better guarantee that post-concentration threats to competition will be unlikely to arise. Another practical advantage from the Commission's point of view is that structural modifications do not require post-concentration scrutiny for compliance whereas behavioural commitments may.

The reason why the Commission has prohibited only a small number of concentrations since the Merger Regulation came into force some ten years ago rests largely with this practice of parties, whose notifications enter a Phase II investigation, agreeing to modify their concentrations, thereby allaying Commission competition fears.

(c) Full-function joint ventures

Where a concentration is in effect a full-function joint venture, then it may have co-operative elements. Since the enactment of the amending Regulation 1301/97, any such co-operative elements will be assessed within the same time limits as the concentrative parts. In conducting such examination, the Commission will assess the concentrative parts of the joint venture under art 2 (ie, does the concentration create or strengthen a dominant position which thereby affects competition) and the co-operative parts under art 2(4) (ie, could the co-operative elements be exempted under art 81 EC). Should the Commission not be satisfied that either legal test is satisfied, it will prohibit the concentration.

In conducting its assessment under art 2(4), the Commission will particularly be mindful of looking at co-operation between the parents, and will attach particular significance to the question of whether the parents retain significant activities in the same or neighbouring markets as the concentration.

Any co-operative elements that are not directly attributable to the concentration fall outside the scope of the regulation, and require a separate notification to the Commission under art 81.

It should not be overlooked either that, full-function joint ventures, which do not have a Community dimension and which do have co-operative elements, will be subject to the full application of art 81 EC because art 22(1) of the Merger Regulation specifically so provides.

3.5.19 COMMISSION ENFORCEMENT POWERS

3.5.19.1 Power to revoke approved concentrations

The Commission has several enforcement powers under the Merger Regulation in respect of revoking approved concentrations:

(a) power to revoke an earlier compatibility decision where undertakings fail to honour an obligation attached to the prior decision (art 8(5));

(b) power to revoke an earlier compatibility decision where undertakings provided false information (art 8(5)), and

(c) power to order the termination of an implemented concentration, whether by way of divestiture or cessation of control of a full-function joint venture, in order to restore effective competition (art 8(4)).

3.5.19.2 Power to request information and search

The Commission has power to request information from both the undertakings and the Member States (art 11) and also has wide powers to conduct dawn raids on undertakings' premises (art 13). It may request Member State competent authorities to undertake investigations on its behalf.

3.5.19.3 Power to fine for breaches of the Merger Regulation

The Commission has wide fining powers under the Merger Regulation.

1,000–50,000 euros

Where any of the following has been determined to occur either intentionally or negligently on the part of an undertaking, the Commission may levy a fine under art 14 in the 1,000–50,000 euro range for:

(i)   failure to notify a concentration;

(ii) notification of incorrect or misleading information;

(iii) failure to supply information or supply of incorrect information in an art 11 investigation;

(iv) failure to produce complete sets of books in art 12 or 13 investigations, and

(v)   failure to submit to an art 13 investigation

In addition to any fines levied in respect of the foregoing breaches, where undertakings fail to comply with art 11 requests for information or fail to submit to an art 13 investigation, art 15(1) gives the Commission additional discretion to impose periodic penalties of up to 25,000 euros per day.

Up to 10 per cent of worldwide turnover

Where any of the following has been determined to have occurred either intentionally or negligently on the part of an undertaking, the Commission may levy a fine of up to 10 per cent of aggregate worldwide turnover under art 14 for:

(i)   failure to comply with commitments given in return for a clearance decision under art 8(2);

(ii) failure to comply with commitments given in return for a derogation from suspensive effect under art 7(4);

(iii) breach of modifications proposed in return for a clearance decision under art 8(2);

(iv) effecting a concentration either before notification, or after notification but before clearance is granted (both are contrary to art 7(1));

(v)   effecting a concentration contrary to its prohibition by the Commission under art 8(3), and

(vi) failure to take cessation or divestiture measures ordered by the Commission under art 8(4).

In addition to any fines levied in respect of the foregoing breaches, where undertakings breach arts 7(4), 8(2) or 8(4) as described above, art 15(2) gives the Commission additional discretion to impose periodic penalties of up to 100,000 euros per day until the breach is remedied.

3.5.20 TAKEOVER PANEL ACT 1997

3.5.20.1 The Irish Takeover Panel

Prior to 1997, the London Stock Exchange's Takeover Panel supervised the orderly conduct of takeovers of Irish companies listed on the Dublin Stock Exchange. However, with the enactment of the Irish Takeover Panel Act 1997 (brought into force by SI 1997/158 and SI 1997/256), the role of the London Panel ceased. In its place, the Irish Takeover Panel was formed under the 1997 Act. It is charged with supervising the conduct of takeovers of companies listed on the Dublin Stock Exchange.

The Panel has adopted its own set of Takeover Rules to govern the orderly conduct of takeovers. Also, it has adopted a separate set of rules, known as the Substantial Acquisition Rules, which govern the acquisition of substantial interests in listed companies.

Companies involved in either the takeover, or acquisition, of a substantial interest in a listed company, must adhere to these rules.

3.5.20.2 Acquisition of control

The Panel's Takeover Rules must be adhered to whenever a transaction will, or does, result in control being acquired in a listed company. 'Control' for the purposes of the Takeover Rules is defined as the holding, whether directly or indirectly, of securities in a listed company which confer in aggregate not less than 30 per cent of the voting rights in the company.

The objective of the Rules is to ensure that the takeover proceeds in an orderly fashion and that, in particular, the interests of the target company's shareholders are treated in a fair fashion.

In this regard, rule 5(1) provides that it is forbidden for a person, either alone or acting in concert with others, to acquire a 30 per cent interest in a listed company unless the person making the acquisition complies with the Rules. In this regard, for example, rule 5(2) provides that where a person makes an acquisition of a controlling interest with the consent of the board of the target company, then this is compatible with the Rules if the person intends immediately afterwards to make a 'firm intention announcement' to purchase all the shares in the company on equal terms.

Rule 5 also prohibits a person who already controls between 30–50 per cent of the voting rights in a listed company from increasing their stake by more than 1 per cent unless the person making the acquisition complies with the rules.

3.5.20.3 Mandatory offer

Where a person increases their stake to 30 per cent, or where, having already acquired control, they increase their control in the company, rule 9 provides that a 'mandatory offer' must be made. A mandatory offer means that the holder of control is obliged to offer to purchase all equity share capital in the company.

Where the Mergers, Take-over and Monopolies (Control) Act 1978 applies to the takeover, then rule 9(3) provides that the transaction may proceed once the Minister has acted, or is deemed under that Act to have acted, in respect of the takeover. In other words, once the Minister has either cleared the takeover, or failed to make a decision (in which event the takeover is deemed to have been cleared), then the transaction may proceed in accordance with the requirements of the Takeover Rules. If the Minister prohibits the takeover, then the Takeover Rules provide that the Panel may order the offeror to reduce its holdings in the company to below 30 per cent.

Where the takeover falls within the jurisdiction of the EC Merger Regulation 4064/89, then rule 9(3) provides that a mandatory offer will lapse where the Commission either opens a four-month Phase II investigation or decides to refer the concentration to the Member State(s) under art 9 of the Merger Regulation. However, the Rules also provide that if the transaction is eventually cleared, then the obligation to make a mandatory offer remains. Should the takeover be prohibited, then the Rules provide that the Panel may order the offeror to reduce its holdings in the company to below 30 per cent.

3.5.20.4 Substantial Acquisition Rules

The purpose of the Substantial Acquisition Rules is to ensure that acquisitions of substantial interests in listed companies take place at an acceptable speed.

A substantial acquisition occurs wherever one acquires, over a seven-day period, securities conferring 10 per cent of the voting rights in the company, in circumstances where those securities, when aggregated with any securities already held by that person, confer on that person 15 to 30 per cent of the voting rights in the company.

The Rules prohibit such an acquisition except in a number of specific situations, the most important of which is that the Rules provide that the person may make a substantial acquisition where immediately after the acquisition, the person announces a firm intention to make an offer under the Takeover Panel Rules in circumstances where the board of the company approves and the acquisition is conditional on the offer being made.

Where a person makes a substantial acquisition, they are obliged to notify the Panel and the Stock Exchange by noon on the business day following the acquisition.

Where a person already holds 30 per cent of the company it is the Takeover Rules rather than the Substantial Acquisition Rules, which apply.

3.5.20.5 The Panel's powers

The Panel is entrusted with a wide range of powers under the Act. It may summon parties under oath to hearings before it, which normally take place in private. The Panel has the power and privileges of the High Court to order witnesses and documents before it. Failure to comply is referable by the Panel to the High Court and, apart from any order the High Court may make, is punishable (if the Panel seeks to prosecute) by up to one year in prison or a fine of up to £1,500.

Under section 9(2) of the 1997 Act, the Panel may give directions on a wide variety of matters in order to ensure compliance with its Rules, on matters such as the acquisition or allotment of securities; the disposal or issue of securities; or a restraint on the exercise of rights attaching to securities; the disclosure of shareholdings or identity of parties.

Where the Panel considers a party is not complying with its rulings or directions, the Panel may request the High Court to make an appropriate order against an errant party.

The decisions of the Panel are subject to a very restrictive form of judicial review. The Act provides that judicial review must be sought within seven days of a Panel decision on any particular matter and that it can only be sought by the parties to the transaction. Furthermore, in an attempt to keep parties away from the High Court, section 15 of the Act further provides that a transaction entered into in contravention of the Rules or the Act cannot be invalidated on that ground – only if the Panel seeks to have the transaction set aside, can the High Court entertain such application.

3.6 Procedure and Enforcement in EU and Irish Competition Law

3.6.1 INTRODUCTION

The objective of this section is to provide an overview of the procedural and enforcement dimensions of EU and Irish competition law. There is a certain degree of overlap between this section and other sections but this is inevitable given the interplay between substantive and procedural law.

The approaches of the EU and Irish systems are very similar so it is useful to examine issues generally and then highlight any specific differences between EU and Irish competition law.

In principle, there should be no departure between the EU and Irish regimes but there are some differences due to, for example, the operation of the Irish Constitution.

Solicitors should be conscious that the procedures associated with the European Commission and the Competition Authority are often more informal than those of the Irish courts. The rules of evidence are often more informal and the standards of proof are often more relaxed. Sometimes, regulators approach matters more informally than judges but undertakings (and their representatives) still have the same legal protections under constitutional and human rights law.

This section examines the following issues:

(a) notifications to regulators;

(b) complaints to regulators;

(c) litigation before the courts, and

(d) dawn-raids by regulators.

3.6.2 NOTIFICATIONS

3.6.2.1 Generally

Undertakings which are party to anti-competitive arrangements may want to have their arrangements exempted or licensed by the Commission or the Competition Authority to ensure the enforceability of the arrangements. This process is known as 'notification' because it involves a notification of an arrangement.

Notifications are rarely compulsory in competition law. The exceptions include the EC's Merger Control Regulation (ie, Regulation 4064/89 as amended) and Ireland's Mergers and Take-overs (Control) Acts 1978-1996. However, notifications under arts 81-82 of the EC Treaty and the Competition Acts 1991-1996 are not compulsory. This means that solicitors must advise clients about the advantages and disadvantages of notifications. The advantages include:

(a) A successful notification process would mean that the arrangement would be enforceable under the relevant provision (ie, art 81 of the EC Treaty or section 4 of the Competition Act 1991).

(b) Parties to the arrangement or third parties would be unable to challenge the arrangement.

The disadvantages include:

(i) the time involved in making notifications to the Commission and the Competition Authority – delays of months and years are not uncommon;

(ii) there is a cost involved in notifications (such as legal and economists' fees as well as the management time involved in making the notification);

(iii) third parties may find out about the arrangement because there may be publicity attached to the process – some clients are very sensitive to this fact and must be advised in advance of publicity, and

(iv) the Commission might decide against granting a legally-binding negative clearance or exemption but rather issue a non-binding 'comfort letter'.

In practice, filing notifications is not simply a form-filling exercise. It often involves a complex legal and economic analysis of the issues involved. It often involves the preparation of a large volume of complicated documentation.

3.6.2.2 EU: anti-competitive arrangements

An undertaking which is party to an arrangement may decide to notify the arrangement to the Commission to determine the compatibility of the arrangement with art 81 of the EC Treaty. Formally, the notification seeks either a negative clearance (ie, a legally-binding instrument that there is no breach of art 81(1)) or an exemption (ie, a legally-binding instrument that there is breach of art 81(1) but there are grounds under art 81(3) allowing the Commission to authorise the arrangement). A certificate is a legally-binding statement that the Commission believes that the arrangement is not in breach of art 81(1). An exemption is a legally-binding statement by the Commission that the arrangement is enforceable under art 81(3). An exemption operates for a period of time and will be subject to conditions. In practice, parties normally indicate in their notification that they would be willing to accept a 'comfort letter' from the Commission. Such a letter is a non-legally-binding statement that the Commission is not proceeding with the case but does not adopt a legally-binding negative clearance or exemption decision.

The notification is made using 'Form A/B'. This is not a form that is filled out. Instead, it is a list of headings each of which must be addressed. The form must contain information on the parties, the market, the arrangements, the reasons why the notification does not breach art 81, and the reasons why an exemption is justifiable.

Only the parties may notify an arrangement to the Commission. Third parties may not notify an arrangement to obtain an exemption or negative clearance but may complain about the arrangement or comment on a notification made by one (or more) of the undertakings party to the arrangement.

The Commission does not charge a fee for notifications. The Commission does not publish a register of notifications that it receives but annual reports will record many of the notifications received and decisions made during the year.

The Commission considers art 82 when deciding whether to grant an exemption or a negative clearance under art 81. An abuse of dominance under art 82 means that an exemption or a negative clearance would not be granted under art 81.

If an arrangement can benefit from an EC block exemption then there is no need for the arrangement to be notified. In practice, it is useful to draft arrangements to comply with a block exemption so as to avoid the need for notification.

It is possible to notify an arrangement under arts 81 and 82 to the Commission. An exemption may only be granted under art 81 while a negative clearance is possible under arts 81 and 82.

At present, only the Commission may grant an exemption. It has proposed the 'decentralisation' of competition law that would involve Member State authorities having the power to grant exemptions. Such a development, were it to happen, would be many years away.

In practice, the Commission annually makes only around a dozen formal decisions. Instead, the Commission often disposes of notifications through comfort letters and discomfort letters. These are administrative letters issued by the Commission rather than formal legal instruments. A comfort letter indicates that the Commission would probably exempt the arrangement had it reached a formal decision. A comfort letter indicates that the Commission would probably refuse to issue a negative clearance or grant an exemption.

3.6.2.3 Ireland: anti-competitive arrangements

The procedure relating to notifications to the Competition Authority of anti-competitive arrangements under Irish competition law is comparable to the EU procedure outlined above with some exceptions. A fee is payable for notifications to the Competition Authority; at present, it is a fee of IR£250. The Competition Authority publishes details of notifications in a daily newspaper each month and ultimately publishes decisions. The Irish form (known as Form CA) is different from the EU's Form A/B so it is not possible to use one form for each system. It is not possible to notify the Competition Authority to obtain a certificate (comparable to an EC negative clearance) in respect of section 5 of the 1991 Act (abuse of dominance). Helpfully, the Competition Authority does not use the 'comfort letter' procedure so that there is a formally-binding decision at the end of each procedure.

3.6.2.4 EU: abuse of dominance

An undertaking may notify the Commission to determine whether or not there is an abuse of dominance under art 82. For example, undertakings might notify an agreement and the Commission may issue a negative clearance or a comfort letter. Such notifications are rare because undertakings do not always wish to alert the Commission about such arrangements. Notifications are made by Form A/B. In practice, notifications in respect of art 82 are made in conjunction with notifications under art 81.

3.6.2.5 Ireland: abuse of dominance

It is not possible to notify the Competition Authority about a possible abuse of dominance under section 5 of the 1991 Act. This means that undertakings always have a possible exposure about a breach of section 5. It is submitted that the Competition Authority must not issue a negative clearance or grant an exemption under section 4 where there is a breach of section 5.

3.6.2.6 EU: mergers and acquisitions

If a merger or acquisition falls within the scope of the Merger Control Regulation (ie, Regulation 4064/89 as amended), then the transaction must be notified to the Commission. Notification is not optional. The notification is made to the Commission – in particular, the Merger Task Force of the European Commission will deal with the matter. The notification uses a form known as 'Form CO' which is not a form in the normal sense of the term but is a list of headings each of which must be addressed. Solicitors should be conscious that the notification is often voluminous with twenty-one copies of the notification being sent to the Commission. The form does not involve the parties making arguments as to why the concentration should be permitted but instead involves a simple explanation by the parties as to the facts.

3.6.2.7 Ireland: mergers and acquisitions

If the EU's Merger Control Regulation does not apply to a transaction then a solicitor advising on a merger or acquisition must consider the possible application of Irish Merger Control law. Irish Merger Control law comprises the Mergers and Take-overs (Control) Acts 1978-1996 and the Competition Acts 1991-1996. The circumstances for the application of the Irish statutes are examined above. This section examines only the notification aspects.

Notifications under the Mergers Acts are made to the Minister for Enterprise, Trade and Employment. Notifications must be made by all enterprises involved in the proposed transaction. The notification must be made within one month of an offer capable of acceptance. The Minister has one month in which to ask any question on the notification. If the Minister has doubts about whether or not the transaction should be permitted then the Minister may ask questions of the parties. If the Minister wants to refer the proposed transaction to the Competition Authority then the referral must be made within thirty days of receiving full answers to any question raised by the Minister. The Minister normally clears transactions within six weeks to two months where the transaction is not referred to the Competition Authority. The Minister gives the Authority one month or so to prepare a report. Ultimately, the Minister decides a proposed transaction on the basis of whether the transaction would be in the public interest having regard to such considerations as competition. A fee of IR£4,000 must accompany each notification to the Minister. Clients should be advised in appropriate cases of the fact that there may be some publicity about the transaction in terms of the annual report of the Minister for Enterprise, Trade and Employment on the application of the Mergers Acts.

The second regime relates to the Competition Acts. A notification is voluntary. A fee of IR£250 is paid with each notification. The notification is made to the Competition Authority. The Authority publishes a list each month in *The Irish Times* of the notifications and decisions made during the previous year. Solicitors should advise clients about the possible publicity. There is no time limit within which decisions must be made and there have been significant delays. The notification is also by way of Form CA. The Competition Authority has to decide whether the transaction falls within the scope of section 4 of the 1991 Act having regard to section 5. If it is possible to fall within the scope of the Competition Authority's Category Certificate in Respect of Sale of Business Agreements (Decision No 489) then there is no need to make a notification. It is possible to withdraw a notification in certain circumstances. Otherwise, a decision, which will be publicly available, will be published.

3.6.2.8 State aid

Potential instances of State aid must be notified to the Commission in certain cases specified in arts 87-89 of the EC Treaty. Only Member States may notify potential cases of State aid. Solicitors acting for clients who may be in receipt of State aid should take all reasonable steps to ensure that the aid is compatible with EU law by contacting both the Member State authorities (often, the Department of Finance) and the European Commission.

3.6.3 COMPLAINTS

Any one who is aggrieved about a breach of competition law may complain to either the Commission (in the case of EU competition law) or the Competition Authority (in the case of Irish competition law).

3.6.3.1 Merits of complaints

Clients should be advised of the merits of complaints. The advantages include:

(a) the complainant may be able to convince the regulator of the seriousness of the issue and the regulator then takes up the issue which may be, from the perspective of the undertaking allegedly in breach of competition law, a more powerful opponent than the complainant; and

(b) the complainant is not liable for the costs of the regulator or the respondent.

The disadvantages include:

(i) the regulator may not take up the complaint;

(ii) even a successful complainant may not recover its costs, and

(iii) the complainant loses control of the complaint because the regulator decides whether or not to proceed with the complaint.

Complainants should carefully consider the interrelationship between the litigation and complaint procedures and decide which avenue to choose.

3.6.3.2 Form of complaint

A complaint may be made to the Commission or the Competition Authority by way of a memorandum or letter. The Commission has Form C for complaints but the Irish Competition Authority does not have a standard form. It would normally be useful to discuss a possible complaint with the relevant regulator before submitting the complaint.

3.6.3.3 Scope of the complaint

Complaints to the European Commission may relate to arts 81, 82 and 87–89 of the EC Treaty. Complaints to the Competition Authority may relate to sections 4 and 5 of the 1991 Act. It is also possible to submit observations to the Minister for Enterprise, Trade and Employment on proposed mergers and acquisitions being considered by the Minister but there is no formal procedure for such observations.

3.6.3.4 Conduct of the procedure

Complainants must remember that the regulator may not take up the complaint. If the regulator takes up the complaint, then the procedure is between the regulator and the respondent; the complainant is a third party to the procedure. This means that the regulator might decide to drop or pursue the case despite the complainant's wishes. Solicitors should advise complainants that they might not be kept informed of developments during the complaint process.

3.6.4 LITIGATION

Competition litigation is involved and technical. It should not be easily undertaken because of the need, in many cases, to adduce considerable factual evidence and complex economic evidence. Nonetheless, there are cases that must be instituted and therefore solicitors must be aware of the practical aspects of litigation. It is worth mentioning that it is often worthwhile instructing specialist counsel, economists and accountants as early as possible. The economists should be experienced in giving evidence in court and the accountants should be able to quantify the losses that may be claimed.

3.6.4.1 EU competition law

It is possible to institute proceedings claiming a breach of arts 81 and 82 before any Irish civil court. In practice, such cases are instituted before the High Court. Similarly, it is possible to defend any case before any Irish court on the basis of EC competition law; for example, a breach of contract action might be defended on the basis that the 'contract' is void and unenforceable under art 81. A preliminary reference under art 234 of the EC Treaty is not compulsory and should only be used in exceptional circumstances where there is a genuine doubt about the state of EU law on a topic. The Commission may intervene in a case before the Irish court in certain circumstances but the circumstances for doing so have not been clearly established.

3.6.4.2 Irish competition law

A claim based on the common law may be instituted before any Irish court. In respect of alleged breaches of the Competition Acts, private claims under section 6 of the 1991 Act may be instituted only by 'aggrieved persons' and may only be instituted against 'under-takings' on the basis of either sections 4 or 5 of the 1991 Act. Section 4 claims may be instituted in the High Court only. Section 5 claims may be instituted in the High Court or the Circuit Court. Private claims under section 6 of the 1991 Act may be for the purposes of recovering damages, exemplary damages, injunctions and declarations. Public claims may be instituted by either the Minister for Enterprise, Trade and Employment or the Competition Authority and the Competition Authority may seek either injunctions or declarations but not damages or exemplary damages. Claims have been made for breaches of the Competition Acts and some have reached judgment but many have been privately settled between the parties.

3.6.5 INVESTIGATIONS

The Commission and the Competition Authority have extensive powers to investigate alleged breaches of EU and Irish competition law. The Commission and Authority may request disclosure, on a voluntary basis, of information from various parties. The Commission and Authority may also conduct an inspection of premises to gather evidence of alleged breaches provided the Commission has a firm decision authorising it to do so and the Authority has been granted a warrant to do so. The inspectors appear unannounced and may stay for several hours or days. They may not seize original documents and may only take copies or extracts. They may copy computer disks. In practice, they do not inspect legally professionally privileged correspondence or communications. Solicitors called by clients to attend such an investigation should at least scrutinise the authority of the investigators, advise the client on the full legislative background to the investigation, advise on the rule against self-incrimination, assist in regard to the logistics of the investigation, advise the clients on questions asked, and ensure that an additional copy is made of all material which has been copied by the officials.

CHAPTER 4

EUROPEAN PRIVATE INTERNATIONAL LAW

4.1   Introduction

Private international law or conflict of laws is the body of rules that govern the relationship between the legal systems of States. These rules are generally contained in national law. Thus, before 1988 most Irish private international law (with the exception of a few international treaties) formed part of the common law. There are now a number of European instruments, which are standardising the private international law rules of EU Member States. This chapter deals with the two most significant – the Brussels Convention on Jurisdiction and the Enforcement of Judgments and the Rome Convention on Choice of Law in Contractual Matters.

4.2   Brussels and Lugano Conventions on Jurisdiction and the Enforcement of Judgments

4.2.1   BRUSSELS CONVENTION GENERALLY

In any legal dispute involving a person from another Member State of the EU – whether it be a dispute arising from a contract between an Irish distributor and an Italian manufacturer or a civil claim arising from a road traffic accident in France involving Irish tourists – the first question to be asked is before which court may an action be brought. In some circumstances an action may be brought before a foreign court, even where the two parties are Irish, or in Ireland even though the two parties are from outside Ireland. The rules for determining where one may sue are laid down in the Brussels Convention of 1968 on Jurisdiction and the Enforcement of Judgments in Civil and Commercial Matters ('the Brussels Convention').

One of the aims of this Convention is to standardise and simplify these rules. Before the adoption of the Brussels Convention, each Member State had its own individual rules for determining jurisdiction which created uncertainty in advising clients. For instance, in Ireland courts required service of a summons within the State or, in certain circumstances, allowed service out of the State under Order 11 of the Rules of the Superior Courts. The Brussels Convention considerably simplified this by providing a common set of rules observed by each Member State. Though it has its critics, who remain attached to the common law rules, which still apply to disputes falling outside its scope, it is a major improvement on those rules.

The other major aim of the Convention is to simplify the enforcement of judgments within the European Union. Before Ireland acceded to the Convention, it was very difficult to enforce a foreign judgment. A foreign judgment for a defined sum of money was viewed as analogous to a debt. It was necessary to commence proceedings against the foreign judgment debtor on foot of a summary summons. Even then, this right was confined to money judgments and foreign revenue judgments were excluded. In contrast, the Brussels Convention operates to create a single law district in Europe where lawyers have defined rules as to where suit should be brought and can simply and speedily enforce a judgment obtained in one Contracting State in another.

4.2.2 IMPLEMENTATION OF THE BRUSSELS CONVENTION

The Jurisdiction of Courts and the Enforcement of Judgments Act 1988 implemented the Brussels Convention into Irish domestic law. The Act took effect on 1 April 1989. Section 2 provides that the Convention is to be treated like any other Irish statute, except that it is to be interpreted in accordance with the decisions of the ECJ. In addition, in interpreting the Convention regard may be had to the interpretative report (which was drawn up by Prof Jenard). The ECJ has jurisdiction to give rulings on the interpretation of the Convention when a court designated in art 2 of the Luxembourg Protocol 1971 (annexed to the Convention) makes a reference.

4.2.3 THE SAN SEBASTIAN CONVENTION

The Convention was subsequently amended by the San Sebastian Convention and this was given effect in Ireland by the Jurisdiction of Courts and Enforcement of Judgments Act 1993. Austria, Sweden and Finland acceded to the Convention in 1996. The Jurisdiction of Courts and Enforcement of Judgments Act 1998 ('the 1998 Act'), implements this Convention into Irish law. This Act consolidates and replaces all the preceding Irish legislation. Annexed to the Act is a consolidated version of the Convention containing all the amendments made to it.

4.2.4 PROPOSALS FOR REVISION

The Brussels Convention is currently being reviewed. On 28 May 1999 the Commission put forward a proposal for revision of the Convention (Proposal for a Council Regulation (EC) on jurisdiction and enforcement of judgments in civil and commercial matters, COM (1999) 348 final). It proposes the replacement of the Convention with a regulation. This would bring the Convention within the framework of EC law. It would also mean that the Regulation would enter into force on its implementation date rather than requiring a number of signatories to implement a Treaty as at present. The accession convention for Austria, Finland and Sweden (which makes a number of minor amendments) has not yet entered into force for this reason. The amendments, which this proposal may make, are set out in the discussion of the appropriate articles.

The legal basis for this proposal is Title IV of the EC Treaty. Measures adopted under this Title are not applicable in Denmark, the UK or Ireland. However, at the Council meeting on 12 March 1999, the UK and Ireland indicated that they would 'opt in' for this and other proposals on judicial co-operation. If Denmark does not opt in the regulation will apply between all other Member States, the Convention between those States and Denmark and the Lugano Convention between the EU and EFTA Member States.

4.2.5 THE LUGANO CONVENTION

There is a parallel Convention – the Lugano Convention – that regulates similar matters between EU and EFTA member States (Norway, Iceland and Switzerland) and between the

EFTA States. This Convention is practically identical to the Brussels Convention. There are some differences but these are relatively minor. The 1993 Act also enabled Ireland to ratify this Convention. The Lugano Convention allows for the accession of future EU and EFTA Member States and even for third States to accede to the Convention. Poland is in the process of acceding to this Convention.

4.2.6 SCOPE OF THE BRUSSELS CONVENTION

4.2.6.1 Civil and commercial matters

Article 1 provides that the Convention applies in civil and commercial matters. Tax, customs and public law matters are expressly excluded. The Convention does not expressly define what a 'civil or commercial matter' is. In Case 29/76 *LTU Lufttransportunternehmen GmbH & Co KG v Eurocontrol* [1976] ECR 1541, the ECJ held that this could not be determined according to national law, but required a supra-national Community-wide approach. The Court decided that, in the first instance, reference would be made to the objectives and schemes of the Convention and, secondly to general principles from national legal systems. In *Eurocontrol*, the Court excluded an action by Eurocontrol, the European aviation authority, to recover charges payable by Lufthansa for the use of its equipment and services. The Court clearly excluded from the application of the Convention actions brought by a public authority acting in the exercise of the regulation of its public powers. Likewise, in Case 814/79 *Netherlands State v Rüffer* [1980] ECR 3807, the ECJ held that the Convention did not cover an action for the recovery of costs incurred by an agent responsible for administering Dutch public waterways when removing a wreck pursuant to an international convention – though Dutch law classified the case as an action in tort.

The ECJ appears to be making a tentative distinction between the exercise of public and private law powers. In Case C-172/91 *Sonntag v Waidmann* [1993] ECR 1963 a German teacher, employed by the State, took a group of students on an excursion to the Italian Alps. One pupil fell and died. Sonntag was charged with manslaughter and brought before the Italian courts. In the course of the proceedings, the next of kin of the deceased intervened claiming damages. Once judgment was obtained the relatives sought to enforce it in Germany. It was argued that the compensation order was an administrative rather than a civil matter as it related to the liability of a public servant acting as such. The ECJ held that this was a civil matter as the standard of care required of Sonntag was one required of all individuals. His liability was derived from ordinary civil liability. If he had been exercising public authority powers, the claim would have fallen outside the scope of the Convention.

4.2.6.2 Exclusions

Article 1 contains a number of express exclusions. These matters are only excluded where they are the main object of proceedings. They are as follows:

The status or capacity of natural persons

Rights in property arising from marriage. This was originally excluded due to the disparity between the family law systems of the Member States. This disparity has lessened and on 8 June 1998 the EU Member States signed the Brussels II Convention on Jurisdiction and the Recognition and Enforcement of Judgments in Matrimonial Matters. The Convention sets out jurisdictional rules in family law cases. It will determine which court can hear particular applications, based on habitual residence, nationality or domicile. It applies to all civil proceedings relating to divorce, legal separation, annulment or parental responsibility. The Brussels II Convention was adopted in the form of a regulation on 29 May 2000. It is due to be implemented by 1 March 2001. This regulation is more fully discussed in the Family Law manual.

This exception does not extend to maintenance orders, which are provided for in art 5(2). The ECJ has spent some time considering the boundaries between the art 1 exclusion and the art 5(2) provision. In Case 143/78 *De Cavel v De Cavel (No 1)* [1979] ECR 1055, the ECJ held that judicial decisions authorising provisional measures in the course of divorce proceedings did not fall within the Convention's scope. They were excluded from the scope of the Convention as they were closely connected with, 'either questions of the status of the persons involved in the divorce proceedings, or proprietary legal relations resulting directly from the matrimonial relationship of the dissolution thereof'. The ECJ reached a similar conclusion in Case 25/81 *CHW v GJH* [1982] ECR 1189. In that case it held that an application for provisional measures to secure up the delivery of a document in order to prevent its use as evidence in proceedings concerning a husband's management of his wife's property was excluded if such management was closely connected with the proprietary relationship resulting directly from the marriage.

In contrast to these decisions is the Court's ruling in Case 120/79 *De Cavel v De Cavel (No 2)* [1980] ECR 731. The Court held that the Convention would be applicable to the enforcement of an interim compensatory order made by the French courts. It reached this conclusion as interim orders were in the nature of maintenance and were designed to provide financial support to the spouse. These ancillary orders came within the Convention's scope as the court deals with them referring to the subject matter of the ancillary application, rather than the subject matter of the primary application. Likewise, a maintenance order after divorce is within the scope of the Convention.

Wills and succession

Bankruptcy and related matters. These matters were excluded, as there were negotiations ongoing for a separate convention on these matters. A regulation on jurisdictional rules in cross-border insolvency proceedings has now been agreed. Insurance and various investment situations are excluded from the scope of this regulation. The regulation provides that the main insolvency proceedings are to be opened in the Member State where the debtor has the centre of his main interests. These proceedings have universal scope and are aimed at encompassing all the debtor's assets. Secondary proceedings can be opened to run in parallel in a Member State where the debtor has an establishment but their effect is limited to assets located in that State. The regulation is to enter into force on 31 May 2002.

Bankruptcy was defined in Case 133/78 *Gourdain v Nadler* [1979] ECR 733. The ECJ held that it included proceedings for the winding up of companies or other legal persons, judicial arrangements, and compositions. It applies to any situation where debtors are unable to meet their liabilities which results in the intervention of national courts and which concludes with a compulsory liquidation of assets. In that case, the Court held that the decision of a French civil court ordering the manager of a company to pay a sum into the assets of the company was given in the context of bankruptcy and therefore excluded from the application of the Convention.

Social security. This exclusion was justified as social security in some States is seen as a matter of public law while in other States, it crosses both public and private law.

Arbitration. Arbitration was excluded, as there is a separate 1958 New York Convention on Arbitration, to which all the Contracting States, with the exception of Portugal, are party. The extent of this exclusion was considered by the ECJ in Case C-190/89 *Marc Rich v Societa Impianti* [1991] ECR I-3855. The case concerned a contract to buy crude oil from Italian defendants. The defendants accepted an offer subject to conditions. The plaintiff confirmed its acceptance of those conditions and then sent a telex setting out terms of a contract that contained an English arbitration clause. The plaintiff claimed that the cargo was contaminated and claimed $7 million compensation. The defendants began Italian proceedings seeking a declaration that they were not liable. The plaintiff applied to the English courts seeking the appointment of an arbitrator. The defendants opposed this and claimed that the Italian courts had jurisdiction under the Convention. The ECJ held that a dispute concerning the existence of an arbitration clause was excluded by the Convention.

4.2.7   JURISDICTIONAL RULES

4.2.7.1   General rule

The general rule of jurisdiction is that persons domiciled in a Member State are to be sued in courts of that State (art 2). 'Domiciled' means ordinarily resident. It does not refer to the common law concept of domicile. The Convention does not define domicile. Article 52 provides that the issue shall be determined by the application of the internal law of each Member State. Section 15 provides that domicile for the purpose of the Convention is defined by Schedule 9 to the Act. Part I of the schedule provides that a person is domiciled in the State if he is ordinarily resident there. Part III provides that the domicile of a company or association is where it was incorporated or where its central management and control is exercised. Part V defines the domicile of a trust as being the system of law of a State with which the trust has its closest and most real connection. The regulation will provide that a company or legal person is domiciled where it has its statutory seat, central administration or principal place of business.

There are a number of exceptions to the general rule allowing a plaintiff a choice of alternative State in which to bring an action. These exceptions are contained in arts 5 and 6.

4.2.7.2   Contract

The first exception is for contracts. Article 5(1) provides that a defendant may be sued in contractual matters either where he is domiciled or in the State which is the place of performance of the obligation in question.

Matters relating to a contract

Article 5(1) applies 'in matters relating to a contract'. This is given quite a wide interpretation. In Case 34/82 *Peters GmbH v Zuid Nederlands AV* [1983] ECR 987, the ECJ held that this had to be given an independent European law meaning. Unfortunately, it did not define it. The case concerned a suit against Peters for money owed to an association of building contractors. The action was brought in the Dutch courts, though Peters was domiciled in Germany. Could an action brought by one member of an association against another be contractual? Dutch law did not view it as such. The ECJ held that it was contractual for the purposes of the Convention.

In Case 9/87 *Arcado v Havilland* [1988] ECR 1539, the ECJ held that a claim flowing from a repudiated contract came within art 5(1). There had been a commercial agency agreement between the plaintiff and defendant. The defendant repudiated the agreement and the plaintiff claimed for unpaid commission and compensation. The Court held that as the claims concerned a commercial agency agreement (albeit a repudiated one), they could be considered as 'matters relating to a contract'.

Article 5(1) may apply even where the existence of the contract is in dispute between the parties. In Case 38/81 *Effner v Kantner* [1982] ECR 825, the defendant argued that the plaintiff had concluded a contract with a third party in his personal capacity and not as agent of the defendant. Therefore, there was no contract and art 5(1) could not be invoked. The ECJ held that art 5(1) applied. To hold otherwise, it said would be to deprive art 5(1) of legal effect as in any dispute one of the parties could claim that there was no contract. The English Court of Appeal applied this case in *Tesam Distribution Ltd v Schuh Mode Team* [1990] ILR 149. The plaintiff claimed that the defendants, a German shoe supplier and a German bank, had entered into a contract with the plaintiff, an English shoe importer and distributor. The defendant bank disputed the existence of a contract. The Court of Appeal followed *Effner*. However, Nicholls LJ did emphasise that frivolous claims of contractual liability asserted to establish jurisdiction under art 5(1) should be closely scrutinised.

The limit of what the ECJ considers contractual was seen in Case C-26/91 *Handte v Traitments Mécano-Chimiques des Surfaces* [1992] 1 ECR 3967. It held that art 5(1) does not extend to a claim by an ultimate purchaser of a product against a manufacturer who was not the direct seller to the plaintiff, based on defects in the product or its unfitness for its intended purpose. A matter relating to a contract could not cover a situation where there is no agreement freely entered into by one party toward another.

There is some uncertainty about whether quasi-contractual/restitutionary claims fall within art 5(1). The matter has not been resolved by the ECJ. Many argue that, following *Arcado*, such claims should be regarded as contractual in nature. Should claims for breach of fiduciary duty, quantum meruit payments or meddling with trust property be viewed as somehow 'contractual' within the meaning of art 5(1), tortious under art 5(3) or totally sui generis, falling under art 2? Unfortunately, the ECJ has not yet undertaken the classification of such equitable claims.

There are a number of decisions of national courts applying art 5(1) to restitutionary claims. The Scots courts in *Engdiv Ltd v G Percy Trentham Ltd* 1990 SLT 617 held that a statutory claim to contribution fell within art 5(1). The English courts have also considered similar matters. In *Atlas Shipping Agency (UK) Ltd and United Shipping Services Ltd v Suisse Atlantique Société, D'Armement Maritime SA, Labuk Bay Shipping Inc and Ulugan Bay Shipping Inc* [1992] 3 WLR 827, a third party to whom a 2 per cent sales commission should have been paid under an agreement for the sale of two ships sought to enforce the agreement. The defendants argued that art 5(1) did not apply on the basis that they were sued on foot of a constructive trust rather than in contract. Rix J held for the plaintiffs, holding that the obligation being enforced was contractual. He said that, 'There is only one contractual obligation in question; there is privity between the parties to it; the obligation was freely entered into by those parties; . . . they both knew the identity and domicile of the plaintiffs and, . . . both intended to benefit them by means of the contracted payment'. He went on to observe that the fact that performance of the obligation was to take place in the broker's domicile is what the buyers must have anticipated. On this basis he held that the buyers were being sued 'in matters relating to a contract' and that the 'obligation in question' was the alleged implied promise given by them that they would pay over the commission to the brokers.

In *Kleinwort Benson v Glasgow City Council* [1999] 1 AC 153, a case that has been of such duration that it is beginning to take on some of the flavour of *Jarndyce v Jarndyce*, the English courts were handed this poisoned chalice. The question of quasi-contract and jurisdiction under the provisions of the Convention came squarely before them.

The plaintiffs sought to recover £807,230 paid in seven interest rate swap transactions to the defendant, a Scots local authority between 7 and 22 September 1982. This action followed on from the House of Lords decision in *Hazell v Hammersmith and Fulham London Borough Council* [1992] 2 AC 1. In that case the House of Lords had held that all such transactions were ultra vires the local authority and void ab initio. The plaintiffs claimed that they were entitled to recover the money on a number of grounds: first, on a restitutionary basis as the consideration for which the agreements were concluded had failed; secondly, the plaintiffs argued that the payments were made under a mistake of fact so that it was unjust and unconscionable that the defendant be entitled to retain the money; thirdly they claimed that the sum in question was money had and received to the use of the plaintiffs; and finally, they claimed that the sum was held by the defendant on an implied or resulting or a constructive trust for the banks and that the banks were entitled to trace it.

The action was initiated in England. Glasgow City Council sought a declaration that the court had no jurisdiction over it in respect of the claims and asked the court to dismiss the action. It asserted that under art 2 of the Convention it should be sued in the place of its domicile, Scotland. It argued that art 5(1) was inapplicable, as the House of Lords had held that there never had been a contract. The plaintiffs argued that the exceptions to art 2 contained in art 5 applied in this situation. One of their primary arguments was that as the court was determining the consequences of the nullity of contracts, art 5(1) was applicable.

Section 16(1) of the Civil Jurisdiction and Judgments Act 1982 applies a somewhat modified version of the Convention for determining jurisdiction between the constituent parts of the United Kingdom. The text of art 5(1) of this modified version is identical.

Section 16(3) provides that in interpreting the Convention in this context regard may be had to decisions of the ECJ concerning it.

In the High Court, Hirst J held that as the transactions were void ab initio there was no contract within the meaning of art 5(1). He said: 'the suggestion that the restitutionary claims in these matters are in matters relating to a contract seems to me to be placing a very severe strain on the language of article 5(1)'. He went on to observe that:

'[T]here must be either a contractual relationship giving rise to actual contractual obligations, or a consensual obligation similar to a contract . . . giving rise to a comparable obligation, for the case to fall within the crucial test in article 5(1)'.

Hirst J therefore held that art 2 applied and that the defendant must be sued in the courts of its place of domicile – Scotland.

In the Court of Appeal a majority (Roch and Millett LJJ) decided to reverse the decision of Hirst J. However, Leggatt LJ vigorously dissented from the majority decision. The Court of Appeal considered the fundamental issue to be whether art 5(1) was to be interpreted by the law of England and Wales or to be interpreted in a wider sense. If the former, the matter could not be considered 'contractual' as it concerned a contract that, under English law, was void ab initio. It accepted that the word 'contract' in art 5(1) should be understood in the wider European sense. Millet LJ observed that the phrase, 'matters relating to a contract' was intentionally indefinite and was designed to avoid technical classifications of causes of action in national law (which differ widely). However, he said that there was a general sense in which 'contract' was understood by the signatories – 'a consensual arrangement intended to create legal relations and to be legally enforceable'. He said that a claim of this nature should fall within art 5(1).

Roch LJ agreed, observing that:

'If the words in article 5(1) "a contract" include a contract void ab initio, then it cannot in my view be doubted that actions to recover moneys paid in the mistaken belief that there was a valid contract between the parties must be "matters in relation to a contract." '

He went on to observe that the word 'obligations' in art 5(1) was not confined to contractual obligations.

Leggatt LJ strongly dissented from the majority opinion. He held that as the dispute turned on the interpretation of Schedule 4, rather than the Convention proper, European law need not necessarily be applied to the dispute. The 1982 Act distinguished between the two, requiring the Convention to be interpreted 'in accordance with' relevant decisions of the ECJ but for the Schedule imposing the lesser interpretative requirement that 'regard shall be had' to relevant decisions of the ECJ. On this basis, he felt that English law should prevail. He said that in this case the cause of action arose as there proved not to be a contractual relationship between the parties. For all these reasons, he agreed with Hirst J that once the contract between the parties had been held void, there never was a contract and that it was therefore impossible to regard a claim for unjust enrichment as a matter relating to a contract. Therefore, the claim falls outside the scope of art 5(1).

The case was then appealed to the House of Lords. By a 3/2 majority, it reversed the decision of the Court of Appeal. The majority held that as the case concerned a void contract, no contract was in existence and the claim could not come within 'matters relating to a contact' in art 5(1). Jurisdiction was to be determined by art 2.

Lord Goff held that:

'In truth, the claim in the present case is simply a claim to restitution, which in English law is based upon the principle of unjust enrichment; and claims of this kind do not per se fall within article 5(1) . . . the vast majority of claims to restitution, . . . are founded simply upon the principles of unjust enrichment. Such is, in my opinion, the present case. No express provision is made in article 5 in respect of claims for unjust enrichment as such; and it is legitimate to infer that this omission is due to the absence of any close connecting factor consistently linking such claims to any jurisdiction other than the defendant's domicile. Article 2 therefore provides the appropriate jurisdiction for such claims.'

In many ways this case muddies the waters for the Irish courts. In the absence of a definitive ruling from the ECJ, there are two very different approaches adopted by different English courts. It is difficult to predict the eventual ruling that will be issued by the ECJ on the question of restitutionary claims.

The obligation in question

Article 5(1) confers jurisdiction on the courts for the place of performance of the 'obligation in question'. What is the 'obligation in question'? One of the first cases to consider this was Case 14/76 *De Bloos v Bouyer* [1976] ECR 1497. A Belgian, De Bloos, was a distributor for a French person, Bouyer. De Bloos sued before a Belgian court claiming that his distributorship had been terminated without proper notice and that therefore he was entitled to compensation and also claiming extra compensation for the goodwill that his efforts had generated. Which of his obligations was relevant for the purpose of considering whether the Belgian court had jurisdiction under art 5(1)? The ECJ held that each obligation had to be considered separately. There was Bouyer's obligation to give proper notice. The Court also considered whether the obligation to pay extra compensation was a contractual obligation. If it was, the national court would have to decide its place of performance and this would determine the court having jurisdiction. The approach in this case was to look at the obligation as one which is imposed on the grantor of the contract and the non-performance of which gives the other party his cause of action.

This matter came up for consideration again in Case 266/85 *Schenavai v Kreischer* [1987] ECR 239. Schenavai was a German architect who sued Kreischer, a Dutch person, for the construction of holiday homes in Germany. The obligation that was the basis of the litigation was the payment of fees. The ECJ followed *De Bloos* but went further. It held that where there are a number of obligations stemming from the one contract one looks to the principal obligation to decide jurisdiction.

The House of Lords applied *Schenavai* in *Union Transport v Continental Lines* [1992] 1 All ER 161. The plaintiffs argued that in December 1983 by means of an exchange of telexes, a charter of a vessel had been agreed with the defendant – the defendant was to nominate the vessel for the carriage of a cargo of telegraph poles from Florida to Bangladesh. The defendant, a Belgian company, denied that a contract had been concluded between the parties. The charterer sued the shipowner for breach of two obligations, ie, to nominate and to provide a vessel. The House of Lords – Lord Goff giving the leading judgment – held that the principal of the two obligations was the obligation to nominate. Therefore, the English courts had jurisdiction as the obligation to nominate a vessel was to be performed in England. This was the case even though it was in Florida that the vessel should have been made available for loading the cargo.

The Irish courts have followed this line. The Supreme Court in *Unidare plc and Unidare Cable Ltd v James Scott Ltd* [1991] 2 IR 88 took a pragmatic approach. In a case concerning payment for the supply of cables, the Court held that the obligation in question was the obligation that was the subject matter of the proceedings – payment for goods supplied. In *Ferndale Films Ltd v Granada Television Ltd* [1993] 3 IR 368 the Supreme Court looked to the principal obligation which was the basis of the action, rather than an ancillary obligation which the plaintiffs relied on in an attempt to give the Irish courts jurisdiction. The defendant, an English company, gave an undertaking to use its best endeavours to promote the film, 'My Left Foot', throughout the entire world with the exception of the United Kingdom and Ireland. As Ireland was not the place of performance of the obligation in question, the Supreme Court declined jurisdiction under art 5(1).

Place of performance

What of the place of performance? In Case 12/76 *Tessili v Dunlop* [1976] ECR 1473, the ECJ held that this is decided according to the conflicts rules of the law governing the obligation in question. This national law approach has been consistently followed since, most recently in Case C-288/92 *Custom Made Commercial Ltd v Stawa Metallbau GmbH* [1994] ECR 2913.

The San Sebastian Convention introduced a new rule relating to employment contracts. Article 5(1) provides that for contracts of employment the place of performance of the obligation in question is the place where the employee habitually carries out his work or, if the employee does not habitually carry out his work in any one country, the employer may also be sued in the courts of the place where the business which engaged the employee was or is now situated. The ECJ considered this in Case C-838/95 *Petrus Wilhelmus Rutten v Cross Medical Ltd* [1997] All ER (EC) 121. It held that the 'place . . . where the employee habitually carries out his work', where an employee works in more than one Member State is the place where the employee has established the effective centre of his working activities. In identifying that place in this case, the Court took into account the fact that he spent most of his working time in one State in which he had an office where he organised his activities for his employer and to which he returned after each business trip to other Member States.

The regulation retains much of the original wording of art 5(1) – jurisdiction is given to the 'place of performance of the obligation in question'. However, in the case of the sale of goods and the provision of services, the regulation defines the place of performance of the obligation in question. For the sale of goods it will be the place where the goods were or should have been delivered. In the case of the provision of services it will be the place where under the contract the services were or should have been provided.

4.2.7.3 Maintenance

If the matter is a maintenance claim the defendant may be sued where the maintenance creditor is domiciled or habitually resident: art 5(2). This provision has been discussed in the context of the art 1 exclusion of property rights arising from marriage.

4.2.7.4 Tort

Choice of jurisdiction

Under art 5(3) in matters relating to tort a plaintiff may sue either in the State of the defendant's domicile or in the State where the harmful event occurred.

The 'place where the harmful event occurred' has been given quite a wide interpretation. In Case 21/76 *Bier v Mines de Potasse* [1976] ECR 1735, the ECJ interpreted this phrase as giving jurisdiction, at the plaintiff's option, to either the courts for the place where the damage occurred or the courts for the place of the 'event giving rise to the damage'. The case concerned cross-border pollution. Mines de Potasse allegedly discharged 11,000 tons of chloride into the river Rhine on a daily basis. Bier ran large garden nurseries near Rotterdam in the Netherlands. It used water from the Rhine to water and irrigate its seedbeds. The high salinity of the Rhine due to the presence of the chlorine in the water damaged Bier's seedbeds. Bier brought an action against Mines de Potasse in the Dutch courts. The French defendant argued that a Dutch court was not competent to hear the dispute. Under art 2 of the Convention the defendant should be sued in the courts of its own domicile. If a tort had been committed, the place of the harmful event was France where the alleged pollutant had been discharged into the Rhine. This argument was successful at first instance. Bier appealed to the Hague Court of Appeal which referred the matter to the ECJ. The Dutch court asked whether 'the place where the harmful event' occurred was to be construed as meaning the place where the damage occurred or where the event which caused the damage took place.

The ECJ first held that 'the place where the harmful event occurred' was to be given an independent interpretation. It looked to its previous decision in *LTU v Eurocontrol* and said that in reaching such an interpretation the Court must look at the objectives and scheme of the Convention. The general rule of the jurisdiction is that of the defendant's domicile in art 2. The Court noted that the special jurisdictional grounds in art 5, which exist by way of an exception to art 2, were introduced due to the existence 'in certain clearly defined situations, of a particularly close connecting factor between a dispute and the court which may be called upon to hear it, with a view to the efficacious conduct of the proceedings'.

The meaning of 'the place where the harmful event occurred' was unclear in the context of a tort, which took place in more than one jurisdiction. The ECJ held that there was a significant connection in relation to both the place of the causal event and the place of injury as each could be helpful in relation to the necessary evidence and the conduct of the proceedings. The Court found it inappropriate to opt for one jurisdiction to the exclusion of the other, as there were significant connecting factors to both. The Court held therefore that:

> 'Where the place of the happening of the event which may give rise to liability in tort, delict or quasi-delict and the place where that event results in damage are not identical, the expression "the place where the harmful event occurred", in article 5(3) . . . must be understood as being intended to cover both the place where the damage occurred and the place of the event giving rise to it.'

The result is that the defendant may be sued, at the option of the plaintiff, either in the courts for the place where the damage occurred or in the courts for the place of the event which gives rise to and is at the origin of that damage.

The ECJ went on to justify its decision. If the place where the harmful event occurred was interpreted as the place of the causal event this would cause some confusion between the scope of art 5(3) and art 2. As both articles would be specifying the same jurisdiction, art 5(3) would lose its effectiveness. If the place of damage was exclusively chosen, this would exclude 'a helpful connecting factor . . . particularly close to the cause of the damage'. Finally the decision reached was in conformity with the approach taken in the national private international law rules of several of the Contracting States.

The plaintiff has the option of suing the defendant in either the place where the damage occurred or in the place of the causal event giving rise to the damage. The ECJ in a simple yet subtle manner accepted the arguments of both the plaintiff and defendant. However, this decision received some criticism as it could lead to fragmentation of jurisdiction.

In *Short v Ireland*, 24 October 1996, Supreme Ct (unreported) the Supreme Court applied *Bier*. The case concerned the proposed construction of a nuclear reprocessing plant at Selafield, Cumbria. The plaintiffs who lived on the Irish coast opposite Cumbria claimed that radioactive contamination from the plant would adversely affect the health of residents. The plaintiffs claimed breaches of directives and customary international law and sought damages for negligence, breach of constitutional rights, trespass and nuisance. The High Court held against the plaintiffs on a number of procedural grounds. On appeal, the Supreme Court held that the plaintiffs' claim was in the nature of a tort action. The cause of action derived not from the reprocessing carried out in the United Kingdom but from the allegedly harmful results of these activities in Ireland. Thus, the Irish courts had jurisdiction to deal with the plaintiffs' claims.

The regulation proposes one small change to art 5(3), which currently provides that in tortious cases jurisdiction is given to the court of the place where the harmful event occurred. The regulation provides that it will cover cases not only where the harmful event has occurred but also those where it may occur.

4.2.7.5 Economic torts

General rules

The ECJ in Case 220/88 *Dumez Bâtiment and Tracona v Hessische Landesbank* [1990] ECR I-49 made it clear that consequential financial loss suffered in one jurisdiction as a result of a tort in another jurisdiction did not found a claim under art 5(3). Ricochet victims are thus excluded. In that case, a French parent company claimed for damages on the basis of losses suffered by its German subsidiary. The parent company claimed that the conduct of a German bank in its dealing with a German subsidiary of the plaintiffs from not carrying out certain contracts had resulted in financial loss to the plaintiffs (as the anticipated profits would have been sent back to the French parent company). The German bank had withdrawn credits to a German property developer. This had caused the halting of a building programme resulting in the insolvency of the German subsidiary. The plaintiffs argued that France was the place of the harmful event and Germany was the place of the causal event. The ECJ held that the French companies were not entitled to bring the action. The victims of the act were the German subsidiaries and only they would be able to sue under art 5(3). The Court held:

> 'the . . . "place where the harmful event occurred" contained in article 5(3) of the Convention may refer to the place where the damage occurred, the latter concept can be understood only as indicating the place where the event giving rise to the damage, and entailing tortious, delictual or quasi-delictual liability, directly produced its harmful effects upon the person who is the immediate victim of that event'.

The ECJ made a similar finding in Case C-364/93 *Marinari v Lloyds Bank plc* [1995] ECR I-2719. The plaintiff had lodged promissory notes with a branch of Lloyds in London. The bank refused to honour the notes or return them. They then advised the police of the existence of the notes and that they were of uncertain origin. The plaintiff was arrested and the notes were sequestrated. After his release he brought an action in Italy against Lloyds seeking compensation for refusal to pay on the notes, for breach of contract, or damage to his reputation and for damage suffered due to his arrest. Lloyds argued that the damage had occurred in Italy. The plaintiff argued that the Italian court could have jurisdiction under art 5(3) as that was where he suffered economic loss as a result of the events in London. The ECJ held:

> 'Whilst it is recognised that the term "place where the harmful event occurred" within the meaning of Article 5(3) of the Convention may cover both the place where the damage occurred and the place of the event giving rise to it, that term cannot, however, be construed so extensively as to encompass any place where the adverse consequences of an event that has already caused actual damage elsewhere can be felt.

> 'Consequently, that term cannot be construed as including the place where, as in the present case the victim claims to have suffered financial loss consequential upon initial damage arising and suffered by him in another Contracting State'.

Defamation

The issue of multi-State defamation arose in Case C-68/93 *Shevill v Presse Alliance* [1995] All ER (EC) 289. The first plaintiff, Fiona Shevill, domiciled in England with her main residence in Yorkshire, was employed at a bureau de change operated by the fourth plaintiff, Chequepoint SARL. Chequepoint SARL is a French enterprise operating a number of bureaux de change in France and elsewhere in Europe. The defendants publish the newspaper, 'France Soir', a daily evening newspaper that has a large circulation in France, in excess of 200,000 copies daily and a smaller daily circulation of approximately 15,500 copies outside France. In relation to this latter circulation, it was claimed that only 230 copies were sold in England and Wales, notably only five in Yorkshire where the first plaintiff resided.

The plaintiff claimed damages for harm caused by the publication of a defamatory newspaper article in 'France Soir' on 27 September 1989. It referred to an alleged investigation by French police into the laundering of money obtained from the sale of drugs by, in particular, the Paris bureau de change in which Ms Shevill was temporarily employed for three months in the summer of 1989, and to whom reference by name was made in the article. In November 1989, the defendants published a retraction and apology in respect of

Ms Shevill and Chequepoint SARL. The action, subsequent to amendments to the statement of claim, related solely to publication in England and Wales, not France. The defendants sought to strike out the claim arguing that there was no jurisdiction as no harmful event had occurred in England.

Before the Court of Appeal, it was argued by counsel for the defendant that none of the plaintiffs had suffered any actual damage so as to constitute a harmful event within the jurisdiction. There was no evidence that there was anyone who could possibly have been affected who knew Ms Shevill or who had access to any copies of the offending newspaper. These submissions were based upon the necessity of demonstrating for the purposes of art 5(3) of the Convention that damage had been actually suffered, an approach which was inconsistent with the English law that assumed that damage had been suffered once the libel had been established.

It was held by the Court of Appeal that, since the action was restricted to publication of the defamatory article in England and Wales, the court could assume jurisdiction under art 5(3) of the Convention once it was shown that there was an arguable case on which each plaintiff could rely to establish a publication carrying with it the presumption of damage.

The defendant appealed to the House of Lords arguing that the French courts had jurisdiction in the dispute under art 2, and that the English courts did not have jurisdiction under art 5(3) as the 'place where the harmful event occurred' was France and no harmful event had taken place in England. The House of Lords, considering that the proceedings raised questions of interpretation of the Convention, decided to stay the proceedings pending a preliminary ruling by the ECJ.

Arising from the questions referred to it by the House of Lords, the ECJ identified two fundamental matters of interpretation. First interpretative guidance was needed on 'the place where the harmful event occurred' in art 5(3), with a view to establishing which court(s) had jurisdiction to hear an action for damages for harm caused to the victim following distribution of a defamatory newspaper article in several Contracting States. Secondly, it had to be decided whether, in determining if it had jurisdiction as court of the place where the damage occurred pursuant to art 5(3), the national court was required to follow specific rules different from those laid down by its national law in relation to the criteria for assessing whether the event in question was harmful and whether specific rules were needed in relation to the evidence required of the existence and extent of the harm alleged by the victim of the defamation.

The ECJ first examined the concept of 'the place where the harmful event occurred'. The ECJ examined in some detail its important earlier decisions in *Bier* and *Dumez* as interpretative aids to establish the place of the harmful event in the international libel context. The harm in *Bier* was material property damage whereas in *Shevill* at issue was non-pecuniary damage to reputation. Nevertheless, the ECJ, by parity of reasoning, applied a similar analysis to art 5(3) irrespective of the type of damage involved. It was expressly stated in *Shevill* that identical principles apply, and the place of the event giving rise to the damage no less than the place where the damage occurred could constitute a significant connecting factor from the point of view of jurisdiction.

Each of them, depending on the circumstances, could be particularly helpful in relation to the evidence and the conduct of the proceedings. The observations made in *Bier* vis à vis physical or pecuniary loss or damage, have now been expressly applied to a case involving injury to reputation and the good name of both natural and legal persons due to a defamatory publication. Where a newspaper article is distributed in several Contracting States then, according to the ECJ, the place of the event giving rise to the damage (causal event), can only be where the miscreant publisher is established, ie, the place where the harmful event originated and from which the libel was issued and put into circulation. The court of the place where the publisher is established has jurisdiction to hear the whole action for all damage caused by the unlawful act. That jurisdiction will, as the ECJ noted, generally coincide in any event with the art 2 jurisdiction based on the defendant's domicile.

The courts of the Contracting State in which the publication was distributed and in which the victim claims to have suffered injury to his reputation have jurisdiction to rule on the injury caused in that State to the victim's reputation. The ECJ held that the State in which the defamatory publication is distributed and in which the victim claims to have suffered injury to his reputation is best suited to assess and determine the corresponding damage.

The second limb of the judgment focused on whether a national court was required to follow specific rules different from those laid down by its national law in relation to the criteria for assessing whether the event in question is harmful and in relation to the evidence required of the existence and extent of the harm alleged by the victim of defamation. The defendants argued that the plaintiff had not suffered any damage so as to constitute 'a harmful event'. There was no evidence that the plaintiff's reputation had actually been harmed or that those who knew the plaintiff had access to any copies of the newspaper. The defendants argued that the principles in English law that assumed that damage is suffered once a libel is established should be disregarded in favour of a common European interpretation of art 5(3) and thus proof of actual damage to qualify England as the place where the 'harmful event' occurred. The ECJ observed that the object of the Convention was not to unify the rules of substantive law and of procedure of the different Contracting States. The effect was that it was for the substantive English law of defamation to determine whether the event in question was harmful and the evidence required to the existence and extent of the harm.

The judgment in *Shevill* achieves suitability of forum. The courts of the place where the damage arises are best placed to assess the harm done to the victim's reputation within their jurisdiction and to determine the extent of the damage. It avoids the difficulty of a court in one State trying to assess the damage caused to the plaintiff by the communication of defamatory material in another State. It would otherwise be extremely difficult to ascertain or assess knowledge of the social conditions and values in another State. If the ECJ had decided that the only State with competence to decide the issue was where the publisher had a place of business, where the material was edited and printed, then it would have been a catalyst to forum shopping by disreputable publishers. Publishers could edit and print material in one State with extremely limited defamation protection for plaintiffs, then distribute widely in other States with tighter plaintiff protection. If by art 5(3), plaintiffs could only sue in the first State then their rights would be inequitably weakened and the publisher could circumvent laws which he disliked.

In *Murray v Times Newspapers*, 29 July 1997, High Ct (unreported) Barron J applied *Shevill*. An Irish plaintiff argued that it was entitled to special damages for harm to its reputation in the UK caused by an allegedly defamatory newspaper article, published in the UK by a UK domiciled defendant. Barron J (and subsequently the Supreme Court) held that art 5(3) did not entitle the plaintiff to seek such damages in the Irish courts.

Barr J applied *Shevill* in the context of an allegedly defamatory statement broadcast on television in *Ewin v Carlton Television* [1997] 2 ILRM 223. The plaintiffs claimed damages in Ireland in respect of a television programme produced by Carlton and broadcast by ITN. The defendant sought to have the Irish proceedings stayed on the basis that the harmful event required by art 5(3) to found jurisdiction took place in the UK. However, approximately 111,000 viewers saw the programme in Ireland as it was distributed by cable and deflector companies and in certain parts of the country could be received by television viewers whose sets received signals from Northern Ireland or Wales. Barr J applied the rule in *Speight v Gospay* (1891) 60 LJQB 231 (as applied in *Turkington v Baron St Osward*, 2 May 1996, NI High Ct (unreported)) that the original publisher of a defamatory statement is liable for its republication or repetition to a third person where this was the natural and probable result of the original publication. Thus, applying *Shevill*, Barr J held that harm had been done in Ireland. Damages in the case would be limited to the harm done to their reputations in Ireland. The only universal jurisdiction where compensation on a worldwide basis could be claimed is the jurisdiction where the publisher is established. The plaintiffs had a choice of jurisdiction under art 5(3) and were free to choose Ireland. He set aside a suggestion that the plaintiffs had been using the Convention to oppress the defendants. He pointed out it could be argued that the motivation of the plaintiffs in choosing jurisdiction was not a matter for the court. In any case, the defendants had not advanced any evidence showing that the plaintiff has been guilty of oppressive or unconscionable behaviour in choosing Ireland.

A similar conclusion was reached by Kelly J in the cases of *Gerry Hunter v Gerald Duckworth & Co Ltd* and *Louis Blom Cooper and Hugh Callaghan v Gerald Duckworth & Co Ltd and Louis Blom Cooper*, 10 December 1999 (unreported). The plaintiffs were two of the Birmingham Six. They argued that statements in a booklet written by the second defendant and published by the first defendant had defamed them. The second defendant contested the jurisdiction of the Irish courts. He argued that he had not authorised publication of the booklet in Ireland and that for a person to be sued in a particular jurisdiction he must have responsibility for the alleged harmful event occurring in that jurisdiction. Kelly J rejected this argument. He pointed out that the author's contract with the publisher authorised the publisher to publish the work worldwide. Thus, applying the rule in *Speight v Gospay*, which had been approved by the court in *Ewin*, the natural and probable consequence of publication of the booklet was its republication in Ireland. Given the proximity of the two countries and the high level of interest in the subject in Ireland it was almost inevitable that it would be republished here. The proceedings had been properly brought in Ireland and applying *Shevill* the plaintiffs could seek damages in respect of the alleged harm done to their reputations in Ireland.

In *Mecklermedia Corporation v DC Congress GmbH* [1998] Ch 40, the English High Court held that an action brought by an English plaintiff against a German defendant for passing off, could be heard by the English courts. England was the jurisdiction where the harmful event occurred as the harm caused to the plaintiff was damage to its goodwill in England.

4.2.7.6 Branch or agency

A company may be sued outside the State in which it is domiciled where a dispute arises from the activities of its branch, agency or other establishment in another Contracting State: art 5(5). In order to qualify as a branch, agency or other establishment the entity must be subject to the control and direction of the company and must be empowered to bind it. In Case 33/78 *Somafer v Saar Ferngas* [1978] ECR 2183, the ECJ enumerated the characteristics of a branch or agency which enable third parties to recognise its existence:

> 'a place of business which has the appearance of permanency, such as the extension of a parent body . . . a management materially equipped to negotiate business with third parties so that the latter, although knowing that there will if necessary be a legal link with the parent body, the head office of which is abroad, do not have to deal directly with such parent body but may transact business at the place of business constituting the extension'.

In Case 139/80 *Blanckaert & Willems v Trost* [1981] ECR 819, the ECJ held that an independent commercial agent whose national law status left him free to organise his own time and, if he so chose, to work for competitors was too independent. Likewise, a sales representative would not fall within this exception, as he generally does not work from an office. In *De Bloos v Bouyer* the ECJ established that art 5(5) does not apply to an exclusive sales distributor, as it is an essential characteristic of a branch or agency that it is subject to the direction and control of the parent body.

4.2.7.7 Multiple defendants

Article 6(1)

A connected claim, which would normally fall within the jurisdiction of another court, may be determined by the court before which the main action is brought. Article 6(1) provides that co-defendants may be sued in the domicile of any one of them. In Case189/87 *Kalfelis v Schroder* [1988] ECR 5565, the ECJ held that for art 6(1) to apply there must be a connection between the actions brought against each of the defendants. The connection must be such that it is expedient to hear the claims against the defendants together. It said that it is for the national court to decide whether this criterion is satisfied in any particular case. Thus, in *Gascoine v Pyrah*, 25 May 1993, CA (unreported) the English Court of Appeal permitted the English purchaser of a French horse, who was suing his English agent who had acted in the purchase, to join as a co-defendant under art 6(1) a German veterinarian who had been engaged to examine and report on the condition of the horse. The claims against both defendants were for negligence in advising in favour of the purchase.

Gannon v B&I Steam Packet Company Ltd [1993] 2 IR 359, demonstrates different judicial approaches to art 6(1) in Ireland. The plaintiff had been injured in a road traffic accident in England. She was on a package holiday organised by the first defendant, injured in the second defendant's bus that had collided with the third defendant's lorry. She argued that the first defendant had a contractual liability to her in relation to its selection, choice and instruction of the coach and driver and that the courts should hear her claim against the other defendants under art 6(1). Denham J in the High Court refused an application from the second and third defendants for dismissal of the proceedings for want of jurisdiction. However, the Supreme Court granted the application. The court held that there were no grounds for suggesting that the selection, choice and instruction of the coach and driver had any causative link with the accident. The court concluded that the sole reason for bringing an action against B&I was so that the other defendants could be joined in under art 6(1) and the jurisdiction of the English courts ousted. The court refused to allow this.

O'Sullivan J took a more flexible approach in *McGee v JWT Ltd*, 27 March 1998 (unreported). A plaintiff claimed to have suffered injuries as a result of a fall on the floor of a hotel bathroom in Lourdes. The plaintiff commenced proceedings in Ireland against JWT (a company domiciled in Ireland) and the French hotel. The hotel sought to have the claim against it set aside on the basis that there was an insufficient connection between the two defendants to enable it to be sued in Ireland on foot of art 6(1). The court held that there was a sufficient connection to justify joining the second defendant in the Irish proceedings.

The regulation proposes a minor change to art 6. It proposes to add the following to art 6:

> *'provided that the claims are so closely connected that it is expedient to hear and determine them together to avoid the risk to irreconcilable judgments resulting from separate proceedings'.*

This follows the consistent interpretation of the original article from *Kalfelis v Schröder*.

Article 6(2)

Article 6(2) relates to third party proceedings. Third party proceedings may be brought in the court of the original proceedings unless those proceedings were instituted with the intention of ousting the jurisdiction. For instance a German exporter delivers goods to Belgium and the Belgian importer resells them. The buyer sues the importer for damages in Belgium and the latter wishes to join the German exporter in the proceedings. Article 6(2) allows him to do so.

4.2.7.8 Insurance

In the case of insurance and consumer contracts, special protection was thought to be necessary for the weaker party. This led to the introduction of two sets of separate jurisdictional rules.

Articles 7 to12 deal with insurance. These articles give a wide choice to the policyholder. He may sue where he is ordinarily resident or in the domicile of the insurer. The insurer may only sue in the courts of the defendant's domicile. This rule was included as many insurance companies operate on a transnational basis. An insurer who is not domiciled in a Contracting State but has a branch, agency or other establishment in one of the Contracting States is deemed to be domiciled in that State in regard to disputes arising out of the operations of the branch, agency or other establishment.

The scope of these provisions has been broadened by the regulation. The right to sue an insurance company in one's own domicile is now extended to the insured person and the beneficiary where they are the applicants. This extension is consistent with the purpose of the article.

4.2.7.9 Certain consumer contracts

A consumer may sue either in the place where he is domiciled or in the courts of the domicile of the other party (arts 13-15). A consumer is defined as a person concluding a contract for a purpose outside his trade or profession. The provisions will apply where the contract is for the sale of goods on instalment credit terms, for a loan repayable by instalments or any other form of credit made to finance the sale of the goods or any other kind of contract for the supply of goods or the supply of services except for transport contracts. In the latter case the contract must have been preceded by a specific invitation to the consumer or advertised in the State of his domicile and he must have taken the steps necessary for the conclusion of the contract in that State.

These provisions were considered by the ECJ in Case C-89/91 *Shearson Lehman Hutton v TVB* [1993] ECR 139. TVB brought an action before a German court against Hutton Inc, a New York brokerage firm, based on an assigned right. The assignor had engaged Hutton to carry out currency futures transactions, in which he had lost considerable sums. TVB, the assignee, started proceedings to recover the money on the basis that Hutton had failed to properly warn the client of the risks involved. The question arose whether TVB was a consumer for the purposes of art 14. The Court held that where a person was acting in the exercise of his profession he is not a consumer.

In Case C-269/95 *Benincasa v Dentalkit* [1996] IL Pr 252, the ECJ, once again, looked at the question of who is a consumer for the purposes of arts 13 and 14. An Italian living in Munich decided to set up a shop there. He entered into a franchise agreement under which he contracted to buy goods from an Italian company. The agreement contained a jurisdiction clause providing that the courts of Florence had jurisdiction over all disputes arising from the contract. He sued the Italian company in Munich seeking to have the contract declared void under German law. He argued that he was suing as a consumer and was thus entitled to sue in the courts of his domicile. The ECJ held that as he had bought the goods with the intention of setting up a business he had not purchased as a consumer.

The scope of the consumer contract provision has been extended in the regulation to offer consumers better protection. The consumer may sue in his own domicile in respect of a contract for the sale of goods on instalment credit terms or in respect of a credit agreement made to finance the sale of goods. The proposed article then goes on to provide that the consumer provisions apply if, in all other cases, the contract has been concluded with a person who pursues commercial or professional activities in the Member State of the consumer's domicile or, by any means, directs such activities to that Member State or to several countries including that Member State, and the contract falls within the scope of such activities.

This is a broader provision than in the original article. Article 13 requires an invitation to purchase addressed to the consumer and requires the consumer to take the necessary steps in his State to conclude the contract. It also confined the provision to contracts for the supply of goods or services. The new provision is designed to take into account consumer contracts concluded through an interactive website accessible in the State of the consumer's domicile. Knowledge of goods or services acquired by a consumer through a passive website accessible in his home State will not be sufficient.

The removal of the requirement that the consumer take the necessary steps to conclude the contract in his home State is also meant to take electronic commerce into account. In the case of contracts concluded through an interactive website it may be difficult or impossible to determine where the steps necessary to conclude the contract were taken.

Those involved in electronic commerce have expressed some concern over this proposed wording. They argue that parties engaged in electronic commerce will be exposed to potential litigation in each Member State or they will have to specify that their products or services are not intended for consumers domiciled in certain Member States. The Commission held a hearing of interested parties on this in late 1999. However, no further amendment has been proposed.

Article 13 excluded transport contracts from its scope. The Regulation retains this exclusion but makes it clear that package holidays do come within the scope of the consumer protection.

4.2.7.10 Exclusive jurisdiction

Certain courts are given exclusive jurisdiction, so that regardless of where the defendant is domiciled only specified courts have jurisdiction. These five situations apply even where the parties are resident outside the EU, provided that the subject matter is situated in one of the Contracting States. The reason for this is that the court given exclusive jurisdiction is so closely connected with the subject matter of the dispute as to justify it having sole control over it.

Property

Article 16(1) provides for exclusive jurisdiction in proceedings concerning in rem rights in immovable property for the State where the property is located. In Case 115/88 *Reichert v Dresdner Bank (No 1)* [1990] I ECR 27, the defendants, a husband and wife, were both domiciled in Germany. They owed money to the plaintiff bank. They owned immovable property in France, which they conveyed to their son as a gift. The bank saw this as an attempt to defraud it. It started proceedings in France claiming that the gift was fraudulent. Did the French court have exclusive jurisdiction? If not the action should have been brought in Germany where the defendants were domiciled. The ECJ held that art 16(1) did not apply because the action in the French courts was not concerned to vindicate any of the policies that justified art 16(1). The claim was essentially a creditor's action, which did not concern the rules and customs of the situs.

A similar decision was handed down in Case C-294/92 *Webb v Webb* [1994] ECR 1717. The plaintiff was an English domiciliary who had acquired a flat in the south of France. For exchange control reasons title to the flat was registered in the name of the defendant, the plaintiff's son. Subsequently the plaintiff wished to have title in the property transferred to him. He commenced proceedings in the English courts seeking a declaration that the defendant held the property on trust for him and an order that the defendant be compelled to transfer title. The defendant contested the jurisdiction of the English courts, arguing that the case fell within art 16(1) and should be tried by the French courts. The Court of Appeal referred the matter to the ECJ. It held that for art 16(1) to apply the action must be based on a right in rem. It was not sufficient for the action to have a link with immovable property or for a right in rem to be involved. The object of the action must be a right in rem. As the aim of the proceedings was to obtain a declaration that the defendant held the flat for the benefit of the plaintiff, the latter was seeking to enforce rights against one person, rather than claiming rights directly enforceable against the whole world. Thus, the action was not one in rem within the meaning of art 16(1).

Though the court's reasoning in this case follows *Reichert* it is open to question. It is strongly arguable that the ECJ is taking too narrow an interpretation of art 16(1).

Tenancies of immovable property

Article 16(1) also applies to disputes concerning tenancies of immovable property. The leading case is Case 241/83 *Rösler v Rottwinkel* [1985] ECR 99. An agreement was drawn up between two Germans, concerning a holiday villa in Italy. The agreement stated that German law was to govern the contract and the German courts were to have jurisdiction. Could the German courts entertain a claim concerning damage and arrears of rent? The ECJ held that the Italian courts had jurisdiction as it concerned rights in rem over immovable property.

In Case C-280/90 *Hacker v Euro-Relais GmbH* [1992] ECR 1111, the ECJ held that a contract for a package holiday fell outside art 16(1). Hacker, a German made an agreement with Euro-Relais, a German travel agency, for the hire of a holiday home in the Netherlands and paid an additional sum for ferry reservations for a sea crossing. Hacker sued claiming that the holiday home fell short of the description given by the travel agent. The matter was referred to the ECJ for a ruling on whether a contract of this nature came within 'tenancy' in art 16(1). The Court held that this was a complex contract in which a range of services was provided in return for a lump sum. Such a contract fell outside the scope of art 16(1). The ECJ noted that the travel agent did not own the holiday accommodation, both parties were domiciled in the same State and the agreement provided for travel services as well as accommodation.

The question of timeshare agreements was considered by the English courts in *Jarrett v Barclays Bank* [1997] 2 All ER 484. The Court of Appeal held that such agreements were tenancies for the purposes of art 16(1). The plaintiffs were three English couples who signed agreements to purchase timeshare properties in Portugal and Spain. The purchases were partly financed by the defendants, a number of English banks. The vendors of the timeshares had made certain misrepresentations to the purchasers. The plaintiffs brought proceedings against the defendants claiming recission of their contracts, repayment of their deposits and damages under the Consumer Credit Act 1974. The defendants contested the action, arguing that it properly fell within art 16(1) as it concerned a tenancy of immovable property. The Court of Appeal held that the object of art 16(1) was that courts of the State in which the property was situated should have exclusive jurisdiction and that the provision was not to be construed any wider than was necessary to achieve that object. The ECJ held that since the timeshare agreement entitled one party to occupy immovable property owned by another for a definite period for payment, such agreements came within the meaning of tenancy in art 16(1). However, the Court held that on the facts of this case at issue was the debtor-creditor agreement with attached statutory rights and not the time-share agreement itself.

Article 16(1)(b) gives jurisdiction in a dispute concerning a short-term tenancy either to the State of the defendant's domicile, or the State in which the property is located. The plaintiff may sue in either State. This is subject to a number of provisos: the tenancy must be for temporary private use; for a maximum of six months; the tenant must be a natural person; and neither party must be domiciled in the Contracting State in which the property is situated. The last two provisos, requiring the tenant to be a natural person and neither party to be domiciled where the property is situated, do not appear in the Lugano Convention. This difference between the Conventions makes the Brussels Convention more restrictive in this area.

Companies

Article 16(2) provides that the courts of the Contracting State in which a company, legal person or association has its seat have jurisdiction

> *in proceedings which have as their object the validity of the constitution, the nullity or the dissolution of companies or other legal persons or associations of natural or legal persons, or the decisions of their organs.*

This provision was considered by the English High Court in *New Therapeutics Ltd v Katz* [1991] 2 All ER 151. The plaintiff was an English medical company that had an agreement to develop a product for AIDS treatment with a French company. This agreement was the main asset of the company. Two of the three directors of the company signed a new agreement with the other company on less favourable terms. One of the two directors subsequently resigned and his severance agreement contained a term on behalf of the company, waiving all claims against him in respect of his performance as a director. The companies subsequently sued the two directors. One claimed that he should have been sued in France where he lived. Knox J held that if the proceedings were concerned with the validity of a decision of an organ of the company, art 16(2) would confer exclusive jurisdiction on the English courts.

4.2.7.11 Agreeing jurisdiction

General rules

Article 17 displaces the jurisdictional rules when the parties to a contract agree that a particular court is to be given exclusive jurisdiction. Generally the jurisdiction clause is required to be in writing. However, there are some limited exceptions to this requirement. Article 17 provides that:

> *Such an agreement conferring jurisdiction shall be either:*
>
> *(a) in writing or evidenced in writing, or*
>
> *(b) in a form which accords with practices which the parties have established between themselves, or*
>
> *(c) in international trade or commerce, in a form which accords with a usage of which the parties are or ought to have been aware and which in such trade or commerce is widely known to, and regularly observed by, parties to contracts of the type involved in the particular trade or commerce concerned.*

The ECJ has adopted a liberal interpretation of art 17 but is anxious to ensure that such clauses show the intent of both parties and do not go unnoticed by one of them. This may be seen in Case 23/78 *Meeth v Glacetal* [1978] ECR 2133. A contract between French and German parties included a clause specifying that an action must be brought in the defendant's State. The Court interpreted art 17 to enable this clause to be effective.

This liberal approach of the ECJ may be seen in Case 312/85 *Fiat v Van Hool* [1986] ECR 3337. A written contract contained a jurisdiction clause. The contract provided that it could only be renewed in writing. The contract expired and was orally renewed. The ECJ held that the contract remained valid provided that its governing law allowed such a renewal. The liberal line of interpretation continued with Case C-214/89 *Powell Duffryn v Petereit* [1992] ECR 1745. An English company, which purchased shares in Germany, went into liquidation. Petereit had been appointed as the liquidator. At issue was whether the liquidator could recover paid dividends. The company argued that the shareholders were bound by a jurisdiction clause in the company's statutes. The ECJ held that a company's statutes could be considered as a contract between the shareholders and between them and the company that they established. The Court held that it satisfied the formal requirements of art 17, provided that it was contained in the company's constitutional documents, which were validly adopted under national law and lodged in a public register or in a place accessible to the shareholders.

In writing

The requirement of writing is satisfied where there is an express jurisdiction clause contained in a written agreement. Where it forms part of a set of general conditions on the back of a contract, it is only regarded as having satisfied this condition if the text of the contract contains an express reference to the general conditions. In Case 71/83 *Russ v Haven*

[1984] ECR 2417 the ECJ held that a jurisdiction clause would only meet the requirement of writing in cases where the written contract contained the jurisdiction clause in its text where the contract had been signed by one party, where the consent of the other party was also in writing either in the original document or a separate one.

Evidenced in writing

In *Russ v Haven*, the question arose of whether a jurisdiction clause in a bill of lading met the requirements of art 17. The ECJ held that it did if the bill came within the framework of a continuing business relationship between the parties, governed by the carrier's general conditions containing the jurisdiction clause, provided that the bills are all issued in pre-printed forms systematically containing the jurisdiction clause.

In Case 25/76 *Galeries Segoura v Bonakdarian* [1976] ECR 1851, the question of an oral contract subsequently confirmed in writing arose. The case concerned a contract for the sale of a batch of carpets. The ECJ ruled that where a contract is concluded orally and then followed by the issue by one party to the other of a purported confirmation in writing, incorporating the former's standard terms, including a jurisdiction clause, the formal requirements of art 17 are not satisfied unless the confirmation is accepted in writing by the other party. However, the Court said that there would be an exception where the oral contract came within the framework of a continuing trading relationship between the parties, which was based on the standard terms of one of them. In such a case, it would be contrary to good faith for the recipient of the confirmation to deny the existence of the agreement on jurisdiction.

The San Sebastian Convention resolved the issue by adding two new subsections to art 17. An agreement conferring jurisdiction may be in a form which accords with the practices which the parties have established between themselves, or in international trade or commerce, in a form which accords with the usage of which the parties are or ought to have been aware and which in such trade or commerce is widely known to, and regularly observed by, parties to contracts of the type involved in the particular trade or commerce concerned.

It is only recently that the ECJ has begun to rule on these new provisions. The first such case was Case C-106/95 *MSG v Les Garvières Rhénanes SARL* [1997] ECR I-911. The case concerned a time charter for the hire of a ship that had been concluded orally between a French company and a German company based in Würzburg. One of the parties sent the other a commercial letter of confirmation containing a pre-printed jurisdiction clause. This party then used invoices containing a similar jurisdiction clause. The other party remained silent and paid the invoices containing the clause.

On the basis of the ECJ's previous case law the jurisdiction clause should have been held invalid. The Court in its decisions has required an acceptance by both parties of a jurisdiction agreement. The Court held that consent was still a necessary element of art 17. However, in this case silence amounted to consent, as the use of the clauses was consistent with a practice in the area of international trade in which the parties were operating and the parties ought to have been aware of this practice. It is for the national court to determine whether there is a practice in international trade or commerce in question and whether the parties are, or ought to have been, aware of it.

The ECJ went on to establish criteria for national courts. In determining the existence of such a practice the court should look to the practice in the area where the activities are being carried on. It is insufficient to look at the national law of one of the parties. A practice may be regarded as existing where businessmen in that area generally and regularly behave in a certain way when concluding contracts of a certain type. Actual or presumed knowledge may be established where parties have previously entered into commercial relations with one another or with other parties in that same area of business or where, in that area of business, such behaviour is generally and regularly followed when concluding contracts of a particular type so that it may be regarded as an established practice.

To invoke art 17 all that is necessary is that at the time of the agreement one of the parties is domiciled in one of the Contracting States.

Article 23 of the regulation reproduces the text of the current art 17. However, it allows parties to agree that a choice of forum clause will not be exclusive. It also takes account of electronic commerce and allows a jurisdiction clause agreed by means of electronic communication to be a durable record on the same basis as a written jurisdiction clause.

Employment contracts

Article 17(5) provides that: 'in matters relating to . . . contracts of employment an agreement conferring jurisdiction shall have legal force only if it is entered into after the dispute has arisen'. This is an employee-oriented provision. The employee has the option of relying on pre-dispute jurisdiction clauses. The employee has a choice of three jurisdictions in which to bring suit. He can choose either the employer's domicile, or the place where she works, or a jurisdiction agreed on after the dispute has arisen.

The proposed regulation retains the same rules on employment contracts. However, they are taken from arts 5 and 17 and grouped together in arts 18 to 21 of the regulation.

4.2.7.12 Submission to jurisdiction

Article 18 gives a Contracting State jurisdiction if the defendant enters an appearance, provided that this does not contravene the exclusive jurisdiction rule and provided that the defendant does not appear merely to protest the jurisdiction. One may protest jurisdiction, lose and proceed with the case. The rules on submission are, however, subject to art 16 on exclusive jurisdiction. The term, 'appearance' is not defined in the Convention. The Jenard Report indicates that its meaning is to be determined by national law. In *Campbell International Trading House Ltd v Peter van Aart* [1992] IR 663, the Supreme Court held that an appearance which does not contest jurisdiction on its face will be taken as a submission under art 18.

The leading case is Case150/80 *Elefanten Schuh v Jacqmain* [1981] ECR 1671. In it the ECJ decided that a valid jurisdiction agreement under art 17 could be overridden by a submission to another forum by a defendant. Thus, art 17 was to be read as subordinate to art 18. The ECJ held that art 18 was applicable where the defendant not only contested the jurisdiction of the court, but also went into matters of substance. The ECJ said that it must be clear that the first line of defence is to contest jurisdiction.

4.2.7.13 Mandatory examination as to jurisdiction

Article 19 provides that if the courts of another Contracting State are seised of the claim and another court has exclusive jurisdiction the first court of its own motion must decline jurisdiction. Thus, in *Rösler v Rottwinkel*, the German courts were obliged to decline jurisdiction in favour of the Italian courts, irrespective of their own wishes and those of the litigants.

4.2.7.14 Lis pendens

Article 21

Article 21 provides that where there are two sets of proceedings involving the same parties and the same cause of action, then the court first seised has exclusive jurisdiction. The ECJ in Case 144/86 *Gubisch Maschinenfabrik v Palumbo* [1987] ECR 4861 held that 'the same cause of action' had to be given an independent European law meaning. This dispute concerned the sale of a machine by a German seller to an Italian buyer. The seller brought an action for payment of the price in the German courts. The buyer brought an action in the Italian courts claiming that the contract had been rescinded. He argued that his offer had been revoked before it reached the buyer or that the delay in the delivery of the machine operated to rescind the contract. The ECJ held that art 21 covered these facts. The same approach was adopted by the ECJ in Case C-402/92 *The Maciej Rataj* [1994] ECR 5439. It held that an action seeking to have the defendant held liable in contract for causing loss to a cargo had the same object as earlier proceedings brought by that defendant seeking a declaration that he was not liable for that loss and was within the scope of art 21.

The English Court of Appeal in *Sarrio v KIA* [1997] 1 Lloyd's Rep 113 pointed out that two different actions may flow from the one business transaction. An action had been brought in Spain arguing that KIA was liable to pay sums due under an option clause. An action was also brought in England claiming damages in tort for oral misstatements, which had induced Sarrio to enter the contract. The Court of Appeal held that there was a clear difference between a claim for damages based on negligent misrepresentation and a claim for sums due for non-performance of a contract. Therefore, the two sets of proceedings, though between the same parties, did not represent the same cause of action.

Article 21 was amended at the suggestion of the EFTA States to deal more effectively with the problem that arises from the fact that the court first seised might not have jurisdiction. There was some danger under the Brussels Convention that the court seised second would decline jurisdiction in favour of the court seised first, as required and it could then emerge that the latter had no jurisdiction and it also had declined to try the case. This would have left the plaintiff with no court in which to bring an action. The amended art 21 solves this possible difficulty by requiring the court seised second to stay its proceedings until the jurisdiction of the court first seised is established. At that point, the court seised second must decline jurisdiction in favour of the first court.

The Convention leaves to national law the question of when the court is seised of the matter. Generally, in civil law countries, the court is seised when the defendant is served, whereas in common law countries the court is seised when proceedings are issued. This problem was considered by the ECJ in Case 129/83 *Zelger v Salinitri (No 2)* [1984] ECR 2397. The Court ruled that the question of whether a court is definitively seised at the time of the issue of the summons or at its service must be determined in accordance with the law of the country to which the court in question belongs.

In *Dresser UK Ltd v Falcongate Freight Management Ltd* [1992] 2 All ER 450 the Court of Appeal interpreted the phrase, 'first seised' as meaning, in general, English courts will only be seised of an action when the originating document has been served on the defendant. This approach has been followed in subsequent cases and brings the common law courts into line with the approach taken by the civil law jurisdictions.

The regulation puts forward a definition of when a court is to be regarded as seised of an action. Article 30 provides that a court is seised either where the document instituting the proceedings is lodged with the court or if the document has to be first served before being lodged, when the server receives the document for service (ie, when a summons is issued). This addresses the procedural differences between the Contracting States.

Article 22

In the case of actions, which are so closely connected that it is expedient to hear and determine them together to avoid the risk of irreconcilable judgments, but which involve different causes of action or are between different parties, art 22 confers discretion on the court subsequently seised. The court subsequently seised may stay its proceedings, so as to enable it to have the benefit of the first court's judgment before it reaches its own decision.

4.2.8 PROVISIONAL AND PROTECTIVE MEASURES

Article 24 concerns protective measures. It makes it possible to apply to the courts of a Contracting State for provisional and protective measures to be taken, even though the courts of another Contracting State have jurisdiction in the main issue. Section 13 of the 1998 Act gives effect to this provision. Probably the most important interim measure is the Mareva injunction. It is now possible for the defendant's assets both in Ireland and abroad to be frozen by such an injunction. This was seen in *Republic of Haiti v Duvalier* [1989] 1 All ER 456. Proceedings were started in the French courts against ex President Jean Paul Duvalier by the new government of Haiti to recover State assets ($120 million) misappropriated by him and members of his family. The plaintiffs sought a Mareva injunction from the English High Court to restrain the defendants from disposing of any assets in England. Staughton LJ held that he had the power to grant such an injunction.

The issue has arisen whether a court may grant protective measures in respect of a defendant who is domiciled outside the Contracting States. In *X v Y* [1989] 3 All ER 689, proceedings were commenced in France against a Saudi Arabian executive who had defaulted on a loan. An application was made in England for a Mareva injunction. The court held that art 24 was not limited to cases where the defendant was domiciled in a Contracting State.

4.2.9 RECOGNITION AND ENFORCEMENT OF JUDGMENTS

4.2.9.1 Generally

One of the central objectives of the Brussels Convention is to create a free market in judgments. Title III concerns the recognition and enforcement of judgments. There is a presumption that a judgment in a civil or commercial matter given by the court of another Contracting State is to be enforced. Only in exceptional circumstances will a judgment debtor be able to prevent enforcement of a judgment. He will only be able to do so if it is contrary to public policy, there is insufficient time to defend the foreign proceedings or there is a risk of the judgment being irreconcilable with a judgment of the enforcing court. Thus, a defendant must raise any jurisdictional challenges before the court which adjudicated the matter.

Article 25 defines a 'judgment' as 'any judgment given by a court or tribunal of a Contracting State'. Unlike the common law it is not confined to money judgments but extends to all forms of judgments in civil and commercial matters given by a court in a Contracting State.

4.2.9.2 Recognition

Article 26 provides that any judgment within the subject matter of the Convention given in a Contracting State may be recognised in any other Contracting State without any special procedure. Recognition occurs when the courts of one Contracting State acknowledge the decision of a court in another Contracting State to be binding and enforceable. In practice, however, if enforcement is not sought as well, recognition is usually just an incidental question in a dispute. The court asked to recognise a foreign judgment is completely bound by the foreign court's findings of facts.

The proposed regulation envisages a certificate being issued by the court giving the judgment in the State of origin, attesting that the judgment to which it relates is enforceable. The court asked to enforce the judgment could not look behind the certificate.

4.2.9.3 Review

Articles 29 and 34 provide that under no circumstances may a foreign judgment be reviewed as to its substance. It may not be argued that a foreign court made a mistake of fact or law. In *Interdesco SA v Nullifire Ltd* [1992] 1 Lloyd's Rep 180, Phillips J made it clear that this means that the defences to enforcement of foreign judgments (set out in art 27) are subordinate to this principle.

4.2.9.4 Appeal

Article 30 provides that a court may stay proceedings for recognition and enforcement if there is an appeal against that judgment. In Case 43/77 *Industrial Diamond Supplies v Riva* [1977] ECR 2175, the ECJ held that appeal means one, the result of which may result in the annulment or amendment of the judgment, which is the subject matter of the recognition or enforcement proceedings. In *Petereit v Babcock International Holdings* [1990] 1 WLR 450, the English courts considered the criteria for a stay in these circumstances. The plaintiff was the receiver of a bankrupt German firm. On 30 September 1988 he obtained a judgment against the defendant. On 17 November the defendant appealed to the Federal District Court. On 22 March 1989 the plaintiff applied for an enforcement order in England. The defendant sought to have proceedings stayed pending the hearing of the appeal. The trial judge held in favour of a stay, ruling that the court had an unfettered discretion to grant a stay.

4.2.9.5 Enforcement

Articles 31 to 35 provide for an application to be made to the relevant judicial authority for recognition and enforcement of a foreign judgment. The judgment to be enforced need not be final. Application may be made for the enforcement of an interim judgment. One must apply by affidavit, giving details of the judgment to be enforced and an address for service within the State. It is an ex parte application in the first instance. A decision is to be given without delay. Enforcement of foreign judgments is almost automatic.

Article 31(1) provides that an application for enforcement of a judgment by a court in a Contracting State other than that in which the judgment was given may only be accepted where the judgment would be enforceable in the Contracting State of origin. Article 32 lists the courts in each Contracting State to which an initial application for enforcement of a judgment should be made. In Ireland this is the High Court.

Article 33 provides that the national law of the Contracting State in which enforcement is sought governs the procedure for enforcement of a judgment. Where the national law of the Contracting State in which enforcement is sought requires it, the applicant must provide an address for service within the jurisdiction of the court seised. Where the national law does not require the provision of an address for service, the applicant must appoint a representative.

Article 46 requires provision of an authentic copy of the judgment and, in the case of default proceedings, an original or a true copy of the document instituting the proceedings, which will establish that the party in default was correctly served. When the required documents are not available to the court, art 48 allows the court, before recognition is sought, to specify a time during which they must be produced or, alternatively, to vary the documents required. If the court considers that it has sufficient evidence before it, it may dispense with the documentary requirements.

As the Convention presumes the enforcement of foreign judgments falling within it, the amended Irish Rules of the Superior Courts reflect this. Section 7 of the Act provides for an application for the enforcement of a foreign judgment under the Convention ex parte to the Master of the High Court. The application must contain (Order 42A, Rule 5, Rules of the Superior Courts):

(a) a certified copy of the foreign judgment;

(b) documents establishing that the judgment is enforceable in its home State and has been served. and

(c) and if it is a default judgment, documents establishing that the defendant has been served in sufficient time to enable him to arrange for his defence.

Such an application will be supported by an affidavit, which must state (Order 42A, Rule 6, Rules of the Superior Courts):

(a) whether the judgment provides for the payment of money;

(b) whether interest is recoverable and if so the rate and the relevant dates, and

(c) the name and address of the judgment debtor and an address within Ireland for service of proceedings on the party making the application.

Article 34 provides that the court to which an application for enforcement is made 'shall give its decision without delay'. The court is obliged to grant an order for enforcement unless one of the grounds in arts 27 and 28 exists. It also excludes the party against whom a judgment is being sought from making any submissions on the application to have the judgment enforced.

The regulation will delete the requirement to produce documents showing that the judgment is enforceable in its State of origin. In its place is a new requirement to produce a certificate in a form annexed to the Convention. The proposal envisages a court issuing a certificate in respect of its own judgment. There will then be a strong presumption that the judgment accompanied by a certificate is enforceable.

4.2.9.6 Defences against recognition and enforcement

The grounds on which a foreign judgment may not be recognised or enforced are set out in art 27.

Public policy

The first defence to enforcement is where the judgment is contrary to the public policy of the enforcing State. This is restricted to circumstances in which a fundamental principle of the national law of the court in which recognition is sought is in question. The Jenard Report states that this defence only applies in exceptional circumstances.

There is no definition of public policy in the Convention. The ECJ has stated that this is a very narrow exception. In Case 145/86 *Hoffman v Krieg* [1988] ECR 645, the Court held that the refusal to recognise a judgment based on public policy should operate only in exceptional circumstances. This was subsequently reflected in *Societé d'Information Service Realisation (SISRO) v Ampersand Software BV* [1996] 2 WLR 30. SISRO had obtained judgment against Ampersand and others in the Tribunal de Grand Instance de Paris for infringement of copyright for computer programs. The defendants had alleged fraud on the part of the plaintiff. When the defendants sought to enforce the judgment in England, the defendants again argued that there had been fraud on the part of the plaintiff. The Court of Appeal held that where a foreign judgment was allegedly obtained by fraud and means of redress were available in the State of origin, there was no breach of public policy in recognising and enforcing the judgment in England.

Even a judgment obtained fraudulently may still have to be enforced. This may be seen in *Interdesco v Nullifire*. The plaintiffs were manufacturers of intumescent paint, which had special fire protection properties. When heated it expanded to form a protective covering over the painted surface and the longer it survived in a fire the better protection it gave. Their best selling product was marketed as SS60, indicating that it gave protection for at least sixty minutes. The defendants, an English company, entered a five-year distribution agreement with the manufacturers under which they were given exclusive distribution rights in the UK and Ireland for Interdesco's paints. Subsequently, the defendants terminated the agreement claiming that Interdesco's SS60 had failed to satisfy the UK's standard for a sixty-minute paint and was therefore unmarketable. Interdesco denied these claims arguing that Nullifire was attempting to replace Interdesco and steal its market. The French Cour d'Appel ignored English tests showing the product to be sub-standard. The plaintiffs applied to the English courts for an enforcement order. The defendant argued that the French judgment had been obtained fraudulently. It said that it had fresh evidence, which had not been produced, to the French court. This purported to show that Interdesco had been a party to fresh tests, which clearly established that its paint was sub-standard.

121

The English court rejected this defence of public policy based on fraud. It held that fundamentally different criteria apply in Convention and non-Convention cases. It held that where a court has ruled on the same matter that a party challenges on grounds of fraud, the Convention estops the English court from reviewing the judgment of the other court. The remedy lies with the foreign court and not the English court.

Recently the ECJ has ruled that a judgment which breaches human rights may fall within the scope of the public policy defence: Case C-7/98 *Dieter Krombach v André Bamberski* 28 March 2000 (unreported). Mr Bamberski is French and Mr Krombach is German. Krombach had been the subject of a preliminary investigation in Germany following the death in Germany of a fourteen-year-old French girl. The investigation was discontinued. Bamberski was the girl's father. At his request the French courts opened an investigation. They then committed Krombach for trial. Krombach did not appear to defend the proceedings. The French court held him in contempt and ordered him to pay 350,000 francs compensation to Bamberski. Bamberski applied to enforce the judgment in Germany. Krombach appealed the German enforcement order. One of the arguments advanced by him was that he had not been allowed to defend the proceedings in France unless he appeared in person and that this was contrary to public policy. The ECJ referred to arts 29 and 34(3), which establish that a foreign judgment cannot be reviewed as to its substance. Thus, a discrepancy between the rules of the forum where the judgment was given and the enforcing forum cannot be taken into account nor can any alleged inaccuracies in findings of law or fact. To successfully invoke art 27(1), there must be a manifest breach of a rule of law regarded as essential in the legal order of the State in which enforcement is seised. The right to be defended is a fundamental right deriving from the constitutional traditions common to the Member States. The European Court of Human Rights has ruled that in criminal cases, the right of the accused to be defended by a lawyer is one of the fundamental elements in a fair trial and that a person does not forfeit entitlement to such a right simply because he is not present at the hearing. Thus, an enforcing court is entitled to invoke art 27 and hold that a refusal to hear the defence of an accused not present at a hearing is a manifest breach of a fundamental right.

The regulation would somewhat narrow the scope of the defences. A foreign judgment must not be 'manifestly' contrary to public policy rather than being contrary to it.

Due service and sufficiency of time (natural justice)

Article 27(2) provides that if there is a default judgment, the creditor must show that the debtor was duly served with the documents in sufficient time to arrange for his defence. This is designed to protect a defendant who has a judgment entered against him in his absence. In judging the questions of whether due service has occurred and whether defective service may be remedied, the court is to apply the law applicable in the State of origin, including any international conventions. Due service consists of two elements – service according to the rules of the first court and service in time.

In Case 166/80 *Klomps v Michel* [1981] ECR 1593, the ECJ held that, in general, the court may judge the timeliness of service by measuring the time available to the defendant from the date of execution to service. Circumstances the court may take into account include the manner in which service was effected, the relationship between the plaintiff and the defendant, and the type of steps that had been taken to try to ensure that judgment was not given in default. The second court may, of course, take account of exceptional circumstances. The ECJ held that the 'document instituting the proceedings' refers to any document, service of which enables the plaintiff to obtain, in default of defence, a judgment capable of being freely recognised and enforced in the Contracting States.

In Case 305/88 *Isabelle Lancray v Peters & Sickert* [1990] 1 ECR 2725, the ECJ confirmed that the requirement of due service and the requirement that the document, which instituted the proceedings, must be served in sufficient time are separate and concurrent safeguards. The plaintiff was a French public limited company that had entered into a contract with a German limited partnership. An express contractual clause conferred jurisdiction on a French commercial court in Nanterre. Proceedings were commenced and a default judgment was obtained. The German authorities issued a certificate of service. This stated that service had been carried out by the delivery of the documents to a secretary in the debtor's office. No German translation was appended to the documents. The German courts refused to enforce the French default judgment. The German courts found that the summons instituting the proceedings had not been served in due form. Substituted service had been used. Under the Hague Convention on Service Abroad of Judicial Documents, such service would only have been acceptable if the document served had been accompanied by a German translation. The matter was referred to the ECJ. It held that the relevant document must not only be served on the defendant in sufficient time for him to arrange a defence but it must also comport with due form. This is necessary to ensure effective protection for the rights of the defendant. It is for the national court to determine whether there has been due service.

Article 27(2) applies whether or not the defendant is domiciled in the State in which the judgment is granted. In Case 49/84 *Debaecker v Bowman* [1985] ECR 1792, the defendant had vacated his rented premises in Antwerp without giving notice or paying the rent due and without leaving a forwarding address. The landlord served the writ at the Antwerp police station in accordance with Belgian procedural law (as the defendant was still registered as resident in Antwerp). After a few days the plaintiff received a registered letter from the defendant repudiating the lease and confirming a new address, which was a post office box number in Essen. The plaintiff did not inform the defendant of the impending hearing or make any effort to serve proceedings on him at his new address. He obtained a default judgment in the Belgian court for over a million Belgian francs. He applied to enforce in the Netherlands. The ECJ stated that the court in which recognition or enforcement is sought could take into account the fact that the plaintiff was informed of the defendant's address four days after having served the document correctly under the Belgian law. There was no overriding obligation on the plaintiff to communicate with the defendant at his new address. However, wilful failure to do so will mean that the recognising court should examine whether art 27(2) is applicable. The national court could also take into account that the defendant was responsible for the failure of the documents served to reach him. The ECJ concluded that it is for the national court 'to assess, in such a case as the present, to what extent the defendant's behaviour is capable of outweighing the fact that the plaintiff was apprised after service of the defendant's new address'.

Irreconcilable judgments

Article 27(3) excludes recognition of a judgment which is irreconcilable with a judgment given in a dispute between the same parties in the Contracting State in which recognition is sought. Pre-eminence is given to the judgment of the judgment-recognising court.

For instance, in *Hoffman v Krieg* a German judgment awarding maintenance on desertion was clearly irreconcilable with a subsequent Dutch divorce. The ECJ took a very narrow approach in Case C-414/92 *Solo Kleinmotoren GmbH v Boch* [1994] ECR 2237. The case involved a dispute between a German manufacturer of agricultural machinery and its Italian retail distributor. The distributor initiated two actions before the Italian courts. In the first case a court in Milan held in its favour. In separate German proceedings an agreed court settlement was drawn up. However, Boch continued with the second Italian case. Once again, it was successful before the court in Bologna. It sought to enforce this judgment in Germany. Solo argued that it was inconsistent with the German settlement and contrary to art 27(3). The ECJ, in a surprising decision, held in favour of Boch. It held that art 27(3) did not apply when the irreconcilable element was a settlement rather than a judgment. This decision confirms the restrictive manner in which the art 27 defences are construed by the ECJ.

4.2.9.7   Security for costs

Article 45 prohibits security for costs in the case of an application for the enforcement of a foreign judgment. This is reflected in Order 29, Rule 8 of the Rules of the Superior Courts.

4.2.9.8 Post-enforcement protective measures

Under art 39, if an order under art 31 is granted, protective measures may be sought. Article 39 provides that:

> During the time specified for an appeal pursuant to art 36 and until any such appeal has been determined, no measures of enforcement may be taken other than protective measures taken against the property of the party against whom enforcement has been sought.

This article was considered in Case 119/84 *Cappelloni v Pelkmans* [1985] ECR 3147. The plaintiff had obtained judgment in the Dutch courts against the defendants for 127,400 Dutch guilders. Leave to enforce the judgment under art 31 was given by the Italian courts but the defendants sought to appeal under art 36. The plaintiff had been granted protective measures under art 39, allowing him to sequestrate the defendant's immovable property. The Italian court refused to confirm these measures, as certain requirements of the Italian Code of Civil Procedure had not been strictly followed. The ECJ upheld the protective measures and held that no national judicial confirmation was necessary. Thus, national courts are obliged to grant such measures and have no discretion.

When applying one must specify the protective measures required. If there is an appeal pending no other measures of enforcement may be taken.

4.2.9.9 Appeal against an order for enforcement

Articles 36 to 38 provide a party against whom enforcement is ordered with a right of appeal. Such an appeal must be made within one month of service of judgment where the defendant is domiciled in the Contracting State in which the decision permitting enforcement is given. Where he is not domiciled in that particular State, he has two months to appeal. Time runs either from the date of service of the decision on him or at his residence. No extension of time is permitted. During this period, no measures of enforcement may be taken other than protective ones. Article 37 sets out the courts to which an appeal may be addressed. In Ireland, the High Court is the appropriate court. There may be a further appeal to the Supreme Court but only on a point of law.

In Case 148/84 *Deutsche Genossenschaftsbank v SA Brasserie du Pêcheur* [1984] ECR 1981, the ECJ confirmed that third parties are excluded from appealing such an order. This is so even where a right of appeal is available under the national law of the court granting the order.

4.2.9.10 Appeal from an order refusing enforcement

Article 40 gives a party seeking enforcement a right of appeal from an order refusing enforcement. The relevant national laws relating to rights of appeal govern the appeal. Article 40(2) requires the court hearing the appeal to summon the party against whom enforcement is sought as well. The court may hear him. Article 41 provides a final right of appeal on a point of law.

4.2.9.11 Partial enforcement

Article 42(1) provides that a court may order partial enforcement in circumstances where enforcement has been requested in respect of several matters but cannot be authorised in all of them. A party may request partial enforcement of a judgment under art 42(2).

4.2.9.12 Judgments of non-Contracting States

In Case C-129/92 *Owens Bank Ltd v Bracco* [1992] 2 AC 443, the ECJ held that the Convention did not apply to proceedings for the enforcement of judgments given in civil and commercial matters in non-Contracting States. Neither did the Convention apply to proceedings or issues arising in proceedings, in Contracting States concerning the recognition and enforcement of judgments given in civil and commercial matters in non-Contracting States.

The plaintiff bank was domiciled in St Vincent. It obtained a judgment of the St Vincent Court ordering the defendant, an Italian who was chairman and managing director of the second defendant, an Italian domiciled company, to repay a loan. Throughout these proceedings, the defendant had alleged that no loan had been made, that the bank's documents were forgeries and that witnesses had perjured themselves. In 1989, the plaintiff sought to enforce the judgment in Italy but the defendant raised the issue of fraud. In 1990, the plaintiff sought a declaration from the English High Court that the judgment of the St Vincent court was enforceable in England. The defendant again raised the issue of fraud and also requested the English court to decline jurisdiction or to stay the proceedings pursuant to arts 21 and 22 of the Convention, pending the conclusion of the Italian proceedings. The High Court and the Court of Appeal refused the application. The defendant appealed to the House of Lords, which referred the matter to the ECJ.

4.3 Rome Convention on the Law Applicable to Contractual Obligations

4.3.1 INTRODUCTION

The Convention on the Law Applicable to Contractual Obligations 1980 ('the Rome Convention') was seen as a sequel to the Brussels Convention. However, it is important to distinguish the two. The purpose of the Rome Convention is to unify the choice of law rules in contracts, whereas the Brussels Convention provides which courts are to have jurisdiction to hear disputes and provides procedures for the easier enforcement of judgments within the Contracting States.

The aim of the Rome Convention is to harmonise rules relating to choice of law provisions in contracts within the EU. Choice of law rules indicate which system of law will apply to decide a dispute concerning a contract. Only States, which are parties to the EU Treaty, may join the Convention. Its application is confined to the European territories of the Contracting States and it does not extend to their overseas colonies or protectorates. The only exception to this is France as the Republic of France includes a number of overseas Departments.

The EU considered that harmonising national choice of law rules would facilitate the working of the common market. Where a contract is concluded between two or more parties in different jurisdictions concerning a matter in another jurisdiction, confusion can arise as to the legal rules to be applied in the case of a dispute. Before the Rome Convention, each EU Member State had its own set of rules to decide whether its law or that of another State was applicable to such a contract. The Convention now takes effect within each ratifying State as a new domestic law code for resolving choice of law problems in contract. With the existence of the Brussels Convention, which means that judgments obtained in one Member State can relatively easily be enforced in another, forum shopping had become more attractive. One of the purposes of the Rome Convention is to prevent forum shopping by providing one set of choice of law rules to be applied in all the Contracting States and thus provide greater legal certainty.

The Convention was implemented in Ireland by way of the Contractual Obligations (Applicable Law) Act 1990. This Act was brought into effect from 1 January 1992. The Act provides that the Convention is to have force of law and sets out its text in a schedule. Professors Guialino and Lagarde drew up an interpretative report on the Convention and the Act provides that the Irish courts may have regard to this when interpreting the Convention. The Act provides that notice is to be taken of all relevant decisions of the ECJ. In appropriate cases the court deciding a matter within the Convention should refer matters of interpretation to the ECJ.

As with the Brussels Convention, it is proposed to replace the Rome Convention with a regulation containing the text of the Convention.

4.3.2 SCOPE OF THE CONVENTION

4.3.2.1 Generally

The Convention's scope is very wide. Article 1 provides that its rules 'apply to contractual obligations in any situation involving a choice between the laws of different countries'. This means that the only choice of law clause not caught by the Convention would be one between two nationals of the one State providing that the law of that State governs their contract. Article 2 provides that any law specified by the Convention is to be applied whether or not it is the law of the Contracting State. These articles give the Convention worldwide effect. This means that it replaced all the rules of Irish private international law applicable to international contracts, whether there is a European Union dimension or not. The Convention has no retrospective effect so that the old rules apply to contracts made before 1 January 1992 (art 17).

The concept of a 'contractual obligation' is not defined in the Convention, nor has there been a definitive ruling of the ECJ on the point. It does not include tortious obligations, property rights and intellectual property rights.

4.3.2.2 Exclusions

There are a number of specific exclusions from the scope of the Convention, set out in arts 1(2) and (3). The exceptions are similar to the Brussels Convention exceptions. These are:

(a) questions involving the status or capacity of natural persons;

(b) contracts relating to succession, matrimonial property, or obligations under family law, including maintenance obligations. This exception is designed to exclude all family law matters. The focus of the Convention is on commercial contracts;

(c) negotiable instruments: this includes obligations arising from bills of exchange, cheques, promissory notes and other negotiable instruments to the extent that the obligations under such other negotiable instruments arise from their negotiable character;

(d) jurisdiction and arbitration clauses: article 17 of the Brussels Convention regulates the validity and form of a choice of forum clause where the courts of any of the Contracting States are chosen. The New York Convention on Arbitral Awards applies to arbitration clauses;

(e) issues covered by company law;

(f) the authority of an agent or organ, as regards the relationship between a principal and third parties;

(g) trusts;

(h) matters relating to evidence and procedure, but not including the burden of proof nor the modes of proof of contracts and other acts, and

(i) contracts of insurance, other than reinsurance, of risks situated within the European Union. Insurance was excluded as directives have been drawn up dealing with life and non-life insurance. These directives include choice of law provisions.

Many of these exclusions appear to be based on the view that the matter in question merited special, and in some cases complex, rules different from those laid down by the Convention. However, the Rome Convention is wider in its application than the Brussels Convention.

4.3.3 PRINCIPAL CHOICE OF LAW RULES

4.3.3.1 Law chosen by the parties: art 3(1)

The principal choice of law rules are contained in arts 3 and 4. In summary these provide that the contract is governed by its proper law. The proper law of a contract is that chosen by the parties expressly or by implication. The parties may choose one law to govern the whole contract or different laws to govern different issues. In the latter case the laws chosen must be logically consistent. 'Split contracts' are rarely used.

In stating that a contract is to be governed by the law chosen by the parties, art 3 follows the approach adopted by most States' private international law rules. Article 3(1) provides that:

> *A contract shall be governed by the law chosen by the parties. The choice must be express or demonstrated with reasonable certainty by the terms of the contract or the circumstances of the case. By their choice the parties can select the applicable law to the whole or a part only of the contract.*

This provision gives the parties great freedom in choosing the law to govern the contracts. Subject to a few exceptions the parties may choose any law.

The choice of law must be expressed or 'demonstrated with reasonable certainty' by the terms of the contract or the circumstances of the case. Reasonable certainty does not mean that in every case there must be an express choice of law clause. If it is clear from the circumstances of the case that both parties accepted that the law of a specific country would be applicable this would be the governing law. However, the requirement of reasonable certainty means that a choice of law clause cannot be implied from minor indications. Article 3(1) was considered in *Egon Oldendorff v Libera Corporation* [1995] 2 Lloyd's Rep 64. The case concerned an agreement between a German commercial partnership and a Japanese corporation for a ten-year charter to the Germans of two Panama bulk carriers to be built for the Japanese corporation in Japan. The charter contained a clause providing for arbitration in London, in the event of any dispute arising under it. The plaintiffs argued that the existence and validity of the contract should be determined by the law which would govern the contract had it been valid. Following the express arbitration clause in favour of London, the plaintiffs argued that a choice of English law could be implied in accordance with art 3(1). Clarke J held that the party relying on art 3(1) must demonstrate with reasonable certainty that the parties have chosen a particular law as the applicable law. He said that it was a crucial factor that the clause was incorporated in a well-known English language form of charterparty, which contained standard clauses with a well-known meaning in English law. Thus, this demonstrated with reasonable certainty that the parties intended English law to apply. He also pointed out that the parties having agreed a 'neutral' forum, the reasonable inference was that the parties intended to apply a 'neutral' law – English law and not German or Japanese law. The 'strong indication' of English choice of law, through the English arbitration clause, became an 'irresistible inference' through the facts of the case.

4.3.3.2 Alteration to governing law: art 3(2)

Article 3(2) provides:

> *The parties may at any time agree to subject the contract to a law other than that which previously governed it, whether as a result of an earlier choice under this Article or of other provisions of this convention. Any variation by the parties of the law to be applied made after the conclusion of the contract shall not prejudice its formal validity under Article 9 or adversely affect the rights of third parties.*

Article 3(2) allows the parties, after the conclusion of the contract, either to alter the previously chosen law, or to choose one where they had failed to do so at the time of contracting. This variation or subsequent choice is not to adversely affect third parties and will not affect the validity of the contract.

4.3.3.3 What happens where the parties have not chosen any law?

In default of an express or implied choice the law of the country with which it is most closely connected will govern the contract. Article 4, which sets out this principle, is quite a complex provision. It provides for a presumption that the contract is most closely connected with the country where the party to it, who will effect the performance which is characteristic of the contract, resides or (if a business) has its central administration. However, this presumption is rebuttable if the characteristic performance cannot be determined or if it appears from the circumstances as a whole that the contract is more closely connected with another country.

What is characteristic performance? No clear definition is given either in the Convention or in the report on it. The report provides that where payment is involved the characteristic performance is the act done for which payment is made. When a contract involves, for instance, the delivery of goods for the payment of money the characteristic performance is the delivery of goods rather than the payment of money. The report also provides that in insurance the insurer is the characteristic performer. Where the characteristic performance cannot be determined the presumption is to be disregarded. In many cases it will not be that difficult to identify the characteristic performance. This may be seen in the Dutch case of *Machinale Glasfabriek De Maas BV v Emaillerie Alsacienne SA* [1985] 2 CMLR 281. The case concerned a contract between a Dutch seller and a French buyer. The contract was held to be governed by Dutch law, as the characteristic performance was the plaintiff's obligation to deliver the goods. The seller had its place of establishment in the Netherlands and thus under art 4(2) the applicable law was Dutch.

Article 4 has been invoked before the English courts. In *Bank of Baroda v Vysya Bank Ltd* [1994] 2 Lloyd's Rep 87, Vysya, India's largest private bank, was instructed by an Indian importer to issue a letter of credit in favour of an Irish company, Granada, with a London office in respect of the purchase of pig iron. The London office of the Bank of Baroda (another Indian bank) eventually confirmed the credit and paid the beneficiary, Granada, on tender of documents, which were then sent to India. The confirmation was notified in writing by notice sent to Granada at its London office. Vysya then withdrew the authorisation to pay on the ground that there had been frauds in the contract of sale and that the documents did not conform to the credit. One of the questions to be decided was the law governing the contract between the two banks. This fell to be decided on the basis of art 4. Baroda argued that the characteristic performance of the contract was its confirmation to the credit and the honouring of the liability thereby accepted. Vysya argued that this argument confused the contract between the two banks and the contract between Baroda and the beneficiary. It argued that characteristic performance was Vysya's obligation to pay Baroda on production of the conforming documents. Mance J said that the performance characteristic of the contract was the confirmation and honouring of the credit in favour of Granada. This performance was to be effected through Baroda's London office. Thus, the presumption was that English law governed the contract. The liability on the part of the issuing bank to reimburse the confirming bank did not characterise the contract but was consequential on its outcome.

There are two exclusions from the presumption that the contract is most closely connected with the State where the characteristic performer has his/her habitual residence. Article 4(3) provides that where the subject matter of the contract is a right in immovable property or a right to use immovable property, it must be presumed that the contract is most closely connected with the State where the immovable property is situated. Article 4(4) excludes contracts for the carriage of goods. In such contracts, if the State in which the carrier has its principal place of business is also the State in which the place of loading or the place of discharge or where the principal place of business of the consignor of the goods is situated, it is presumed that the contract is most closely connected with that State.

Article 4(5) provides that: 'the presumptions in paragraphs 2, 3 and 4 shall be disregarded if it appears from the circumstances as a whole that the contract is more closely connected with another country'. This gives judges a certain discretion to reject the presumptions. This provision was applied in *Bank of Baroda v Vysya Bank Ltd*. The court also examined the contract between Vysya and Granada. Under art 4(2), the presumption was that Indian law governed the contract, as Vysya was the party to effect characteristic performance. This would have meant that two different legal systems would govern two contracts relating to the same provision of credit. Mance J looked to art 4(5), saying that it was a classic demonstration of its appropriateness and the need for such a provision. The court held that from the circumstances as a whole the contract was most closely connected with England. Therefore, English law applied to the contract.

4.3.3.4 Application of the governing law

Once we decide that a particular law governs the contract what are the consequences of that decision? Articles 8 to 10 specify that subject to certain exceptions, the proper law shall govern the existence and validity of a contract and its interpretation and performance. Thus, once you determine what the governing law of the contract is under arts 3 and 4 it is necessary to turn to arts 8 to 10 to examine its application.

Article 8 provides that the existence and validity of a contract is to be determined by the governing law. This covers such matters as whether a contract was validly formed whether it is invalidated by mistake or misrepresentation, or whether consideration is necessary to make the agreement legally binding. Article 8(2) sets out that by way of exception 'a party may rely upon the law of the country in which he has his habitual residence to establish that he did not consent if it appears from the circumstances that it would not be reasonable to determine the effect of his conduct in accordance' with the governing law. An example of a situation where a court may invoke art 8(2) would be where a party has failed to expressly accept a contract and the other party stipulates that the contract shall be governed by a law that recognises silence as acceptance.

Article 8 was considered by the English courts in *Egon Oldendorff v Libera Corporation*. The defendants invoked art 8(2). They argued that under art 8(2), Japanese law should be applied to establish that they did not consent to any contract or to any arbitration clause on the basis that it would not be reasonable to determine the effect of their conduct in accordance with English law. Mance J held that the onus was on the party invoking art 8(2) to negative consent to bring himself within the scope of that article. In this case there were very strong reasons not to apply Japanese law. The arbitration clause carried with it the natural implication that English law governed. To ignore it would be contrary to ordinary commercial expectations.

Article 9 provides that a contract is formally valid if it satisfies the requirements of either the governing law or the law of the country where it was concluded. This rule of alternative reference reflects the existing private international law rules and is designed to ensure validation of contracts. Formal validity includes matters such as a requirement that certain contracts be in writing, notarised or registered with some official body.

Article 10 provides that the governing law will determine questions of interpretation, performance, breach of contract, nullity, damages and periods of limitation. This is qualified by art 10(2) which provides that, in relation to the manner of performance and the steps to be taken in the event of defective performance, regard shall be had to the law of the State in which the performance took place. The Giuliano and Lagarde Report indicates that this is intended to cover rules governing public holidays, the manner in which goods are to be examined and the steps to be taken if they are rejected. The forum has a discretion to apply the laws of the place of performance in order to do justice. Therefore it seems that the court will only apply the law of the State in which performance takes place to questions of minor importance.

4.3.4 EVIDENTIAL AND PROCEDURAL ASPECTS

Evidence and procedure generally fall outside the scope of the Convention and are governed by the rules of the State in whose courts the dispute is being heard (known as the forum). However, art 14 modifies this exclusion in two ways. Article 14(1) provides that 'the law governing the contract under this Convention applies to the extent that it contains, in the law of contract, rules which raise presumptions of law or determine the burden of proof'.

Article 14(2) provides that:

> *a contract or an act intended to have legal effect may be proved by any mode of proof recognised by the laws of the forum or by any of the laws referred to in art 9 under which that contract or act is formally valid provided that such mode of proof can be administered by the forum.*

The effect of art 14(2) is that a forum's rules as to modes of proof are not to have the effect of invalidating a contract formally valid under the terms of art 9.

4.3.5 MANDATORY RULES

The Convention applies a State's mandatory rules rather than the governing law in one case. Article 3(3) provides:

> *The fact that the parties have chosen a foreign law, whether or not accompanied by the choice of a foreign tribunal, shall not, where all the other elements relevant to the situation at the time of the choice are connected with one country only, prejudice the application of rules of the law of that country which cannot be derogated from by contract, hereinafter called 'mandatory rules'.*

Thus, if a contract is in all respects Irish save for the fact that the parties chose a foreign law, then the parties will be unable to evade Irish mandatory rules. This will be so even if the matter is litigated in England or France.

A mandatory rule is one that the parties cannot opt out of in a domestic situation. The report gives as examples of mandatory rules those relating to cartels, competition, restrictive practices, consumer protection and the carriage of goods. In Ireland some provisions of the Sale of Goods and Supply of Services Act 1980 or the Consumer Credit Act 1995 would come under this heading.

4.3.6 PUBLIC POLICY

The Convention derogates from the general rule that it lays down in arts 3 and 4 that a contract should be governed by its proper law, by making in art 16 a proviso in favour of the forum's public policy. Article 16 provides that the application of a rule of law of any State specified by the Convention may be refused only if such application is manifestly incompatible with the public policy of the forum. This includes the policy of the EU as a whole. It seems to be designed to deal with two types of situation; first, where the foreign rules are offensive to the State's conception of justice and, secondly, where application of the foreign rule would jeopardise the conduct of the forum State's international relations.

In relation to the first category, art 16 will enable the Irish courts to refuse to apply a rule contained in a foreign governing law where they find the nature of the foreign rules to be intolerably offensive to the Irish judicial conscience. In relation to the second kind of case, art 16 will continue in operation the rules which prevent a court from enforcing in any way a contract which was actually intended by the parties to be performed in defiance of the criminal law of the place at which performance was intended to be carried out, or from enforcing a contract whose performance would infringe the criminal law of the place at which the contract required the performance to take place. This applies even if the parties contracted without knowing of the prohibition, or even if the prohibition was imposed after the contract was concluded.

4.3.7 PARTICULAR TYPES OF CONTRACT

With a view to protecting consumers and employees, who are considered to stand in a weak position via-à-vis their suppliers or employers, arts 5 and 6 of the Convention lay down special choice of law rules applicable to consumer contracts, which fulfil certain requirements, and to all individual contracts of employment.

4.3.7.1 Consumer contracts

Article 5 provides a measure of consumer protection. Its aim is to protect consumers, being the weaker party in a contract. Article 5(2) provides that a consumer is not to be deprived of the mandatory rules of the State of his habitual residence if any one of three conditions is fulfilled. The first is that transnational canvassing and advertising take place. An instance would be where an Irish consumer placed an order with a local agent having seen an advertisement on a satellite channel. The second condition deals with local branches and agencies established in one State, even if only on a purely temporary basis, such as a trade stand at a fair or exhibition. The third condition deals with cross-border excursion selling.

Article 5(3) provides that for persons in these categories, in the absence of choice, the applicable law shall be that of the habitual residence of the consumer. Article 5(5) makes it clear that the article does apply to package holidays.

4.3.7.2 Contracts of employment

Article 6 of the Convention applies to all individual contracts of employment. It makes applicable for the employee's benefit mandatory rules of the law of the State where he habitually carries out his work or, if does not habitually carry out his work in any one State, by the law of the State in which the place of business through he was engaged is situated. He has the benefit of these rules even if there is an express or implied choice of law. Article 6(2) provides that, in the absence of such choice, there are three presumptions to discover the governing law. First, the law of the place where he habitually works will govern the contract. Secondly, if he does not habitually work in any one State, the law of the State in which the place of business through which he was engaged is situated applies. Thirdly, if it appears from the circumstances as a whole that the contract is more closely connected with another State, the law of that State governs the contract.

Article 6(2) also establishes another presumption that in the absence of a choice of law 'the law of the country in which the employee habitually carries out his work in pursuance of his contract, even if he is temporarily employed in another country', shall govern the contract of employment.

4.3.8 NON-CONTRACTUAL OBLIGATIONS

The Rome Convention determines the law applicable to contractual obligations. Non-contractual obligations are currently subject to national private international law rules. The Commission has announced that it will propose a regulation setting out a common set of rules on the law applicable to non-contractual obligations. The parties will be free to choose the applicable law but, in the absence of such a choice, the law will be that of the State which has the strongest links with the act creating the obligation. This presumption may be rebutted by certain factors, such as place of residence. The proposal will not apply to family law, intellectual property and succession.

4.4 Proposed Regulation of Service of Judicial and Extrajudicial Documents in Civil or Commercial Matters

4.4.1 HAGUE CONVENTION

Most Member States of the EU are signatories of the Hague Convention on the Service Abroad of Judicial and Extrajudicial Documents in Civil and Commercial Matters 1965. The purpose of the Hague Convention is to simplify the serving of judicial documents of one State in another. Such documents include summons, pleadings and other documents used in civil litigation. It sets out procedures to ensure proper service and that proof of service is provided. The Convention requires each of the Contracting States to appoint a central authority to receive requests for service from other Contracting States.

Ireland implemented this Convention through two statutory instruments which amended the Rules of the Superior Courts (SI 1994/101) and the District Court Rules (District Court (Service Abroad of Documents in Civil and Commercial Matters) Rules 1994, SI 1994/120). The Master of the High Court is designated as the central authority under the Convention. Irish judicial documents must be forwarded to the Central Authority of the State concerned by a 'judicial officer' in Ireland. For Ireland, a practising solicitor, a County Registrar, a District Court Clerk or the Master of the High Court are deemed to be judicial officers. Service of foreign judicial documents in Ireland can be effected through the Master of the High Court, by a solicitor or by post.

4.4.2 EU APPROACH

In addition to signing the Hague Convention many EU Member States also agreed a number of bilateral or regional instruments on service of judicial documents. This led to conflicting rules and some confusion. As a result the EU drew up a draft convention, which would supersede the Hague Convention and other treaties within the EU. In May 1997 the Member States signed a convention on the service of judicial and extrajudicial documents. This convention was never ratified. In early 2000, the Commission proposed a directive, which incorporated the text of this convention. This was referred to the European Parliament, which proposed some amendments, the most significant being its adoption as a regulation. The Commission, in March 2000, put an amended proposal forward. This was adopted by the Council on 29 May 2000 and is to be implemented in Member States by 31 May 2001.

The proposed regulation will apply within the EU and within it will prevail over any other service convention such as the Hague Convention. The Hague Convention will continue to apply to service of judicial documents outside the EU.

The regulation asks States to designate public officers, authorities or other persons as 'transmitting agencies' and 'receiving agencies'. As their names suggest these agencies will be competent for transmitting judicial documents to be served in another State or for receipt of judicial documents from another State for service in their own State. If Ireland was to follow the same approach as with the Hague Convention, it could appoint solicitors as such agencies. Documents are to be transmitted through these agencies and are to be accompanied by a standard form set out in the annex to the regulation. Service by the receiving agency is to take place as soon as possible.

The regulation allows States to accept service of such documents by post. The document to be served must be in the language of the place of service or in a language the addressee knows.

CHAPTER 5

FREE MOVEMENT

The principles of free movement of goods, capital, persons, and services within the EU are the building blocks of the single European market.

5.1 The Free Movement of Goods

5.1.1 QUANTITATIVE RESTRICTIONS

5.1.1.1 Scope of the prohibition: art 28

Article 28 prohibits Member States from imposing quantitative restrictions (or measures of equivalent effect) on imports of goods between Member States. Article 29 imposes a similar prohibition in so far as exports are concerned. In this chapter, for the sake of simplicity, quantitative restrictions are discussed in the context of affecting imports (simply because these are the measures more likely to be imposed by a State rather than restrictions on exports). However, any such references may also be taken to include restrictions on exports.

Neither art 28 nor art 29 defines what constitutes a 'quantitative restriction'. It would appear from the case law of the ECJ that 'quantitative restrictions' within the meaning of art 28, contemplate quotas, product content rules, minimum and maximum pricing laws and such like. Quantitative restrictions do not include fiscal or pecuniary charges imposed by Member States unilaterally on goods when they cross a border. The ECJ's case law on customs duties defines a customs duty (or charge of equivalent effect) as being a fiscal or pecuniary charge unilaterally imposed by a Member State on goods by virtue of the fact that they cross a border (Cases 2 and 3/69 *Sociaal Fonds voor de Diamantarbeiders v SA Brachfield & Sons* [1969] ECR 211). Such measures fall to be considered under the regime of art 25 rather than under art 28.

The ECJ has elaborated in its case law on what constitutes a quantitative restriction. The case law demonstrates how, in the early days of the Court's foray into this area, the Court adopted an expansionist approach, holding a wide range of measures to be quantitative restrictions or measures of equivalent effect. However, of late the Court has adopted a more conservative approach because it is now recognised that certain Member State measures do not constitute quantitative restrictions but rather are measures concerned with the orderly operation of social and economic life in the Member States.

One of the classic judgments which exemplifies the ECJ's early determination to give art 28 a wide scope is the seminal decision in Case 8/74 *Procureur du Roi v Dassonville* [1974] ECR 837 where the Court pronounced:

'All trading rules enacted by Member States which are capable of hindering, directly or indirectly, actually or potentially, intra-Community trade are to be considered as measures having an effect equivalent to quantitative restrictions'.

In that judgment, the ECJ held that Belgian regulations which prohibited the importation of goods bearing an indication of origin (in this case Scotch whisky) unless the importer was in possession of a certificate of authenticity from the authorities in the State of origin constituted a quantitative restriction contrary to the free movement of goods. The reason the ECJ adopted this position was because such a measure potentially discriminated against parallel importers who would be unlikely to be in possession of such documentation.

Although the Court acknowledged that quantitative restrictions might be justified if it could be shown that they were not arbitrarily discriminatory or a disguised restriction on trade between Member States (as, for example, in certain cases proof of authenticity is necessary in order to prevent unfair trading practices), nevertheless the Court was signalling that a wide range of measures would fall to be condemned as quantitative restrictions.

We shall now see how the ECJ divides its consideration of quantitative restrictions into two separate categories. This is important because, should a quantitative restriction constitute a discriminatory quantitative restriction, then it is illegal unless it can be justified under art 30. Whereas, on the other hand, should a quantitative restriction constitute an indistinctly applicable quantitative restriction, then it is illegal unless it can be justified under the 'mandatory requirements' jurisprudence enunciated by the ECJ in its case law.

5.1.1.2 Discriminatory quantitative restrictions

The ECJ has readily condemned discriminatory quantitative restrictions, ie, measures that aim to inhibit imports in favour of domestic products. Such measures may take a variety of forms. What follows is not an exhaustive exposition of the ECJ's voluminous case law on this area but rather a consideration of some of the more high profile examples of the Court's case law which illustrate the extremely broad scope of art 28's prohibition.

Practices conducted by State-supported bodies

Case 249/81 *Commission v Ireland* [1983] ECR 4005 provides a typical example of a situation where the ECJ condemned the practices of a State-supported entity. In this judgment, the ECJ considered the campaign run by the Irish Goods Council, a body whose members were appointed by the State, and whose activities were largely funded by the State. The Council's campaign encouraged Irish consumers to switch their preference from foreign to Irish products. Notwithstanding that evidence was adduced to show that the campaign utterly failed in its objective, the Court nevertheless condemned the campaign as constituting a quantitative restriction on trade between Member States because the objective of the campaign was to encourage domestic consumers to switch their preference from foreign to Irish goods. Furthermore, the Court made it clear that the activities of the Goods Council were attributable to the State because at the time the Council was supported and appointed by the State. The Court also rejected argument to the effect that the Council's campaign was a non-binding one, because the Court emphasised that the prohibition in art 28 is so wide that even measures which are non-binding may be capable of influencing the conduct of traders and consumers and thus frustrate the free movement of goods between Member States contrary to art 28.

Origin-marking

In Case 207/83 *Commission v United Kingdom* [1985] ECR 1201 the ECJ condemned the United Kingdom's requirement that certain goods not be sold in retail outlets unless they were marked with their country of origin. The rationale for the Court's judgment was that not only would such a requirement drive up costs for foreign producers, but furthermore, it would allow UK consumers to assert any prejudices they might have in favour of domestically produced products. Indication of product origin regulations will only be acceptable where they signify that the origin denotes a certain quality in the goods or that they were manufactured in a certain unique manner (Case 113/80 *Commission v Ireland* [1981] ECR 1625).

Administrative practices

Not only will art 28 condemn State laws and rules, it also extends to cover the administrative actions of State bodies, as was seen in Case 21/84 *Commission v France* [1985] ECR 1355. In this judgment the ECJ condemned the French postal administration's practices whereby imported postal franking machines were invariably subjected to long approval delays by the French authorities. The ECJ indicated that where a consistently systematic level of tardiness in considering equipment-approval applications may be demonstrated, then such practice may well constitute a quantitative restriction.

Failure by the State to prevent illegal interference with free movement of goods

Although art 28 only applies to Member States, Case 249/81 *Commission v Ireland* [1983] ECR 4005, discussed above, demonstrates that bodies or institutions which are associated with the State will also fall within the scope of its prohibition. While art 28 cannot apply to purely private actions, the judgment of the ECJ in Case C-265/95 *Commission v France* [1997] ECR I-6959 demonstrates how art 28 may be invoked against the State where it may be demonstrated that the State has failed to do all in its power to prevent the actions of private parties who are interfering with the free movement of goods. In this case, French farming activists had been interrupting imports of agricultural products for a number of years in circumstances where the French State authorities had taken very little counter-action to prevent such disruption. Using arts 10 and 28 as legal base, the Court found that France had violated art 28 by not taking sufficient action to counteract the farmers' actions that de facto, amounted to a quantitative restriction.

5.1.1.3   Justifying discriminatory quantitative restrictions

Article 30 provides the legal basis for justifying quantitative restrictions which are discriminatory in nature. The ECJ has made it clear in its case law that art 30 will only be invocable in the most narrow of circumstances, and that Member States cannot invoke it to serve economic ends nor where the Commission has completed a programme of harmonisation of trading rules in any particular field (Case 72/83 *Campus Oil Ltd v Minister for Industry and Energy* [1984] ECR 2727).

Article 30: three prerequisites to be satisfied

In order for a discriminatory quantitative restriction to be justified under art 30 (and hence compatible with the Treaty) it must satisfy three prerequisites.

First, it must fall within one of the six exceptional categories listed in art 30:

(a)   protection of public morality, or

(b)   protection of public policy, or

(c)   protection of public security, or

(d)   protection of health and life of humans, animals or plants, or

(e)   protection of national treasures possessing artistic, historic or archaeological value, or

(f)   protection of industrial or commercial property.

No new art 30 categories may be judicially created (Case 113/80 *Commission v Ireland* [1981] ECR 1625).

Secondly, the quantitative restriction must not constitute a disguised restriction on trade between Member States.

Thirdly, the quantitative restriction must not be arbitrarily discriminatory.

To demonstrate how art 30 has been applied, the following examples shall be considered.

Measures to protect public morality

Cases such as Case 34/79 *R v Henn and Darby* [1979] ECR 3795 and Case 121/85 *Conegate Ltd v Commissioners of Customs and Excise* [1986] ECR 1007 were concerned with the public morality justification.

In *Henn and Darby* the ECJ made it clear that each Member State is free to decide what is, or is not, contrary to public morality. Consequently, the Court upheld as justifiable United Kingdom regulations that prohibited the importation of pornographic materials. The Court found that the ban on such items imposed by the UK authorities was not a means of disguising a restriction on trade in such goods from other Member States because the manufacture and marketing of such goods was prohibited internally in the UK also. Consequently, the UK ban was not arbitrarily discriminatory against imports.

However, an opposite decision was reached in the later case of *Conegate* where it was argued that the seizure by UK authorities of imports of obscene materials (on the grounds that such goods were subject to an importation ban) was contrary to art 28 as it was a disguised restriction on trade between Member States. The ECJ agreed, as it found that the UK had failed to demonstrate that an equivalent ban on domestically produced obscene items was in force. Attempts by the UK to successfully invoke art 30 to justify the seizures failed because the Court found that a similarly strict regime was not in force to counteract the manufacture and marketing of domestically produced obscene items. Hence, the contested measure (the prohibition on imports) was arbitrarily discriminatory and constituted a disguised restriction on trade between Member States. Consequently, art 30 could not be invoked by the Member State to justify the importation ban and seizure of the goods.

One point worth noting is that the ECJ also held that a Member State measure will not fail to satisfy art 30 merely because the State applies equivalent, though not identical, legal restrictions to imports than apply to similar domestic products: merely as long as the regime that applies is equivalent in its effect vis à vis both domestic products and imports it is sufficient for the State to succeed in arguing that its measure is not arbitrarily discriminatory or a disguised restriction on trade between Member States.

Measures to protect public security

The plea of public security and public policy was advanced in *Campus Oil Ltd v Minister for Industry and Energy*. In that decision Ireland argued that its regime, whereby oil importers were obliged to purchase a significant proportion of their requirements from the State's only oil refinery, was justifiable under art 30. The ECJ agreed but emphasised that art 30 was only invocable in this case because, were petrol supplies to be interrupted, a massive threat to the public security and the stability of the State's economy would arise if the State did not have the regime in place to ensure continuity of supplies for a certain period.

The Court also emphasised that art 30 may only be invoked on non-economic grounds. In other words, art 30 may not be invoked merely on the grounds that as the common market develops, a Member State's economy may become threatened by the importation of cheaper imports arising out of the lowering of barriers to trade between Member States. However, in the instant case, the Court took the view that art 30 was not being invoked in order to keep an uneconomic refinery operating, but rather the State was invoking it in order to justify a regime which would ensure that a certain minimum level of strategic petroleum supplies was present on the national territory in the event of an interruption of international oil supplies.

Measures to protect humans, animals and plants

The plea of protection of humans, animals and plants is one that States often attempt to invoke, generally without success. In Case 40/82 *Commission v United Kingdom* [1982] ECR 2793 the ECJ rejected UK pleas advanced to justify the UK's ban imposed on poultry imports from other Member States. The UK argued that the ban was imposed in order to protect the national turkey population from the spread of Newcastle disease. However, the Court found that the UK ban was motivated by a desire to protect national producers, particularly as other Member States had effective measures in place to combat the spread of the disease and there was undoubtedly pressure from domestic producers on the UK authorities to ban imports in the run-up to Christmas.

Member States may often try to interfere with the free movement of goods by imposing a requirement that goods may not be marketed unless they have been certified to have been treated, and so certified, to the satisfaction of the State's own legislative or regulatory authorities' requirements. Or perhaps the State may go further and require goods not checked or treated in the State to be subjected to rechecking or retreatment when they enter the national territory before they may go on sale, even though they may have already undergone a similar check or treatment process in their country of origin. For example, in Case 124/81 *Commission v United Kingdom* [1983] ECR 203 the UK would only permit certain types of milk product to be sold and marketed provided they had been certified as having gone through certain treatment processes. Because the imported product would have to undergo extra expense in the UK in order to obtain the requisite certification from the UK authorities, effectively this regime amounted to a ban on the import of milk products as it made it unattractive for importers to import milk product into the UK even though it had undergone a similar treatment process in its Member State of origin.

The ECJ held that if the milk products underwent equivalent treatment processes in their country of origin, then the UK ban might well be disproportionate (in other words, a disguised restriction on trade of an arbitrarily discriminatory nature) because the UK concerns about milk treatment could be satisfied by less restrictive means which would constitute less of a hindrance to inter-State trade. For example, the production of certification from the authorities in the Member State where the products originated as to the products' product-worthiness would be less of a hindrance to inter-State trade. It should be noted that while this judgment of the Court does not mean that the Member States are obliged to accept certification from other Member States in order to remain on the right side of art 30, nevertheless the ECJ was clearly signalling that a failure to take such certification into consideration, accompanied by the imposition and maintenance of an importation ban, may well constitute a disguised restriction on trade between Member States which cannot be justified under art 30.

5.1.1.4 Indistinctly applicable quantitative restrictions

Article 28's prohibition of quantitative restrictions applies not only to measures that obviously discriminate against imports (or exports in the case of art 29) but also to quantitative restrictions of an indistinctly applicable nature. Indistinctly applicable quantitative restrictions are measures which hinder the free movement of goods, notwithstanding the fact that they appear to apply equally to both imports and domestic products alike. Unlike discriminatory measures, an indistinctly applicable measure's application does not appear to be predicated on the place of origin of the goods.

At first glance, indistinctly applicable measures would not appear to be incompatible with the Treaty because they do not seem to have a discriminatory rationale. However, it must not be forgotten that it is not the discriminatory intent or objective that is the basis for the prohibition on quantitative restrictions found in art 28, but rather the fact that a measure hinders the free movement of goods. On this basis, therefore, indistinctly applicable measures will be incompatible with art 28 on the ground that they hinder free movement. This raises the interesting question of how such measures may be justified, if at all.

5.1.1.5 Justifying indistinctly applicable quantitative restrictions: 'mandatory requirements'

The Treaty does not provide an analogous provision to art 30 for justifying indistinctly applicable quantitative restrictions. Article 30 cannot be used to justify indistinctly applicable measures: Case 788/79 *Italy v Gilli and Andres* [1980] ECR 2071. However, the ECJ has developed a justification theory for such measures, known as 'mandatory requirements'. In so doing, the Court recognises that in some instances indistinctly applicable quantitative restrictions are necessary in order to provide for the orderly regulation of the economy and the conduct of business generally.

In order to understand where the mandatory requirements justification emanated from, the classic judgment in the area of indistinctly applicable measures, Case 120/78 *Rewe-Zentral AG v Bundesmonopolverwalthung fur Branntwein 'Cassis de Dijon'* [1979] ECR 649 must be considered.

The birth of mandatory requirements theory

In *Cassis de Dijon* the German authorities refused the applicant's request for permission to import Cassis de Dijon liqueur from France for sale in Germany. The grounds for refusal were that the Cassis product was too weak in alcohol strength and that to permit it to go on sale in Germany would constitute a violation of German regulations, which prohibited the sale of such products below a certain alcohol strength.

At this point it must be borne in mind that the German authorities were not singling out foreign liqueurs, because all liqueurs, German or otherwise, had to satisfy the minimum alcohol requirement by law. In attempted justification, the German authorities claimed that such a requirement was, inter alia, designed to protect the young from alcohol tolerance by preventing weak alcohol products coming on to the market. The ECJ rejected this on the ground that German consumers diluted strong alcohol products, thereby showing that such an argument was ill founded.

Next, the German authorities argued that the aim of the rules was to protect German consumers from unfair marketing as they might unwittingly purchase a weak liqueur when their real preference may have been for liqueur with much stronger alcohol content. The Court rejected this line of argument, indicating that proper labelling could adequately protect consumers in this regard as opposed to a complete ban on the sale of low alcohol products.

However, the most significant point that emanated from the ECJ's judgment was the Court's pronouncement that Member States cannot prevent products from other Member States being imported and put on sale merely because they do not satisfy local product content rules. Only where local product rules can be demonstrated to satisfy a 'mandatory requirement' could justification be made. In elaborating this justification theory, the Court was enunciating a judicially created set of exceptional categories under which indistinctly applicable quantitative restrictions could be justified.

The ECJ's mandatory requirements justification theory, allowing indistinctly applicable measures to be justified, is predicated on the rationale that such measures are not designed to discriminate against foreign products, but rather pursue an objective that is compatible with Community objectives, in circumstances where the parameters of the measure employed to pursue such objective are proportionate rather than disproportionate.

In *Cassis de Dijon* the Court laid down four examples of such exceptional categories. These are measures taken to ensure the effectiveness of fiscal supervision, the protection of public health, the fairness of commercial transactions and the defence of the consumer. In so doing, the ECJ made it clear that these categories are not exhaustive, and indeed in its subsequent case law, has added further categories to the four elaborated in the judgment.

Requirement for the measure to be proportionate

Where a mandatory requirement is pleaded, the State will not succeed where the measure employed to pursue the mandatory requirement is disproportionate to the objective to be achieved. The judgment in *Gilli and Andres* (above) is illustrative. Italy prosecuted importers of vinegar on the grounds that they imported vinegar made from apples rather than from wine for sale in Italy, thereby allegedly misleading consumers. Italy claimed that its prosecution was designed to protect consumers. Apart from finding that apple vinegar is not a threat to human health, the Court also found that the Italian regime was disproportionate in pursuing the objective of safeguarding consumers because consumers could be adequately informed by the more proportionate means of requiring vinegar producers/importers to adequately label the product such that consumers' attention would be drawn to the fact that the product was apple rather then wine based.

Additional mandatory requirements

The ECJ has added to its list of mandatory requirements in various cases. For example, in Cases 60 & 61/84 *Cinéthèque SA v Federation National des Cinémas Français* [1985] ECR 2605 the Court found that a French law which banned the sale and hire of newly released films on video, without distinction as to the State of origin of the film video, for a one-year period after the film was released in the cinemas was acceptable, provided that it was in pursuit of the (newly recognised) mandatory requirement of 'encouraging cinematographic distribution of film'. In recognising this new mandatory requirement, the ECJ was taking the view that the French measures were compatible with the mandatory requirements justification theory as long as they were proportionate in their scope.

In Case C-145/88 *Torfaen Borough Council v B&Q plc* [1989] ECR 3851 the ECJ recognised a further mandatory requirement, that of prohibiting Sunday opening of certain retail-trading premises. The Court found this restriction compatible with Community law because the measure was not designed to hinder the free movement of goods between Member States, but rather reflected certain social and political choices in a Member State to have Sunday as a day of rest. Such a mandatory requirement would be compatible with Community objectives and with art 28, provided that the measure was not disproportionate. The fact that the Sunday trading ban might lower the volume of goods imported from other Member States (as the opportunity to retail them was confined to six days per week) did not cause the Court to regard the ban on Sunday trading as being a quantitative restriction designed to hinder inter-State trade in goods. Rather, held the Court, it was an indistinctly applicable measure, which also affected sales of domestic goods, and was imposed not for the purpose of affecting inter-State trade, but rather to pursue a social objective. Provided the national court found such a measure to be proportionate in pursuing such objective, then the ban was compatible with art 28.

However, the difficulty with this approach was that it was being left up to national courts to decide whether a contested indistinctly applicable measure was proportionate or not. This led to conflicting decisions and difficult choices having to be made by national judges. Furthermore, the ECJ experienced a dramatic increase in both the volume and novelty of cases referred to it from national courts arising out of importers and traders art 28-inspired challenges to indistinctly applicable measures. Consequently, in its judgment in Cases C-267 & 268/91 *Criminal proceedings against Keck and Mithouard* [1993] ECR I-6097 the Court changed its approach dramatically.

5.1.1.6 **Indistinctly applicable measures falling outside scope of art 28**

In *Keck* the ECJ found that French legislation designed to prohibit sales of goods at a loss was not a measure of equivalent effect to a quantitative restriction. This was a ground-breaking judgment because the Court was, in effect, finding that certain indistinctly applicable measures will not constitute quantitative restrictions in the first place, hence the question of their attempted justification does not arise.

There has been much debate since this judgment over whether the ECJ has abandoned some of its mandatory requirements case law, because the Court expressly admitted in its judgment that it was ruling contrary to what it had decided in previous cases. However, the problem was that the Court did not indicate which cases it was overruling.

What is helpful though, is that the ECJ referred to national rules which it described as 'selling arrangements' and distinguished these from rules such as were found in the Cassis judgment which concerned *product content characteristics* (*Cassis de Dijon*). It seems the point the Court was making in *Keck* is that national rules which affect the selling (rather than the content or characteristics) of products fall outside the scope of art 28 altogether. Hence, such measures may not be challenged under art 28, in which event the question of their attempted justification does not arise. The reason why the Court is happy to accept this position is because it pronounced that provided such indistinctly applicable measures apply to all traders (ie, domestic and foreign) in law and in fact in the same manner and to the same extent, then such rules do not impede imports from accessing a Member State's market any more than they impede the access of domestic products to that market.

In subsequent decisions the ECJ found that national rules that governed the opening and closing hours of petrol stations (Cases C-401 & 402/92 *Tankstation 't Heustke vof and J.B.E. Boermans* [1994] ECR I-2199) and retail shops would not constitute quantitative restrictions provided they applied to all traders (domestic and foreign) in the same manner. In this light, one may query whether the *Torfaen Borough Council v B&Q plc* judgment (for example) on the UK Sunday trading ban has now effectively been overruled, such that a measure such as a Sunday trading ban should more properly be regarded as a measure which falls outside art 28 altogether, rather than one which is deemed a quantitative restriction under art 28 and thereby is compatible with art 28 (and hence maintained in force) provided it is proportionate in effect.

In the years since *Keck* the ECJ has had to face many difficult issues. For example, what constitutes a 'selling arrangement'? In Case C-368/95 *Vereingte Familiapress Zeitungsverlags und Vertreibs GmbH v Heinrich Bauer Verlag* [1997] ECR I-3689 the Court held that an Austrian law which prohibited publishers including competition prizes in their newspapers did not constitute a 'selling arrangement' type measure but rather a measure as to product content, hence art 28 was in principle still applicable.

Another interesting issue that arose was whether a national measure which reduces sales of imported goods because it limits the opportunities in which outlets, which sell such goods, may open (and thereby by implication reduces the volume of imports of such goods) was a quantitative restriction. In Cases C-418/93 & 332/94 *Semeraro Casa Uno Srl v Sindaco del Commune Di Erbusco* [1996] ECR I-2975 the Court held that merely because national measures (limiting the trading hours of out-of-town shopping malls) incidentally limit the volume of imports, that is not a ground for classifying the measure as a quantitative restriction in circumstances where the measure affects domestic producers and importers in the same manner in law and in fact.

5.1.2 CUSTOMS DUTIES AND INTERNAL TAXATION: ARTS 25 AND 90

5.1.2.1 Generally

Until now, the art 28 regime that applies to prohibit obstacles to the free movement of goods which are non-pecuniary in nature has been considered, ie, 'quantitative restrictions or measures of equivalent effect'.

However, Member States may attempt to interfere with the free movement of goods between Member States using other fiscal means, ie, by using pecuniary measures. This may be attempted in one of two ways. Either the Member State may impose a customs duty or charge of equivalent effect, or, alternatively, it may use its internal taxation system to, in some way, discriminate against goods originating in another Member State (or destined for export to another Member State).

Article 25 provides that:

Customs duties on imports and exports and charges of equivalent effect shall be prohibited between Member States. This prohibition shall also apply to customs duties of a fiscal nature.

Article 90 provides that:

(1) No Member State shall impose, directly or indirectly, on the products of other Member States any internal taxation of any kind in excess of that imposed directly or indirectly on similar domestic products.

(2) Furthermore, no Member State shall impose on the products of other Member States any internal taxation of such a nature as to afford indirect protection to any other products.

Thus, it is evident that while the Treaty appears to prohibit customs duties and charges of equivalent effect absolutely (art 25), measures imposed by way of a State's internal taxation regime may be tolerated provided certain parameters are respected (art 90). Hence, it is very important at the outset to be able to determine accurately whether a charge is a customs duty (or charge of equivalent effect) or a measure of internal taxation.

5.1.2.2   Definition of customs duties and charges of equivalent effect: art 25

Customs duties are absolutely prohibited by art 25. In Case 7/68 *Commission v Italy* [1968] ECR 423, the ECJ demonstrated how widely it intended art 25's prohibition to apply when it ruled that Italy's imposition of a tax on the export of archaeological treasures constituted a customs duty, and thus was prohibited. Italy argued that the purpose of the scheme was purely benevolent (to protect Italy's cultural and archaeological heritage). Rejecting this line of argument, the Court made it clear that the fiscal intent behind the charge was irrelevant. It constituted a fiscal barrier to the free movement of artistic and historical items and, as such items could be regarded as 'goods' within the meaning of the Treaty (being items which have a monetary value), hence the charge constituted a customs duty which interfered with the free movement of goods and hindered the development of the common market between Member States. While one may have some sympathy for the efforts of the Italian authorities, the Court was not prepared to restrict the scope of art 25 merely for the sake of national sentiment or higher cultural motives.

Not only are customs duties prohibited, but so too are charges of equivalent effect. In Case 24/68 *Commission v Italy* [1969] ECR 193 the ECJ demonstrated that any charge imposed on goods by virtue of the fact that they cross a national border constitutes a charge prohibited by art 25 and, furthermore, that the purpose behind the imposition of the duty or charge is irrelevant. The ECJ stated that a charge of equivalent effect is:

'any pecuniary charge, however small and whatever its mode of designation and mode of application, which is imposed unilaterally on goods by reason of the fact that they cross a frontier, and which is not a customs duty in the strict sense, constitutes a charge of equivalent effect within the meaning of . . . the Treaty, even if it is not imposed for the benefit of the State, is not discriminatory or protective in effect and if the product on which the charge is imposed is not in competition with any domestic product'.

However, as we shall see shortly below, notwithstanding the strictness of this pronouncement the ECJ did create judicial exceptions to this prohibition.

Before considering such exceptions, first it is appropriate to consider how a charge imposed on goods may not be classified as an art 25-type charge at all where it constitutes a different animal entirely – a 'measure of internal taxation' covered by art 90's regime.

141

5.1.2.3 Definition of measure of internal taxation: art 90

As measures of internal taxation are subject to a more lenient regime under the Treaty – they remain compatible with the Treaty provided the tax respects the parameters set by art 90 – the question arises as to how such pecuniary measures are defined, and furthermore, how are they to be distinguished from an art 25 customs duty/charge of equivalent effect.

Case 132/78 *Denkavit Loire Sarl v France* [1979] ECR 1923 provides guidance on this issue. In this judgment the ECJ was called upon to consider whether a charge imposed by France on a consignment of animal lard was a measure of internal taxation or a customs duty. France imposed a tax whenever an animal was slaughtered in a French abattoir, and so, apparently to equalise the playing field, France imposed a similar charge on imported lard products in an effort to ensure that the imported product was subject to similar taxation treatment as the domestically slaughtered (French) product. The Court held the charge imposed on the imported lard was an art 25 charge of equivalent effect to a customs duty, not an art 90 measure of internal taxation. According to the ECJ, measures of internal taxation concern measures, which relate to a general system of internal taxation, applied systematically and in accordance with the same objective criteria to domestic products and imports alike. What the Court meant by this was that the taxes must be levied at the same stage of marketing or production of both imports and domestic products alike, such that the chargeable event is the same for both products. The ECJ further found that it is not sufficient (in order for a measure to be classified as an art 90 measure rather than an art 25 customs duty or equivalent charge) that the objective of the charge imposed on imported products is to compensate for a charge imposed on domestic products, particularly where the 'tax' is imposed at a production or marketing stage which is different from that at which the domestic products were taxed. Consequently, the Court held that the charge imposed on the imported lard, not being classifiable as an art 90 measure of internal taxation, could only be an art 25 customs duty or charge of equivalent effect (and hence be subject to a much more rigorous regime).

5.1.2.4 Exceptions to the prohibition in art 25

Notwithstanding that art 25 appears to admit of no exceptions (and the fact that the ECJ, in the early days of its art 25 jurisprudence-building, stated that there were no exceptions: Case 24/68 *Commission v Italy* [1969] ECR 193), nevertheless the ECJ over time recognised a number of situations whereby a charge would not be prohibited by art 25. While these exceptions would appear to be significant upon first examination, as a matter of substance, however, they have proven very difficult for Member States to invoke successfully.

Fee charged in return for service rendered to the importer/exporter

The ECJ has recognised that where an importer (or exporter) is charged a fee by Member State authorities and in return receives a benefit, then the fee will not be regarded as a charge of the kind prohibited by art 25. However, as will now be seen when the case law is examined, in practice it is very difficult to satisfy this requirement that a specific benefit to the importer be demonstrated to exist. Furthermore, even if this hurdle is overcome, it must also be demonstrated that the fee charged is no more than the cost of the actual inspection. Member States typically have found this a difficult hurdle to satisfy also, because often the means used in the past to charge for services has been on an approximate (unacceptable) basis rather than on a precise cost-of-provision of the service basis (acceptable).

Specific benefit to the importer/exporter. So far as demonstrating that a specific benefit accrues to the importer is concerned, in order for the State to succeed in this argument, the State must demonstrate that the benefit arising out of the performance of the service for the importer (for which the fee is levied by the State) accrues to the importer specifically, rather than to merely society or the wider economy generally.

In *Commission v Italy* the ECJ rejected a claim by Italy that Italy was entitled to impose a fee on importers and exporters in order to help recover the costs incurred by the Italian authorities who were engaged in the collection of statistical information on the destination of goods entering and leaving Italy. Italy claimed it was performing a service, which was ultimately of benefit to all importers and exporters because such information would be of use to them. The Court held that in order for such a charge imposed for such a service to fall outside the art 25 prohibition, a specific benefit to each specific importer/exporter would have to be demonstrated. The benefit, if any, arising from the collection of the statistics, was so general in nature, that it was impossible to determine whether it was a benefit to each individual trader. Hence, the fee charged to cover the collection of the information was prohibited as being contrary to art 25.

Similarly in Case 87/75 *Bresciani v Amministrazione Italiana delle Finanze* [1976] ECR 129, the ECJ held that a charge imposed to cover the inspection of imported cowhides into Italy, while of benefit to the general public (protecting public health), could not be categorised as a charge compatible with art 25 because no specific benefit to the individual importer could be demonstrated. The inspection was necessitated by the need to protect public health, not by the need to provide a specific service to the individual importer. Consequently, any fee charged for providing such an inspection should come from the public purse and not from the importer who was receiving no specific benefit from the service (ie, the public health inspection).

Charge levied must be no more than the actual cost of providing the benefit. Furthermore, the ECJ also imposes a further condition before a charge will be regarded as falling outside art 25: the charge or fee must be no more than the cost of providing the benefit or service in question. This issue was dealt with in the ECJ's judgment in Case 18/87 *Commission v Germany* [1988] ECR 5427 where the ECJ held that where a charge is imposed, it will be prohibited under art 25 if it cannot be demonstrated that it relates to the actual cost of the specific service rendered to the importer/exporter.

The difficulty that this creates for Member States is that this effectively prevents them using 'rule of thumb' calculations of an approximate nature (such as charges levied on the basis of the quality or quantity of goods inspected). In *Bresciani* the ECJ rejected Italian arguments that a fee was compatible with art 25 where it was levied on the basis that it was proportionate to the quantity of goods inspected rather than their invoice value. Rejecting such argument, the Court ruled that the fee charged must be no more than the actual cost of the inspection rendered for the service performed for the individual importer. Otherwise, it is incompatible with art 25.

Where State levies charge or fee to recover costs arising out of EU obligations

However, the ECJ does recognise that where the State performs a service in order to comply with obligations imposed on the State by EU law, such as a directive which specifically requires the inspection of imported goods, then the State is entitled to impose a fee for performing such obligation provided certain parameters are respected. In *Commission v Germany* the Court stated that where the State is obliged to perform a service in order to comply with EU law obligations (in this case, the inspection of live animal imports), then the State is entitled to levy a fee for this purpose provided that the fee does not exceed the cost of the inspections; the inspections are obligatory throughout the EU; the inspections are in the general interest of the EU, and the inspections promote the free movement of goods. One implication of this ruling is that if EU law does not impose a mandatory obligation on the State to perform the service in question, then the State cannot rely on *Commission v Germany* as authority for mandating the levying of a charge or fee.

Where a Member State is obliged to conduct inspections on goods pursuant to international conventions, then they will only be compatible with EU law provided they satisfy the rules set out above (Case 46/76 *Bauhuis v Netherlands* [1977] ECR 5; Case 89/76 *Commission v Netherlands* [1977] ECR 1355).

143

5.1.3 INTERNAL TAXATION

5.1.3.1 Generally

Where a Member State's pecuniary measure is determined to be an art 90 measure of internal taxation, as opposed to an art 25 customs duty or charge of equivalent effect, then its prospects of being found compatible with the Treaty are much improved. The basic proposition on which art 90 is based is that internal taxation is permitted as long as it does not discriminate against imported goods coming from other Member States. Thus the contrast with art 25 is starkly evident: art 25 does not permit customs duties or equivalent charges (unless the narrow judicially-developed exceptions discussed above apply), whereas art 90 does permit internal taxation to be levied provided the taxation respects the parameters set by art 90. (The legal test for determining whether a measure is an art 90 measure of internal taxation or, alternatively, an art 25 customs duty/charge of equivalent effect has already been discussed above in the context of the ECJ's judgment in Case 132/78 *Denkavit Loire Sarl v France* [1979] ECR 1923.)

Under art 90(1), where goods are 'similar' then internal taxation may be levied on imports provided it is no more than is levied on similar domestic products. Where products are not similar but are 'competing', then higher taxation may be levied on the competing import provided that the higher level of taxation does not give a 'protective effect' to the competing domestic product.

5.1.3.2 Wide judicial approach to interpreting article 90 prohibition

Before considering the parameters of art 90(1) and (2), it should be noted that the ECJ has adopted a wide approach to interpreting the prohibitions in art 90. Thus, for example, where a State allows domestic traders more time to pay taxes than was allowed to importers of similar goods, this constitutes discriminatory taxation in violation of art 90 even though the level of tax levied may be identical (Case 55/79 *Commission v Ireland* [1980] ECR 481).

Similarly, in Case 21/79 *Commission v Italy* [1980] ECR 1, the ECJ ruled that Italy was in breach of art 90 by refusing to allow imported regenerated oil to benefit from an environmentally friendly lower taxation regime afforded to domestically regenerated oil products. Consequently, imported regenerated oil product was taxed on the higher tax scale along with imported and domestically produced non-regenerated oil products. The Italian authorities had argued they could not differentiate between imported non-regenerated oil products and imported regenerated oil products (whereas this was possible with domestically produced products because the Italian authorities could inspect their place and method of production). Rejecting such argument, the ECJ found that the Italians could have devised a verification process to allow the imported regenerated product to be objectively identified, and hence benefit from the lower tax regime which domestically produced regenerated oil products enjoyed. In this regard, the ECJ suggested that the Italian authorities could require importers to produce a certificate of authenticity from the authorities in the Member State of origin of the product, which would verify that the imported oil product was of the regenerated variety. As the Italian authorities had failed to implement such a system, maintaining the higher tax on such product in such circumstances constituted a breach of art 90.

Another classic example of the ECJ's wide approach preventing Member States finding a way around art 90 is to be found in Case 112/84 *Humblot v Directeur des Services Fiscaux* [1985] ECR 1367. France operated a progressively increasing system of taxation for motor cars based on engine capacity. It operated on a sliding scale with the tax progressively increasing as the engine capacity increased. However, once an engine capacity rose above 1,600 cc, the tax multiplied by several times. It so happened that no French-produced cars had engine capacity above the 1,600 cc level. The French authorities argued that the taxation regime was not discriminatory because it was not predicated on the origin of goods and therefore could not be labelled as 'discriminatory'. However, the Court rejected this argument, finding that although the taxation regime was not overtly based on the origin of the goods (and hence did not appear discriminatory on a superficial examination), nevertheless it was discriminatory because the 1,600 cc point appeared to have been chosen in order to effectively deter French consumers from purchasing imported cars whose engine capacity was more than 1,600 cc and favour the purchase of French-produced cars, ie, those with an engine capacity of under 1,600 cc. This violated art 90 because, for example, if a French consumer was faced with purchasing a French car with an engine in the 1,500–1,599 cc range and a foreign comparable car with a slightly more powerful engine (ie, just above 1,600 cc) the consumer would be deterred from purchasing the imported car by the punitive tax burden applying to the (imported) car whose engine capacity was over the 1,600 cc threshold.

That *Humblot* does not condemn progressively increasing taxation systems per se was made clear in Case 132/88 *Commission v Greece* [1990] ECR I-1567. In this judgment the ECJ did not condemn a progressively increasing taxation system imposed on motor cars in Greece because the Court found that the engine capacity levels at which the tax increased substantially were not set at a point where Greek consumers would be deterred from purchasing a foreign car and 'encouraged' to purchase a comparable Greek produced car. In this case, the tax rose substantially once engine capacity rose above 1,800 cc. The most powerful Greek car was 1,600 cc: hence the Court found that Greek consumers could still purchase a comparable imported car even with a more powerful engine (ie, up to 1,800 cc) without the national taxation system acting as a prohibitive deterrent.

5.1.3.3   Creation of judicial exceptions to article 90's prohibitions

The ECJ has recognised that art 90 clearly allows Member States to continue to levy internal taxation on imports, albeit within the parameters set by art 90. As part of this recognition, the ECJ has in some instances, permitted national taxation systems to favour national products. However this is not because they are domestically produced (that would be discrimination contrary to art 90), but rather because the products have some characteristics, which permit the State to claim that there is an objective justification for such a regime. However, in order to prevent Member States attempting to abuse this objective justification exception, the ECJ requires that where an imported product has similar characteristics, or is produced in similar circumstances, to those of the domestic product, then it too must also be allowed the benefit of the more lenient tax regime. Otherwise, the national system will in reality be discriminatory (Case 148/77 *Hansen GmbH & Co v Hauptzollampt Flensburg* [1978] ECR 1787).

In *Commission v Greece* and Case 140/79 *Chemial Farmaceutici v DAF SpA* [1981] ECR 1 and Case 196/85 *Commission v France* [1987] ECR 1597 the ECJ accepted that the State's favouring of particular products under national lower taxation schemes was objectively justified.

In *Commission v Greece* the ECJ accepted that a Member State could use the national taxation regime for motor cars in order to promote consumers to purchase cars with smaller engines because they were more environmentally friendly. Combating air pollution using the national taxation system is compatible with EU objectives, provided the means used to achieve it are not discriminatory against imported goods. In promoting such an objective, the Greek taxation regime was not discriminating against imported cars because Greek consumers could continue to buy them at the same tax levels as applied to comparable domestic cars. Hence the Greek regime was objectively justified and thus compatible with art 90.

In *Chemial Farmaceutici v DAF SpA* the ECJ found that Italy's favourable treatment of ethyl alcohol produced from fermented agricultural products, and its less favourable tax treatment of such product produced from petroleum derivatives, was objectively justified. The ECJ found that the Italian regime was not discriminatory because domestically produced ethyl alcohol produced by non-fermentation methods was as highly taxed as imported non-fermented product (thus precluding any allegation that Italy was using the national taxation system to protect domestic production of non-fermented product). Furthermore, the Italian authorities permitted imported fermented product to also benefit from the lower tax regime applicable to the domestic equivalent product. Taking the foregoing into account, the ECJ took the view that the Italian taxation regime was taxing fermented ethyl alcohol according to the raw materials and production processes used, and that this was an objective justification for treating it differently for taxation purposes from petroleum-derived ethyl alcohol products.

5.1.3.4 'Similar' or 'Competing'?

Under art 90(1), where goods are 'similar' then internal taxation may be levied on imports provided it is no more than is levied on similar domestic products. Where products are not similar but are 'competing', then higher taxation may be levied on the competing import provided that the higher level of taxation does not give a protective effect to the competing domestic product. Hence, it is vitally important to determine whether goods are 'similar' or 'competing'.

Where a Member State is found to have violated art 90(1), then its duty is to equalise the taxes, not by equalising upwards (ie, raising the level of tax on the domestic product up to that imposed on the similar import), but rather by equalising downwards (ie, reduce the tax on the import to the level imposed on the domestic product) (Cases 2 & 3/62 *Commission v Luxembourg and Belgium* [1965] ECR 425).

Where a Member State is found to have violated art 90(2), its obligation is to remove the 'protective' effect occasioned by the imposition of the higher tax imposed on the competing import, and that may, depending on the particular circumstances of each case, mean that the tax on the import is either reduced, and thus made the same as that imposed on the competing domestic product, or that the tax on the import is merely reduced somewhat such that the 'protective' element occasioned by the initial taxation level is negated. All depends therefore on the particular facts of each case as to what is required in order to remove the 'protective' effect.

While the tax rate is the most obvious indicator of discrimination, naturally the foregoing also applies to the mode of assessment of the tax, or the time for its payment (*Commission v Ireland* [1980] ECR 481 discussed above), or indeed any other conditions under which the tax is levied or collected.

5.1.3.5 Similar

Goods are similar where they are similar in terms of consumer perception, their objective characteristics such as content and raw materials used, and the method of production employed. For example, in Case 184/85 *Commission v Italy* [1987] ECR 2013 the ECJ found that bananas were not similar to other fruits because bananas have certain characteristics which objectively differentiate them from other fruit products. For example, the banana contains certain minerals, which other fruits do not possess, and hence the Court suggested that this was one of the reasons why consumers consume the product in preference to other fruits. In Case 243/84 *John Walker v Ministeriet for Skatter* [1986] ECR 875 the ECJ found that whisky and fruit liqueur wine were not similar as, although both were alcohol products, they were produced by different methods, their alcohol content was very different, and consumers did not perceive them to be similar.

Sometimes, however, the ECJ does not indicate definitively whether a product is 'similar' or merely 'competing'. For example, in Case 168/78 *Commission v France* [1980] ECR 347 the ECJ did not firmly indicate whether spirit products made from grain (mostly imported into France) and alcohol products made from fruit (mostly domestically produced) were similar or merely competing. While the ECJ took the view that the taxation regime employed in that case would violate both paragraphs of art 90, nevertheless it is not beyond the bounds of reason that a case may arise where a clear indication of which paragraph of art 90 is applicable may be vitally important as, otherwise, the offending Member State will not be sure as to whether it must equalise the taxes (art 90(1)) or merely act to remove the protective effect (art 90(2)).

5.1.3.6 Competing products – protective effect must be removed

Products are 'competing' where there is some degree of competition between them in the sense that, although consumers may not regard them as the same, nevertheless consumers may be willing to switch their preference to the other product should the price become a competitive one. The classic judgment in this area is Case 170/78 *Commission v United Kingdom* [1983] ECR 2265 where the ECJ considered that although wine (mostly imported) and beer (mostly domestically produced) were not 'similar' on account of their different alcohol levels, taste, consumption patterns, method of production, raw materials used and consumer perception, nevertheless the ECJ did regard cheaper light alcohol wines as 'competing' with beer products for the purposes of art 90(2). The ECJ took the view that beer and light wines could meet identical needs, and hence must be to some degree interchangeable and thus deemed 'competing' within the meaning of art 90(2) (though they could not be termed 'similar' within the meaning of art 90(1) on account of the aforementioned differences).

The ECJ then proceeded to consider whether the United Kingdom's high taxation of wine protected beer contrary to art 90(2). It found that because the tax burden imposed on wine was so high relative to that imposed on beer, consumers could not regard wine to be 'competing' with beer on account of the major price differential between the products, such differential being chiefly due to the taxation system's imposition of such high taxes on wine.

However, notwithstanding, the ECJ stated that where a Member State has used national taxation policy in such a way as to cause consumers not to regard products being interchangeable due to price differential, that will not prevent the Court from finding that the products are nevertheless 'competing'. Were it to be otherwise, the ECJ indicated it would be allowing Member States to use national taxation policy to crystallise consumer tastes to the detriment of the free movement of goods in the EU. There was little doubt but that the United Kingdom tax regime was 'protective' of beer contrary to art 90(2).

The ECJ has not indicated a hard and fast rule to indicate when tax on a competing import is in fact 'protective'. All depends on the individual circumstances of each case. In *Commission v United Kingdom*, the tax on wine was obviously protective as it was several times the level of the tax on beer. In *Commission v Italy* (the banana case discussed at **5.1.3.5** above) the consumption tax imposed on bananas was protective because it was 50 per cent greater than the level of tax imposed on other fruits. However, in Case 356/85 *Commission v Belgium* [1987] ECR 3299 the ECJ held there was no protective effect where the tax differential was relatively small (6 per cent) and the cost of the products was substantially different such that their overall prices were very different, with the tax component of the difference being therefore relatively minor.

5.1.4 DISTINGUISHING CUSTOMS DUTIES AND INTERNAL TAXES

5.1.4.1 Legal test

As already discussed above, the legal test for distinguishing between art 25 customs duties, or equivalent charges, on one hand, and art 90 internal taxes on the other lies in the application of the *Denkavit* test:

(a) Is the leviable event where the tax is applied part of a system of general taxation whereby the tax is applied systematically to categories of products in accordance with the same objective criteria to both domestic and imported products at the same stage of production or marketing and irrespective of origin of the products? (If so, art 90 applies, in which event the tax is assessed for compatibility under art 90(1) or (2) depending on whether the products are adjudged to be either 'similar' or competing'), or alternatively,

(b) Is the so-called tax in fact a pecuniary charge unilaterally imposed on goods by virtue of the fact that they cross a border, regardless of the intent behind the levying of the charge? (If so, art 25 applies, in which event the measure is prohibited under art 25 unless one of the narrow judicially recognised exceptions applies).

5.1.4.2 No comparable domestic product

However, what is the situation where a Member State levies a tax on an imported product in circumstances where no similar or competing domestic equivalent exists. Will such charge be condemned as a customs duty? All depends on the circumstances of each case. Where the State can demonstrate that the tax category into which the product falls is part of the system of general taxation, which is not predicated on the origin of the product, then the tax will be considered under art 90, notwithstanding that it appears to affect imports only. In Case 193/85 *Co-operative Co-Frutta v Amministrazione delle Finanze dello Stato* [1987] ECR 2085 the ECJ, when called upon to consider how an Italian consumption tax applicable to bananas which were almost exclusively imported should be classified, stated that:

'[T]he prohibition laid down by [art 25] in regard to charges having an equivalent effect covers any charge exacted at the time of or on account of importation which, being borne specifically by an imported product to the exclusion of the similar domestic product, has the result of altering the cost price of the imported product, thereby producing the same restrictive effect on the free movement of goods as a customs duty.

'The essential feature of a charge having an equivalent effect to a customs duty which distinguishes it from an internal tax therefore resides in the fact that the former is borne solely by an imported product as such whilst the latter is borne both by imported and domestic products.'

The ECJ, however, recognised that even a charge which is borne by a product imported from another Member State, when there is no identical or similar domestic product, does not constitute a charge having equivalent effect but internal taxation within the meaning of art 90 of the Treaty if it relates to a general system of internal dues applied systematically to categories of products in accordance with objective criteria irrespective of the origin of the products. As the Court observed:

'A tax on consumption of the type at issue in the main proceedings does form part of a general system of internal dues. The nineteen taxes on consumption are governed by common tax rules and are charged on categories of products irrespective of their origin in accordance with an objective criterion, namely the fact that the product falls into a specific category of goods . . . Whether those goods are produced at home or abroad does not seem to have a bearing on the rate, the basis of assessment or the manner in which the tax is levied. The revenue from those taxes is not earmarked for a specific purpose; it constitutes tax revenue identical to other tax revenue and like it, helps to finance State expenditure generally in all sectors.'

Thus, the ECJ held that, notwithstanding that the product taxed had no domestic equivalent (effectively the Court disregarded domestic production of bananas as such production was of negligible quantities), it would nevertheless not automatically regard such a tax as an art 25 measure, but rather would allow it to be scrutinised in order to see if it was in substance a measure that more properly fell within the ambit of art 90. Having so found that the consumption tax was indeed a measure which fell to be scrutinised under art

90 (as opposed to art 25) the ECJ nevertheless proceeded to condemn it as being protective contrary to 90(2).

5.2 Free Movement of Capital and Economic and Monetary Union

5.2.1 FREE MOVEMENT OF CAPITAL

The wording of the Treaty articles on liberalisation of national Member State laws concerning the free movement of capital was not as rigorous as the wording of the other freedoms. Thus, matters such as national exchange controls on the movement of capital were only gradually dismantled in the 1960s and 1970s. The infamous Joined Cases 286/82, 26/83 *Luisi and Carbone v Ministero del Tesoro* [1984] ECR 377 demonstrates how even until the 1980s national provisions were maintained which inhibited the free movement of capital. In that judgment, the ECJ condemned as being contrary to the Treaty's provision on free movement of services provisions of Italian law under which the applicants were being prosecuted for having exported currency abroad in order to pay for medical services they were receiving in another Member State.

However, since the Treaty on European Union, the original Treaty articles on liberalisation of capital movements have been replaced by the more forthright art 56 which states, inter alia, that:

> *Within the framework of the provisions set out in this Chapter, all restrictions on the movement of capital between Member States and between Member States and third countries shall be prohibited.*

However, upon closer inspection art 58 reveals exceptions to art 56. Provided that Member States do not use tax laws in an arbitrarily discriminatory way or as a means of disguising restrictions on the free movement of capital, Member States shall be free to apply their tax laws which distinguish between taxpayers who are not in the same situation with regard to their place of residence or with regard to the place where their capital is invested. Furthermore, Member States shall be free to take all requisite measures under art 58 (again subject to them not being arbitrarily discriminatory or being a disguised restriction on trade between Member States) to prevent infringements of national law, in particular in the field of taxation and the prudential supervision of financial institutions. It is also provided that the State may require, for administrative or statistical purposes, the declaring of capital movements, or take measures necessary to protect public policy or security.

5.2.2 ECONOMIC AND MONETARY UNION

Monetary union has been in train in various forms since the 1970s. It is not proposed to recount the historical ground in this regard apart from merely noting its passing. In 1978 the European Monetary System was established. It utilised the Exchange Rate Mechanism whereby each national currency had a fixed value against a new currency unit, the ECU. Each national currency was obliged to remain within a central exchange rate band with the ECU with a defined margin for fluctuation. However, the EMS came under severe pressures in the early 1990s when certain currencies weakened and were forced to leave the ERM.

The Maastricht Treaty set the stage for Economic and Monetary Union, which will culminate in January 2002 with the introduction of the new EU single currency, the Euro. In order to prepare for the advent of the Euro, Member States are obliged to adhere to common monetary policies to ensure price stability and low inflation in their national economies. They are also obliged to ensure that their economies are open to competition and that they co-ordinate their economic policies in order to ensure stability in the internal market.

Central to this grand plan is the irrevocable fixing of exchange rates as between Member States for the purpose of introducing the Euro as the sole European currency unit. The national currencies will be abolished once the Euro is introduced. At the time of writing, eleven Member States (excluding Britain, Greece, Sweden and Denmark) have committed to joining the Euro in 2002.

As part of this Economic and Monetary Union, the national central banks of the participating Member States have lost autonomy over the setting of national interest rates. This function is now performed solely by the European Central Bank (ECB) based in Frankfurt. Article 108 of the Treaty provides that the ECB shall be independent in its decision-making and shall not take instruction from the Member States. The Governors of the national Central Banks sit on the ECB's Governing Council and the national Central Banks shall form part of the European System of Central Banks (ECSB) whose function, inter alia, under the Treaty is to ensure the implementation of the Community's monetary policies, conduct foreign exchange operations, manage the official reserves of the Member States and contribute to the operation of the prudential system governing the prudential supervision of credit institutions and the stability of the financial system.

Member States are now obliged to avoid excessive budget deficits and promote price stability policies in order to ensure optimal conditions for the arrival of the Euro.

5.3   Free Movement of Workers

5.3.1   SCOPE

The principles of free movement of goods, capital, persons, and services within the EU are essential to the establishment of a common market. Part of the motivation behind the establishment of a common market was to ensure the integration of the European peoples. Without free movement of workers, the internal labour market within the Union would remain inconsistent, with areas of unemployment and low wages and other areas of high wages and labour shortages and no means of ensuring that workers could migrate from the one area to another.

The basic principle of free movement of persons is contained in art 3(c) of the EC Treaty. This seeks to establish 'an internal market, characterised by the abolition, as between Member States, of obstacles to the free movement of goods, persons, services and capital'. These provisions are fleshed out in arts 39–42 on workers, arts 43–48 on rights of establishment and arts 49–55 on services.

The right to freedom of movement is granted to workers, those exercising rights of establishment and those providing services within the Community. They must be nationals of one of the Member States of the Community. A right of free movement is also granted to those with independent means. Directive 90/364 gives effect to this requiring a person exercising the right of residence in another Member State to have sufficient resources, so as not to require social assistance from the State concerned.

The ECJ regards the principle of free movement of persons as fundamental. The provisions of the Treaty relating to free movement of persons have been given a generous interpretation by the Court.

5.3.2 LEGISLATIVE FRAMEWORK

Article 39 provides that:

1. Freedom of movement for workers shall be secured within the Community by the end of the transitional period at the latest.

2. Such freedom of movement shall entail the abolition of any discrimination based on nationality between workers of the member States as regards employment, remuneration and other conditions of work and employment.

3. It shall entail the right, subject to limitations justified on grounds of public policy, public security or public health:

(a) to accept offers of employment actually made;

(b) to move freely within the territory of Member States for this purpose;

(c) to stay in a Member State for the purpose of employment in accordance with the provisions governing the employment of nationals of that State laid down by law, regulation or administrative action;

(d) to remain in the territory of a Member State after having been employed in that State, subject to conditions which shall be embodied in implementing Regulations to be drawn up by the Commission.

4. The provisions of this Article shall not apply to employment in the public service.

Secondary legislation was introduced to give substance to these principles. The principal measures are Directive 68/360 governing rights of entry and residence, Regulation 1612/68 governing access to and conditions of employment, Regulation 1251/70 governing rights to remain in the territory of a Member State after having been employed there and Directive 64/221 governing Member States' right to derogate from the free movement provisions on grounds of public policy, public security or public health.

5.3.3 WHAT IS A WORKER?

The rights granted under art 39 and the secondary legislation are granted to 'workers' and their families. Neither the Treaty nor legislation in this area defines a 'worker'. Thus, it has been left to the ECJ to fill the legislative gap. In Case 53/81 *Levin v Staatssecretaris van Justitie* [1982] ECR 1035 the ECJ held that 'worker' has to be given a Community definition, independent of its meaning in the laws of Member States. As there was no authoritative definition of 'worker' in the Treaty or secondary legislation, it claimed for itself the task of making such a definition. The Court has given the term a wide interpretation.

In Case 66/85 *Lawrie Blum v Land Baden-Württemberg* [1986] ECR 2121, the ECJ held that the essential characteristic of a worker is that he performs a service of some economic value for, and under the direction of, another for remuneration. The worker must be a national of one of the Member States. In this case, the worker was a probationary music teacher. In Case 75/63 *Hoekstra (née Unger) v BBDA* [1964] ECR 177 the ECJ held that the term 'worker' included a person who has lost his/her job but is capable of taking another.

In *Levin* the ECJ held that the term included permanent, seasonal and part-time workers. In the case of part-time workers the occupation must be really genuine. However, it does include employment yielding an income less than that State considers necessary for subsistence. In Case 139/85 *Kempf v Staatssecretaris van Justitie* [1986] ECR 1741, the ECJ further refined its definition, holding that it did not matter that the person earned a small amount of money, provided that he was engaged in a genuine and effective activity. The Court held that a part-time music teacher was a worker. It held that free movement of workers was one of the fundamental freedoms and should be defined broadly. It was irrelevant that the income of the worker was supplemented by state benefits. However, in Case C-357/89 *Raulin* [1992] ECR I 1027 the ECJ held that the duration of the activity concerned was a factor that could be taken into account in assessing whether the employment was effective and genuine or so limited as to be marginal or ancillary.

In Case 196/87 *Steymann v Staatssecretaris van Justitie* [1988] ECR 6195 the ECJ held that the occupation of a member of a religious community who received his keep and 'pocket money' was an effective and genuine activity where commercial activity is an inherent part of membership of that community. In contrast, in Case 344/87 *Battray v Staatssecretaris van Justitie* [1989] ECR 1621 paid activity provided by the State as part of a compulsory drug rehabilitation programme was held not to be 'real and genuine economic activity'. This was not an economic activity as the primary purpose of the scheme was to reintegrate potential workers into the labour market. The objective was social and not economic.

In more recent cases, the ECJ has clarified the concept further, applying objective criteria to the test of 'genuine and effective' work. This could include someone in occupational training if there was proof that the trainee had worked long enough to become fully acquainted with the job performed.

5.3.4   THE FAMILY OF A WORKER

EU legislation provides that the rules on entry and residence for workers, those seeking to establish themselves or provide or receive a service apply, irrespective of nationality, to their spouses and offspring of their own or their spouses who are under the age of twenty-one or who are dependants. Article 10(1) of Regulation 1612/68 defines families as a worker's 'spouse and their descendants who are under the age of twenty-one years or are dependants', and 'dependent relatives in the ascending line of the worker and his spouse'.

5.3.4.1   Spouse

The rights given to spouses of workers are not generally extended to cohabitees. In Case 59/85 *Netherlands State v Reed* [1985] ECR 1283 the ECJ held that the term spouse in art 10(1) only referred to a marital relationship and did not apply to cohabitees. However, the Court held that since aliens cohabiting with Dutch nationals were entitled to reside in the Netherlands it would be discriminatory not to accord the same treatment to workers of other Member States.

Separation, in itself, is insufficient to deprive a spouse of residence rights. In Case 267/83 *Diatta v Land Berlin* [1985] ECR 567, a separated wife, intending to obtain a divorce and living apart from her husband, did not lose her rights of residence in Germany. The ECJ held that even though the spouses were living separately the marital relationship had not dissolved.

The ECJ has made no absolute decision on the effects of divorce on the status of a spouse of a worker. A divorce could be held to have ended the marital bond, thus depriving a spouse of any rights derived from the worker. However, in *R v Secretary of State for the Home Department, ex parte Sandhu* [1982] 2 CMLR 553 Comyn J in the English High Court held that divorce did not necessarily end the marital bond. He said that if a non-EU spouse lost his residence rights through divorce this would 'add a new terror to marriage'. The Court of Appeal and House of Lords disagreed, holding that when his spouse left the country in which he was resident he lost his rights of residence.

Case C-370/90 *R v Immigration Appeal Tribunal and Singh, ex parte Secretary of State for the Home Department* [1992] ECR I-4265 was a similar case. An Indian national living in the United Kingdom had married a United Kingdom national. The couple separated and obtained a decree nisi. Before the divorce became absolute Mr Singh was threatened with deportation from the United Kingdom. The ECJ found in his favour but did not consider the effects of the divorce, which became final after the proceedings.

Article 11 states that:

> *Where a national of a Member State is pursuing an activity as an employed or self-employed person in the territory of another Member State, his spouse and those of the children who are under the age of 21 years or dependent on him shall have the rights to take up any activity as an employed person throughout the territory of that same State, even if they are not nationals of any Member State.*

In Case 131/85 *Emir Gül v Regierungsprasident Düsseldorf* [1986] ECR 1573, a Turkish Cypriot, married to an English woman working in Germany, wished to practise medicine in Germany. He was refused permission because of his nationality. He was a qualified doctor who had already practised part time in Germany. The ECJ held that if he was adequately qualified for the occupation he wished to take up, then under art 11, as a spouse of an EU national, he was entitled to practise.

Article 12 of the regulation, which gives equal access to educational, vocational or training courses, has been extended to spouses by the ECJ. A spouse succeeded in claiming such a right in Case 152/82 *Forcheri v Belgium* [1982] ECR 2323. Forcheri was the wife of an Italian working in Brussels. She was given a place on a social work training course in Brussels, but was required to pay an additional fee, which was not charged, to Belgian students. She claimed that this was discriminatory on the basis of arts 12 and 39 and art 12 of the regulation. The Court held that to require of a national of another Member State, lawfully established in the first Member State, a fee which is not required of its own nationals is discrimination by reason of nationality which is prohibited by art 12.

5.3.4.2 Children

Article 12 provides that children are entitled to non-discriminatory access to general educational, apprenticeship and vocational training courses. The entitlement includes entitlement both to admission to courses and also such funding as may be available to aid in attendance. In Case 42/87 *Commission v Belgium (re higher education funding)* [1989] 1 CMLR 457 the Court held that children of migrant EU workers are entitled to full national treatment as regards all forms of state education, even if the working parent has retired or died. In Cases 389 & 390/87 *Echternach and Moritz v Minister van Onderwijis en Wetenschapper* [1989] ECR 723 children of German parents working in the Netherlands wished to remain there to complete their college studies when their parents moved back to Germany. The ECJ held that they could. The Court held that the integration of the children of migrant workers into the education system and society of the host nation was of great importance, and the value of this would be lost if, when the parents decided to leave the host State, their children were in some way disadvantaged. In such cases, the children would retain their status as 'children of a family', even where the workers had returned to their home State – though this status would cease on completion of the course of education.

A similar approach was taken in Case C-7/94 *Gaal* [1995] ECR I-1031. It was held that the orphaned child of a deceased Belgian worker, living in Germany, who was over the age of twenty-one and not financially dependent on the remaining parent, was entitled to claim equality with nationals under art 25 in order to obtain finance from the German authorities for studies in Scotland. The ECJ held that the definition of family could not be invoked to limit financial assistance to students by age or dependency.

5.3.5 RIGHTS OF ENTRY AND RESIDENCE

5.3.5.1 General rights

Directive 68/360 regulates rights of entry and residence. They comprise the following rights for the worker and his family:

1. To leave their home State in order for the worker to pursue activities as an employed person in another Member State (art 2).

153

2.   To enter the territory of another Member State 'simply on production of a valid identity card or passport' (art 3(1)). Entry visas may not be demanded except for members of the family who are not nationals of a Member State. Member States are required to accord to such persons every facility for obtaining the necessary visas (art 3(2)). In Case 157/79 *R v Pieck* [1980] ECR 2171 a requirement by the UK authorities that individuals from other Member States should obtain a written 'leave' to enter the UK was held by the ECJ to be contrary to art 3(2).

3.   To obtain a residence permit on the production of the document with which the worker entered the country and a confirmation of engagement from the employer or a certificate of employment (art 4(3)(a)). Members of his/her family must produce their documents of entry, a document of entry proving their relationship to the worker, to be issued by the competent authority of the State of origin or the State from which they came. Dependants must also produce a document from the same authorities testifying that they are dependent on the worker or that they live under his roof in that country (art 4(3)(c), (d) and (e)).

The residence permit must be valid throughout the territory of the Member State which issued it. It must be valid for at least five years from the date of issue and it must be automatically renewable (art 6(1)). Breaks in residence not exceeding six months and absence on military service are not to affect the validity of a residence permit (art 6(2)).

Residence permits may not be withdrawn from a worker on the grounds that he is no longer in employment, due to illness or accident or because he is involuntarily unemployed (art 7(1)). When the residence permit is renewed for the first time the period of residence may be restricted (but not to less than twelve months) if the worker has been involuntarily unemployed for more than twelve consecutive months.

Temporary workers (working from two to twelve months) are entitled to temporary residence permits for the duration of their employment (art 6(3)). Seasonal workers and those working for less than three months are entitled to reside during the period of their employment without a residence permit (art 8).

5.3.5.2   Case law

These provisions have been given a generous interpretation by the ECJ. In Case 48/75 *Procureur du Roi v Royer* [1976] ECR 497 the ECJ held that the right of entry in art 3, included a right to enter 'in search of work'. Case C-292/89 *R v Immigration Appeal Tribunal, ex parte Antonnissen* [1991] ECR I-745, established that art 39 protects an individual who migrates in order to seek work. The Court in that case suggested that after a period of six months a person could be deported if he/she had not found work and has no genuine prospect of finding it. However, the ECJ did not impose a specific time limit.

Though the right to enter a Member State in search of work is available to all EU citizens, the right to a residence permit would appear to be conditional on the finding of employment. However, once in employment, the ECJ has held that a worker's right to reside in the State where he is employed is not dependent on his possession of a residence permit. The right to residence is derived from art 39 and not from implementing legislation or from documents issued by national authorities. Thus, neither a worker nor his family may be denied entry to, or be deported from, a Member State merely because they do not possess a valid residence permit. As long as the worker has a right of residence as a worker, he will be entitled to reside as long as he would have been entitled had he been in possession of a residence permit (normally five years in addition to a minimum of one further year). As long as the worker is entitled to stay, so will his family.

However, a State is entitled to demand that migrant workers and their families comply with its administrative formalities on immigration, and may even impose penalties in the form of fines for non-compliance, provided that the penalties are not disproportionate. In Case 265/88 *Messner* [1989] ECR 4209 a time limit of three days from crossing the frontier in which aliens were required to register their presence with Italian police, sanctioned by criminal penalties, was found to be unreasonable.

Article 7(1) of Directive 68/360 provides that a valid residence permit cannot be withdrawn if the worker becomes incapable of work through illness or accident or involuntary unemployment. However, it implies that the right will be lost if he is *voluntarily* unemployed. The 'competent employment office' is to determine whether unemployment is voluntary or involuntary. In Case 171/91 *Dimitrios Tsiotras* [1993] ECR I-2925 an unemployed Greek who had worked in Germany before Greece's accession to the EC, but who was unemployed at the time of accession and subsequently and had no reasonable prospect of obtaining employment in Germany, was held by the ECJ not to have acquired a right to reside in Germany.

Directive 68/360 makes special provision for temporary and seasonal workers. A temporary worker who works from three to twelve months in another Member State is entitled to a temporary residence permit in that State, to coincide with the expected period of employment (art 6(3)). Those who work for less than three months in another State, or who work only seasonally, are entitled to reside in that State during the period of employment, but are not entitled to a residence permit (art 8).

5.3.6 REGULATION 1612/68

5.3.6.1 Purpose of Regulation

Regulation 1612/68 was passed to implement arts 39(2) and (3)(a) and (b). Its preamble states that the free movement of workers requires: 'the abolition of any discrimination based on nationality between workers of the Member States as regards employment, remuneration and other conditions of work and employment'. It also requires, in order that the right to free movement may be exercised 'in freedom and dignity', equality of treatment in 'all matters relating to the actual pursuit of activities as employed persons' and that 'obstacles to the mobility of workers shall be eliminated, in particular as regards the worker's right to be joined by his family and the conditions for the integration of that family into the host country'. The ECJ has placed great reliance on this preamble in interpreting the regulation.

5.3.6.2 Eligibility for employment

Article 1 of the regulation provides that any national of a Member State has the right to take up activity as an employed person, and pursue such activity, in the territory of another Member State under the same conditions as nationals of that State. A Member State may not discriminate, overtly or covertly, against non-nationals, by limiting applications and offers of employment (art 3(1)), or by prescribing special recruitment procedures or limiting advertising or in any other way impeding recruitment of non-resident workers (art 3(2)). Member States may not restrict by number or percentage the number of foreign nationals to be employed in any activity or area of activity (art 4). In Case 169/73 *Commission v France (re French merchant seamen)* [1975] ECR 117 the ECJ held that a requirement of the French Code du Travail Maritime 1926 requiring a ratio of three French to one non-French person serving on crews of French merchant ships was in breach of EU law.

Member States must offer non-national applicants the same assistance in seeking employment as are available to nationals (art 5). However, States may impose conditions on non-nationals 'relating to linguistic knowledge required by reason of the nature of the post to be filled' (art 3(1)). In Case 379/87 *Groener v Minister for Education* [1989] ECR 3967 the ECJ held that a requirement of Irish law that teachers in vocational schools in Ireland should be proficient in the Irish language would be permissible under art 3(1) in view of the clear policy of national law to maintain and promote the use of the Irish language as a means of expressing national identity and culture. The Irish language was the first official language of Ireland. Such a requirement must not be disproportionate to the objective to be pursued. A similar approach was taken in Case 272/92 *Maria Chiara Spotti* [1993] ECR I-5185. This case concerned a challenge to a German law permitting contracts of limited duration for foreign language teaching assistants. The ECJ held that such contracts would only be permitted if they were objectively justified. The ECJ found these contracts not to be justified, as the justification put forward was that they ensured up-to-date tuition.

An employer may require a non-national to undergo a vocational test provided he expressly requests this when making his offer of employment (art 6(2)). However, this provision cannot be used as a means of hidden discrimination.

5.3.6.3 Conditions of work

Article 7(1) of the regulation provides that:

> *A worker who is a national of a Member State may not, in the territory of another Member State, be treated differently from national workers by reason of his nationality in respect of any conditions of employment and work, in particular as regards remuneration, dismissal, and should he become unemployed, reinstatement or re-employment.*

This article covers both direct and indirect discrimination. In Case 15/69 *Württembergische Milchverwertung-Südmilch-AG v Ugliola* [1969] ECR 363, a condition whereby a German employer took into account, for the purposes of calculating seniority, employees' periods of national service in Germany, thereby prejudicing an employee such as Ugliola, who was required to perform his national service in Italy, was held unlawful under this article. In Case 152/73 *Sotgiu v Deutsche Bundespost* [1974] ECR 153, the German post office's decision to pay increased separation allowances only to workers living away from home in Germany, was held to be capable of breaching art 7(1).

5.3.6.4 Social advantages

Article 7(2) of Regulation 1612/68 provides that a migrant worker 'shall enjoy the same social and tax advantages as national workers'. This term has been interpreted very widely by the ECJ. In Case 32/75 *Fiorini v SNCF* [1975] ECR 1985 the ECJ held that unlike some of the provisions under art 7(1), the rights granted under art 7(2) do not have to be related to some contract of employment and may remain even when the worker dies so that his family may benefit from them. The case concerned a claim by an Italian woman, the widow of an Italian who had worked for the French railways and who was living in France, for a special fare reduction card issued by the French railways to parents of large families. Her husband had claimed it while he was alive. She was refused the card, as she was not a French national. She claimed discrimination in breach of art 12 of the Treaty and art 7(2) of the Regulation. The ECJ held that since the family had a right to remain in France under EU law (Regulation 1251/70), they were entitled under art 7(2) to equal 'social advantages'.

This was followed in Case 207/78 *Ministère Public v Even* [1979] ECR 2109. The ECJ stated that the social advantages, which accrued under art 7(2), could be taken to mean all advantages 'generally granted to national workers primarily because of their objective status as workers or by virtue of the mere fact of their residence on national territory'. On the basis of this reasoning migrant workers have been held entitled to, amongst other things, a special discretionary childbirth loan which was purported to be payable only to German nationals in Germany (Case 65/81 *Reina v Landeskreditbank Baden-Württemberg* [1982] ECR 33); a payment made to all old people in Belgium (Case 261/83 *Castelli v ONPTS* [1984] ECR 3199); a Belgian minimum income payment; a tiding-over allowance payable to young job seekers; and a scholarship to study abroad which was part of a reciprocal agreement between Belgium and Germany (Case 235/87 *Matteucci v Communauté Luxembourg* [1988] ECR 5889).

The right to social benefit on the same basis as national workers was restricted by Case 316/ 85 *Centre Public de l'Aide Sociale de Courcelles v Lebon* [1987] ECR 2811. In that case the ECJ held that the rights given under art 7(2) were only for the benefit of workers and not for nationals of Member States migrating in search of employment. The latter are not entitled to full equality of treatment. It concerned the claim of a French national, Lebon, for the Belgian minimex (Belgian minimum income payment). She was living in Belgium and based her claim on the fact that she was looking for work there.

5.3.6.5 Access to training

Article 7(3) provides that migrant workers may avail themselves of vocational training and retraining courses, which are provided for national workers. The ECJ has given this article a very broad interpretation. In Case 9/74 *Casagrande v Landeshauptstadt München* [1974] ECR 773 the Court held that the right to be admitted to educational, vocational and training courses included not only admission but 'general measures to facilitate attendance'. This included grants. Since then, it has become accepted that grants and loans are 'social advantages' under art 7(2) and require no special treatment under art 7(3). This was the approach taken by the ECJ in Case 197/86 *Brown* [1988] ECR 3205 and Case 39/86 *Lair* [1989] ECR 3161. Brown had obtained a place at the University of Cambridge to study engineering and Lair obtained a place at the University of Hanover to study languages. They claimed maintenance grants from the UK and German authorities. Lair was French and Brown, though he had dual French/English nationality, had for many years been domiciled in France. Before taking up his place Brown had obtained sponsorship from, and worked for, a Scots company. The job lasted for eight months and was intended as a preparation for his studies. Lair had worked intermittently in Germany for over five years, with spells of involuntary unemployment. Both were refused a grant and challenged that refusal on the basis of arts 7(2) and 7(3). The ECJ took a narrow interpretation of art 7(3) and said that it applied only to vocational training – institutions offering sandwich or apprenticeship courses. The Court held that neither course would constitute vocational training. The ECJ held that a university maintenance grant could be considered a social advantage under art 7(2). Were the applicants 'workers'? The Court said that while Brown might be regarded as a worker, he was not entitled to claim the grant as a social advantage as he had acquired the status of worker exclusively as a result of his having been accepted for admission to university. His employment was ancillary to the studies to be financed by a grant. In relation to Lair, the ECJ drew a distinction between a migrant worker, who was involuntarily unemployed and legitimately resident, and one who gave up his work in order to undertake further training in the host State. The latter might only claim a grant for such a course if there was some link between the studies to be pursued and his previous work activity.

5.3.6.6 Trade union rights

Article 8 provides that workers should be entitled to avail themselves of membership of trade unions and attendant rights without discrimination.

5.3.6.7 Housing

Article 9 provides that both public and private housing should be made available to migrant workers on the same terms and conditions that are given to nationals of the host State.

5.3.7 FREE MOVEMENT OF NON WORKERS

The EU is increasingly moving away from economic justifications for the conferring of rights towards a more social-minded approach. There are now a number of measures to facilitate the free movement of those who are not economically active but wish to have the freedom to move between, and to take up residence in, any of the Member States.

5.3.7.1 Retired

Regulations 1251/70 and 90/365 provide that under certain circumstances nationals of a Member State who have worked as employed persons in another Member State and their families as defined in Regulation 1612/68 may continue to reside in the host Member State at the end of their employment there. There are three conditions to be met:

1. the worker must have resided in the host Member State for the last twelve months, have resided there for the last thirty-six months and have now retired, or

2. have resided in the host Member State for the last twenty-four months and have ceased employment due to a permanent incapacity preventing work, or

3. after thirty-six months employment and residence in the host Member State take up employment in another Member State while continuing to reside in the host State.

The worker's family may continue to reside in the host Member State after the death of the worker if, at the time of his death, he had acquired the right to reside there under this regulation. Even where the worker had not acquired such a right his family will have a right of residence if he had resided there continuously for twenty-four months prior to his death, or he died as a result of an occupational illness or accident, or his surviving spouse is a national of the host Member State.

Periods of absence from the host Member State of less than three months do not count against continuity of residence, nor do absences due to obligatory military service. Neither does involuntary unemployment nor absences due to illness or accidents.

5.3.7.2 Students and the economically inactive

Directives to ensure a right of movement for students and those not economically active were adopted in 1990 and came into force in 1992. Directive 93/96 confers a right of residence for students and Directive 90/364 confers a general right of residence for the economically inactive.

Directive 93/96 gives students the right to move freely in the EU in order to attend a training course in another Member State. Students, their spouses and dependent children are granted a residence permit for the duration of their studies.

Before a student may rely on the terms of the directive, he must first of all be accepted to attend a vocational training course in the host Member State. The student is also required to assure the authorities by means of a declaration that:

(a) he has sufficient resources to avoid becoming a burden on the host State's social assistance system during the period of residence;

(b) he is enrolled in a recognised educational establishment for the principal purpose of following a vocational training course there, and

(c) he is covered by sickness insurance in respect of all risks in the host State.

The right of residence may be limited in time to the duration of the studies pursued and may be granted only for the purpose of the studies. Article 2(2) of the directive allows Member States to derogate from the provisions of the directive on grounds of public policy, public security or public health.

5.3.7.3 Residual category

Directive 90/3645 grants a right of residence to nationals of Member States who do not enjoy this right under other provisions of EU law. The directive requires that the person have sufficient resources to avoid becoming a burden on the social assistance system of the host Member State. Persons seeking to rely on the directive must also have sickness insurance cover.

The spouse and dependent children of a beneficiary of the directive are entitled to take up any employment or self-employed activity within the host State, even if they are not EU nationals. Member States may derogate from the terms of the directive on grounds of public policy, public security or public health.

5.3.8 RIGHTS OF CITIZENSHIP

The Maastricht Treaty introduced the concept of community citizenship. The citizenship provisions are now contained in arts 18–21 of the EC Treaty. They provide that 'every citizen holding the nationality of a Member State shall be a citizen of the Union'. A number of rights are attached to this citizenship, including a general right to free movement, a right to stand for election and vote in municipal and European Parliament elections, and a right of residence. Article 18 provides that:

> every citizen of the Union shall have the right to move and reside freely within the territory of the Member States, subject to the limitations and conditions laid down in this Treaty and by the measures adopted to give it effect.

The limitations on free movement in the Treaty apply to the rights of citizens. These rights are relatively new as yet and are not very well developed.

5.3.9 LIMITATIONS ON RIGHT TO FREE MOVEMENT OF WORKERS

5.3.9.1 Generally

The Treaty itself places certain limitations on the provisions relating to free movement of workers. Article 39(3) sets out the rights attaching to freedom of movement for workers, but states that these are 'subject to limitations justified on grounds of public policy, public security or public health'.

Directive 64/221 ([1963-4] OJ Spec Ed 117) was adopted on 25 February 1965 pursuant to art 46(2), which provides for the issuing of directives to co-ordinate the public policy, security and health measures. It gives substance to the restrictions provided for in the Treaty. Though the preamble to the Directive only refers to art 46 it covers workers, the self-employed and the recipients of services.

The scope of the Directive is twofold. First, it lays down the principles on which a State may refuse entry or residence to those who would otherwise be eligible, on grounds of public policy, public security or public health. Secondly, it sets out very strict procedural safeguards, which must be followed by States when they are seeking to exclude non-nationals. The Directive applies to all those coming within the free movement provisions of the Treaty. It applies to the employed, the self-employed, their families, those who move within the EU as 'recipients of services', persons of independent means, the retired and students.

The Directive lays down the circumstances in which measures taken by Member States on the grounds of public policy, public security or public health, may and may not be taken. 'Measures' taken on grounds of public policy, public security or public health were defined in Case 30/77 *R v Bouchereau* [1977] ECR 1999 as any action affecting the rights of persons coming within the field of application of art 39 to enter and reside freely in a Member State on the same conditions as apply to nationals of the host State.

The permitted grounds must not be invoked for economic reasons (art 2(2) of the Directive). A person has the right to be informed of the reasons for refusal of entry or expulsion, the right of appeal to a court of law and the right, except in cases of urgency, to remain for at least fifteen days (entry) or a month (expulsion).

Article 3(3) provides that 'Expiry of the identity card or passport used by the person concerned to enter the host country and to obtain a residence permit shall not justify expulsion from the territory'. In Case 48/75 *Procureur du Roi v Royer* [1976] ECR 497 the ECJ noted that the right of residence does not depend on the possession of a residence permit – it merely provides proof of such a right, which is derived from the Treaty. The same principle applies to identity cards and passports. The ECJ held in Case 118/75 *Watson & Belmann* [1976] ECR 1185 that Member States are free to require foreign nationals to comply with registration procedures. However, it also held that if these procedures limited the free movement of workers or restricted their rights of residence they would contravene art 39. In Case 8/77 *Sagulo, Brenca and Bakhouche* [1977] ECR 1495, the ECJ held that German legislation imposing penalties on non-nationals who did not acquire identity documents did not violate art 39. The Court once again pointed out that the penalties must not be 'so severe as to cause an obstacle to the freedom of entry and residence provided for in the Treaty'. Case 157/79 *R v Pieck* [1980] ECR 2171 establishes that a State is not free to deny entry on the basis that the persons concerned do not have residence permits.

5.3.9.2 Public policy

The meaning of the terms 'public security' and 'public health' are relatively clear (see section **5.3.9.2** and **5.3.9.3**). However, the meaning of the public policy derogation is less clear.

In Case 41/74 *Van Duyn v Home Office* [1974] ECR 1337, the ECJ held that the concept of public policy must be interpreted strictly. Member States cannot determine its scope unilaterally, without being subject to control by EU institutions.

Personal conduct

Measures adopted upon grounds of public policy or public security must be based exclusively upon an individual's 'personal conduct'. Article 3(1) of the directive requires measures taken on grounds of public policy (or public security) to be based exclusively on the personal conduct of the individual concerned. Personal conduct does not have to be illegal. In *Van Duyn* the ECJ was disinclined to regard a person's past association with an organisation as amounting to personal conduct. Van Duyn was a Dutch national, who was refused entry into the United Kingdom on grounds of public policy. She wished to take up a job with the Church of Scientology. Scientology was not illegal in the UK but it was regarded as socially undesirable. The matter was referred to the ECJ, which was asked whether membership of an organisation could count as 'personal conduct' and whether the conduct should be illegal to justify exclusion on public policy grounds. The Court distinguished between past association and present association, stating that the former cannot be seen as personal conduct whereas the latter can. The Court also held that conduct does not have to be illegal to justify exclusion of non-nationals provided that the State has made it clear that it considers the activities to be 'socially harmful' and has taken administrative measures to counteract them. This definition must be read in the light of a more restrictive test advanced in Case 30/77 *R v Bouchereau* [1977] ECR 1999. The activities must be sufficiently socially harmful to pose a genuine and sufficiently serious threat to the requirements of public policy affecting one of the fundamental interests of society.

The kind of evidence required to prove that a particular activity is considered by the State to be sufficiently harmful to justify exclusion on the grounds of public policy was considered by the ECJ in Cases 115 & 116/81 *Adoui and Cornuaille v Belgian State* [1982] ECR 1665. Two prostitutes appealed against the Belgian authorities' refusal to grant them a residence permit in Belgium where they were seeking to practise their trade. The ECJ held that Member States could not deny residence to non-nationals by reason of conduct which, when attributable to a State's own nationals, did not give rise to repressive measures or other genuine and effective measures to combat such conduct. Thus, evidence of measures of this nature will have to be adduced to prove that the public policy justification is genuine.

Article 3(2) of the directive requires something more than previous convictions in order to justify reliance on public policy to justify a derogation. This was underlined by Case 36/75 *Ruitili v Ministre de l'Intérieur* [1975] ECR 1219. Ruitili, an Italian political agitator, had been restricted by the Minister to certain regions of France. The ECJ held that restrictions could not be imposed on the right of a national of a Member State to enter the territory of another Member State, to stay there and to move within it, unless his presence represents a 'genuine and sufficiently serious threat to public policy'.

The ECJ has also established that current criminal convictions in themselves may not be sufficient to justify a derogation. In Case 67/74 *Bonsignore v Oberstadtdirektor of the City of Cologne* [1975] ECR 297, an Italian worker living in Germany bought a pistol in breach of German firearms law and accidentally shot his brother. He was fined for unlawful possession of a firearm and his deportation was ordered. Germany argued that his deportation was necessary as a general preventative measure to deter other immigrants from committing similar offences. The ECJ disagreed. It held that the concept of personal conduct expresses the requirement that a deportation order may only be made for breaches of the peace and public security, which might be committed by the individual concerned. Deportation could not be based on reasons of a general preventative nature.

In *Bouchereau* a French worker in the UK was convicted of two drugs offences. An English magistrate wished to recommend his deportation. There was a reference to the ECJ on the meaning of art 3(2) of the Directive. The Court held that

'[T]he existence of a previous criminal conviction can, therefore, only be taken into account in so far as the circumstances which gave rise to that conviction are evidence of personal conduct constituting a present threat to the requirements of public policy'.

The ECJ defined public policy for this purpose and said that there must be 'a genuine and sufficiently serious threat affecting one of the fundamental interests of society'.

5.3.9.3 Public health

The only diseases or disabilities which may justify refusal of entry (but not expulsion) are those listed in the annex to the directive. Member States may not add unilaterally to the list. The annex lists a number of 'highly infectious or contagious' diseases, such as tuberculosis and syphilis and then refers to 'other infectious diseases'. It also includes drug addiction and profound mental disturbance. However, art 4(2) provides that diseases or disabilities occurring after a residence permit has been issued 'shall not justify refusal to renew the residence permit or expulsion from the territory'. Article 6 requires the person concerned to be informed of the public health grounds on which he is refused entry or a residence permit.

5.3.9.4 Public security

The same considerations apply to the ground of public security as to public policy, discussed above. A decision to exclude on grounds of public security must be based on personal conduct.

The ECJ seems to have laid the foundations of another restriction in *Ruitili*. In that case, the Court looked to the European Convention on Human Rights. The ECJ held that the public policy limitation was a specific manifestation of the more general principle contained in arts 8, 9, 10 and 11 of the Convention and art 2 of the Fourth Protocol to the Convention. According to these provisions, no restrictions in the interests of public security could be placed on the rights given by these articles other than such as are necessary for the protection of those interests 'in a democratic society'. From the tenor of this judgment, it would appear that the public security exception may only be relied on if to do so would be necessary in a democratic society.

5.3.9.5 Procedural rights

Directive 64/221 provides extensive procedural safeguards for parties seeking to assert rights of entry or residence in Member States. These are as follows:

Temporary residence

Where a person's identity card or passport has expired or the nationality of the holder is in dispute the State that issued that identity card or passport must allow its holder to re-enter its territory without formalities (art 3(4)).

A person awaiting a decision to grant or refuse a first residence permit in a Member State must be allowed to remain temporarily in that State pending that decision. The decision must be taken as soon as possible and not more than six months from the date of application (art 5(1)).

In the event of a decision to refuse the issue of a residence permit or to expel a person from the territory of a Member State that person shall be allowed, 'save in cases of urgency', not less than fifteen days (if he had not yet been granted a residence permit), or one month (in all other cases), in which to leave the country (art 7).

Reasons for decisions

Article 6 provides that:

> *The person concerned shall be informed of the grounds of public policy, public security or public health upon which the decision taken in his case is based, unless this is contrary to the interests of the security of the State involved.*

In *Rutili* the ECJ held that the authority making the decision must give the applicant a precise and comprehensive statement of the grounds for the decision, to enable the applicant to take effective steps to prepare his defence.

Remedies: rights of defence

Article 8 provides:

> *The person concerned shall have the same legal remedies in respect of any decision concerning entry, or refusing the issue or renewal of a residence permit, or ordering expulsion from the territory, as are available to nationals of the State concerned in respect of acts of the administration.*

Therefore, all domestic public law remedies must be made available to him/her.

Article 9(1) provides:

> *Where there is no right of appeal to a court of law, or where such an appeal may be only in respect of the legal validity of the decision, or where the appeal cannot have suspensory effect, a decision refusing renewal of a permit from the territory shall not be taken by the administrative authority, save in cases of urgency, until an opinion has been obtained from a competent authority of the host country before which the person concerned enjoys such rights of defence and of assistance or representation as the domestic law of that country provides for.*
>
> *This authority shall not be the same as that empowered to take the decision refusing renewal of the residence permit or ordering expulsion.*

Where the remedies provided by art 8 are insufficient, art 9 provides a safety net, incorporating the minimum requirements of natural justice. Questions concerning the scope of art 9 were raised in Case 131/79 *R v Secretary of State for the Home Department, ex parte Santillo* [1980] ECR 1585. Santillo, an Italian, had been convicted in the UK of a number of crimes of violence. He was sentenced to eight years in jail, with a recommendation for deportation at the end of his sentence. Nearly five years later the UK Government made a deportation order against him. He applied for a judicial review to quash this decision. The issue arose as to whether the judge's recommendation was an 'opinion from a competent

162

authority' as required by art 9 and whether the lapse of time would deprive it of this status if it was. The ECJ held that it was. It also held that the safeguard in art 9 could only be a real one if that opinion were sufficiently proximate in time to the decision recommending deportation to ensure that the factors justifying deportation still existed at the time when the order was made.

The scope of art 9(2) was more recently considered in Case C-175/94 *R v Secretary of State for the Home Department, ex parte Gallagher* [1995] ECR I-4253. Gallagher had been convicted in Ireland for the possession of rifles for unlawful purposes. He subsequently went to England and took up employment there. He was arrested and deported. On arrival in Dublin, he challenged the deportation decision as unlawful. At his request, the Home Secretary reconsidered his case but the deportation decision was not reversed. He challenged the decision under art 9, questioning the status of those bodies as 'competent authorities'. The ECJ found that the matter fell within art 9(2), which provides for challenge before a competent authority after the deportation decision had been made, and only at the request of the person concerned. Article 9 does not specify how the competent authority should be appointed or what its composition should be. However, it was essential that it should be independent of the authority empowered to take the measure concerning deportation, and that the person concerned should be able to submit his or her defence. There was no need to notify the claimant of the identity of the authority as long as the national court was in a position to determine whether it was impartial.

5.3.9.6 Public service

Article 39(4) states that the provisions of art 39 do not apply to those working in the public service. The ECJ defines this restrictively. The provision was included in the Treaty to protect certain essential positions within the public service of Member States. Article 39(4) does not apply to all positions in the public service. When a national of another Member State is employed within the host nation's public services, he cannot be discriminated against on the basis of his nationality. In Case 152/73 *Sotgiu v Deutsche Bundespost* [1974] ECR 153 the ECJ stated that art 39(4) did not apply to all public service positions, being restricted to 'certain activities', connected with the exercise of official authority. Sotgiu had argued that German post office rules giving extra allowances to workers living apart from their families were discriminatory. The ECJ held that art 39(4) only applied to conditions of access.

The ECJ expanded on this in Case 149/79 *Commission v Belgium (re public employees)* [1980] ECR 3881. In that case Belgium argued that the term 'public service posts', restricted by Belgian law to Belgian nationals, covered a considerable range of positions including nurses, plumbers, electricians, unskilled workers and architects. France and Germany supported the arguments of the Belgian government. The ECJ rejected this argument, holding that public service was an EU concept rather than one of the Member States and that art 39(4) only referred to those positions, which involved safeguarding the interests of the State. The Court held that:

> '[I]t removes from the ambit of article 39(1)-(3) a series of posts which involve direct or indirect participation in the exercise of powers conferred by public law and duties designed to safeguard the general interests of the State or of other public authorities. Such posts in fact presume on the part of those occupying them the existence of a special relationship of allegiance to the State and reciprocity of rights and duties which form the bond of nationality.'

In the opinion of the ECJ plumbers, electricians and the like did not carry out such weighty tasks. In later decisions the Court has held that regardless of how they are viewed by the Member States, nurses, school teachers and university lecturers are not employees in the public service with regard to the aim of art 39(4). Similar proceedings were successfully brought against France in Case 307/84 *Commission v France (re French nurses)* [1986] ECR 1725. The French law in question had limited the appointment of nurses in French hospitals to French nationals.

When a particular job involves the 'exercise of official authority' is not always clear. It does not apply to civil servants generally. To constitute employment in the public service, employees must be charged with the exercise of powers conferred by public law or must be responsible for 'safeguarding the general interests of the State'. In Case C-4/91 *Bleis v Ministère de l'Education* [1991] ECR I-5627 the ECJ held that the concept of public service 'presumes on the part of those occupying such posts the existence of a special relationship of allegiance to the State and reciprocity of rights and duties which form the foundation of the bond of nationality.'

In 1988, the Commission published a notice (88/C 72/02, OJ 1988 C72/2) stating that it intended to examine employment in public health care services, teaching in State educational establishments, research for non-military purposes in public establishments and public bodies responsible for administering commercial services. The Commission stated that the ECJ had demonstrated that these types of employment were sufficiently far away from the activities which art 39(4) was supposed to protect to fall very rarely under that proviso. It advised that nationals of other Member States be permitted access to posts in bodies which administer public services, such as public transport, supply of electricity and gas, airlines and shipping lines, post and telecommunications and in radio and television companies, public health care services, state education and research for non-military purposes conducted in public establishments.

The restrictive interpretation of the public services exception has recently been re-affirmed by the ECJ in three joined cases – Case C-473/93 *Commission v Grand Duchy of Luxembourg* [1996] ECR I-3207, Case C-173/94 *Commission v Kingdom of Belgium* [1996] ECR I-3265 and Case C-290/94 *Commission v Hellenic Republic* [1996] ECR I-3285. Despite the Commission notice and ensuing correspondence, Luxembourg, Belgium and Greece had persisted in a blanket exclusion of non-nationals from jobs in such areas as health, transport, teaching, post and telecommunications and the distribution of water, gas and electricity. In Greece the exclusion extended to membership of the Athens Opera and municipal and local orchestras. The ECJ held that these posts were too remote from the specific activities of the public service to avail of art 39(4). It therefore held that Luxembourg, Belgium and Greece had acted in breach of art 39 and art 1 of Regulation 1612/68.

5.4 Establishment and Services

The right of establishment and the freedom to provide services are generally dealt with together as they have so many common features. Articles 43–48 of the Treaty deal with the right of establishment. Articles 49–55 deal with the right to provision of services.

5.4.1 ESTABLISHMENT

Article 43 provides:

> *Within the framework of the provisions set out below, restrictions on the freedom of establishment of nationals of a Member State in the territory of another Member State shall be prohibited. Such prohibition shall also apply to restrictions on the setting-up of agencies, branches or subsidiaries by nationals of any Member State established in the territory of any Member State.*

> *Freedom of establishment shall include the right to take up and pursue activities as self-employed persons and to set up and manage undertakings, in particular companies and firms within the meaning of the second paragraph of Article 48, under the conditions laid down for its own nationals by the law of the country where such establishment is effected, subject to the provisions of the Chapter relating to capital.*

'Companies and firms' are defined in art 48 as being bodies which have been formed under civil or commercial law. This includes co-operative societies and other legal persons. An exception is made for non-profit making bodies.

5.4.2 SERVICES

Article 49 provides:

Within the framework of the provisions set out below, restrictions on freedom to provide services within the Community shall be prohibited in respect of nationals of Member States who are established in a State of the Community other than that of the person for whom the services are provided.

Article 50(3) provides:

Services shall be considered to be 'services' within the meaning of this Treaty where they are normally provided for remuneration, insofar as they are not governed by the provisions relating to freedom of movement for goods, capital and persons.

'Services' shall in particular include:

(a) activities of an industrial character;

(b) activities of a commercial character;

(c) activities of craftsmen;

(d) activities of the professions.

Without prejudice to the provisions on the Chapter relating to the right of establishment, the person providing a service may, in order to do so, temporarily pursue his activity in the State where the service is provided, under the same conditions as are imposed by that State on its own nationals.

The differences between the right of establishment and the right to provide services are minimal. Both apply to business and professional activity pursued for 'profit' or 'remuneration'. A right of establishment is the right to install oneself, to 'set up shop' in another Member State, permanently or semi-permanently, whether as an individual, a partnership or a company, for the purpose of performing a particular activity there. In contrast, the right to provide services involves the provision of services in one State, on a temporary or periodical basis, by a person established in another State. For the provision of services, it is not necessary to reside, even temporarily, in the State in which the service is provided. Thus, an Irish solicitor moving to Scotland to set up a firm specialising in advising Scots companies how to deal with Irish law would be exercising the right to establish. In Case C-55/94 *Gebhard v Consiglio dell'Ordine degli Avvocati e Procuratori di Milano* [1995] ECR I - 4165 a German lawyer opened an office in Italy. The ECJ held that he was exercising his right to establishment. It is possible to be established in more than one State through a second professional base.

These rights are accorded under the Treaty to EU nationals and to companies formed according to the law of one of the Member States. In Case 205/84 *Commission v Germany ('insurance services')* [1986] ECR 3755, the ECJ suggested that an enterprise would fall within the concept of 'establishment' where its presence consisted of an office managed by the enterprise's own staff or by an independent person who is authorised to work on a permanent basis for the enterprise.

The ECJ has described the right to provide services and the right of establishment as 'fundamental Community rights'. The principle on which these rights are based is the principle of non-discrimination on grounds of nationality, whether arising from legislation, regulation or administrative practice. Both provisions are directly effective.

Secondary legislation has been enacted granting rights of entry and residence to the self-employed. Directive 73/148 (OJ (Special Edition) 1975 L 14/10) gives rights of entry and residence into Member States. Article 4(1) of the Directive provides that those who establish themselves are entitled to a residence permit to be valid for not less than five years from the date of issue and automatically renewable. Article 4(2) provides that in the case of services the right of residence 'is of equal duration with the period during which the services are provided'. Directive 75/34 gives the right to remain permanently in a Member State after having been self-employed there.

5.4.3 LIMITATIONS

5.4.3.1 General

The right of establishment and freedom to provide services are not absolute. Both are subject to derogations on the grounds of public policy, public security or public health. These derogations are found in arts 46 and 55 and in Directive 64/221. Economic grounds cannot be used to justify restrictions and any measures taken must be proportionate to the aims to be achieved. Both rights are also expressed not to apply to 'activities which in that State are connected, even occasionally, with the exercise of official authority'.

These rights are also subject to another limitation. The right to equality of opportunity may only be exercised 'under the conditions laid down for its own nationals by the law of the country where such establishment is effected' (art 43(2)) or 'under the same conditions as are imposed by that State on its own nationals' (art 50(3)). The difficulty for non-nationals seeking to establish themselves in another Member State or to provide services there is that they may not be able to satisfy the conditions laid down in that State for the practice of the particular trade or profession which they wish to exercise. The relevant conditions are those prescribed by trade or professional bodies relating to the education and training required for qualification for the job and rules of professional conduct. These vary greatly from State to State. The need to comply with them is a strong barrier to freedom of movement for the self-employed.

Due to these difficulties, the Treaty provided for the abolition of existing restrictions on freedom of establishment and freedom to provide services. These rights have been in evidence in the move to harmonise professional qualifications and higher educational qualifications throughout the EU.

5.4.3.2 Professional bodies

Professional bodies lay down rules governing the conduct of their profession, relating both to access to the profession and practice within it. These rules are normally justified on the basis of the common good. However, they represent barriers to free movement of persons, as compliance by persons who have qualified and practised according to the rules of another Member State may be both difficult and expensive. They, therefore, have a discriminatory effect. The burden on those wishing to provide services is even greater, as they will generally be subject to professional regulation in the State in which they are established. In some cases, where national rules restrict the categories of persons entitled to practise certain professions the practice of a profession in which a person is fully qualified in his home State may be impossible.

The ECJ has sought to impose some limits on a Member State's powers to demand observance of its own professional rules by persons providing services and even by those seeking establishment in its territory. In Case 33/74 *Van Binsbergen* [1974] ECR 1229, it was acknowledged, in the context of a residence requirement imposed by the Dutch Bar on those seeking to provide legal services in the Netherlands, that specific requirements imposed on a person providing services would not infringe arts 49 and 50 where they have as their purpose the application of professional rules justified by the common good. This would apply, in particular, to rules relating to organisation, ethics, qualifications, supervision and liability, which are binding on any person established in the Member State in which the service is provided. Therefore, even a permanent residence requirement for persons engaged in certain activities could be permissible where it was objectively justified by the need to ensure the observance of professional rules of conduct.

However, a residence requirement could not be imposed if the desired objectives could be achieved by less restrictive means. Professional rules, which inhibit the free provision of services, are permissible only if they are non-discriminatory, objectively justified and not disproportionate. The ECJ added to this test in Case 279/80 *Webb* [1981] ECR 3305. It said that, in ascertaining whether its own rules are justified, the host State must take into account the justifications and safeguards already provided by the applicant in order to pursue the activity in question in his State of establishment. In the *Co-insurance Cases* (Case 205/84 *Commission v Germany (re insurance services)* [1986] ECR 3755; Case 206/84 *Commission v Ireland (re co-insurance services)* [1986] ECR 773; Case 220/83 *Commission v France* [1986] ECR 3663; and Case 252/83 *Commission v Denmark (re insurance services)* [1986] ECR 3713) these principles were developed. The actions were based on alleged infringements of arts 49 and 50 and Directive 78/473 (Insurance Directive) by the defendant Member States in their rules regulating the provision of insurance services. The rules and the alleged breaches in each State were similar. These rules generally required that a person providing direct insurance must be established and authorised to practise in the State in which the service is provided.

The ECJ created a fundamental difference between the freedom of establishment and the freedom to provide services. It held that in relation to the provision of services arts 49 and 50 require the removal, not only of all discrimination based on nationality, but also 'all restrictions on his freedom to provide services imposed by reason of the fact that he is established in a Member State other than that in which the services are provided'. Due to this, the Court held that not all the legislation applicable to nationals or those engaged in permanent activities could be applied to the temporary activities of enterprises established in another Member State. It could only be applied if three criteria were satisfied:

(a) it is justified by imperative reasons relating to the public interest;

(b) the public interest is not already protected by the rules of the State of establishment; and

(c) the same result cannot be attained by less restrictive means.

Applying this approach in Case C-351/90 *Commission v Luxembourg* [1992] ECR I-3945, the ECJ found that a 'single surgery rule' was not justified in the interests of good professional practice. The rule prohibited doctors, dentists and veterinary surgeons established outside Luxembourg from opening surgeries in Luxembourg on the basis that it was good professional practice to ensure that such professionals should be located in proximity to their patients. The Court found such a general prohibition 'unduly restrictive' and 'too absolute and too general'.

In Case C-76/90 *Säger v Dennemeyer & Co Ltd* [1991] ECR I-421, the ECJ considered rules considering the granting of licences for the performance of various services in Germany. Dennemeyer was a patent renewal agent based in the UK. He provided patent renewal services in Germany without the licence, which Germany requires for the provision of legal services. Such licences were not normally granted to patent renewal agents. Dennemeyer's right to provide such services in Germany was challenged by a German patent agent operating in Germany, Säger. Dennemeyer argued that the German rules were a hindrance to the free movement of services, contrary to arts 49 and 50(3). Advocate General Jacobs accepted that art 49 applied to discriminatory rules but said that it was not yet clear whether it applied to rules which were applicable to all providers of services, whether established in the State in which the service was provided or not. The ECJ held that:

> 'Article 49 requires not only the abolition of all discrimination against a person providing
> services on the ground of his nationality but also the abolition of any restriction, even if
> applied without distinction to national providers of services and to those of other
> Member States, when it is liable to prohibit or otherwise impede the activities of a

provider of services established in another Member State where he lawfully provides similar services.'

The Court went on to hold that:

'Having regard to the particular characteristics of certain specific provisions of services, specific requirements imposed on the provider cannot be regarded as incompatible with the Treaty. [However] the freedom to provide services may be limited only by rules which are justified by imperative reasons relating to the public interest and which apply to all persons and undertakings pursuing an activity in the State of destination in so far as that interest is not protected by rules to which the person providing the service is subject in the State in which he is established. In particular, these requirements must be objectively necessary in order to ensure compliance with professional rules and must not exceed what is necessary to attain those objectives.'

These principles have been followed in a succession of cases in which national or professional rules likely to 'prohibit or otherwise impede' the free provision of services have been tested for their compatibility with art 49. For instance, in Case C-154/89 *Commission v France* [1991] ECR I-659 a requirement of French law that tourist guides must obtain a licence by examination, although justifiable in principle in the interest of consumers as contributing to a 'proper appreciation of places and things of interest', was found to be disproportionate. The licence requirement went further than was necessary to protect this interest. In Case C-43/93 *Vander Elst v Office des Migrations Internationales* [1994] ECR I-3803 the requirement of a French work permit for third-country nationals seeking to work in France was held not to be justified by 'overriding reasons in the general interest' since the workers in question were already in possession of a work permit obtained in Belgium. In Case C-384/93 *Alpine Investments BV v Minister van Financiën* [1995] ECR I-1141, a Dutch prohibition on 'cold calling' by providers of financial services was held to be justified in order to protect consumers and the reputation of the Netherlands' security market and was not disproportionate.

5.4.4 DRAWING TOGETHER RULES ON ESTABLISHMENT AND SERVICES

The principles established in *Säger* appeared only to apply to the provision of services. The ECJ suggested that:

'a Member State may not make the provision of services in its territory subject to the conditions required for establishment . . . and thereby deprive of all practical effectiveness the provisions of the Treaty whose object is, primarily, to provide services'.

This implied that persons who established themselves in a Member State must comply with the conditions laid down in that State for its own nationals. However, in the more recent case of *Gebhard* this was changed. A German lawyer, who was a member of the Stuttgart Bar, challenged a decision of the Milan Bar Council prohibiting him practising in Italy from an Italian office using the title 'avvocato'. He claimed that the rules of the Milan Bar breached art 49 and/or art 43. The ECJ held that this was a matter concerning establishment. To what extent could the rules of the Italian Bar relating to qualifications and professional practice be enforced against him? The Court held that the possibility for a national of a Member State to exercise his right of establishment, and the conditions for the exercise of that right, had to be determined in the light of the activities which he intended to pursue on the territory of the host Member State. Where an activity was not subject to any rules in the host State, a national of another Member State was entitled to establish himself on the territory of the first State and pursue his activities there. Where the activity was subject to rules in the host State, a national of another Member State intending to pursue that activity must in principle comply with those rules. The ECJ held that national rules, which hinder or make less attractive the exercise of fundamental freedoms guaranteed by the Treaty, must fulfil four conditions:

1. They must be applied in a non-discriminatory manner.

2. They must be justified by imperative requirements in the general interest.

3. They must be suitable for securing the attainment of the objective, which they pursue.

4. They must not go beyond what it necessary in order to attain it.

States must take into account the equivalence of diplomas and if necessary compare the knowledge and qualifications required by their national rules and those of the person concerned.

Gebhard brings the rules relating to establishment into line with those relating to services.

5.4.5 ACTIVITIES CONNECTED WITH EXERCISE OF OFFICIAL AUTHORITY

Article 45 provides that:

> *The provisions of this Chapter [right of establishment] shall not apply, so far as any given Member State is concerned, to activities which in that State are connected, even occasionally, with the exercise of official authority.*

Article 45 also applies to the provision of services (art 56). This derogation is very similar to that for workers (art 39(4)). As in the case of workers, the derogation has been given a very narrow scope.

It was invoked in Case 2/74 *Reyners v Belgium* [1974] ECR 631. One of the defences put forward by the Belgian government in defending the Belgian Bar's rule restricting the profession of avocat to Belgian nationals was that the profession of avocat fell within art 45 in that it was connected to official authority. The ECJ disagreed. It held that art 45 only applied to 'activities' connected with the exercise of official authority. It did not apply to professions or occupations as a whole. The Court held that the derogation was aimed at the exercise of 'prerogative power'. While the exercise of judicial power would represent an exercise of official authority, the activities of an avocat would not.

5.4.6 FREEDOM TO PROVIDE SERVICES AND THE EXERCISE OF INDUSTRIAL PROPERTY RIGHTS

It was held in Case 62/79 *SA Compagnie, Générale pour la Diffusion de la Télévision Coditel v Ciné Vog Films (No 1)* [1980] ECR 881 that the freedom to provide services granted by art 49 could not be invoked to prevent the legitimate exercise of industrial property rights. Vog Films was a Belgian film distribution company, which owned performing rights in several Belgian films including 'Le Boucher'. Vog sought to prevent Coditel, a Belgian cable television company, from picking up 'Le Boucher' from German television and transmitting it in Belgium in breach of Vog's copyright. Coditel argued that to prevent it from so doing would be an interference with its freedom to provide services in breach of art 49. The ECJ held that art 49 does not restrict the use of trademarks or copyright, except where they are a means of arbitrary discrimination or a disguised restriction on trade between Member States. This would be the case if that application enabled parties to an assignment of copyright to create artificial barriers to trade between Member States. This was not found to be the case with Vog.

The ECJ protects the legitimate use of industrial property rights but not their misuse.

5.4.7 RIGHT TO RECEIVE SERVICES

5.4.7.1 Cross-border services

The freedoms provided by arts 49 and 50 are expressed in terms of the freedom to 'provide' services. The ECJ has extended the services provisions to those who wish to avail of cross-border services as well as those who provide such services.

In Case 26/83 *Luisi and Carbone v Ministero del Tesoro* [1984] ECR 377 the ECJ accepted that the freedom to move within the EU to receive services was the necessary corollary to the freedom to provide services. The case concerned criminal proceedings in Italy against Luisi and Carbone for breach of Italian currency regulations. They were accused of taking foreign currency out of Italy, more than the maximum permitted amount. They had taken the money for the purposes of tourism and medical treatment. The Court was asked whether payment for such services was a movement of capital under the Treaty, or payment for the provision of services. If the latter, was it governed by arts 49-55? Advocate General Mancini argued that art 49 was concerned with the receipt of services as well as their provision. The ECJ followed his recommendation. It held that the money was for payment for services. It held that freedom to provide services, as provided for in art 49, included the freedom, for recipients of services, to travel to another Member State in order to receive a service there. Recipients of such services were held to include tourists, persons receiving medical treatment and persons travelling for the purposes of education and business.

This case established the right to enter and remain in another Member State for the purpose of receiving services in that State. Directive 64/221 and Directive 73/148 refer to a right to receive services. Directive 64/221 provides that there should be 'freedom of movement for employed or self-employed persons or the recipients of services'. Directive 73/148 provides a right for nationals of Member States to go to another Member State to receive a service. Article 4(2) of the Directive permits the recipient of the service to stay while the service is being provided.

5.4.7.2 Publicly-funded services

Difficulties arise with publicly funded services, such as education or health. Are nationals of Member States entitled to travel to other States to receive such services?

The matter was considered in the context of the availability of free vocational training in a Member State to nationals of other Member States. Case 293/83 *Gravier v City of Liège* [1985] ECR 593 concerned a French student who had been given a place on a four-year course in strip cartooning at the Liège Academie des Beaux-Arts. She was charged the 'minerval' – a fee payable by foreign students, but not by Belgian students or EU nationals working in Belgium or their families. She brought an action before the Belgian courts claiming that the fee was discriminatory. She argued that it was an obstacle to her freedom of movement to receive services. She also argued that it was discriminatory to charge higher prices for vocational training to EU nationals who were not Belgian citizens or resident in Belgium. The ECJ found for her on the second argument. It held that access to vocational training was a matter covered by EU law and that it was an essential element in promoting freedom of movement throughout the EU. The Court's definition of vocational education was very wide. It was held to include all forms of teaching which prepares for, and leads directly to, a particular profession, trade or employment, or which provides the necessary skills for such profession, trade or employment, even if the programme of instruction includes an element of general education.

Most university courses would meet these criteria. The only exception would be courses designed for persons seeking to 'improve their general knowledge rather than prepare themselves for an occupation'.

This was followed by Case 24/86 *Blaziot v University of Liège* [1988] ECR 379 where the Court held that certain university courses could constitute vocational training. University courses would be considered vocational where the final examination provided a qualification for a particular job or even where the studies provided training needed for the pursuit of a trade or profession. The claim was brought by university students of veterinary science for reimbursement of the 'minerval'.

In Case 263/86 *Belgium v Humbel* [1988] ECR 5365 the ECJ considered fees paid for secondary education by a French national living in Luxembourg for his son who attended secondary school in Belgium. The Court held that any course of general education could be held to be vocational if it is part of an overall programme of vocational education.

5.4.8 MUTUAL RECOGNITION OF QUALIFICATIONS

5.4.8.1 Generally

Significant barriers to the right of establishment and the freedom to provide services under arts 43 and 49 are national requirements that access to certain 'regulated' trades or professions depends upon qualifications, which nationals of other Member States are unlikely to possess. This is a very significant barrier to freedom of movement for the self-employed. It also hinders the free movement of the employed who may wish to work as employees in a trade or profession, which is regulated at a national level.

The Commission wished to create a Community, which would be genuinely open to those wishing to exercise a trade, profession or other self-employed activity in any Member State other than that in which the qualification was obtained. Initially it sought to proceed on the basis of harmonisation. It tried to obtain agreement from all the Member States on the minimum standard needed for the education and training necessary for a qualification in that field. For each sector two directives were to be passed – one specifying the general level of the education and training necessary to pursue that activity or profession and the second listing the qualifications and diplomas awarded in the various Member States which satisfied those conditions for recognition.

The Council has now adopted a number of directives in different sectors harmonising national rules on educational or professional qualifications, thus enabling a person qualified in one Member State to establish himself or provide a service in another Member State. These mutual recognition directives cover a variety of different areas.

This process of sectoral harmonisation proved to be very time consuming and, in some sectors where national traditions varied, widely impossible. The Architects Directive alone took seventeen years to pass. In 1974 the Council adopted a resolution on the mutual recognition of formal qualifications, expressing the wish that future work on mutual recognition be based on 'flexible and qualitative criteria' and that directives should, 'resort as little as possible to the prescription of detailed training requirements': [1974] OJ C98/1.

As an instance of the ineffectiveness of sectoral harmonisation, I propose taking a brief look at the Lawyers Provision of Services Directive. This is a very short directive covering the situation where a lawyer established in one Member State provides legal services in another. It has been implemented in a very restrictive way by almost every Member State. For instance, art 5 provides that Member States *may* require the visiting lawyer to be introduced to the court where services are to be provided and to work in conjunction with a lawyer practising within that ECJ's jurisdiction. All Member States have exercised the 'working in conjunction' requirement. In Case 427/85 *Commission v Germany* [1988] ECR 1123 the German implementation of this provision was challenged by the Commission as being too restrictive on the visiting lawyer and too generous to the local lawyer. The ECJ held that the requirement had been designed to enable the visiting lawyer to carry out his tasks on behalf of his client effectively. The Court found incompatible with art 5, German requirements that the local lawyer had to be appointed as representative of the visiting lawyer's client and that the visiting lawyer could not present a case in court or make a prison visit without the presence of the local lawyer.

The Legal Services Directive was implemented into Irish law by the European Communities (Freedom to Provide Services) (Lawyers) Regulations 1979 (SI 1979/50). Legal services may be provided in Ireland by lawyers established in other EU Member States with the exception of conveyancing and probate work. Rights of audience before the Irish courts may only be exercised in conjunction with a practising Irish barrister or solicitor.

5.4.8.2 Direct reliance on Treaty articles

As the right of establishment and the right to provide services provided under arts 43 and 49 appeared to be conditional on the issuing of directives under arts 47(1) and (2) it was thought that individuals could not invoke these rights until such directives had been passed. This matter was tested in *Reyners*. Reyners was a Dutch man, born, educated and resident in Belgium and the holder of a doctorate in Belgian law. He was refused admission to the Belgian Bar, as he was not a Belgian national. He challenged the decision, arguing that it was in breach of art 43. The Belgian government argued that he could not invoke art 43 as it depended for its effect on the issuing of directives under art 47. The ECJ held that individuals were entitled to invoke art 43. It held that the provisions of art 47 were complementary to art 43; they were not a necessary pre-condition. The purpose of art 43 was to facilitate the increase of freedom of establishment; taken together with art 12 it required that the actual conditions imposed could not be stricter than those imposed on the State's own nationals.

The same principle was applied in the context of services in Case 33/74 *Van Binsbergen* [1974] ECR 1229. The plaintiff, Van Binsbergen, a Dutch national qualified as a Dutch advocate, wished to invoke arts 49(1) and 50(3) to challenge a rule of the Dutch Bar that persons representing certain clients must reside in the State in which that service is supplied. Van Binsbergen had lived and worked in the Netherlands but had moved to Belgium. As a result, he was denied the right to represent clients before social security tribunals in the Netherlands. The ECJ held that he was entitled to rely directly on arts 49(1) and 50(3).

Thus, even though recognition and harmonisation are not achieved in a particular profession, arts 43, 49 and 50 together with art 12 may be invoked to challenge a national rule (whether in the form of a nationality or residence requirement), which is discriminatory. The principle applies to both direct and indirect discrimination and applies not only to the taking up of an activity but to pursuit of that activity in the widest sense. This was seen in Case 197/84 *Steinhauser v City of Biarritz* [1985] ECR 1819. Steinhauser, a German artist, was resident in Biarritz. He applied to the Biarritz authorities to rent an exhibition space. He was turned down on the basis of his nationality as the exhibition venue could only be rented by French nationals. The ECJ held that freedom of establishment provided under art 43 related not only to the taking up of an activity as a self-employed person but also the pursuit of that activity in the widest sense. Thus, the right to equal treatment was held to include the right to rent premises.

5.4.8.3 Professional qualifications

These cases formed the backdrop for the development of the principle of 'equivalence' of qualifications. This means that while the Member States may still regulate qualifications and professional or academic titles, a person seeking to establish himself in a 'regulated' trade or profession in another Member State has the right to have his existing qualifications taken into account. The competent authorities of the host Member State must consider whether those qualifications, even if different, are 'equivalent' to those required of home nationals, and may refuse authorisation only if they decide on reasonable grounds that they are insufficient. Any refusal must be reasoned and subject to judicial review. Otherwise, it may be discriminatory in breach of arts 43 or 49 and 50 together with art 12. Where the existing qualifications are equivalent in some aspects but not in others, the person is entitled to pursue further training to make up the difference.

Equivalence may be seen in operation in a number of cases. In Case 71/76 *Thieffry v Conseil de l'ordre des advocats à la Cour de Paris* [1977] 2 CMLR 373 the ECJ held that the French Bar Council could not refuse to allow Thieffry, a Belgian national with a Belgian law degree, to undertake practical training for the French Bar. Thieffry had been able to establish equivalence as his degree had been recognised by the University of Paris and he had acquired a qualifying certificate in France for the profession of avocat. Case 11/77 *Patrick v Ministre des Affaires Culturelles* [1977] ECR 1199 was a similar case. Patrick was an Englishman with an architect's qualification obtained in the UK. French law required a diplomatic convention with another State before recognising professional qualifications from that State. However, despite the absence of such a convention or a directive Patrick was able to demonstrate equivalence on foot of a Ministerial Decree of 1964.

Where a directive has been issued for mutual recognition or harmonisation of qualifications in a particular profession that profession may no longer insist on compliance with its own requirements by persons who have qualified in another Member State according to the terms of the directive. For professions where such directives exist the ECJ is unsympathetic to the protectionist aims of professional organisations and Member States.

Thus, in Case 246/80 *Broekmeulen v Huisarts Registratie Commissie* [1981] ECR 2311 a Dutch doctor's committee was unable to refuse Broekmeulen, a Belgian doctor, permission to practise in the Netherlands. Dutch regulations require three years specialised training, which Belgian doctors did not have to undergo. However, EC Directive 75/362 did not require doctors to undergo training additional to their original qualification. The ECJ held that where a specific directive has been issued for mutual recognition or harmonisation of qualifications in a profession, a Member State professional body may not insist on requirements above and beyond those required in the directive.

5.4.8.4   New approach

As progress on harmonisation had been so slow the EU in 1984 decided on a new approach. The Commission decided to approach the problem, not from the perspective of harmonisation, but on the basis of the mutual recognition of qualifications. This new approach was not to apply to individual professions but to all areas of activity where a higher education diploma was required.

Directive 89/48 (1989) OJ L19/16, based on these principles, was approved in December 1988. It came into effect on 1 January 1991. It creates a 'general' system for 'mutual recognition' of higher education diplomas. Its basic thrust is that if a national of a Member State wishes to pursue a regulated profession in any Member State, the competent authorities in that State may not refuse permission on the grounds of inadequate qualifications if the person meets certain conditions. The directive applies only to regulated professional activities, though it is sufficient if the activity is regulated in only one of the Member States. It does not apply to professions, which were already subject to separate directives providing for mutual recognition.

The directive applies to higher education diplomas awarded on completion of professional education and training of at least three years duration, or the equivalent period part time. Where, in the host State, the taking up and pursuit of a regulated profession is subject to the possession of a diploma, the competent authority of that State may not refuse to authorise a national of a Member State to take up and pursue that profession on the same conditions as apply to its own nationals, provided the applicant holds a diploma required in another State for the pursuit of the profession in question, or has pursued that profession for at least two years in a State which does not regulate that profession (art 3). Thus, all professionals whose qualifications are within its scope will be entitled to recognition of their qualifications within the other Member States.

Where the applicant's education and training is at least one year shorter than that which is required by the host State or where there is a shortfall in the period of supervised practice required by the host State, the applicant may be required to provide evidence of professional experience. This may not exceed the shortfall in supervised practice nor twice the shortfall in duration of education and training required by the home State.

The host State may also require an 'adaptation period' not exceeding three years where:

(a) matters covered by the applicant's education and training differ substantially from those covered by those of the host State, or

(b) the activities regulated in the host State are not regulated in the applicant's State of origin, or

(c) the profession regulated in the host State comprises activities which are not pursued in the State from which the applicant originates.

In the latter two situations, the difference must correspond to specific education and training required in the host State and cover matters which differ substantially from those covered by the evidence of formal qualification (art 4(1)(b)).

Instead of the adaptation period, the applicant may opt for an aptitude test. For professions whose practice requires precise knowledge of national law and in which the giving of advice on national law is an essential and constant aspect of that activity, a State may stipulate either an adaptation period or an aptitude test (art 4(1)(b)). The requirements of periods of professional experience and adaptation cannot be applied cumulatively. Thus, the total period cannot exceed four years. The host State has discretion, on the basis of equivalence, to permit the period of supervised professional practice to be undertaken in the host State (art 5).

The directive has been supplemented by Directive 92/51, which extends the same principles of mutual recognition to qualifications of less than three years. The directive was adopted in 1992 and Member States were required to implement this directive by 18 July 1994.

A person who has qualified in a non-Member State cannot invoke either the directives or the principle of mutual recognition even though the qualification has been recognised in a particular Member State and the person has been practising the profession within that State. The Council has issued a recommendation encouraging Member States to recognise diplomas and other evidence of formal qualifications obtained by nationals of Member States in non-Member States (OJ L 19/24, 1989).

However, there have also been some difficulties in the implementation of this directive. Professions throughout Europe have expressed a fondness for aptitude tests. These have proved to be very difficult. For instance, Germany requires lawyers to take three written examinations of five hours each on civil law, public or criminal law and one other paper from a choice provided. In addition, there is an oral examination comprising a fifty-minute presentation and a forty-minute discussion on professional conduct. The Commission is taking steps to ensure that the system established under the directive applies fairly.

The Irish implementing measure for foreign lawyers wishing to qualify as solicitors was the Solicitors Acts 1954 and 1960 (European Community) Regulations 1991 (SI 1991/85). These regulations allows for the admission of solicitors from Northern Ireland and England and Wales. All other EU lawyers are required to sit an aptitude test. This consists of five written papers and an oral examination in professional conduct. The written papers are in:

1. Constitutional Law and, at the option of the applicant, either Criminal Law or Company Law;

2. Contract and Tort;

3. Land Law and Conveyancing;

4. Probate and Taxation; and

5. Solicitors' Accounts.

Provision is made for exemptions to be given. On foot of these regulations, large numbers of English and Northern Irish solicitors have qualified as Irish solicitors. The English and Northern Irish Law Societies implemented the directive in much the same way and large numbers of Irish solicitors have also availed of this qualification route.

In some professional sectors, the Commission is introducing specific directives to overcome the difficulties that they have encountered.

5.4.8.5 Establishment Directive for Lawyers

One instance of this is the Commission's introduction of a specific Establishment Directive for lawyers. It went through the Council on a qualified majority with Luxembourg voting against. Its implementation date is 14 March 2000.

In brief, the directive entitles lawyers to move to any other EU Member State and practise law under their home title. After a period of three years the visiting lawyer may choose to take out the local qualification and cannot be required to pass any examination or test in order to do so.

Article 3 of the Directive requires the visiting lawyer to register with the competent authority in the State in which he is practising. The competent authority may look for proof of his qualification and must inform the competent authority in his State of origin. Where a competent authority publishes the names of its own lawyers, it is also to publish the names of these registered lawyers.

Article 5 provides that the immigrant lawyer can carry on the same activities, as he would be entitled to in his home State. He can advise on the law of the host State as well as that of his home State. Article 5(2) provides that in States where conveyancing and probate work is reserved to a certain category of lawyers, lawyers coming from other States, where such activities are carried on by non-lawyers, may be excluded from practising such activities.

Article 5(3) provides for another restriction where, as in Ireland, representation of clients in court is reserved to lawyers licensed to practise in that State. In these States, in order to appear in court, the immigrant lawyer may be required to 'work in conjunction' with a local lawyer.

Article 6(1) provides that the immigrant lawyer is subject to the rules of professional conduct, which apply to lawyers in the host State. Thus, immigrant lawyers in Ireland will be subject to the solicitors' professional conduct rules, if they register with the Law Society.

Article 7 provides that if the 'obligations in force in the host Member State' are not complied with the rules of procedure, penalties and remedies provided for in the host Member State shall apply. However, art 7(2) provides that before the host State competent authority commences disciplinary proceeding, it is to inform the competent authority in the home Member State, furnishing it with all the relevant details. Article 7(3) provides that the two competent authorities are to co-operate in these proceedings. The home competent authority may make submissions to any appellate body. Article 7(4) provides that the competent authority in the home Member State shall decide what action to take, under its own rules, in the light of a decision of the competent authority in the host Member State.

Article 6(2) provides that the immigrant lawyer shall be granted appropriate representation. At a minimum, this involves the right to vote in elections to the competent authority's governing body.

Article 6(3) provides that the immigrant lawyer may be required 'either to take out professional indemnity insurance or to become a member of a professional guarantee fund in accordance with the rules which that state lays down for professional activities pursued in its territory'. The immigrant lawyer is to be exempted from this requirement if he can show that he is covered by insurance taken out or a guarantee provided in his home Member State, in so far as the insurance or guarantee is equivalent in terms of the conditions and extent of cover. If the equivalence is only partial, the immigrant lawyer may be required to take out additional insurance or an additional guarantee to cover those elements not covered by his home insurance or guarantee.

Article 10 is the single most complex provision of the directive. It provides two means of being integrated into the host State profession (such as being admitted as a solicitor).

Under art 10(1) an immigrant lawyer is entitled to be exempted from taking the aptitude test if he can show that he has 'effectively and regularly' pursued an activity in the law of the host State for a period of three years. This includes EU law.

The immigrant lawyer is to furnish the host competent authority with proof of this. He is to provide the competent authority with any relevant information and documents, notably on the number of cases dealt with and their nature. The competent authority may verify the nature of the activity pursued. If necessary it can request the applicant to provide orally, or in writing, clarification or further details on the information and documents provided.

Article 10(3) provides for another method of obtaining admission where the immigrant lawyer has effectively and regularly pursued a professional activity in the host State for a period of three years but for a lesser period in the law of the host State. The competent authority is required to take into account the professional work undertaken during the three-year period and 'any knowledge and professional experience of the law of the host Member State and any attendance at lectures or seminars on the law of the host Member State, including the rules regarding professional practice and conduct'. As in art 10(1), the applicant is obliged to provide any relevant information and documents, notably on the cases he has dealt with. An assessment of the immigrant lawyer's effective and regular activity in the host Member State and the assessment of his capacity to continue the activity he had pursued, may be carried out by means of an interview for verification purposes.

The article gives very limited grounds for refusal. Article 10(4) provides that a refusal may be made by a reasoned decision, subject to appeal, where this is in the public interest, notably because of disciplinary proceedings, complaints or incidents of any kind. This right of refusal appears to be premised on conduct of the applicant, rather than legal competence or knowledge.

The Establishment Directive is being implemented in Ireland through amendments to the Solicitors Acts 1954 to 1994 and statutory instrument.

APPENDIX 1

Further Reading

GENERAL

There is a wealth of legal materials available in the area of EU law. Two general texts, which we recommend are:

Craig & De Burca: *EU Law, Text, Cases and Materials* (2nd edn, 1998, OUP)
Steiner & Woods: *Textbook on EC Law* (7th edn, 2000, Blackstone).

The EU's own web site (www.europa.eu.int) contains a great deal of information on current and pending legislation as well as details of cases decided by the CFI and ECJ. The Eurlegal section of the Law Society's Gazette carries regular updates on European cases and legislation of interest to practitioners as well as longer articles analysing recent developments.

We have listed further reading (articles and books) for those who would like to explore the issues raised in the sections of this book in greater depth.

CHAPTER 2: ASSERTING EUROPEAN UNION LAW RIGHTS

Craig: 'Once More unto the Breach: the Community, the State and Damages Liability in the Court of Justice' (1997) 105 Law Quarterly Review 67
Steiner: 'From Direct Effects to Francovich: Shifting Means of Enforcement of Community Law' (1993) 18 European Law Review 3

CHAPTER 3: COMPETITION LAW

Butterworths Competition Law (looseleaf; Freeman & Whish (eds))
Cahill: *Corporate Finance Law* (2000, Roundhall Sweet & Maxwell) Chapter 9
Cook and Kerse: *EC Merger Control* (3rd edn, 1999, Sweet & Maxwell)
Goyder: *EC Competition Law* (3rd edn, 1998, Oxford)
Kerse: *EEC Antitrust Procedure* (3rd edn, 1994, Sweet & Maxwell)
Rose (ed) *Bellamy and Child on Common Market Law of Competition* (4th edn, 1996, Sweet & Maxwell)

CHAPTER 4: EUROPEAN PRIVATE INTERNATIONAL LAW

Mayss & Reed: *European Business Litigation* (1998, Ashgate)
Reed & Kennedy: 'International Torts and Shevill: The Ghost of Forum Shopping Yet to Come' [1996] Lloyds Maritime and Commercial Law Quarterly 108

FURTHER READING

CHAPTER 5: FREE MOVEMENT

Handoll: *Free Movement of Persons in the European Union* (1995, Chancery)
Oliver: *Free Movement of Goods in the EC* (3rd edn, 1996, Sweet & Maxwell)
Usher: *The Law of Money and Financial Services in the European Community* (1994, Oxford)

APPENDIX 2

Commercial Agents Regulations

Council Directive 86/653/EEC of 18 December 1986 on the coordination of the laws of the Member States relating to self-employed commercial agents

of the Member State relating to self-employed commercial agents (86/653/EEC)

THE COUNCIL OF THE EUROPEAN COMMUNITIES,

Having regard to the Treaty establishing the European Economic Community, and in particular Articles 57(2) and 100 thereof,

Having regard to the proposal from the Commission,

Having regard to the opinion of the European Parliament,

Having regard to the opinion of the Economic and Social Committee,

Whereas the restrictions on the freedom of establishment and the freedom to provide services in respect of activities of intermediaries in commerce, industry and small craft industries were abolished by Directive 64/224/EEC;

Whereas the differences in national laws concerning commercial representation substantially affect the conditions of competition and the carrying-on of that activity within the Community and are detrimental both to the protection available to commercial agents vis-à-vis their principals and to the security of commercial transactions; whereas moreover those differences are such as to inhibit substantially the conclusion and operation of commercial representation contracts where principal and commercial agents are established in different Member States;

Whereas trade in goods between Member States should be carried on under conditions which are similar to those of a single market, and this necessitates approximation of the legal systems of the Member States to the extent required for the proper functioning of the common market; whereas in this regard the rules concerning conflict of laws do not, in the matter of commercial representation, remove the inconsistencies referred to above, nor would they even if they were made uniform, and accordingly the proposed harmonization is necessary notwithstanding the existence of those rules;

Whereas in this regard the legal relationship between commercial agent and principal must be given priority;

Whereas it is appropriate to be guided by the principles of Article 117 of the Treaty and to maintain improvements already made, when harmonizing the laws of the Member States relating to commercial agents;

Whereas additional transitional periods should be allowed for certain Member States which have to make a particular effort to adapt their regulations, especially those concerning indemnity for termination of contract between the principal and the commercial agent, to the requirements of this Directive,

HAS ADOPTED THIS DIRECTIVE:

COUNCIL DIRECTIVE 86/653/EEC

CHAPTER I. SCOPE

Article 1

1. The harmonization measures prescribed by this Directive shall apply to the laws, regulations and administrative provisions of the Member States governing the relations between commercial agents and their principals.

2. For the purposes of this Directive, 'commercial agent' shall mean a self-employed intermediary who has continuing authority to negotiate the sale or the purchase of goods on behalf of another person, hereinafter called the 'principal', or to negotiate and conclude such transactions on behalf of and in the name of that principal.

3. A commercial agent shall be understood within the meaning of this Directive as not including in particular:

   - a person who, in his capacity as an officer, is empowered to enter into commitments binding on a company or association,

   - a partner who is lawfully authorized to enter into commitments binding on his partners,

   - a receiver, a receiver and manager, a liquidator or a trustee in bankruptcy.

Article 2

1. This Directive shall not apply to:

   - commercial agents whose activities are unpaid,

   - commercial agents when they operate on commodity exchanges or in the commodity market, or

   - the body known as the Crown Agents for Overseas Governments and Administrations, as set up under the Crown Agents Act 1979 in the United Kingdom, or its subsidiaries.

2. Each of the Member States shall have the right to provide that the Directive shall not apply to those persons whose activities as commercial agents are considered secondary by the law of that Member State.

CHAPTER II. RIGHTS AND OBLIGATIONS

Article 3

1. In performing has activities a commercial agent must look after his principal's interests and act dutifully and in good faith.

2. In particular, a commercial agent must:

   (a) make proper efforts to negotiate and, where appropriate, conclude the transactions he is instructed to take care of;

   (b) communicate to his principal all the necessary information available to him;

   (c) comply with reasonable instructions given by his principal.

Article 4

1. In his relations with his commercial agent a principal must act dutifully and in good faith.

2. A principal must in particular:

   (a) provide his commercial agent with the necessary documentation relating to the goods concerned;

   (b) obtain for his commercial agent the information necessary for the performance of the agency contract, and in particular notify the commercial agent within a reasonable period once he anticipates that the volume of commercial transactions will be significantly lower than that which the commercial agent could normally have expected.

3. A principal must, in addition, inform the commercial agent within a reasonable period of his acceptance, refusal, and of any non-execution of a commercial transaction which the commercial agent has procured for the principal.

Article 5

The parties may not derogate from the provisions of Articles 3 and 4.

CHAPTER III. REMUNERATION

Article 6

1. In the absence of any agreement on this matter between the parties, and without prejudice to the application of the compulsory provisions of the Member States concerning the level of remuneration, a commercial agent shall be entitled to the remuneration that commercial agents appointed for the goods forming the subject of his agency contract are customarily allowed in the place where he carries on his activities. If there is no such customary practice a commercial agent shall be entitled to reasonable remuneration taking into account all the aspects of the transaction.

2. Any part of the remuneration which varies with the number or value of business transactions shall be deemed to be commission within the meaning of this Directive.

3. Articles 7 to 12 shall not apply if the commercial agent is not remunerated wholly or in part by commission.

Article 7

1. A commercial agent shall be entitled to commission on commercial transactions concluded during the period covered by the agency contract:

   (a) where the transaction has been concluded as a result of his action; or

   (b) where the transaction is concluded with a third party whom he has previously acquired as a customer for transactions of the same kind.

2. A commercial agent shall also be entitled to commission on transactions concluded during the period covered by the agency contract:

   – either where he is entrusted with a specific geographical area or group of customers,

   – or where he has an exclusive right to a specific geographical area or group of customers,

   and where the transaction has been entered into with a customer belonging to that area or group.

   Member States shall include in their legislation one of the possibilities referred to in the above two indents.

Article 8

A commercial agent shall be entitled to commission on commercial transactions concluded after the agency contract has terminated:

(a) if the transaction is mainly attributable to the commercial agent's efforts during the period covered by the agency contract and if the transaction was entered into within a reasonable period after that contract terminated; or

(b) if, in accordance with the conditions mentioned in Article 7, the order of the third party reached the principal or the commercial agent before the agency contract terminated.

Article 9

A commercial agent shall not be entitled to the commission referred to in Article 7, if that commission is payable, pursuant to Article 8, to the previous commercial agent, unless it is equitable because of the circumstances for the commission to be shared between the commercial agents.

Article 10

1. The commission shall become due as soon as and to the extent that one of the following circumstances obtains:

   (a) the principal has executed the transaction; or

   (b) the principal should, according to his agreement with the third party, have executed the transaction; or

   (c) the third party has executed the transaction.

2. The commission shall become due at the latest when the third party has executed his part of the transaction or should have done so if the principal had executed his part of the transaction, as he should have.

3. The commission shall be paid not later than on the last day of the month following the quarter in which it became due.

4. Agreements to derogate from paragraphs 2 and 3 to the detriment of the commercial agent shall not be permitted.

Article 11

1. The right to commission can be extinguished only if and to the extent that:

   – it is established that the contract between the third party and the principal will not be executed, and

   – that fact is due to a reason for which the principal is not to blame.

2. Any commission which the commercial agent has already received shall be refunded if the right to it is extinguished.

3. Agreements to derogate from paragraph 1 to the detriment of the commercial agent shall not be permitted.

Article 12

1. The principal shall supply his commercial agent with a statement of the commission due, not later than the last day of the month following the quarter in which the commission has become due. This statement shall set out the main components used in calculating the amount of commission.

2. A commercial agent shall be entitled to demand that he be provided with all the information, and in particular an extract from the books, which is available to his principal and which he needs in order to check the amount of the commission due to him.

3. Agreements to derogate from paragraphs 1 and 2 to the detriment of the commercial agent shall not be permitted.

4. This Directive shall not conflict with the internal provisions of Member States which recognize the right of a commercial agent to inspect a principal's books.

CHAPTER IV. CONCLUSION AND TERMINATION OF THE AGENCY CONTRACT

Article 13

1. Each party shall be entitled to receive from the other on request a signed written document setting out the terms of the agency contract including any terms subsequently agreed. Waiver of this right shall not be permitted.

2. Notwithstanding paragraph 1 a Member State may provide that an agency contract shall not be valid unless evidenced in writing.

Article 14

An agency contract for a fixed period which continues to be performed by both parties after that period has expired shall be deemed to be converted into an agency contract for an indefinite period.

Article 15

1. Where an agency contract is concluded for an indefinite period either party may terminate it by notice.

2. The period of notice shall be one month for the first year of the contract, two months for the second year commenced, and three months for the third year commenced and subsequent years. The parties may not agree on shorter periods of notice.

3. Member States may fix the period of notice at four months for the fourth year of the contract, five months for the fifth year and six months for the sixth and subsequent years. They may decide that the parties may not agree to shorter periods.

4. If the parties agree on longer periods than those laid down in paragraphs 2 and 3, the period of notice to be observed by the principal must not be shorter than that to be observed by the commercial agent.

5. Unless otherwise agreed by the parties, the end of the period of notice must coincide with the end of a calendar month.

6. The provision of this Article shall apply to an agency contract for a fixed period where it is converted under Article 14 into an agency contract for an indefinite period, subject to the proviso that the earlier fixed period must be taken into account in the calculation of the period of notice.

Article 16

Nothing in this Directive shall affect the application of the law of the Member States where the latter provides for the immediate termination of the agency contract:

(a) because of the failure of one party to carry out all or part of his obligations;

(b) where exceptional circumstances arise.

COUNCIL DIRECTIVE 86/653/EEC

Article 17

1. Member States shall take the measures necessary to ensure that the commercial agent is, after termination of the agency contract, indemnified in accordance with paragraph 2 or compensated for damage in accordance with paragraph 3.

2. (a) The commercial agent shall be entitled to an indemnity if and to the extent that:

   – he has brought the principal new customers or has significantly increased the volume of business with existing customers and the principal continues to derive substantial benefits from the business with such customers, and

   – the payment of this indemnity is equitable having regard to all the circumstances and, in particular, the commission lost by the commercial agent on the business transacted with such customers. Member States may provide for such circumstances also to include the application or otherwise of a restraint of trade clause, within the meaning of Article 20;

   (b) The amount of the indemnity may not exceed a figure equivalent to an indemnity for one year calculated from the commercial agent's average annual remuneration over the preceding five years and if the contract goes back less than five years the indemnity shall be calculated on the average for the period in question;

   (c) The grant of such an indemnity shall not prevent the commercial agent from seeking damages.

3. The commercial agent shall be entitled to compensation for the damage he suffers as a result of the termination of his relations with the principal.

   Such damage shall be deemed to occur particularly when the termination takes place in circumstances:

   – depriving the commercial agent of the commission which proper performance of the agency contract would have procured him whilst providing the principal with substantial benefits linked to the commercial agent's activities,

   – and/or which have not enabled the commercial agent to amortize the costs and expenses that he had incurred for the performance of the agency contract on the principal's advice.

4. Entitlement to the indemnity as provided for in paragraph 2 or to compensation for damage as provided for under paragraph 3, shall also arise where the agency contract is terminated as a result of the commercial agent's death.

5. The commercial agent shall lose his entitlement to the indemnity in the instances provided for in paragraph 2 or to compensation for damage in the instances provided for in paragraph 3, if within one year following termination of the contract he has not notified the principal that he intends pursuing his entitlement.

6. The Commission shall submit to the Council, within eight years following the date of notification of this Directive, a report on the implementation of this Article, and shall if necessary submit to it proposals for amendments.

Article 18

The indemnity or compensation referred to in Article 17 shall not be payable:

(a) where the principal has terminated the agency contract because of default attributable to the commercial agent which would justify immediate termination of the agency contract under national law;

(b) where the commercial agent has terminated the agency contract, unless such termination is justified by circumstances attributable to the principal or on grounds

184

of age, infirmity or illness of the commercial agent in consequence of which he cannot reasonably be required to continue his activities;

(c) where, with the agreement of the principal, the commercial agent assigns his rights and duties under the agency contract to another person.

Article 19

The parties may not derogate from Articles 17 and 18 to the detriment of the commercial agent before the agency contract expires.

Article 20

1. For the purposes of this Directive an agreement restricting the business activities of a commercial agent following termination of the agency contract is hereinafter referred to as a restraint of trade clause.

2. A restraint of trade clause shall be valid only if and to the extent that:

    (a) it is concluded in writing; and

    (b) it relates to the geographical area or the group of customers and the geographical area entrusted to the commercial agent and to the kind of goods covered by his agency under the contract.

3. A restraint of trade clause shall be valid for not more than two years after termination of the agency contract.

4. This Article shall not affect provisions of national law which impose other restrictions on the validity or enforceability of restraint of trade clauses or which enable the courts to reduce the obligations on the parties resulting from such an agreement.

CHAPTER V. GENERAL AND FINAL PROVISIONS

Article 21

Nothing in this Directive shall require a Member State to provide for the disclosure of information where such disclosure would be contrary to public policy.

Article 22

1. Member States shall bring into force the provisions necessary to comply with this Directive before 1 January 1990. They shall forthwith inform the Commission thereof. Such provisions shall apply at least to contracts concluded after their entry into force. They shall apply to contracts in operation by 1 January 1994 at the latest.

2. As from the notification of this Directive, Member States shall communicate to the Commission the main laws, regulations and administrative provisions which they adopt in the field governed by this Directive.

3. However, with regard to Ireland and the United Kingdom, 1 January 1990 referred to in paragraph 1 shall be replaced by 1 January 1994.

    With regard to Italy, 1 January 1990 shall be replaced by 1 January 1993 in the case of the obligations deriving from Article 17.

EC (COMMERCIAL AGENTS) REGULATIONS 1994

Article 23

This Directive is addressed to the Member States.

Done at Brussels, 18 December 1986.
For the Council
The President
M.JOPLING

SI No 33 of 1994
European Communities (Commercial Agents) Regulations 1994

I, RUAIRÍ QUINN, Minister for Enterprise and Employment, in exercise of the powers conferred on me by section 3 of the European Communities Act 1972 (No 27 of 1972) for the purpose of giving effect to Council Directive 86/653/EEC of 18 December 1986, on the co-ordination of the laws of the Member States relating to self-employed commercial agents, hereby make the following Regulations:

1. These Regulations may be cited as the European Communities (Commercial Agents) Regulations 1994.

2. (1) In these Regulations:

    'commercial agent' means a self-employed intermediary who has continuing authority to negotiate the sale or purchase of goods on behalf of another person, hereinafter called 'the principal', or to negotiate and conclude such transactions on behalf of and in the name of the principal;

    the term 'commercial agent' does not include –

    (a) a person who, in the capacity of an officer of a company or association, is empowered to enter into commitments binding on that company or association;

    (b) a partner who is lawfully authorised to enter into commitments binding on the partners;

    (c) a receiver, a receiver and manager, a liquidator or an examiner, as defined in the Companies Acts, 1963 to 1990, or a trustee in bankruptcy;

    (d) a commercial agent whose activities are unpaid;

    (e) a commercial agent operating on commodity exchanges or in the commodity market; or

    (f) a consumer credit agent or a mail order catalogue agent for consumer goods, whose activities, pursuant to paragraph (2) of this Regulation, are considered secondary;

    'the Directive' means Council Directive 86/653 EEC of 18 December 1986.

    (2) The activities of an agent of a category described in paragraph (1) (f) of this Regulation shall be presumed, unless the contrary is established, to be secondary for the purposes of these Regulations.

3. The Directive shall, subject to these Regulations, apply to the relations between commercial agents and their principals from 1 January 1994.

4. In the application of Article 7 (2) of the Directive, a commercial agent shall be entitled to commission on commercial transactions concluded during the period covered by the agency contract only where the agent has an exclusive right to a specific geographical

186

area or group of customers and where the transaction has been entered into with a customer belonging to that area or group.

5. The agency contract shall not be valid unless it is evidenced in writing.

GIVEN under my Official Seal, this 21st day of February 1994.

RUAIRÍ QUINN,
Minister for Enterprise and Employment.

SI No 31 of 1994
European Communities (Commercial Agents) Regulations 1997

I, RICHARD BRUTON, Minister for Enterprise and Employment, in exercise of the powers conferred on me by section 3 of the European Communities Act, 1972 (No 27 of 1972), for the purpose of giving effect to Council Directive No 86/653/EEC of 18 December 1986, on the co-ordination of the laws of the Member States relating to self-employed commercial agents, hereby make the following Regulations:

1. (1) These Regulations may be cited as the European Communities (Commercial Agents) Regulations, 1997.

   (2) The European Communities (Commercial Agents) Regulations, 1994 (S.I. No. 33 of 1994) and these Regulations shall be construed as one and may be cited together as the European Communities (Commercial Agents) Regulations, 1994 and 1997.

2. It is hereby confirmed that, pursuant to Regulation 3 of the European Communities (Commercial Agents) Regulations, 1994, a commercial agent shall, after termination of the agency agreement, be entitled to be compensated for damage in accordance with Article 17 (3) of the Directive subject, insofar as they are relevant to such compensation, to the provisions of that Article and of Articles 18, 19 and 20 of the Directive.

GIVEN under my Official Seal, this 7th day of January, 1997.

RICHARD BRUTON,
Minister for Enterprise and Employment.

APPENDIX 3

Competition Law and Mergers

COMPETITION ACT 1991

Number 24 of 1991

ARRANGEMENT OF SECTIONS

PART I. PRELIMINARY

PART II. RULES OF COMPETITION

PART III. THE COMPETITION AUTHORITY

PART IV. MERGERS, TAKE-OVERS AND MONOPOLIES

COMPETITION ACT 1991

PART V. GENERAL

20. Authorised officers.
21. Powers of authorised officers.
22. Repeals.
23. Regulations.
24. Expenses.

SCHEDULE. COMPETITION AUTHORITY

AN ACT TO PROHIBIT, BY ANALOGY WITH ARTICLES 85 AND 86 OF THE TREATY ESTABLISHING THE EUROPEAN ECONOMIC COMMUNITY, AND IN THE INTERESTS OF THE COMMON GOOD, THE PREVENTION, RESTRICTION OR DISTORTION OF COMPETITION AND THE ABUSE OF DOMINANT POSITIONS IN TRADE IN THE STATE, TO ESTABLISH A COMPETITION AUTHORITY, TO AMEND THE MERGERS, TAKE-OVERS AND MONOPOLIES (CONTROL) ACT, 1978, AND TO PROVIDE FOR OTHER MATTERS CONNECTED WITH THE MATTERS AFORESAID.

[22nd July 1991]

BE IT ENACTED BY THE OIREACHTAS AS FOLLOWS:

PART I. PRELIMINARY

1. Short title

This Act may be cited as the Competition Act, 1991.

2. Commencement

(1) This Act shall come into operation on such day or days as may be fixed therefor by order or orders of the Minister, either generally or with reference to a particular purpose or provision, and different days may be so fixed for different purposes and different provisions of this Act.

(2) An order under *subsection* (1) may as respects the repeal effected by section 22 of the provisions of the Act of 1972 fix different days for the repeal of different provisions of that Act or for the repeal for different purposes of any provision of that Act.

3. Interpretation

(1) In this Act, unless the context otherwise requires

'the Act of 1972' means the Restrictive Practices Act, 1972;

'the Act of 1978' means the Mergers, Take-overs and Monopolies (Control) Act, 1978;

'the Act of 1987' means the Restrictive Practices (Amendment) Act, 1987;

'authorised officer' means a person appointed under *section 20*;

'the Authority' means the Competition Authority established by *section 10*;

'the Court' means the High Court or, in the case of an appeal, the Supreme Court;

'the Minister' means the Minister for Industry and Commerce;

'prescribed' means prescribed by regulations made by the Minister;

'undertaking' means a person being an individual, a body corporate or an unincorporated body of persons engaged for gain in the production, supply or distribution of goods or the provision of a service.

(2) In this Act a reference to a section or Schedule is to a section of, or Schedule to, this Act unless it is indicated that a reference to some other provision is intended.

(3) In this Act a reference to a subsection or paragraph is to the subsection or paragraph of the provision in which the reference occurs, unless it is indicated that reference to another provision is intended.

(4) In this Act a reference to any other enactment is to that enactment as amended by any other enactment including this Act.

PART II. RULES OF COMPETITION

4. Anti-competitive agreements, decisions and concerted practices

(1) Subject to the provisions of this section, all agreements between undertakings, decisions by associations of undertakings and concerted practices which have as their object or effect the prevention, restriction or distortion of competition in trade in any goods or services in the State or in any part of the State are prohibited and void, including in particular, without prejudice to the generality of this subsection, those which

    (a) directly or indirectly fix purchase or selling prices or any other trading conditions;

    (b) limit or control production, markets, technical development or investment;

    (c) share markets or sources of supply;

    (d) apply dissimilar conditions to equivalent transactions with other trading parties thereby placing them at a competitive disadvantage;

    (e) make the conclusion of contracts subject to acceptance by the other parties of supplementary obligations which by their nature or according to commercial usage have no connection with the subject of such contracts.

(2) The Competition Authority established by this Act ('the Authority') may in accordance with *section 8* grant a licence for the purposes of this section in the case of—

    (a) any agreement or category of agreements,

    (b) any decision or category of decisions,

    (c) any concerted practice or category of concerted practices,

which in the opinion of the Authority, having regard to all relevant market conditions, contributes to improving the production or distribution of goods or provision of services or to promoting technical or economic progress, while allowing consumers a fair share of the resulting benefit and which does not—

    (i) impose on the undertakings concerned terms which are not indispensable to the attainment of those objectives;

    (ii) afford undertakings the possibility of eliminating competition in respect of a substantial part of the products or services in question.

(3) (a) A licence under *subsection (2)* shall, while it is in force, and in accordance with its terms, permit the doing of acts which would otherwise be prohibited and void under *subsection (1)*.

    (b) Where a licence under *subsection (2)* covers a category of agreements, decisions or concerted practices, any agreements, decisions or concerted practices (as the case may be) within that category which comply with the terms of the licence need not be notified under *section 7* to benefit from the licence while it is in force.

(4) The Authority may certify that in its opinion, on the basis of the facts in its possession, an agreement, decision or concerted practice notified under *section 7* does not offend against *subsection (1)*.

(5) Before granting a licence or issuing a certificate under this section, the Authority may invite any Minister of the Government concerned with the matter to offer such observations as he may wish to make.

(6) On granting a licence or issuing a certificate under this section, the Authority shall forthwith give notice in the prescribed manner to every body to which it relates stating the terms and the date thereof and the reasons therefor and cause the notice to be published in *Iris Oifigiúil* and cause notice of the grant of the licence or issue of the certificate, as the case may be, to be published in one daily newspaper published in the State.

(7) The prohibition in *subsection* (1) shall not prevent the Court, in exercising any jurisdiction conferred on it by this Act concerning an agreement, decision or concerted practice which contravenes that prohibition and which creates or, but for this Act, would have created legal relations between the parties thereto, from applying, where appropriate, any relevant rules of law as to the severance of those terms of that agreement, decision or concerted practice which contravene that prohibition from those which do not.

(8) In respect of an agreement, decision or concerted practice such as is referred to in *subsection* (7) a court of competent jurisdiction may make such order as to recovery, restitution or otherwise between the parties to such agreement, decision or concerted practice as may in all the circumstances seem just, having regard in particular to any consideration or benefit given or received by such parties on foot thereof.

5. Abuse of dominant position

(1) Any abuse by one or more undertakings of a dominant position in trade for any goods or services in the State or in a substantial part of the State is prohibited.

(2) Without prejudice to the generality of *subsection* (1), such abuse may, in particular, consist in

    (a) directly or indirectly imposing unfair purchase or selling prices or other unfair trading conditions;

    (b) limiting production, markets or technical development to the prejudice of consumers;

    (c) applying dissimilar conditions to equivalent transactions with other trading parties, thereby placing them at a competitive disadvantage;

    (d) making the conclusion of contracts subject to the acceptance by other parties of supplementary obligations which by their nature or according to commercial usage have no connection with the subject of such contracts.

6. Right of action

(1) Any person who is aggrieved in consequence of any agreement, decision, concerted practice or abuse which is prohibited under *section 4* or *5* shall have a right of action for relief under this section against any undertaking which is or has at any material time been a party to such agreement, decision or concerted practice or has been guilty of such abuse.

(2) (a) Subject to *paragraph (b)*, an action under this section shall be brought in the High Court.

    (b) An action under this section may be brought in the Circuit Court in respect of any abuse which is prohibited under *section 5* but any relief by way of damages, including exemplary damages, shall not, except by consent of the necessary parties in such form as may be provided for by rules of court, be in excess of the limit of the jurisdiction of the Circuit Court in an action founded on tort.

(3) The following reliefs, or any of them, may be granted to the plaintiff in an action under this section:

(a) relief by way of injunction or declaration,

(b) subject to *subsection (6)*, damages, including exemplary damages.

(4) The Minister shall have a right of action, in respect of an agreement, decision or concerted practice or an abuse which is prohibited under *section 4 or 5*, for the reliefs specified in *subsection (3)(a)*.

(5) (a) Where in proceedings under this section it is finally decided by the Court that an agreement, decision or concerted practice which is in question infringes the prohibition in *section 4 (1)*, any certificate in force under *section 4 (4)* in relation to that agreement, decision or concerted practice shall thereupon cease to have force and effect as from the date of the order of the Court and the Court shall cause a certified copy of the said order to be served on the Authority.

(b) The Authority shall, as soon as may be, cause notice of the fact that, pursuant to *paragraph (a)*, its certificate has ceased to have force and effect to be published in *Iris Oifigiúil*.

(6) Where there is or has been in force a certificate pursuant to *section 4 (4)* in relation to an agreement, decision or concerted practice, and that certificate has not been revoked under *section 8 (6) (b)*, a claimant shall not be entitled to damages pursuant to this section for a contravention of the prohibition in *section 4 (1)* in any proceedings under this section commenced after the issue of that certificate for loss suffered in consequence of that agreement, decision or concerted practice in respect of the period during which the certificate is or has been in force, but this subsection shall not prejudice any right to damages for a contravention of the prohibition in *section 5*.

(7) This section shall not apply to any agreement, decision or concerted practice to which *section 7 (2)* applies which has been duly notified to the Authority until the Authority has decided to grant or refuse to grant a licence under *section 4 (2)*, or to issue a certificate or not to issue a certificate under *section 4 (4)*, in relation thereto and any appeal to the Court under *section 9* in relation to the licence or the certificate has been concluded.

(8) The Authority shall as soon as may be cause to be published in *Iris Oifigiúil* any decision of the Authority referred to in *subsection (7)* and a copy of any such notice shall be *prima facie* evidence of the making and content of such decision and of the date thereof in any action under this section.

7. Notification of agreements, decisions and concerted practices to Authority

(1) Every agreement, decision and concerted practice of a kind described in *section 4 (1)* which comes into existence after the commencement of that section in respect of which the parties thereto request a licence under *section 4 (2)* or a certificate under *section 4 (4)* of that section shall be notified to the Authority.

(2) Every agreement, decision and concerted practice of a kind described in *section 4 (1)* which is in existence at the commencement of that section and in respect of which the parties seek a licence under *section 4 (2)* or a certificate under *section 4 (4)* shall be notified to the Authority within year of such commencement.

(3) A licence under *section 4 (2)* or a certificate under *section 4 (4)* shall not be granted until the agreement, decision or concerted practice (as the case may be) has been notified to the Authority but any such licence may in the case of an agreement, decision or concerted practice to which *subsection (1)* applies be made retrospective to the date of notification under that subsection.

(4) A notification in accordance with this section shall be accompanied by such fee as may be prescribed.

(5) For the purpose of the exercise of its functions in relation to licences under *section 4 (2)* and certificates under *section 4 (4)* the Authority may accept such observations or submissions from persons claiming to be interested as it may think proper.

(6) The functions of the Authority under this Act shall be carried out in accordance with such procedures, if any, as may be prescribed.

8. Licence of Authority under *section 4 (2)* and certificate of Authority under *section 4 (4)*

(1) A licence of the Authority under *section 4 (2)* shall be granted for a specified period subject to such conditions as may be attached to and specified in the licence.

(2) The Authority may from time to time, on the application of a party to a request under *section 7*, extend the period of a licence if it is of opinion that the requirements of *section 4 (2)* continue to be fulfilled and the Authority shall, as soon as may be, cause to be published in *Iris Oifgiúil* notice of any such extension.

(3) Where the Authority is of the opinion that, having regard to the requirements of *section 4 (2)* and to the basis upon which a licence under that subsection was granted

    (a) there has been a material change in any of the circumstances on which the decision was based,

    (b) any party commits a breach of any obligation attached to the decision,

    (c) the licence was based on materially incorrect or misleading information, or

    (d) any party abuses the permission granted to it by the licence,

the Authority may revoke or amend the licence and, without prejudice to the generality of this subsection, may in particular insert in a licence conditions the effect of which is to prohibit specific acts by any party thereto which would otherwise be authorised pursuant to such a licence.

(4) The Authority shall as soon as may be cause to be published in *Iris Oifgiúil* notice of every revocation or amendment of a licence under *section 4 (2)*.

(5) Every licence under *section 4 (2)* shall have effect in accordance with its terms, subject to any amendment thereof including any conditions inserted therein under *subsection (3)* of this section.

(6) The Authority may revoke a certificate under *section 4 (4)* where it is of opinion that—

    (a) there has been a material change in any of the circumstances on which the certificate was based, or

    (b) the certificate was based on materially incorrect or misleading information.

(7) The Authority shall as soon as may be cause to be published in *Iris Oifgiúil* notice of every revocation under *subsection (6)*.

9. Appeal to High Court

(1) Any undertaking or association of undertakings concerned, or any other person aggrieved by a licence or a certificate of the Authority under *section 4 (2)* or *(4)*, or the Minister, may appeal to the High Court within 28 days of publication pursuant to this Act of the licence or certificate and on the hearing of any such appeal the Court may confirm, amend or revoke the licence so appealed against, or, in the case of such a certificate, may cancel or refuse to cancel the certificate.

(2) The right of appeal in relation to a licence under *section 4 (2)* includes the right to appeal against the insertion or exclusion of conditions attaching to any exemption granted.

(3) The Court may order that a licence or certificate in respect of which an appeal has been brought under this section shall be suspended pending the hearing and conclusion of the appeal.

(4) Any undertaking or association of undertakings concerned or the Minister may within 28 days of the notification or publication pursuant to this Act of a revocation or amendment by the Authority, pursuant to *section 8 (3)*, of a licence under *section 4 (2)*, or of a revocation by the Authority, pursuant to *section 8 (6)*, of a certificate under *section 4 (4)*, appeal to the High Court

(5) The Court may extend the time specified in *subsection (1)* or *(4)* in any case where it seems just and convenient to do so.

PART III. THE COMPETITION AUTHORITY

10. Establishment of Competition Authority

(1) There shall be a body to be known as the Competition Authority to exercise the functions assigned to it by this Act.

(2) The Authority shall stand established on such day as the Minister may by order appoint.

(3) The Authority shall in particular discharge any function of the Fair Trade Commission under the Act of 1972 not completed at the commencement of this section and, accordingly, sections 7 and 8 of the Act of 1978 are amended by the substitution of references to the Authority for references to the Fair Trade Commission.

(4) The provisions of the *Schedule* shall have effect in relation to the Authority.

11. Studies and analyses by Authority

The Authority may, at the request of the Minister, study and analyse and, when requested by the Minister, report to him the results of any such study or analysis, any practice or method of competition affecting the supply and distribution of goods or the provision of services. A study or analysis may consist of, or include, a study or analysis of any development outside the State.

12. Reports

(1) The Authority shall submit to the Minister an annual report of its activities within four months of the end of each year.

(2) The Minister shall lay before each House of the Oireachtas a copy of every such report within four months of receiving the report.

PART IV. MERGERS, TAKE-OVERS AND MONOPOLIES

13. Construction with Act of 1978

This Part shall be construed as one with the Act of 1978 and with the other Parts of this Act.

14. Investigation of abuse of dominant position

(1) Where the Minister is of the opinion that there is, contrary to *section 5*, an abuse of a dominant position he may request the Authority to carry out an investigation and the Authority shall comply with the request.

(2) Where the Authority holds an investigation pursuant to a request under *subsection (1)* it shall report thereon to the Minister and the report shall state whether in the opinion of the Authority—

(a) a dominant position exists, and

(b) if it does, whether that dominant position is being abused.

(3) The Minister, having considered a report of the Authority under *subsection* (2), may, if the interests of the common good so warrant, after consultation with any other Minister of the Government concerned, by order either

    (a) prohibit the continuance of the dominant position except on conditions specified in the order, or

    (b) require the adjustment of the dominant position, in a manner and within a period specified in the order, by a sale of assets or otherwise as he may specify.

(4) An order under this section shall state the reasons for making the order.

(5) The Minister may by order revoke an order under this section and may, with the agreement of every enterprise concerned, amend an order under this section.

(6) An order under this section shall not have effect unless and until it is confirmed by a resolution of each House of the Oireachtas.

(7) References in section 12 and 13 of the Act of 1978 to section 11 of that Act shall be construed as references to this section and the expression 'monopoly' shall be construed as a reference to an abuse of a dominant position.

(8) Compliance with an order under this section shall be a good defence to an action under *section 6* in respect of any period after such compliance, in so far as such action is in respect of any matter which is the subject of such compliance.

(9) A right of action for relief under *section 6* includes a right of action for contravention of an order under this section.

(10) The Minister shall publish a report under *subsection* (2), with due regard to commercial confidentiality, within two months of its being furnished to him by the Authority.

(11) Sections 10 and 11 of the Act of 1978 are hereby repealed.

15. Definitions in Act of 1978

(1) 'Service' in section 1 (1) of the Act of 1978 shall not include the owning and transfer of land where this activity is the sole activity of the enterprise in which control is being sought.

(2) Section 1 (3) of the Act of 1978 is hereby amended by the substitution for paragraph (*c*) of the following:

    '(c) Without prejudice to paragraph (*b*), where an enterprise (in this paragraph referred to as "the first enterprise"), whether by means of acquisition or otherwise, obtains the right in another enterprise (in this paragraph referred to as "the second enterprise") which is a body corporate—

        (i) to appoint or remove a majority of the board or committee of management of the second enterprise, or

        (ii) to shares of the second enterprise which carry voting rights, except where the voting rights in the second enterprise which are controlled by the first enterprise—

            (I) are not after the acquisition more than 25 per cent of the total of such voting rights, or

            (II) are before the acquisition more than one half of the total of such voting rights,

    the said enterprises shall be deemed to have been brought under common control.'.

(3) Section 1 (3) (*e*) of the Act of 1978 is hereby amended by the insertion after 'acquisition' at the end of the paragraph of 'and the value of those assets or the value of the turnover generated therefrom, exceeds the thresholds referred to in section 2 (1) (*a*).'.

16. Notification of proposed merger or take-over

The Act of 1978 is hereby amended by the substitution, for section 5, of the following section:

'5.—(1) Each of the enterprises involved in a proposed merger or take-over shall notify the Minister in writing of the proposal, and provide full details thereof within the specified period of the offer capable of acceptance having been made, the effect of which would bring the enterprises under common control.

(2) Where, having received a notification under this section from each of the enterprises involved, the Minister is of opinion that in order to consider for the purposes of this Act a proposed merger or take-over he requires further information he may, within one month of the date of receipt by him of the notification, or of the last of such notifications, as the case may be, request such further information in writing from any one or more of the enterprises concerned, each of which shall provide the information within a period to be stated to them by the Minister in writing.

(3) (a) Where there is a contravention of subsection (1) or (2) the person in control of an enterprise failing to notify the Minister within the specified period or failing to supply the information requested within the period stated by the Minister shall be guilty of an offence and shall be liable

    (i) on summary conviction, to a fine not exceeding £1,000 and, for continued contravention, to a daily default fine not exceeding £100, or

    (ii) on conviction on indictment, to a fine not exceeding £200,000 and, for continued contravention, to a daily default fine not exceeding £20,000.

(b) Where a person is liable to a daily default fine he shall be guilty of contravening the provision on every day on which the contravention continues after the specified period has elapsed.

(c) For the purposes of this subsection the person in control of an enterprise is—

    (i) in the case of a body corporate, any officer of the body corporate who knowingly and wilfully authorises or permits the contravention,

    (ii) in the case of a partnership, each partner who knowingly and wilfully authorises or permits the contravention,

    (iii) in the case of any other form of enterprise, any individual in control of that enterprise who knowingly and wilfully authorises or permits the contravention.

(4) For the purposes of this section the specified period shall be one month, or such other period as the Minister may specify.

(5) A notification for the purposes of subsection (1) shall not be valid where any information provided or statement made under subsection (1) or (2) is false or misleading.'

17. Amendment of sections 6, 7 and 8 of the Act of 1978

(1) Section 6 of the Act of 1978 is hereby amended by the insertion after 'section 3' of 'or section 7'.

(2) The Act of 1978 is hereby amended by the substitution of the following for section 7:

'7.—Upon receipt of a notification under section 5 the Minister shall—

(a) as soon as practicable inform the enterprises which made the notification and any other enterprise involved which enquires of him that he has decided not to make an order under section 9 in relation to the proposed merger or take-over, or

(b) within 30 days of the commencement of the relevant period refer the notification to the Authority for investigation.'.

(3) Section 8 (1) of the Act of 1978 is hereby amended by the insertion after the word 'date' of 'not being less than 30 days after the reference'.

(4) Section 8 of the Act of 1978 is hereby amended by the substitution for subsection (2) of the following:

'(2) (a) A report of the Authority under subsection (1) shall state its opinion as to whether or not the proposed merger or take-over concerned would be likely to prevent or restrict competition or restrain trade in any goods or services and would be likely to operate against the common good.

(b) The Authority shall give its views on the likely effect of the proposed merger or take-over on the common good in respect of:

(i) continuity of supplies or services,

(ii) level of employment,

(iii) regional development,

(iv) rationalisation of operations in the interests of greater efficiency,

(v) research and development,

(vi) increased production,

(vii) access to markets,

(viii) shareholders and partners,

(ix) employees,

(x) consumers.'.

(5) The Minister shall publish any such report, with due regard to commercial confidentiality, within two months of its being furnished to him by the Authority.

(6) The Schedule to the Act of 1978 is hereby repealed.

18. Amendment of section 9 of the Act of 1978

Section 9 (1) (a) of the Act of 1978 is hereby amended by the insertion after 'so warrant', of the following, 'which shall include, but is not confined to, the criteria in section 8,'.

19. Control of concentrations

(1) The transmission to the Minister by the Commission of the European Communities of a copy of a notification made under Council Regulation (EEC) No. 4064/89 on the control of concentrations between undertakings shall constitute a notification under section 5 of the Act of 1978 (as inserted by *section 16* of this Act).

(2) The relevant period in respect of such a notification shall not commence until the Commission of the European Communities makes a decision under either Article 9 or 21 (3) of that Regulation.

PART V. GENERAL

20. Authorised officers

The Minister and the Authority with the consent of the Minister may appoint persons to be authorised officers for the purposes of this Act.

21. Powers of authorised officers

(1) For the purpose of obtaining any information necessary for the exercise by the Authority or the Minister of any of their functions under this Act, an authorised officer may, on production of a warrant issued by a Justice of the District Court expressly authorising him to do so—

(a) enter and inspect premises at or vehicles in or by means of which any activity in connection with the business of supplying or distributing goods or providing a service, or in connection with the organisation or assistance of persons engaged in any such business, is carried on,

(b) require the person who carries on such activity and any person employed in connection therewith to produce to the authorised officer any books, documents or records relating to such activity which are in that person's power or control, and to give to the authorised officer such information as he may reasonably require in regard to any entries in such books, documents and records,

(c) inspect and copy or take extracts from any such books, documents and records,

(d) require a person mentioned in *paragraph (b)* to give to the authorised officer any information he may require in regard to the persons carrying on such activity (including in particular, in the case of an unincorporated body of persons, information in regard to the membership thereof and its committee of management or other controlling authority) or employed in connection therewith,

(e) require a person mentioned in *paragraph (b)* to give to the authorised officer any information which the officer may reasonably require in regard to such activity.

(2) A Justice of the District Court may issue a warrant under *subsection (1)*, if satisfied by information on oath that it is proper for him to do so for the purposes of that subsection.

(3) A person who obstructs or impedes an authorised officer in the exercise of a power conferred by this section or does not comply with a requirement under this section shall be guilty of an offence and shall be liable on summary conviction to a fine not exceeding £1,000 or imprisonment for a period not exceeding twelve months or, at the discretion of the Court, to both such fine and imprisonment.

22. Repeals

The provisions of the Act of 1972 and every order made under that Act and sections 5 and 6 and sections 8 to 23 of the Act of 1987 are hereby repealed.

23. Regulations

(1) The Minister may by regulations provide for any matter referred to in this Act as prescribed or to be prescribed.

(2) Every regulation made by the Minister under this section shall be laid before each House of the Oireachtas as soon as may be after it is made and, if a resolution annulling the regulation is passed by either House within the next 21 days on which that House has sat after the regulation is laid before it, the regulation shall be annulled accordingly, but without prejudice to the validity of anything previously done thereunder.

24. Expenses

Any expenses incurred by the Minister in the administration of this Act shall, to such extent as may be sanctioned by the Minister for Finance, be paid out of moneys provided by the Oireachtas.

SCHEDULE. COMPETITION AUTHORITY

1. (1) The permanent members of the Authority shall consist of a chairman and not less than two and not more than four other members each of whom shall be appointed by the Minister.

   (2) Whenever it appears to the Minister that a permanent member is temporarily unable to discharge his duties, the Minister may appoint a temporary member to act in his place during such inability or for such shorter period as the Minister thinks proper.

   (3) The Minister may also appoint additional temporary members for such period and on such terms and conditions as he may specify in the appointment.

2. (1) The term of office of a permanent member shall be fixed by the Minister when appointing him and shall not exceed five years.

   (2) An outgoing permanent member shall be eligible for reappointment.

   (3) Each member shall hold office on such conditions as may be fixed by the Minister after consultation with the Minister for Finance.

   (4) A member may be paid such remuneration as the Minister with the consent of the Minister for Finance determines.

   (5) The Civil Service Commissioners Act, 1956 and the Civil Service Regulation Acts, 1956 and 1958, shall not apply to the office of member.

3. If a member is personally interested in a particular matter with which the Authority is dealing, he shall inform the Minister accordingly and shall not act as a member during the consideration of the matter, unless the Minister, being of opinion that the member's interest is not such as to interfere with the impartial performance of his duties, authorises him to act.

4. (1) The Minister may remove from office a member who has become incapable through ill-health of performing efficiently his duties as such member or whose removal appears to the Minister to be necessary in the interests of the effective and economical performance of the functions of the Authority.

   (2) Where the Minister removes a member from office he shall lay before each House of the Oireachtas a statement in writing of the reasons for such removal.

   (3) A member may resign his office.

   (4) Where a member of the Authority is—

      (a) nominated as a member of Seanad Éireann, or

      (b) elected as a member of either House of the Oireachtas or of the European Parliament, or

      (c) regarded pursuant to section 15 (inserted by the European Assembly Elections Act, 1984) of the European Assembly Elections Act, 1977, as having been elected to the European Parliament to fill a vacancy,

      he shall thereupon cease to be a member of the Authority.

(5) A person who is, for the time being, entitled under the Standing Orders of either House of the Oireachtas to sit therein or who is a member of the European Parliament shall be disqualified from being a member of the Authority.

(6) A member shall be disqualified from holding and shall cease to hold office if he is adjudged bankrupt or makes a composition or arrangement with his creditors, or is sentenced by a court of competent jurisdiction to suffer imprisonment or penal servitude or ceases to be ordinarily resident in the State.

5. (1) The Minister shall, with the consent of the Minister for Finance, as soon as may be make and carry out a scheme for the granting of pensions, gratuities or other allowances to or in respect of members of the Authority ceasing to hold office other than members in respect of whom an award under the Superannuation Acts, 1934 to 1963, may be made.

(2) A scheme under this paragraph may provide that the termination of the appointment of a member of the Authority during the member's term of office shall not preclude the award to him of a pension, gratuity or other allowance.

(3) The Minister may, with the consent of the Minister for Finance, amend a scheme made by him under this paragraph.

6. (1) The quorum for a meeting of the Authority shall be—

(a) three permanent members unless the Minister otherwise authorises,

(b) three permanent members for decisions on requests for a licence or certificate under *section 4*.

(2) The Authority may act notwithstanding vacancies in its membership.

(3) Subject to this Act, the Authority may regulate its own procedure.

(4) The Authority may, with the consent of the Minister, appoint officers of the Minister to be authorised officers for the purposes of this Act.

7. (1) The Authority may, for the purposes of its functions under this Act and the Act of 1978, do all or any of the following things—

(a) summon witnesses to attend before it,

(b) examine on oath (which any member is hereby authorised to administer) the witnesses attending before it,

(c) require any such witness to produce to the Authority any document in his power or control,

(d) perform such of its functions as it deems proper through or by any officer of the Minister duly authorised by it in that behalf.

(2) A witness before the Authority shall be entitled to the same immunities and privileges as if he were a witness before the High Court.

(3) A summons shall be signed by at least one member.

(4) Any person who—

(a) on being duly summoned as a witness before the Authority makes default in attending, or

(b) being in attendance as a witness refuses to take an oath legally required by the Authority to be taken, or to produce any document in his power or control legally required by the Authority to be produced by him, or to answer any question to which the Authority may legally require an answer, or

(c) does any other thing which would, if the Authority were a court, having power to commit for contempt of court, be contempt of such court,

shall be guilty of an offence and shall be liable on summary conviction to a fine not exceeding £1,000 or imprisonment for a period not exceeding six months or, at the discretion of the court, to both such fine and imprisonment.

8. Any person may make a submission to the Authority in the manner prescribed by its rules in relation to the subject matter of any investigation.

9. (1) No person shall disclose information available to him by virtue of the powers of obtaining information conferred by this Act or by any other enactment conferring functions on the Authority or through being present at a meeting of the Authority held in private.

(2) *Subparagraph (1)* shall not apply to—

(i) a communication made by a member of the Authority in the execution of his functions under this Act, or

(ii) the disclosure of information in a report of the Authority or for the purpose of legal proceedings under this Act or pursuant to an order of a court of competent jurisdiction for the purposes of any proceedings in that court.

(3) If any person contravenes this paragraph he shall be guilty of an offence and shall be liable on summary conviction to a fine not exceeding £1,000 or imprisonment for a period not exceeding six months or, at the discretion of the court, to both such fine and imprisonment.

10. (1) The Minister, with the consent of the Minister for Finance, may appoint such officers and servants as he thinks necessary to assist the Authority in the performance of its functions.

(2) The officers and servants so appointed shall hold office on such terms and receive such remuneration as the Minister for Finance determines.

11. The Authority shall be entitled, in any proceedings, to the same privilege in respect of a communication to or by the Authority, any member of the Authority or any of its officers or servants as any Minister of the Government.

COMPETITION (AMENDMENT) ACT 1996

Number 19 of 1996

AN ACT TO AMEND AND EXTEND THE COMPETITION ACT 1991, AND THE MERGERS, TAKE-OVERS AND MONOPOLIES (CONTROL) ACTS 1978 AND 1987, AND TO PROVIDE FOR RELATED MATTERS.

[*3rd July* 1996]

BE IT ENACTED BY THE OIREACHTAS AS FOLLOWS:

1. Interpretation

(1) In this Act—

'the Act of 1978' means the Mergers, Take-overs and Monopolies (Control) Act, 1978;

'director' includes a person in accordance with whose directions or instructions the directors of the undertaking concerned are accustomed to act but does not include such a person if the directors are accustomed so to act by reason only that they do so on advice given by the person in a professional capacity;

'the Principal Act' means the Competition Act, 1991.

(2) In this Act references, however expressed, to an act that is done with the consent of a person shall be construed as including references to an act that is done with the connivance of a person.

(3) In this Act a reference to any other enactment shall be construed as a reference to that enactment as amended, extended or adapted by or under any subsequent enactment (including this Act).

2. Offences in respect of breaches of rules of competition

(1) In this section—

'agreement', 'decision' and 'concerted practice' mean, respectively, an agreement, decision and concerted practice of a kind described in section 4 (1) of the Principal Act;

'certificate' means a certificate under section 4 (4) of the Principal Act;

'licence' means a licence under section 4 (2) of the Principal Act.

(2) (a) An undertaking shall not—

   (i) enter into, or implement, an agreement, or

   (ii) make or implement a decision, or

   (iii) engage in a concerted practice.

(b) An undertaking that contravenes this subsection shall be guilty of an offence.

(c) In proceedings for an offence under this subsection, it shall be a good defence to prove that—

   (i) the defendant did not know, nor, in all the circumstances of the case, could the defendant be reasonably expected to have known, that the effect of the agreement, decision or concerted practice concerned would be the prevention, restriction or distortion of competition in trade alleged in the proceedings, or

   (ii) at all material times a licence or certificate was in force in respect of the agreement, decision or concerted practice concerned and, in the case of a licence—

      (I) the terms and conditions of the licence were at all material times being complied with by the defendant, or

      (II) subject to *subsection (3)* of this section, in case any terms or conditions of the licence were not being so complied with—

         (A) those terms or conditions are terms or conditions that had been amended, or inserted in the licence, under section 8 of the Principal Act,

         (B) the defendant was complying with the terms and conditions of the licence immediately before the making of such amendments or insertions, and

         (C) the defendant began to take, within 14 days after the date of publication, in accordance with the said section 8, of notice of the amendment or insertion of terms or conditions aforesaid, all reasonable steps for the purposes of complying with those terms or conditions and was proceeding with due expedition on the date on which the offence is alleged to have been committed with the completion of any step remaining for those purposes,

   or

   (iii) subject to *subsections (3)* and *(4)* of this section, in the case of an agreement, decision or concerted practice in respect of which a licence or certificate has been granted and such a licence has been revoked or suspended or, as the case may be, such a certificate has been revoked, the defendant began to take, within 14 days after—

(I) in the case of the revocation of a licence or certificate, the date of publication, in accordance with section 8 of the Principal Act, of notice of such revocation, or

(II) in the case of the suspension of a licence, the date of the order of the High Court or, as may be appropriate, the Supreme Court providing for such suspension,

all reasonable steps for the purposes of ensuring that any arrangements that had been made and which were necessary for the implementation of the agreement or decision or, as the case may be, which constituted the concerted practice were discontinued and was proceeding with due expedition on the date on which the offence is alleged to have been committed with the completion of any step remaining for those purposes.

(3) The defence provided for by *subparagraph (ii) (II)* or, as the case may be, *subparagraph (iii)* of *subsection (2) (c)* of this section shall not be available to a defendant if the date on which the offence concerned is alleged to have been committed is more than 2 months after the date of publication of the notice concerned referred to in *subclause (C)* of the said *subparagraph (ii) (II)* or, as the case may be, *clause (I)* of the said *subparagraph (iii)* or, where appropriate, the date of the order concerned referred to in *clause (II)* of the said *subparagraph (iii)*.

(4) The defence provided for by *subsection (2) (c) (iii)* of this section shall not be available to a defendant the doing of any act or the making of any omission by whom constituted the grounds for the revocation of the licence or certificate concerned.

(5) (a) An undertaking that is a party to an agreement, decision or concerted practice in respect of which a licence is in force shall comply with the terms and conditions of the licence.

(b) An undertaking that contravenes this subsection shall be guilty of an offence.

(c) Subject to *subsection (6)* of this section, where, in proceedings for an offence under this subsection, the terms or conditions of the licence which it is alleged were not complied with are terms or conditions that had been amended, or inserted in the licence, under section 8 of the Principal Act, it shall be a good defence to prove that—

(i) the defendant was complying with the terms and conditions of the licence immediately before the making of such amendments or insertions, and

(ii) the defendant began to take within 14 days after the date of publication, in accordance with the said section 8, of notice of the amendment or insertion of terms or conditions aforesaid, all reasonable steps for the purposes of complying with those terms or conditions and was proceeding with due expedition on the date on which the offence is alleged to have been committed with the completion of any step remaining for those purposes.

(6) The defence provided for by *subsection (5)* of this section shall not be available to a defendant if the date on which the offence concerned is alleged to have been committed is more than 2 months after the date of publication of the notice concerned referred to in *paragraph (c) (ii)* of that subsection.

(7) (a) An undertaking that acts in a manner prohibited by section 5 (1) of the Principal Act or which contravenes an order under section 14 of that Act shall be guilty of an offence.

(b) In proceedings for an offence under this subsection (being an offence which consists of the doing of an act in a manner prohibited by section 5 (1) of the Principal Act), it shall be a good defence to prove that—

    (i) the defendant did not know, nor, in all the circumstances of the case, could the defendant be reasonably expected to have known, that the act or acts concerned done by the defendant would constitute the abuse of the dominant position in trade for goods or services alleged in the proceedings, or

    (ii) the said act was done in compliance with the provisions of an order under section 14 of the said Act ('the first-mentioned order'), or

    (iii) subject to *subsection (8)* of this section, in case any of those provisions were not being complied with—

        (I) those provisions are provisions that had been amended, or inserted in the first-mentioned order, by another order under the said section 14 ('the second-mentioned order'),

        (II) the defendant was complying with the provisions of the first-mentioned order immediately before the commencement of the second-mentioned order and

        (III) the defendant began to take, within 14 days after the commencement of the second-mentioned order, all reasonable steps for the purposes of complying with the provisions so amended or inserted and was proceeding with due expedition on the date on which the offence is alleged to have been committed with the completion of any step remaining for those purposes, or

    (iv) subject to *subsection (8)* of this section, in case an order under section 14 of the said Act prohibited the continuance of the act concerned except on conditions specified in that order and that order has been revoked by another order under the said section 14 ('the second-mentioned order'), the defendant began to take, within 14 days after the commencement of the second-mentioned order, all reasonable steps for the purposes of discontinuing the act concerned and was proceeding with due expedition on the date on which the offence is alleged to have been committed with the completion of any step remaining for those purposes.

(c) Subject to *subsection (8)* of this section, where, in proceedings for an offence under this subsection (being an offence which consists of the contravention of an order under section 14 of the Principal Act ('the first-mentioned order')), the provisions of that order which it is alleged were not complied with are provisions that had been amended, or inserted in that order, by another order under the said section 14 ('the second-mentioned order'), it shall be a good defence to prove that—

    (i) the defendant was complying with the provisions of the first-mentioned order immediately before the commencement of the second-mentioned order, and

    (ii) the defendant began to take, within 14 days after the commencement of the second-mentioned order, all reasonable steps for the purposes of complying with the provisions so amended or inserted and was proceeding with due expedition on the date on which the offence is alleged to have been committed with the completion of any step remaining for those purposes.

(8) The defence provided for by *subparagraph (iii)* or *(iv)* of *paragraph (b)*, or, as the case may be, by *paragraph (c)*, of *subsection (7)* of this section shall not be available to a defendant if the date on which the offence concerned is alleged to have been committed is more than 2 months after the commencement of the order concerned secondly referred to in the said *subparagraph (iii)* or *(iv)* or the said *paragraph (c)*, as the case may be.

(9) For the purpose of determining liability for an offence under this section, any act done by an officer or an employee of an undertaking for the purposes of, or in connection with, the business or affairs of the undertaking shall be regarded as an act done by the undertaking.

(10) References in this section to an order under section 14 of the Principal Act shall, where the context admits, be construed as including references to an order under subsection (2) of section 12 (as adapted by the Principal Act) of the Act of 1978.

3. Penalties, proceedings, etc., in relation to offences under section 2

(1) An undertaking guilty of an offence under *section 2* of this Act shall be liable—

    (a) on summary conviction—

        (i) to a fine not exceeding £1,500, or

        (ii) in the case of an individual, to such a fine or, at the discretion of the court, to imprisonment for a term not exceeding 6 months or to both such fine and such imprisonment,

    (b) on conviction on indictment—

        (i) to a fine not exceeding whichever of the following amounts is the greater, namely, £3,000,000 or 10 per cent of the turnover of the undertaking in the financial year ending in the 12 months prior to the conviction, or

        (ii) in the case of an individual, to a fine not exceeding whichever of the following amounts is the greater, namely, £3,000,000 or 10 per cent of the turnover of the individual in the financial year ending in the 12 months prior to the conviction or, at the discretion of the court, to imprisonment for a term not exceeding 2 years or to both such fine and such imprisonment.

(2) If the contravention in respect of which an undertaking is convicted in summary proceedings of an offence under section 2 of this Act is continued after the conviction, the undertaking shall be guilty of a further offence on every day on which the contravention continues and for each such offence the undertaking shall be liable, on summary conviction to a fine not exceeding £1,500.

(3) (a) Where a court imposes a fine or affirms or varies a fine imposed by another court for an offence under section 2 of this Act in proceedings brought by the Authority, it shall, on the application of the Authority (made before the time of such imposition, affirmation or variation), provide by order for the payment of the amount of the fine to the Authority and such payment may be enforced by the Authority as if the payment were due to it on foot of a decree or order made by the court in civil proceedings.

    (b) The amount of any fine paid to, or recovered by, the Authority under this subsection shall be disposed of by it in such manner as the Minister for Finance directs.

(4) (a) Where an offence under *section 2* of this Act has been committed by an undertaking and the doing of the acts that constituted the offence has been authorised, or consented to, by a person, being a director, manager, or other similar officer of the undertaking, or a person who purports to act in any such capacity, that person as well as the undertaking shall be guilty of an offence and shall be liable to be proceeded against and punished as if he or she were guilty of the first-mentioned offence.

    (b) Where a person is proceeded against as aforesaid for such an offence and it is proved that, at the material time, he or she was a director, manager or other similar officer of the undertaking concerned, or a person who purported to act in any such capacity, it shall be presumed, until the contrary is proved, that that person consented to the doing of the acts by the undertaking which constituted the commission by it of the offence concerned under *section 2* of this Act.

   (c) Where the affairs of a body corporate are managed by its members, this subsection shall apply in relation to the acts or defaults of a member in connection with his or her functions of management as if he or she were a director of the body corporate.

(5) The Authority or an authorised officer appointed under section 20 of the Principal Act may carry out an investigation into any contravention of *subsection (2), (5)* or *(7)* of *section 2* of this Act that the Authority or the authorised officer suspects has occurred or is occurring.

(6) (a) Summary proceedings for an offence under *section 2* of this Act may be brought by the Minister or the Authority.

   (b) An action under section 6 of the Principal Act may be brought whether or not there has been a prosecution for an offence under *section 2* of this Act in relation to the matter concerned and such an action shall not prejudice the initiation of a prosecution for any such offence.

   (c) Notwithstanding section 10 (4) of the Petty Sessions (Ireland) Act, 1851, summary proceedings for an offence under *section 2* of this Act may be instituted within 2 years from the date of the offence.

(7) In this section 'turnover' does not include any payment in respect of value-added tax on sales or the provision of services or in respect of duty of excise.

4. Provision as respects expert evidence

(1) In proceedings for an offence under *section 2* of this Act, the opinion of any witness who appears to the court to possess the appropriate qualifications or experience as respects the matter to which his or her evidence relates shall, subject to *subsection (2)* of this section, be admissible in evidence as regards any matter calling for expertise or special knowledge that is relevant to the proceedings and, in particular and without prejudice to the generality of the foregoing, the following matters, namely—

   (a) the effects that types of agreements, decisions or concerted practices may have, or that specific agreements, decisions or concerted practices have had, on competition in trade,

   (b) an explanation to the court of any relevant economic principles or the application of such principles in practice, where such an explanation would be of assistance to the judge or, as the case may be, jury.

(2) Notwithstanding anything contained in *subsection (1)* of this section, a court may, where in its opinion the interests of justice require it to so direct in the proceedings concerned, direct that evidence of a general or specific kind referred to in the said subsection shall not be admissible in proceedings for an offence under *section 2* of this Act or shall be admissible in such proceedings for specified purposes only.

5. Certificates in respect of agreements, decisions or concerted practices

Section 4 of the Principal Act is hereby amended by the substitution of the following subsection for subsection (4):

  '(4) (a) The Authority may certify that in its opinion, on the basis of the facts in its possession—

       (i) an agreement, decision or concerted practice, or

      (ii) a category of agreements, decisions or concerted practices, does not contravene subsection (1).

(b) Where a certificate under this subsection covers a category of agreements, decisions or concerted practices, any agreements, decisions or concerted practices (as the case may be) within that category need not be notified under section 7 to benefit from the certificate.'.

6. Amendment of section 6 of Principal Act

Section 6 (7) of the Principal Act is hereby amended by the insertion after 'has been concluded' of; 'in respect of such an agreement, decision or concerted practice that has been so notified, no relief may be granted under this section in respect of the period beginning on the commencement of section 4 and ending on the date that the Authority makes a decision as aforesaid or, as the case may be, an appeal as aforesaid is concluded', and the said subsection (7), as so amended, is set out in the Table to this section.

TABLE

(7) This section shall not apply to any agreement, decision or concerted practice to which section 7 (2) applies which has been duly notified to the Authority until the Authority has decided to grant or refuse to grant a licence under section 4 (2), or to issue a certificate or not to issue a certificate under section 4 (4), in relation thereto and any appeal to the Court under section 9 in relation to the licence or the certificate has been concluded; in respect of such an agreement, decision or concerted practice that has been so notified, no relief may be granted under this section in respect of the period beginning on the commencement of section 4 and ending on the date that the Authority makes a decision as aforesaid or, as the case may be, an appeal as aforesaid is concluded.

7. Conferral of right of action on Competition Authority

Section 6 of the Principal Act is hereby amended—

(a) by the substitution of the following subsection for subsection (1):

'(1) Any person who is aggrieved in consequence of any agreement, decision, concerted practice or abuse which is prohibited under section 4 or 5 shall have a right of action for relief under this section against either or both of the following, namely

(a) any undertaking which is or has at any material time been a party to such an agreement, decision or concerted practice or has been guilty of such an abuse,

(b) any director, manager or other officer of such an undertaking, or a person who purported to act in any such capacity, who authorised or consented to, as the case may be, the entry by the undertaking into, or the implementation by it of, the agreement or decision, the engaging by it in the concerted practice or the doing by it of the act that constituted the abuse.',

(b) in subsection (4), by the substitution for 'The Minister' of 'Each of the following, namely, the Minister and the Authority,',

(c) by the insertion after subsection (4) of the following subsection:

'(4A) Where in an action under this section it is proved that the act complained of was done by an undertaking it shall be presumed, until the contrary is proved, that each (if any) director, manager and similar officer of the undertaking, and any other person who purported to act in any such capacity at the material time, consented to the doing of the said act.', and

(d) in subsection (5) (a), by the insertion after 'the Court shall' of '(unless the Authority is a party to the proceedings)',

and the said subsections (4) and (5) (a), as so amended, are set out in *paragraphs 1* and *2*, respectively, of the Table to this section.

TABLE

1. (4) Each of the following, namely, the Minister and the Authority, shall have a right of action, in respect of an agreement, decision or concerted practice or an abuse which is prohibited under section 4 or 5, for the reliefs specified in subsection (3) (*a*).

2. (5) (a) Where in proceedings under this section it is finally decided by the Court that an agreement, decision or concerted practice which is in question infringes the prohibition in section 4 (1), any certificate in force under section 4 (4) in relation to that agreement, decision or concerted practice shall thereupon cease to have force and effect as from the date of the order of the Court and the Court shall (unless the Authority is a party to the proceedings) cause a certified copy of the said order to be served on the Authority.

8. Studies and analyses by Competition Authority

The following section is hereby substituted for section 11 of the Principal Act:

'11.—(1) The Authority may and, at the request of the Minister, shall, study and analyse any practice or method of competition affecting the supply and distribution of goods or the provision of services and which, in the case of a request by the Minister, is specified in the request. Such a study or analysis may consist of, or include, a study or analysis of any development outside the State.

(2) The Authority shall, at the request of the Minister, report to the Minister the results of a study or analysis referred to in subsection (1).'

9. Amendment of Schedule to Principal Act

Paragraph 1 of the Schedule to the Principal Act is hereby amended by the insertion after subparagraph (1) of the following subparagraph:

'(1A) The Minister may assign to one permanent member of the Authority the title, 'Director of Competition Enforcement', and such a member to whom the Minister assigns the said title shall, without prejudice to his membership of the Authority, have the following functions, namely—

(a) to carry out an investigation, whether on his own initiative or as a result of a complaint to him from any person, into any contravention of section 4 or 5, or *subsection (2), (5)* or *(7)* of *section 2* of the *Competition (Amendment) Act, 1996*, that he suspects has occurred or may occur,

(b) to make recommendations and give advice to the Authority as respects the institution by the Authority of proceedings under—

(i) section 6 in relation to any matter, or

(ii) *section 3 (6)* of the *Competition (Amendment) Act, 1996*, in relation to an offence under *subsection (2), (5)* or *(7)* of *section 2* of that Act, and the enforcement generally of the provisions of this Act, and

(c) subject to the provisions of this Act, to carry out such other duties as the Authority may from time to time assign to him.'.

10. Amendment of section 5 of Act of 1978

Section 5 (inserted by the Principal Act) of the Act of 1978 is hereby amended by the insertion of the following subsection after subsection (1):

'(1A) A notification in accordance with this section shall be accompanied by such fee as the Minister may prescribe by regulations.'.

COMPETITION (AMENDMENT) ACT 1996

11. Miscellaneous amendments

(1) The Act of 1978 is hereby amended by the deletion in section 1 (1) of the definition of 'monopoly'.

(2) The Principal Act is hereby amended—

(a) in section 14, by the substitution of the following subsection for subsection (7):

'(7) References in—

(a) sections 12 and 13 (1) of the Act of 1978 to section 11 of that Act shall be construed as references to this section, and

(b) the said section 12 to subsections (1) and (5) of the said section 11 shall be construed as references to subsections (3) and (6), respectively, of this section.',

(b) by the insertion in sections 20 and 21 after 'this Act', in each place where those words occur, of 'the *Competition (Amendment) Act, 1996*, or the Act of 1978', and

(c) in section 21, by the addition of the following subsections after subsection (3):

'(4) In this section "records" includes, in addition to records in writing—

(a) discs, tapes, sound-tracks or other devices in which information, sounds or signals are embodied so as to be capable (with or without the aid of some other instrument) of being reproduced in legible or audible form,

(b) films, tapes or other devices in which visual images are embodied so as to be capable (with or without the aid of some other instrument) of being reproduced in visual form, and

(c) photographs,

and a reference to a copy of records includes, in the case of records falling within paragraph (*a*) only, a transcript of the sounds or signals embodied therein, in the case of records falling within paragraph (*b*), a still reproduction of the images embodied therein and, in the case of records falling within both of those paragraphs, such a transcript and such a still reproduction.

(5) In—

(a) an action under section 6, or

(b) proceedings for an offence under the *Competition Acts, 1991* and *1996*, or the Act of 1978,

the production to the court of a document purporting to be a warrant or other document whereby the Minister or the Authority appointed, on a specified date, a person under section 20 to be an authorised officer for the purposes of an enactment specified in that section shall, without proof of any signature on it or that the signatory was the proper person to sign it, be sufficient evidence, until the contrary is proved, that the first-mentioned person is or, as the case may be, was at all material times (but not earlier than the date aforesaid) a person appointed under section 20 to be an authorised officer for the purposes of the said enactment.'.

12. Provision for avoidance of doubt: Part II of Principal Act

(1) For the avoidance of doubt, it is hereby declared that—

(a) references in Part II of the Principal Act to the parties to an agreement, decision or concerted practice of a kind described in section 4 (1) of that Act include, and shall be deemed always to have included, references to one or more of the parties to such an agreement, decision or concerted practice,

210

(b) an agreement or decision as aforesaid which a person proposes to conclude or make with one or more other persons may be notified to the Authority under section 7 of the said Act and shall be deemed always to have been capable of being so notified.

(2) *Subsection (1) (a)* of this section is without prejudice to section 11 (*a*) of the Interpretation Act, 1937.

13. Provision with respect to fees payable under Principal Act or Act of 1978

The Public Offices Fees Act, 1879, shall not apply to fees payable under the Principal Act or the Act of 1978.

14. Saving

Nothing in this Act shall prejudice any legal proceedings instituted before the date of its passing.

15. Repeals

The following provisions of the Act of 1978 are hereby repealed, namely—sections 2 (2), 6 (2) and 8 (3).

16. Short title, construction and collective citation

(1) This Act may be cited as the Competition (Amendment) Act, 1996.

(2) The Principal Act and, in so far as it amends the said Act, this Act shall be construed together as one and may be cited together as the Competition Acts, 1991 and 1996.

(3) The Mergers, Take-overs and Monopolies (Control) Acts, 1978 and 1987, and, in so far as they amend the said Acts, The Principal Act and this Act shall be construed together as one and may be cited together as the Mergers and Take-overs (Control) Acts, 1978 to 1996.

MERGERS, TAKE-OVERS AND MONOPOLIES (CONTROL) ACT, 1978

Number 17 of 1978

AN ACT TO PROVIDE FOR THE CONTROL BY THE MINISTER FOR INDUSTRY, COMMERCE AND ENERGY IN THE INTERESTS OF THE COMMON GOOD OF CERTAIN TAKEOVERS, MERGERS AND MONOPOLIES, TO EXTEND THE RESTRICTIVE PRACTICES ACT, 1972, AND TO PROVIDE FOR OTHER MATTERS CONNECTED WITH THE AFORESAID MATTERS.

[*3rd July* 1978]

BE IT ENACTED BY THE OIREACHTAS AS FOLLOWS:

1. Interpretation

(1) In this Act—

'the Act of 1972' means the Restrictive Practices Act, 1972;

'the Commission' means the Restrictive Practices Commission;

'conditional order' means an order under section 9 prohibiting a proposed merger or take-over except on conditions specified in the order;

'enterprise' means—

(i) a person or partnership engaged for profit in the supply or distribution of goods or the provision of services, including—

> > (a) a society, including a credit union, registered under the Industrial and Provident Societies Acts, 1893 to 1971,
>
> > (b) society registered under the Friendly Societies Acts, 1896 to 1977, and
>
> > (c) society established under the Building Societies Act, 1976, or
>
> (ii) a holding company within the meaning of section 155 of the Companies Act, 1963;
>
> 'the Examiner' means the Examiner of Restrictive Practices;
>
> 'the Minister' means the Minister for Industry, Commerce and Energy;
>
> 'monopoly' means an enterprise or two or more enterprises under common control, which supply or provide, or to which is supplied or provided, not less than one-half of goods or services of a particular kind supplied or provided in the State in a particular year, according to the most recent information available on an annual basis, but does not include any enterprise at least 90 per cent of whose output is exported from the State or any enterprise at least 90 per cent of whose output comprises components for products which are exported from the State:
>
> 'the scheduled criteria' means the matters specified in the Schedule to this Act:
>
> 'service' includes any professional service, but does not include—
>
> (i) any service provided by the holder of a licence under section 9 of the Central Bank Act, 1971,
>
> (ii) any service provided by a trustee savings bank certified under the Trustee Savings Banks Acts, 1863 to 1965,
>
> (iii) any service provided under a contract of employment,
>
> (iv) the supplying of electricity,
>
> (v) any transport service provided or operated by Córas Iompair Éireann,
>
> (vi) any air service or service ancillary thereto,
>
> (vii) any transport service provided by the holder of a licence under the Road Transport Act, 1932, or the Road Transport Act, 1933,
>
> (viii) any service provided by a harbour authority within the meaning of the Harbours Act, 1946, or by a pilotage authority constituted under the Pilotage Act, 1913, or
>
> (ix) any service provided by a local authority within the meaning of section 2 of the Local Government Act, 1941.

(2) For the purposes of this Act, a merger or take-over shall be deemed to be proposed when an offer capable of acceptance is made.

(3) (a) For the purposes of this Act, but subject to section 3, a merger or take-over shall be taken to exist when two or more enterprises, at least one of which carries on business in the State, come under common control.

> (b) Enterprises shall be deemed to be under common control if the decision as to how or by whom each shall be managed can be made either by the same person, or by the same group of persons acting in concert.

> (c) Without prejudice to paragraph (*b*), the acquisition by an enterprise (in this paragraph referred to as 'the first enterprise') in another (in this paragraph referred to as 'the second enterprise') which is a body corporate—

> > (i) of the right to appoint or remove a majority of the board or committee of management of the second enterprise, or

> > (ii) of shares of the second enterprise which carry voting rights, except where the voting rights in the second enterprise which are controlled by the first enterprise—

(A) are not after the acquisition more than 30 per cent of the total of such voting rights, or

(B) are before the acquisition more than one-half of the total of such voting rights,

shall be deemed to bring those enterprises under common control.

(d) For the purposes of paragraph (c)—

(i) 'voting rights' do not include voting rights which arise only in specified circumstances; and

(ii) voting rights shall be deemed to be controlled by an enterprise when it can determine how the votes concerned shall be cast.

(e) Subject to section 3, where the assets, including goodwill, (or a substantial part of the assets) of an enterprise are acquired by another enterprise, the acquisition shall be deemed to constitute a merger or take-over for the purposes of this Act if upon the acquisition a result of the acquisition is to place the second-mentioned enterprise in the position to replace (or substantially to replace) the first-mentioned enterprise in the business in which that enterprise was engaged immediately before the acquisition.

(f) This subsection does not apply to a case where enterprises come under common control (or are deemed to come under common control) either because the person referred to in paragraph (b) is a receiver or liquidator acting as such or because the person making an acquisition referred to in paragraph (c) is an underwriter or jobber acting as such, or because the person making an acquisition referred to in paragraph (e) is a receiver or liquidator acting as such.

(g) This subsection does not apply to two or more bodies corporate, each of which is a wholly-owned subsidiary of the same body corporate.

(4) In this Act a reference to a section is to a section of this Act unless it is indicated that reference to some other enactment is intended.

(5) In this Act a reference to a subsection, paragraph, subparagraph or clause is to the subsection, paragraph, subparagraph or clause of the provision in which the reference occurs, unless it is indicated that reference to some other provision is intended.

2. Application of Act

(1) (a) This Act shall apply to a proposed merger or take-over if in the most recent financial year the value of the gross assets of each of two or more of the enterprises to be involved in the proposal is not less than £1,250,000 or the turnover of each of those two or more enterprises is not less than £2,500,000.

(b) For the purposes of this subsection, 'turnover' does not include any payment in respect of value-added tax on sales or in respect of duty of excise.

(2) This Act shall apply to a monopoly where in the most recent financial year the monopoly's sales or purchases of the goods or services concerned exceed £1,500,000.

(3) This Act shall not apply to enterprises coming under common control where this occurs solely as a result of a testamentary disposition or an intestacy.

(4) The Minister may from time to time by order amend subsection (1) or subsection (2) by the substitution for an amount mentioned in that subsection of another amount, not being in any case a smaller amount than the amount for which it is substituted.

(5) (a) Where he is of opinion that the exigencies of the common good so warrant, the Minister may by order declare that, notwithstanding subsection (1), this Act shall

apply to a proposed merger or take-over of a particular class specified in the order and, upon the making of such an order, this Act shall apply to a proposed merger or take-over of that class.

(b) The Minister may by order amend or revoke an order under this subsection.

(6) Every order under this section shall have effect on and from the date on which it is made and shall be laid before each House of the Oireachtas as soon as may be after it is made and, if a resolution confirming the order is not passed by each such House within the next 21 days after each House has sat after the order is laid before it, the order shall lapse, but without prejudice to the validity of anything previously done thereunder.

3. Limitation on commencement of merger or take-over

(1) In relation to a proposed merger or take-over, title to any shares or assets concerned shall not pass until—

(a) the Minister, in pursuance of section 7 (a), has stated in writing that he has decided not to make an order under section 9 in relation to the proposed merger or take-over, or

(b) the Minister has stated in writing that he has made a conditional order in relation to the proposed merger or take-over, or

(c) the relevant period within the meaning of section 6 has elapsed without the Minister's having made an order under section 9 in relation to the proposed merger or take-over,

whichever first occurs.

(2) A statement under subsection (1) (a) shall cease to have effect at the end of the period of 12 months beginning on the date of the statement if the enterprises the subject of the proposed merger or take-over referred to in the statement have not come under common control during that period.

4. Right of purported vendor of shares to damages

Where a purported sale of shares is rendered invalid under section 3, the purported vendor shall be entitled to recover from the purported purchaser any damages the purported vendor suffers by reason only of the invalidity, unless the purported purchaser satisfies the court that before the purported sale he had notified the purported vendor of circumstances relating to the proposed sale which gave rise to the possibility of such an invalidity.

5. Notification of proposed mergers and take-overs to Minister

(1) Where a merger or take-over is proposed each of the enterprises involved and having knowledge of the existence of the proposal shall notify the Minister in writing of the proposal as soon as may be.

(2) Where, having received a notification under this section, the Minister is of opinion that in order to consider for the purposes of this Act a proposed merger or take-over he requires further information he may, within one month of the date of receipt by him of the notification, request such further information in writing from any one or more of the enterprises concerned.

(3) (a) Where there is a contravention of subsection (1) the person in control of an enterprise failing to notify the Minister shall be guilty of an offence and shall be liable on summary conviction to a fine not exceeding £500 or on conviction on indictment to a fine not exceeding £5,000.

(b) For the purposes of this subsection the person in control of an enterprise shall be—

(i) in the case of a body corporate, any officer of the body corporate who knowingly and wilfully authorises or permits the contravention,

(ii) in the case of a partnership, each partner who knowingly and wilfully authorises or permits the contravention.

6. Relevant period for purpose of section 3

(1) For the purpose of section 3, the relevant period in relation to a particular merger or take-over shall be the period of three months beginning on the date on which the Minister first receives a notification under section 5 (1) or, where the Minister requests further information under section 5 (2), the date of receipt by him of such information.

(2) Where a person involved in a proposed merger or take-over which is being investigated by the Examiner under section 8 applies, by virtue of that section, to the High Court for a declaration under section 15 of the Act of 1972, the period beginning on the date of the application and ending on the date of the decision of the High Court, or (where that decision is appealed) the date of the decision of the Supreme Court, on the application shall, notwithstanding any other provision of this section, not be reckoned in calculating the relevant period for the purposes of this section.

7. Reference to Examiner of proposed merger or take-over

Upon receipt of a notification under section 5 the Minister shall as soon as practicable either—

(a) inform the enterprises which made the notification and any other enterprise involved which enquires of him that he has decided not to make an order under section 9 in relation to the proposed merger or take-over, or

(b) refer the notification to the Examiner for investigation in relation to the scheduled criteria and inform those enterprises of such reference.

8. Report by Examiner to Minister

(1) As soon as practicable after a reference to him under section 7, the Examiner shall investigate the proposal so referred and shall, before such date, if any, as the Minister specifies, furnish the Minister with a report of his investigation.

(2) A report of the Examiner under subsection (1) shall state his opinion as to whether or not the proposed merger or take-over concerned would operate against the common good in respect of the scheduled criteria.

(3) Section 15 of the Act of 1972, which relates to inspection of premises and records, shall for the purposes of an investigation under this section apply to a person authorised in writing by the Examiner.

9. Order by Minister prohibiting proposed merger or take-over

(1) (a) The Minister, having considered a report of the Examiner under section 8 (1), may, if he thinks that the exigencies of the common good so warrant, after consultation with any other Minister of the Government appearing to him to be concerned, by order prohibit a proposed merger or take-over either absolutely or except on conditions specified in the order.

(b) The conditions referred to in paragraph (a) shall include a condition requiring the proposed merger or take-over to be effected within 12 months of the making of the order.

(2) An order under this section shall state the reasons for making the order and, in the case of a conditional order, may have retrospective effect.

(3) Before making an order under this section the Minister shall have regard to any relevant international obligations of the State.

(4) The Minister may by order revoke an order under this section and may, with the agreement of the enterprise or enterprises concerned, amend an order under this section.

(5) Every order under this section shall be laid before each House of the Oireachtas as soon as may be after it is made and, if a resolution annulling the order is passed by either such House within the next twenty-one days on which that House has sat after the order is laid before it, the order shall be annulled accordingly, but without prejudice to the validity of anything previously done thereunder.

10. Commission's enquiry and report on monopoly

(1) (a) Where the Minister is of opinion that an enquiry should be held into an apparent monopoly—

    (i) he may request the Commission through the Examiner to hold such an enquiry, and

    (ii) the Commission shall comply with the request.

(b) The following provisions shall apply in relation to a request under subsection (1) (a):—

    (i) where the Minister so directs, a request shall be transmitted forthwith by the Examiner to the Commission;

    (ii) a request may be accompanied by such report, if any, as the Minister may provide, and the report shall be transmitted by the Examiner to the Commission with the request;

    (iii) nothing in this subsection shall be construed as preventing the Examiner from making available to the Commission any relevant information in his possession.

(2) Where the Examiner states in a report under section 16 (1) of the Act of 1972 that he is of opinion that a monopoly exists which should be the subject of an enquiry by the Commission, or where the Commission holds an enquiry pursuant to a request under subsection (1), a report of the Commission under section 5 of the Act of 1972 of an enquiry held under that section shall state whether in the opinion of the Commission—

(a) a monopoly exists,

(b) if it does, it prevents or restricts competition or endangers the continuity of supplies or services or restrains trade or the provision of any service, or is likely to do any of these things,

(c) any interference or likely interference with competition, the provision of services or the continuity of supplies or services or any restraint of trade or of the provision of a service such as are mentioned in paragraph (b) is or would be unfair or operates or would operate against the common good.

(3) Any enquiry held by the Commission by virtue of this section shall be deemed to be an enquiry under section 5 of the Act of 1972.

11. Order by Minister relating to monopoly

(1) The Minister, having considered a report of the Commission (being a report referred to in section 10), may, if he thinks that the exigencies of the common good so warrant,

after consultation with any other Minister of the Government appearing to him to be concerned, by order either—

(a) prohibit the continuance of the monopoly except on conditions specified in the order, or

(b) require the division, in a manner and within a period specified in the order, of the monopoly by a sale of assets or as otherwise so specified.

(2) An order under this section shall state the reasons for making the order.

(3) Before making an order under this section the Minister shall have regard to any relevant international obligations of the State.

(4) The Minister may by order revoke an order under this section and may, with the agreement of the enterprise or enterprises concerned, amend an order under this section.

(5) An order under this section shall not have effect unless it is confirmed, by Act of the Oireachtas but, upon being so confirmed, it shall have the force of law in accordance with its terms.

12. Appeal to High Court against orders of Minister

(1) Where the Minister makes an order under section 9 (1) or 11 (1), an appeal on a point of law may be made to the High Court against the order within one month of the coming into effect of the order by any enterprise referred to in the order.

(2) Where the High Court allows an appeal under this section, the Minister shall by order amend or revoke (as may be appropriate) the order the subject of the appeal as soon as practicable.

(3) Where pursuant to subsection (2) the Minister makes an order following an appeal, section 9 (5) (in the case of an appeal against an order under section 9 (1)) or section 11 (5) (in the case of an appeal against an order under section 11 (1)) shall not apply to the order under subsection (2).

(4) An appeal against a decision of the High Court under this section shall not lie to the Supreme Court.

13. Provisions relating to orders under section 9 or 11

(1) (a) It shall be lawful for a court of competent jurisdiction to grant an injunction on the motion of the Minister or of any other person to enforce compliance with the terms of an order under section 9 or 11 for the time being in force.

(b) This subsection shall not affect any other right of the Minister or other person to bring proceedings (whether civil or criminal) for the enforcement of compliance with the terms of an order under section 9 or 11.

(2) A person who contravenes (whether by act or omission) a provision of an order under section 9 or 11 for the time being in force shall be guilty of an offence under this section and shall be liable—

(a) on summary conviction, to a fine not exceeding £500 (together with, in the case of a continuing offence, a fine not exceeding £100 for every day on which the offence is continued) or, at the discretion of the court, to imprisonment for a term not exceeding six months, or to both such fine and such imprisonment, or

(b) on conviction on indictment, to a fine not exceeding £5,000 together with, in the case of a continuing offence, a fine not exceeding £500 for every day on which the offence is continued) or, at the discretion of the court, to imprisonment for a term not exceeding two years or to both such fine and such imprisonment.

(3) (a) Where a person is convicted of an offence under this section by reason of his failure, neglect or refusal to comply with a provision in an order requiring him to perform a specified act within a specified period or before a specified date, and the act remains, after the date of conviction, unperformed by him, the person shall be guilty of an offence and shall be liable on summary conviction to a fine not exceeding £100, or on conviction on indictment to a fine not exceeding £500, for each day, after the date of the first-mentioned conviction, on which the act remains unperformed by him or, at the discretion of the court, to imprisonment for a term not exceeding six months.

(b) An offence under this section shall be a continuing offence and, accordingly, fresh proceedings in respect thereof may be taken from time to time.

(4) Every person who aids, abets or assists another person, or conspires with another person, to do anything (whether by way of act or of omission), the doing of which is an offence by virtue of subsection (2) or (3) shall himself be guilty of an offence under this section and shall be liable on conviction to the penalties specified in subsection (2) or (3).

(5) (a) Summary proceedings in relation to an offence under this section may be prosecuted by the Minister.

(b) Notwithstanding section 10 (4) of the Petty Sessions (Ireland) Act, 1851, summary proceedings for an offence under this section may be instituted within twelve months from the latest day on which the offence was committed.

(6) Where an offence under this section which is committed by a body corporate or by a person purporting to act on behalf of a body corporate or an unincorporated body of persons is proved to have been so committed with the consent or connivance of, or to be attributable to any neglect on the part of, any person who is a director, manager, secretary, member of the committee of management or other controlling authority of any such body, or who is any other similar officer of any such body, that person shall also be guilty of the offence and shall be liable to be proceeded against and punished accordingly.

14. Application of certain statutory provisions relating to amalgamation

(1) Nothing in the Companies Acts, 1963 to 1977, the Industrial and Provident Societies Acts, 1893 to 1971, the Building Societies Act 1976, or the Friendly Societies Acts, 1896 to 1977, shall be construed as relieving an enterprise of the obligation to comply with section 5.

(2) An order under section 201 of the Companies Act, 1963, shall not be made in respect of a proposed amalgamation (being a proposed merger or take-over to which this Act applies) until either—

(a) the Minister has stated in writing that he has decided not to make an order under section 9 in relation to the proposed amalgamation, or

(b) the Minister has stated in writing that he has made a conditional order in relation to the proposed amalgamation, or

(c) the relevant period within, the meaning of section 6 has elapsed without the Minister's having made an order under section 9 in relation to the proposed amalgamation,

whichever first occurs.

(3) (a) A copy of a special resolution under section 53 of the Act of 1893, providing for the amalgamation of, or the transfer of engagements between, two or more societies registered under that Act (being a proposed merger or take-over to which this Act applies) shall not be registered under section 56 of the Act of 1893 until either—

(i) the Minister has stated in writing that he has decided not to make an order under section 9 in relation to the proposed amalgamation or transfer of engagements, or

(ii) the Minister has stated in writing that he has made a conditional order in relation to the proposed amalgamation or transfer of engagements, or

(iii) the relevant period within the meaning of section 6 has elapsed without the Minister's having made an order under section 9 in relation to the proposed amalgamation or transfer of engagements,

whichever first occurs.

(b) In this subsection 'the Act of 1893' means the Industrial and Provident Societies Act, 1893.

(4) (a) A copy of a special resolution under section 70 of the Act of 1896, providing for the amalgamation of, or the transfer of engagements between, two or more societies registered under that Act (being a proposed merger or take-over to which this Act applies) shall not be registered under section 75 of the Act of 1896 until either—

(i) the Minister has stated in writing that he has decided not to make an order under section 9 in relation to the proposed amalgamation or transfer of engagements, or

(ii) the Minister has stated in writing that he has made a conditional order in relation to the proposed amalgamation or transfer of engagements, or

(iii) the relevant period within the meaning of section 6 has elapsed without the Minister's having made an order under section 9 in relation to the proposed amalgamation or transfer of engagements,

whichever first occurs.

(b) In this subsection 'the Act of 1896' means the Friendly Societies Act, 1896.

(5) (a) A union of two or more societies which are registered under the Act of 1976, a transfer of engagements between two such societies or an undertaking by one such society to fulfill the engagements of another such society (being in each case a proposed merger or take-over to which this Act applies) shall not be registered under section 25 (2), 26 (2) or section 27 (6) of the Act of 1976 until either—

(i) the Minister has stated in writing that he has decided not to make an order under section 9 in relation to the proposed union, transfer or undertaking, or

(ii) the Minister has stated in writing that he has made a conditional order in relation to the proposed union transfer or undertaking, or

(iii) the relevant period within the meaning of section 6 has elapsed without the Minister having made an order under section 9 in relation to the proposed union, transfer or undertaking,

whichever first occurs.

(b) In this subsection 'the Act of 1976' means the Building Societies Act, 1976.

15. Annual report by Minister

(1) The Minister shall furnish to each House of the Oireachtas an annual report stating the number and the nature of investigations under section 8.

(2) It shall be lawful for the Minister to omit from an annual report under this section any information the publication of which would in his opinion materially injure the legitimate interests of an enterprise, if the information is not essential to the full understanding of the investigation to which it relates, and a statement indicating the general character of information so omitted shall be included in the report.

16. Amendment of Second Schedule to Act of 1972

Paragraph 8 of the Second Schedule to the Act of 1972 is hereby amended by the insertion in subparagraph (1) after 'under section 14' and in subparagraph (2) after 'under this Act' of 'or under the Mergers, Take-overs and Monopolies (Control) Act, 1978', and that paragraph as so amended is set out in the Table to this section.

TABLE

8.—(1) No person shall disclose information available to him through being present at an investigation held by the Examiner under section 14 or under the Mergers. Take-overs and Monopolies (Control) Act, 1978.

(2) Subparagraph (1) does not apply to a communication made by the Examiner or an authorised officer in the execution of his duties under this Act or under the Mergers, Take-overs and Monopolies (Control) Act, 1978, or to the disclosure of information in a report by the Examiner or for the purpose of legal proceedings under this Act or under the Mergers, Take-overs and Monopolies (Control) Act, 1978.

(3) If any person contravenes this paragraph he shall be guilty of an offence and shall be liable on summary conviction to a fine not exceeding one hundred pounds or imprisonment for a period not exceeding six months or, at the discretion of the court, to both such fine and imprisonment.

17. Expenses

Any expenses incurred by the Minister in the administration of this Act shall, to such extent as may be sanctioned by the Minister for Finance, be paid out of moneys provided by the Oireachtas.

18. Short title

This Act may be cited as the Mergers, Take-overs and Monopolies (Control) Act, 1978.

SCHEDULE

Criteria for purposes of section 7 (b) and 8 (2)

(a) The extent to which the proposed merger or take-over would be likely to prevent or restrict competition or to restrict trade or the provision of any service.

(b) The extent to which the proposed merger or take-over would be likely to endanger the continuity of supplies or services.

(c) The extent to which the proposed merger or take-over would be likely to affect employment and would be compatible with national policy in relation to employment.

(d) The extent to which the proposed merger or take-over is in accordance with national policy for regional development.

(e) The extent to which the proposed merger or take-over is in harmony with the policy of the Government relating to the rationalisation, in the interests of greater efficiency, of operations in the industry or business concerned.

(f) Any benefits likely to be derived from the proposed take-over or merger and relating to research and development, technical efficiency, increased production, efficient distribution of products and access to markets.

(g) The interests of shareholders and partners in the enterprises involved.

(h) The interests of employees in the enterprises involved.

(i) The interests of the consumer.

Council Regulation (EEC) No 4064/89 of 21 December 1989 on the control of concentrations between undertakings

THE COUNCIL OF THE EUROPEAN COMMUNITIES,

Having regard to the Treaty establishing the European Economic Community, and in particular Articles 87 and 235 thereof,

Having regard to the proposal from the Commission,

Having regard to the opinion of the European Parliament,

Having regard to the opinion of the Economic and Social Committee,

(1) Whereas, for the achievement of the aims of the Treaty establishing the European Economic Community, Article 3(f) gives the Community the objective of instituting 'a system ensuring that competition in the common market is not distorted';

(2) Whereas this system is essential for the achievement of the internal market by 1992 and its further development;

(3) Whereas the dismantling of internal frontiers is resulting and will continue to result in major corporate reorganizations in the Community, particularly in the form of concentrations;

(4) Whereas such a development must be welcomed as being in line with the requirements of dynamic competition and capable of increasing the competitiveness of European industry, improving the conditions of growth and raising the standard of living in the Community;

(5) Whereas, however, it must be ensured that the process of reorganization does not result in lasting damage to competition; whereas Community law must therefore include provisions governing those concentrations which may significantly impede effective competition in the common market or in a substantial part of it;

(6) Whereas Articles 85 and 86, while applicable, according to the case-law of the Court of Justice, to certain concentrations, are not, however, sufficient to control all operations which may prove to be incompatible with the system of undistorted competition envisaged in the Treaty;

(7) Whereas a new legal instrument should therefore be created in the form of a Regulation to permit effective control of all concentrations from the point of view of their effect on the structure of competition in the Community and to be the only instrument applicable to such concentrations;

(8) Whereas this Regulation should therefore be based not only on Article 87 but, principally, on Article 235 of the Treaty, under which the Community may give itself the additional powers of action necessary for the attainment of its objectives, including with regard to concentrations on the markets for agricultural products listed in Annex II to the Treaty;

(9) Whereas the provisions to be adopted in this Regulation should apply to significant structural changes the impact of which on the market goes beyond the national borders of any one Member State;

(10) Whereas the scope of application of this Regulation should therefore be defined according to the geographical area of activity of the undertakings concerned and be limited by quantitative thresholds in order to cover those concentrations which have a Community dimension; whereas, at the end of an initial phase of the application of this Regulation, these thresholds should be reviewed in the light of the experience gained;

(11) Whereas a concentration with a Community dimension exists where the combined aggregate turnover of the undertakings concerned exceeds given levels worldwide and within the Community and where at least two of the undertakings concerned have their sole or main fields of activities in different Member States or where, although the undertakings in question act mainly in one and the same Member State, at least one of them has substantial operations in at least one other Member State; whereas that is also the case where the concentrations are effected by undertakings which do not have their principal fields of activities in the Community but which have substantial operations there;

(12) Whereas the arrangements to be introduced for the control of concentrations should, without prejudice to Article 90(2) of the Treaty, respect the principle of non-discrimination between the public and the private sectors; whereas, in the public sector, calculation of the turnover of an undertaking concerned in a concentration needs, therefore, to take account of undertakings making up an economic unit with an independent power of decision, irrespective of the way in which their capital is held or of the rules of administrative supervision applicable to them;

(13) Whereas it is necessary to establish whether concentrations with a Community dimension are compatible or not with the common market from the point of view of the need to maintain and develop effective competition in the common market; whereas, in so doing, the Commission must place its appraisal within the general framework of the achievement of the fundamental objectives referred to in Article 2 of the Treaty, including that of strengthening the Community's economic and social cohesion, referred to in Article 130a;

(14) Whereas this Regulation should establish the principle that a concentration with a Community dimension which creates or strengthens a position as a result of which effective competition in the common market or in a substantial part of it is significantly impeded is to be declared incompatible with the common market;

(15) Whereas concentrations which, by reason of the limited market share of the undertakings concerned, are not liable to impede effective competition may be presumed to be compatible with the common market; whereas, without prejudice to Articles 85 and 86 of the Treaty, an indication to this effect exists, in particular, where the market share of the undertakings concerned does not exceed 25% either in the common market or in a substantial part of it;

(16) Whereas the Commission should have the task of taking all the decisions necessary to establish whether or not concentrations with a Community dimension are compatible with the common market, as well as decisions designed to restore effective competition;

(17) Whereas to ensure effective control undertakings should be obliged to give prior notification of concentrations with a Community dimension and provision should be made for the suspension of concentrations for a limited period, and for the possibility of extending or waiving a suspension where necessary; whereas in the interests of legal certainty the validity of transactions must nevertheless be protected as much as necessary;

(18) Whereas a period within which the Commission must initiate proceedings in respect of a notified concentration and periods within which it must give a final decision on the compatibility or incompatibility with the common market of a notified concentration should be laid down;

(19) Whereas the undertakings concerned must be afforded the right to be heard by the Commission when proceedings have been initiated; whereas the members of the management and supervisory bodies and the recognized representatives of the employees of the undertakings concerned, and third parties showing a legitimate interest, must also be given the opportunity to be heard;

(20) Whereas the Commission should act in close and constant liaison with the competent authorities of the Member States from which it obtains comments and information;

(21) Whereas, for the purposes of this Regulation, and in accordance with the case-law of the Court of Justice, the Commission must be afforded the assistance of the Member States and must also be empowered to require information to be given and to carry out the necessary investigations in order to appraise concentrations;

(22) Whereas compliance with this Regulation must be enforceable by means of fines and periodic penalty payments; whereas the Court of Justice should be given unlimited jurisdiction in that regard pursuant to Article 172 of the Treaty;

(23) Whereas it is appropriate to define the concept of concentration in such a manner as to cover only operations bringing about a lasting change in the structure of the undertakings concerned; whereas it is therefore necessary to exclude from the scope of this Regulation those operations which have as their object or effect the coordination of the competitive behaviour of undertakings which remain independent, since such operations fall to be examined under the appropriate provisions of the Regulations implementing Articles 85 and 86 of the Treaty; whereas it is appropriate to make this distinction specifically in the case of the creation of joint ventures;

(24) Whereas there is no coordination of competitive behaviour within the meaning of this Regulation where two or more undertakings agree to acquire jointly control of one or more other undertakings with the object and effect of sharing amongst themselves such undertakings or their assets;

(25) Whereas this Regulation should still apply where the undertakings concerned accept restrictions directly related and necessary to the implementation of the concentration;

(26) Whereas the Commission should be given exclusive competence to apply this Regulation, subject to review by the Court of Justice;

(27) Whereas the Member States may not apply their national legislation on competition to concentrations with a Community dimension, unless this Regulation makes provision therefor; whereas the relevant powers of national authorities should be limited to cases where, failing intervention by the Commission, effective competition is likely to be significantly impeded within the territory of a Member State and where the competition interests of that Member State cannot be sufficiently protected otherwise by this Regulation; whereas the Member States concerned must act promptly in such cases; whereas this Regulation cannot, because of the diversity of national law, fix a single deadline for the adoption of remedies;

(28) Whereas, furthermore, the exclusive application of this Regulation to concentrations with a Community dimension is without prejudice to Article 223 of the Treaty, and does not prevent the Member States from taking appropriate measures to protect legitimate interests other than those pursued by this Regulation, provided that such measures are compatible with the general principles and other provisions of Community law;

(29) Whereas concentrations not covered by this Regulation come, in principle, within the jurisdiction of the Member States; whereas, however, the Commission should have the power to act, at the request of a Member State concerned, in cases where effective competition could be significantly impeded within that Member State's territory;

COUNCIL REGULATION (EEC) NO 4064/89

(30) Whereas the conditions in which concentrations involving Community undertakings are carried out in non-member countries should be observed, and provision should be made for the possibility of the Council giving the Commission an appropriate mandate for negotiation with a view to obtaining non-discriminatory treatment for Community undertakings;

(31) Whereas this Regulation in no way detracts from the collective rights of employees as recognized in the undertakings concerned,

HAS ADOPTED THIS REGULATION:

Article 1

Scope

1. Without prejudice to Article 22 this Regulation shall apply to all concentrations with a Community dimension as defined in paragraph 2.

2. For the purposes of this Regulation, a concentration has a Community dimension where:

   (a) the combined aggregate worldwide turnover of all the undertakings concerned is more than ECU 5,000 million; and

   (b) the aggregate Community-wide turnover of each of at least two of the undertakings concerned is more than ECU 250 million,

   unless each of the undertakings concerned achieves more than two-thirds of its aggregate Community-wide turnover within one and the same Member State.

3. The thresholds laid down in paragraph 2 will be reviewed before the end of the fourth year following that of the adoption of this Regulation by the Council acting by a qualified majority on a proposal from the Commission.

Article 2

Appraisal of concentrations

1. Concentrations within the scope of this Regulation shall be appraised in accordance with the following provisions with a view to establishing whether or not they are compatible with the common market.

   In making this appraisal, the Commission shall take into account:

   (a) the need to maintain and develop effective competition within the common market in view of, among other things, the structure of all the markets concerned and the actual or potential competition from undertakings located either within or outwith the Community;

   (b) the market position of the undertakings concerned and their economic and financial power, the alternatives available to suppliers and users, their access to supplies or markets, any legal or other barriers to entry, supply and demand trends for the relevant goods and services, the interests of the intermediate and ultimate consumers, and the development of technical and economic progress provided that it is to consumers' advantage and does not form an obstacle to competition.

2. A concentration which does not create or strengthen a dominant position as a result of which effective competition would be significantly impeded in the common market or in a substantial part of it shall be declared compatible with the common market.

3. A concentration which creates or strengthens a dominant position as a result of which effective competition would be significantly impeded in the common market or in a substantial part of it shall be declared incompatible with the common market.

Article 3

Definition of concentration

1. A concentration shall be deemed to arise where:

   (a) two or more previously independent undertakings merge, or

   (b) – one or more persons already controlling at least one undertaking, or

   – one or more undertakings

   acquire, whether by purchase of securities or assets, by contract or by any other means, direct or indirect control of the whole or parts of one or more other undertakings.

2. An operation, including the creation of a joint venture, which has as its object or effect the coordination of the competitive behaviour of undertakings which remain independent shall not constitute a concentration within the meaning of paragraph 1 (b).

   The creation of a joint venture performing on a lasting basis all the functions of an autonomous economic entity, which does not give rise to coordination of the competitive behaviour of the parties amongst themselves or between them and the joint venture, shall constitute a concentration within the meaning of paragraph 1(b).

3. For the purposes of this Regulation, control shall be constituted by rights, contracts or any other means which, either separately or in combination and having regard to the considerations of fact or law involved, confer the possibility of exercising decisive influence on an undertaking, in particular by:

   (a) ownership or the right to use all or part of the assets of an undertaking;

   (b) rights or contracts which confer decisive influence on the composition, voting or decisions of the organs of an undertaking.

4. Control is acquired by persons or undertakings which:

   (a) are holders of the rights or entitled to rights under the contracts concerned; or

   (b) while not being holders of such rights or entitled to rights under such contracts, have the power to exercise the rights deriving therefrom.

5. A concentration shall not be deemed to arise where:

   (a) credit institutions or other financial institutions or insurance companies, the normal activities of which include transactions and dealing in securities for their own account or for the account of others, hold on a temporary basis securities which they have acquired in an undertaking with a view to reselling them, provided that they do not exercise voting rights in respect of those securities with a view to determining the competitive behaviour of that undertaking or provided that they exercise such voting rights only with a view to preparing the disposal of all or part of that undertaking or of its assets or the disposal of those securities and that any such disposal takes place within one year of the date of acquisition; that period may be extended by the Commission on request where such institutions or companies can show that the disposal was not reasonably possible within the period set;

   (b) control is acquired by an office-holder according to the law of a Member State relating to liquidation, winding up, insolvency, cessation of payments, compositions or analogous proceedings;

   (c) the operations referred to in paragraph 1(b) are carried out by the financial holding companies referred to in Article 5(3) of the Fourth Council Directive 78/ 660/EEC of 25 July 1978 on the annual accounts of certain types of companies, as last amended by Directive 84/569/EEC, provided however that the voting rights in respect of the holding are exercised, in particular in relation to the appointment of members of the management and supervisory bodies of the undertakings in which they have holdings, only to maintain the full value of those investments and not to determine directly or indirectly the competitive conduct of those undertakings.

Article 4

Prior notification of concentrations

1. Concentrations with a Community dimension defined in this Regulation shall be notified to the Commission not more than one week after the conclusion of the agreement, or the announcement of the public bid, or the acquisition of a controlling interest. That week shall begin when the first of those events occurs.

2. A concentration which consists of a merger within the meaning of Article 3(1)(a) or in the acquisition of joint control within the meaning of Article 3(1)(b) shall be notified jointly by the parties to the merger or by those acquiring joint control as the case may be. In all other cases, the notification shall be effected by the person or undertaking acquiring control of the whole or parts of one or more undertakings.

3. Where the Commission finds that a notified concentration falls within the scope of this Regulation, it shall publish the fact of the notification, at the same time indicating the names of the parties, the nature of the concentration and the economic sectors involved. The Commission shall take account of the legitimate interest of undertakings in the protection of their business secrets.

Article 5

Calculation of turnover

1. Aggregate turnover within the meaning of Article 1(2) shall comprise the amounts derived by the undertakings concerned in the preceding financial year from the sale of products and the provision of services falling within the undertakings' ordinary activities after deduction of sales rebates and of value added tax and other taxes directly related to turnover. The aggregate turnover of an undertaking concerned shall not include the sale of products or the provision of services between any of the undertakings referred to in paragraph 4.

   Turnover, in the Community or in a Member State, shall comprise products sold and services provided to undertakings or consumers, in the Community or in that Member State as the case may be.

2. By way of derogation from paragraph 1, where the concentration consists in the acquisition of parts, whether or not constituted as legal entities, of one or more undertakings, only the turnover relating to the parts which are the subject of the transaction shall be taken into account with regard to the seller or sellers.

   However, two or more transactions within the meaning of the first subparagraph which take place within a two-year period between the same persons or undertakings shall be treated as one and the same concentration arising on the date of the last transaction.

3. In place of turnover the following shall be used:

   (a) for credit institutions and other financial institutions, as regards Article 1(2)(a), one-tenth of their total assets

   As regards Article 1(2)(b) and the final part of Article 1(2), total Community-wide turnover shall be replaced by one-tenth of total assets multiplied by the ratio between loans and advances to credit institutions and customers in transactions with Community residents and the total sum of those loans and advances.

As regards the final part of Article 1(2), total turnover within one Member State shall be replaced by one-tenth of total assets multiplied by the ratio between loans and advances to credit institutions and customers in transactions with residents of that Member State and the total sum of those loans and advances;

    (b) for insurance undertakings, the value of gross premiums written which shall comprise all amounts received and receivable in respect of insurance contracts issued by or on behalf of the insurance undertakings, including also outgoing reinsurance premiums, and after deduction of taxes and parafiscal contributions or levies charged by reference to the amounts of individual premiums or the total volume of premiums; as regards Article 1(2)(b) and the final part of Article 1(2), gross premiums received from Community residents and from residents of one Member State respectively shall be taken into account.

4. Without prejudice to paragraph 2, the aggregate turnover of an undertaking concerned within the meaning of Article 1(2) shall be calculated by adding together the respective turnovers of the following:

    (a) the undertaking concerned;

    (b) those undertakings in which the undertaking concerned, directly or indirectly:

        – owns more than half the capital or business assets, or

        – has the power to exercise more than half the voting rights, or

        – has the power to appoint more than half the members of the supervisory board, the administrative board or bodies legally representing the undertakings, or

        – has the right to manage the undertakings' affairs;

    (c) those undertakings which have in the undertaking concerned the rights or powers listed in (b);

    (d) those undertakings in which an undertaking as referred to in (c) has the rights or powers listed in (b);

    (e) those undertakings in which two or more undertakings as referred to in (a) to (d) jointly have the rights or powers listed in (b).

5. Where undertakings concerned by the concentration jointly have the rights or powers listed in paragraph 4(b), in calculating the aggregate turnover of the undertakings concerned for the purposes of Article 1(2):

    (a) no account shall be taken of the turnover resulting from the sale of products or the provision of services between the joint undertaking and each of the undertakings concerned or any other undertaking connected with any one of them, as set out in paragraph 4(b) to (e);

    (b) account shall be taken of the turnover resulting from the sale of products and the provision of services between the joint undertaking and any third undertakings. This turnover shall be apportioned equally amongst the undertakings concerned.

Article 6

Examination of the notification and initiation of proceedings

1. The Commission shall examine the notification as soon as it is received.

    (a) Where it concludes that the concentration notified does not fall within the scope of this Regulation, it shall record that finding by means of a decision.

    (b) Where it finds that the concentration notified, although falling within the scope of this Regulation, does not raise serious doubts as to its compatibility with the common market, it shall decide not to oppose it and shall declare that it is compatible with the common market.

(c) If, on the other hand, it finds that the concentration notified falls within the scope of this Regulation and raises serious doubts as to its compatibility with the common market, it shall decide to initiate proceedings.

2. The Commission shall notify its decision to the undertakings concerned and the competent authorities of the Member States without delay.

Article 7

Suspension of concentrations

1. For the purposes of paragraph 2 a concentration as defined in Article 1 shall not be put into effect either before its notification or within the first three weeks following its notification.

2. Where the Commission, following a preliminary examination of the notification within the period provided for in paragraph 1, finds it necessary in order to ensure the full effectiveness of any decision taken later pursuant to Article 8(3) and (4), it may decide on its own initiative to continue the suspension of a concentration in whole or in part until it takes a final decision, or to take other interim measures to that effect.

3. Paragraphs 1 and 2 shall not prevent the implementation of a public bid which has been notified to the Commission in accordance with Article 4(1), provided that the acquirer does not exercise the voting rights attached to the securities in question or does so only to maintain the full value of those investments and on the basis of a derogation granted by the Commission under paragraph 4.

4. The Commission may, on request, grant a derogation from the obligations imposed in paragraphs 1, 2 or 3 in order to prevent serious damage to one or more undertakings concerned by a concentration or to a third party. That derogation may be made subject to conditions and obligations in order to ensure conditions of effective competition. A derogation may be applied for and granted at any time, even before notification or after the transaction.

5. The validity of any transaction carried out in contravention of paragraph 1 or 2 shall be dependent on a decision pursuant to Article 6(1)(b) or Article 8(2) or (3) or on a presumption pursuant to Article 10(6).

This Article shall, however, have no effect on the validity of transactions in securities including those convertible into other securities admitted to trading on a market which is regulated and supervised by authorities recognized by public bodies, operates regularly and is accessible directly or indirectly to the public, unless the buyer and seller knew or ought to have known that the transaction was carried out in contravention of paragraph 1 or 2.

Article 8

Powers of decision of the Commission

1. Without prejudice to Article 9, all proceedings initiated pursuant to Article 6(1)(c) shall be closed by means of a decision as provided for in paragraphs 2 to 5.

2. Where the Commission finds that, following modification by the undertakings concerned if necessary, a notified concentration fulfils the criterion laid down in Article 2(2), it shall issue a decision declaring the concentration compatible with the common market.

It may attach to its decision conditions and obligations intended to ensure that the undertakings concerned comply with the commitments they have entered into vis-à-vis the Commission with a view to modifying the original concentration plan. The decision declaring the concentration compatible shall also cover restrictions directly related and necessary to the implementation of the concentration.

3. Where the Commission finds that a concentration fulfils the criterion laid down in Article 2(3), it shall issue a decision declaring that the concentration is incompatible with the common market.

4. Where a concentration has already been implemented, the Commission may, in a decision pursuant to paragraph 3 or by separate decision, require the undertakings or assets brought together to be separated or the cessation of joint control or any other action that may be appropriate in order to restore conditions of effective competition.

5. The Commission may revoke the decision it has taken pursuant to paragraph 2 where:

   (a) the declaration of compatibility is based on incorrect information for which one of the undertakings is responsible or where it has been obtained by deceit; or

   (b) the undertakings concerned commit a breach of an obligation attached to the decision.

6. In the cases referred to in paragraph 5, the Commission may take a decision under paragraph 3, without being bound by the deadline referred to in Article 10(3).

Article 9

Referral to the competent authorities of the Member States

1. The Commission may, by means of a decision notified without delay to the undertakings concerned and the competent authorities of the other Member States, refer a notified concentration to the competent authorities of the Member State concerned in the following circumstances.

2. Within three weeks of the date of receipt of the copy of the notification a Member State may inform the Commission, which shall inform the undertakings concerned, that a concentration threatens to create or to strengthen a dominant position as a result of which effective competition would be significantly impeded on a market, within that Member State, which presents all the characteristics of a distinct market, be it a substantial part of the common market or not.

3. If the Commission considers that, having regard to the market for the products or services in question and the geographical reference market within the meaning of paragraph 7, there is such as distinct market and that such a threat exists, either:

   (a) it shall itself deal with the case in order to maintain or restore effective competition on the market concerned; or

   (b) it shall refer the case to the competent authorities of the Member State concerned with a view to the application of that State's national competition law.

   If, however, the Commission considers that such a distinct market or threat does not exist it shall adopt a decision to that effect which it shall address to the Member State concerned.

4. A decision to refer or not to refer pursuant to paragraph 3 shall be taken:

   (a) as a general rule within the six-week period provided for in Article 10(1), second subparagraph, where the Commission, pursuant to Article 6(1)(b), has not initiated proceedings; or

   (b) within three months at most of the notification of the concentration concerned where the Commission has initiated proceedings under Article 6(1)(c), without taking the preparatory steps in order to adopt the necessary measures under Article 8(2), second subparagraph, (3) or (4) to maintain or restore effective competition on the market concerned.

5. If within the three months referred to in paragraph 4(b) the Commission, despite a reminder from the Member State concerned, has not taken a decision on referral in accordance with paragraph 3 nor has taken the preparatory steps referred to in paragraph 4(b), it shall be deemed to have taken a decision to refer the case to the Member State concerned in accordance with paragraph 3(b).

6. The publication of any report or the announcement of the findings of the examination of the concentration by the competent authority of the Member State concerned shall be effected not more than four months after the Commission's referral.

7. The geographical reference market shall consist of the area in which the undertakings concerned are involved in the supply and demand of products or services, in which the conditions of competition are sufficiently homogeneous and which can be distinguished from neighbouring areas because, in particular, conditions of competition are appreciably different in those areas. This assessment should take account in particular of the nature and characteristics of the products or services concerned, of the existence of entry barriers of consumer preferences, of appreciable differences of the undertakings' market shares between the area concerned and neighbouring areas or of substantial price differences.

8. In applying the provisions of this Article, the Member State concerned may take only the measures strictly necessary to safeguard or restore effective competition on the market concerned.

9. In accordance with the relevant provisions of the Treaty, any Member State may appeal to the Court of Justice, and in particular request the application of Article 186, for the purpose of applying its national competition law.

10. This Article will be reviewed before the end of the fourth year following that of the adoption of this Regulation.

Article 10

Time limits for initiating proceedings and for decisions

1. The decisions referred to in Article 6(1) must be taken within one month at most. That period shall begin on the day following that of the receipt of a notification or, if the information to be supplied with the notification is incomplete, on the day following that of the receipt of the complete information.

   That period shall be increased to six weeks if the Commission receives a request from a Member State in accordance with Article 9(2).

2. Decisions taken pursuant to Article 8(2) concerning notified concentrations must be taken as soon as it appears that the serious doubts referred to in Article 6(1)(c) have been removed, particularly as a result of modifications made by the undertakings concerned, and at the latest by the deadline laid down in paragraph 3.

3. Without prejudice to Article 8(6), decisions taken pursuant to Article 8(3) concerning notified concentrations must be taken within not more than four months of the date on which proceedings are initiated.

4. The period set by paragraph 3 shall exceptionally be suspended where, owing to circumstances for which one of the undertakings involved in the concentration is responsible, the Commission has had to request information by decision pursuant to Article 11 or to order an investigation by decision pursuant to Article 13.

5. Where the Court of Justice gives a Judgment which annuls the whole or part of a Commission decision taken under this Regulation, the periods laid down in this Regulation shall start again from the date of the Judgment.

6. Where the Commission has not taken a decision in accordance with Article 6(1)(b) or (c) or Article 8(2) or (3) within the deadlines set in paragraphs 1 and 3 respectively, the concentration shall be deemed to have been declared compatible with the common market, without prejudice to Article 9.

Article 11

Requests for information

1. In carrying out the duties assigned to it by this Regulation, the Commission may obtain all necessary information from the Governments and competent authorities of the Member States, from the persons referred to in Article 3(1)(b), and from undertakings and associations of undertakings.

2. When sending a request for information to a person, an undertaking or an association of undertakings, the Commission shall at the same time send a copy of the request to the competent authority of the Member State within the territory of which the residence of the person or the seat of the undertaking or association of undertakings is situated.

3. In its request the Commission shall state the legal basis and the purpose of the request and also the penalties provided for in Article 14(1)(c) for supplying incorrect information.

4. The information requested shall be provided, in the case of undertakings, by their owners or their representatives and, in the case of legal persons, companies or firms, or of associations having no legal personality, by the persons authorized to represent them by law or by their statutes.

5. Where a person, an undertaking or an association of undertakings does not provide the information requested within the period fixed by the Commission or provides incomplete information, the Commission shall by decision require the information to be provided. The decision shall specify what information is required, fix an appropriate period within which it is to be supplied and state the penalties provided for in Articles 14(1)(c) and 15(1)(a) and the right to have the decision reviewed by the Court of Justice.

6. The Commission shall at the same time send a copy of its decision to the competent authority of the Member State within the territory of which the residence of the person or the seat of the undertaking or association of undertakings is situated.

Article 12

Investigations by the authorities of the Member States

1. At the request of the Commission, the competent authorities of the Member States shall undertake the investigations which the Commission considers to be necessary under Article 13(1), or which it has ordered by decision pursuant to Article 13(3). The officials of the competent authorities of the Member States responsible for conducting those investigations shall exercise their powers upon production of an authorization in writing issued by the competent authority of the Member State within the territory of which the investigation is to be carried out. Such authorization shall specify the subject matter and purpose of the investigation.

2. If so requested by the Commission or by the competent authority of the Member State within the territory of which the investigation is to be carried out, officials of the Commission may assist the officials of that authority in carrying out their duties.

COUNCIL REGULATION (EEC) NO 4064/89

Article 13

Investigative powers of the Commission

1. In carrying out the duties assigned to it by this Regulation, the Commission may undertake all necessary investigations into undertakings and associations of undertakings.

   To that end the officials authorized by the Commission shall be empowered:

   (a) to examine the books and other business records;

   (b) to take or demand copies of or extracts from the books and business records;

   (c) to ask for oral explanations on the spot;

   (d) to enter any premises, land and means of transport of undertakings.

2. The officials of the Commission authorized to carry out the investigations shall exercise their powers on production of an authorization in writing specifying the subject matter and purpose of the investigation and the penalties provided for in Article 14(1)(d) in cases where production of the required books or other business records is incomplete. In good time before the investigation, the Commission shall inform, in writing, the competent authority of the Member State within the territory of which the investigation is to be carried out of the investigation and of the identities of the authorized officials.

3. Undertakings and associations of undertakings shall submit to investigations ordered by decision of the Commission. The decision shall specify the subject matter and purpose of the investigation, appoint the date on which it shall begin and state the penalties provided for in Articles 14(1)(d) and 15(1)(b) and the right to have the decision reviewed by the Court of Justice.

4. The Commission shall in good time and in writing inform the competent authority of the Member State within the territory of which the investigation is to be carried out of its intention of taking a decision pursuant to paragraph 3. It shall hear the competent authority before taking its decision.

5. Officials of the competent authority of the Member State within the territory of which the investigation is to be carried out may, at the request of that authority or of the Commission, assist the officials of the Commission in carrying out their duties.

6. Where an undertaking or association of undertakings opposes an investigation ordered pursuant to this Article, the Member State concerned shall afford the necessary assistance to the officials authorized by the Commission to enable them to carry out their investigation. To this end the Member States shall, after consulting the Commission, take the necessary measures within one year of the entry into force of this Regulation.

Article 14

Fines

1. The Commission may by decision impose on the persons referred to in Article 3(1)(b), undertakings or associations of undertakings fines of from ECU 1 000 to 50 000 where intentionally or negligently

   (a) they fail to notify a concentration in accordance with Article 4;

   (b) they supply incorrect or misleading information in a notification pursuant to Article 4;

 (c) they supply incorrect information in response to a request made pursuant to Article 11 or fail to supply information within the period fixed by a decision taken pursuant to Article 11;

 (d) they produce the required books or other business records in incomplete form during investigations under Article 12 or 13, or refuse to submit to an investigation ordered by decision taken pursuant to Article 13.

2. The Commission may by decision impose fines not exceeding 10% of the aggregate turnover of the undertakings concerned within the meaning of Article 5 on the persons or undertakings concerned where, either intentionally or negligently, they:

 (a) fail to comply with an obligation imposed by decision pursuant to Article 7(4) or 8(2), second subparagraph;

 (b) put into effect a concentration in breach of Article 7(1) or disregard a decision taken pursuant to Article 7(2);

 (c) put into effect a concentration declared incompatible with the common market by decision pursuant to Article 8(3) or do not take the measures ordered by decision pursuant to Article 8(4).

3. In setting the amount of a fine, regard shall be had to the nature and gravity of the infringement.

4. Decisions taken pursuant to paragraphs 1 and 2 shall not be of criminal law nature.

Article 15

Periodic penalty payments

1. The Commission may by decision impose on the persons referred to in Article 3(1)(b), undertakings or associations of undertakings concerned periodic penalty payments of up to ECU 25 000 for each day of delay calculated from the date set in the decision, in order to compel them:

 (a) to supply complete and correct information which it has requested by decision pursuant to Article 11;

 (b) to submit to an investigation which it has ordered by decision pursuant to Article 13.

2. The Commission may by decision impose on the persons referred to in Article 3(1)(b) or on undertakings periodic penalty payments of up to ECU 100 000 for each day of delay calculated from the date set in the decision, in order to compel them:

 (a) to comply with an obligation imposed by decision pursuant to Article 7(4) or Article 8(2), second subparagraph, or

 (b) to apply the measures ordered by decision pursuant to Article 8(4).

3. Where the persons referred to in Article 3(1)(b), undertakings or associations of undertakings have satisfied the obligation which it was the purpose of the periodic penalty payment to enforce, the Commission may set the total amount of the periodic penalty payments at a lower figure than that which would arise under the original decision.

Article 16

Review by the Court of Justice

The Court of Justice shall have unlimited jurisdiction within the meaning of Article 172 of the Treaty to review decisions whereby the Commission has fixed a fine or periodic penalty payments; it may cancel, reduce or increase the fine or periodic penalty payments imposed.

Article 17

Professional secrecy

1. Information acquired as a result of the application of Article 11, 12, 13 and 18 shall be used only for the purposes of the relevant request, investigation or hearing.

2. Without prejudice to Articles 4(3), 18 and 20, the Commission and the competent authorities of the Member States, their officials and other servants shall not disclose information they have acquired through the application of this Regulation of the kind covered by the obligation of professional secrecy.

3. Paragraphs 1 and 2 shall not prevent publication of general information or of surveys which do not contain information relating to particular undertakings or associations of undertakings.

Article 18

Hearing of the parties and of third persons

1. Before taking any decision provided for in Articles 7(2) and (4), Article 8(2), second subparagraph, and (3) to (5) and Articles 14 and 15, the Commission shall give the persons, undertakings and associations of undertakings concerned the opportunity, at every stage of the procedure up to the consultation of the Advisory Committee, of making known their views on the objections against them.

2. By way of derogation from paragraph 1, a decision to continue the suspension of a concentration or to grant a derogation from suspension as referred to in Article 7(2) or (4) may be taken provisionally, without the persons, undertakings or associations of undertakings concerned being given the opportunity to make known their views beforehand, provided that the Commission gives them that opportunity as soon as possible after having taken its decision.

3. The Commission shall base its decision only on objections on which the parties have been able to submit their observations. The rights of the defence shall be fully respected in the proceedings. Access to the file shall be open at least to the parties directly involved, subject to the legitimate interest of undertakings in the protection of their business secrets.

4. In so far as the Commission or the competent authorities of the Member States deem it necessary, they may also hear other natural or legal persons. Natural or legal persons showing a sufficient interest and especially members of the administrative or management bodies of the undertakings concerned or the recognized representatives of their employees shall be entitled, upon application, to be heard.

Article 19

Liaison with the authorities of the Member States

1. The Commission shall transmit to the competent authorities of the Member States copies of notifications within three working days and, as soon as possible, copies of the most important documents lodged with or issued by the Commission pursuant to this Regulation.

2. The Commission shall carry out the procedures set out in this Regulation in close and constant liaison with the competent authorities of the Member States, which may express their views upon those procedures. For the purposes of Article 9 it shall obtain information from the competent authority of the Member State as referred to in paragraph 2 of that Article and give it the opportunity to make known its views at every

stage of the procedure up to the adoption of a decision pursuant to paragraph 3 of that Article; to that end it shall give it access to the file.

3. An Advisory Committee on concentrations shall be consulted before any decision is taken pursuant to Article 8(2) to (5), 14 or 15, or any provisions are adopted pursuant to Article 23.

4. The Advisory Committee shall consist of representatives of the authorities of the Member States. Each Member State shall appoint one or two representatives; if unable to attend, they may be replaced by other representatives. At least one of the representatives of a Member State shall be competent in matters of restrictive practices and dominant positions.

5. Consultation shall take place at a joint meeting convened at the invitation of and chaired by the Commission. A summary of the case, together with an indication of the most important documents and a preliminary draft of the decision to be taken for each case considered, shall be sent with the invitation. The meeting shall take place not less than 14 days after the invitation has been sent. The Commission may in exceptional cases shorten that period as appropriate in order to avoid serious harm to one or more of the undertakings concerned by a concentration.

6. The Advisory Committee shall deliver an opinion on the Commission's draft decision, if necessary by taking a vote. The Advisory Committee may deliver an opinion even if some members are absent and unrepresented. The opinion shall be delivered in writing and appended to the draft decision. The Commission shall take the utmost account of the opinion delivered by the Committee. It shall inform the Committee of the manner in which its opinion has been taken into account.

7. The Advisory Committee may recommend publication of the opinion. The Commission may carry out such publication. The decision to publish shall take due account of the legitimate interest of undertakings in the protection of their business secrets and of the interest of the undertakings concerned in such publication's taking place.

Article 20

Publication of decisions

1. The Commission shall publish the decisions which it takes pursuant to Article 8(2) to (5) in the Official Journal of the European Communities.

2. The publication shall state the names of the parties and the main content of the decision; it shall have regard to the legitimate interest of undertakings in the protection of their business secrets.

Article 21

Jurisdiction

1. Subject to review by the Court of Justice, the Commission shall have sole jurisdiction to take the decisions provided for in this Regulation.

2. No Member State shall apply its national legislation on competition to any consideration that has a Community dimension.

   The first subparagraph shall be without prejudice to any Member State's power to carry out any enquiries necessary for the application of Article 9(2) or after referral, pursuant to Article 9(3), first subparagraph, indent (b), or (5), to take the measures strictly necessary for the application of Article 9(8).

3. Notwithstanding paragraphs 1 and 2, Member States may take appropriate measures to protect legitimate interests other than those taken into consideration by this Regulation and compatible with the general principles and other provisions of Community law.

Public security, plurality of the media and prudential rules shall be regarded as legitimate interests within the meaning of the first subparagraph.

Any other public interest must be communicated to the Commission by the Member State concerned and shall be recognized by the Commission after an assessment of its compatibility with the general principles and other provisions of Community law before the measures referred to above may be taken. The Commission shall inform the Member State concerned of its decision within one month of that communication.

Article 22

Application of the Regulation

1. This Regulation alone shall apply to concentrations as defined in Article 3.

2. Regulation No 17, (EEC) No 1017/68, (EEC) No 4056/86 and (EEC) No 3975/87 shall not apply to concentrations as defined in Article 3.

3. If the Commission finds, at the request of a Member State, that a concentration as defined in Article 3 that has no Community dimension within the meaning of Article 1 creates or strengthens a dominant position as a result of which effective competition would be significantly impeded within the territory of the Member State concerned it may, in so far as the concentration affects trade between Member States, adopt the decisions provided for in Article 8(2), second subparagraph, (3) and (4).

4. Articles 2(1)(a) and (b), 5, 6, 8 and 10 to 20 shall apply. The period within which proceedings may be initiated pursuant to Article 10(1) shall begin on the date of the receipt of the request from the Member State. The request must be made within one month at most of the date on which the concentration was made known to the Member State or effected. This period shall begin on the date of the first of those events.

5. Pursuant to paragraph 3 the Commission shall take only the measures strictly necessary to maintain or store effective competition within the territory of the Member State at the request of which it intervenes.

6. Paragraphs 3 to 5 shall continue to apply until the thresholds referred to in Article 1(2) have been reviewed.

Article 23

Implementing provisions

The Commission shall have the power to adopt implementing provisions concerning the form, content and other details of notifications pursuant to Article 4, time limits pursuant to Article 10, and hearings pursuant to Article 18.

Article 24

Relations with non-member countries

1. The Member States shall inform the Commission of the general difficulties encountered by their undertakings with concentrations as defined in Article 3 in a non-member country.

2. Initially not more than one year after the entry into force of this Regulation and thereafter periodically the Commission shall draw up a report examining the treatment

accorded to Community undertakings, in the terms referred to in paragraphs 3 and 4, as regards concentrations in non-member countries. The Commission shall submit those reports to the Council, together with any recommendations.

3. Whenever it appears to the Commission, either on the basis of the reports referred to in paragraph 2 or on the basis of other information, that a non-member country does not grant Community undertakings treatment comparable to that granted by the Community to undertakings from that non-member country, the Commission may submit proposals to the Council for an appropriate mandate for negotiation with a view to obtaining comparable treatment for Community undertakings.

4. Measures taken under this Article shall comply with the obligations of the Community or of the Member States, without prejudice to Article 234 of the Treaty, under international agreements, whether bilateral or multilateral.

Article 25

Entry into force

1. This Regulation shall enter into force on 21 September 1990.

2. This Regulation shall not apply to any concentration which was the subject of an agreement or announcement or where control was acquired within the meaning of Article 4(1) before the date of this Regulation's entry into force and it shall not in any circumstances apply to any concentration in respect of which proceedings were initiated before that date by a Member State's authority with responsibility for competition.

This Regulation shall be binding in its entirety and directly applicable in all Member States.
Done at Brussels, 21 December 1989.
For the Council
The President
E. CRESSON

Council Regulation (EC) No 1310/97 of 30 June 1997 amending Regulation (EEC) No 4064/89 on the control of concentrations between undertakings

(EEC) No 4064/89 on the control of concentrations between undertakings

THE COUNCIL OF THE EUROPEAN UNION,

Having regard to the Treaty establishing the European Community, and in particular Articles 87 and 235 thereof,

Having regard to the proposal from the Commission,

Having regard to the opinion of the European Parliament,

Having regard to the opinion of the Economic and Social Committee,

(1) Whereas concentrations with a significant impact in several Member States that fall below the thresholds referred to in Council Regulation (EEC) No 4064/89 of 21 December 1989 on the control of concentrations between undertakings may qualify for examination under a number of national merger control systems; whereas multiple notification of the same transaction increases legal uncertainty, effort and cost for companies and may lead to conflicting assessments;

(2) Whereas extending the scope of Community merger control to concentrations with a significant impact in several Member States will ensure that a 'one-stop shop' system applies and will allow, in compliance with the subsidiarity principle, for an appreciation of the competition impact of such concentrations in the Community as a whole;

COUNCIL REGULATION (EC) NO 1310/97

(3) Whereas additional criteria should be established for the application of Community merger control in order to meet the above mentioned objectives; whereas those criteria should consist of new thresholds established in terms of the total turnover of the undertakings concerned achieved world-wide, at Community level and in at least three Member States;

(4) Whereas at the end of the initial phase of application of this Regulation the Commission should report to the Council on the implementation of all applicable thresholds and criteria, so that the Council is in a position, acting in accordance with Article 145 of the Treaty, to change the criteria or adjust the thresholds laid down in this Regulation;

(5) Whereas it is appropriate to define the concept of concentration in such a manner as to cover operations bringing about a lasting change in the structure of the undertakings concerned; whereas in the specific case of joint ventures it is appropriate to include within the scope and procedure of Regulation (EEC) No 4064/89 all full-function joint ventures; whereas, in addition to the dominance test set out in Article 2 of that Regulation, it should be provided that the Commission apply the criteria of Article 85 (1) and (3) of the Treaty to such joint ventures, to the extent that their creation has as its direct consequence an appreciable restriction of competition between undertakings that remain independent; whereas, if the effects of such joint ventures on the market are primarily structural, Article 85 (1) does not as a general rule apply; whereas Article 85 (1) may apply if two or more parent companies remain active in the market of the joint venture, or, possibly, if the creation of the joint venture has as its object or effect the prevention, restriction or distortion of competition between the parent companies in upstream, downstream or neighbouring markets; whereas, in this context, the appraisal of all competition aspects of the creation of the joint venture must be made within the same procedure;

(6) Whereas, for the purposes of calculating the turnover of credit and financial institutions, banking income is a better criterion than a proportion of assets, because it reflects more accurately the economic reality of the whole banking sector;

(7) Whereas it should be expressly provided that decisions taken at the end of the first phase of the procedure cover restrictions directly related and necessary for the implementation of a concentration;

(8) Whereas the Commission may declare a concentration compatible with the common market in the second phase of the procedure, following commitments by the parties that are proportional to and would entirely eliminate the competition problem; whereas it is also appropriate to accept commitments in the first phase of the procedure where the competition problem is readily identifiable and can easily be remedied; whereas it should be expressly provided that in these cases the Commission may attach to its decision conditions and obligations; whereas transparency and effective consultation of Member States and interested third parties should be ensured in both phases of the procedure;

(9) Whereas, to ensure effective control, concentrations should be suspended until a final decision has been taken; whereas, on the other hand, it should be possible to waive a suspension, where appropriate; whereas, in deciding whether or not to grant a waiver, the Commission should take account of all pertinent factors, such as the nature and gravity of damage to the undertakings concerned by a concentration or to third parties, and the threat to competition posed by the concentration;

(10) Whereas the rules governing the referral of concentrations between the Commission and Member States should be reviewed at the same time as the additional criteria for implementation of Community merger control are established; whereas these rules protect the competition interests of the Member States in an adequate manner and take due account of legal security and the 'one-stop shop' principle; whereas, however, certain aspects of the referral procedures should be improved or clarified;

(11) Whereas, in particular, the Commission can declare a concentration incompatible with the common market only if it impedes effective competition in a substantial part thereof; whereas the application of national competition law is, therefore, particularly appropriate where a concentration affects competition on a distinct market within a Member State that does not constitute a substantial part of the common market; whereas in this case it should not be necessary to demonstrate, in the request for referral, that the concentration threatens to create or to strengthen a dominant position on this distinct market;

(12) Whereas it should be possible to suspend exceptionally the period within which the Commission must take a decision within the first phase of the procedure;

(13) Whereas it should be expressly provided that two or more Member States may make a joint request pursuant to Article 22 of Regulation (EEC) No 4064/89; whereas to ensure effective control, provision should be made for the suspension of concentrations referred to the Commission by one or more Member States;

(14) Whereas the Commission should be given the power to adopt implementing provisions where necessary,

HAS ADOPTED THIS REGULATION:

Article 1

Regulation (EEC) No 4064/89 is hereby amended as follows:

1. in Article 1:

    (a) paragraph 1 shall be replaced by the following:

    '1. Without prejudice to Article 22, this Regulation shall apply to all concentrations with a Community dimension as defined in paragraphs 2 and 3.';

    (b) paragraph 3 shall be replaced by the following:

    '3. For the purposes of this Regulation, a concentration that does not meet the thresholds laid down in paragraph 2 has a Community dimension where:

    (a) the combined aggregate worldwide turnover of all the undertakings concerned is more than ECU 2 500 million;

    (b) in each of at least three Member States, the combined aggregate turnover of all the undertakings concerned is more than ECU 100 million;

    (c) in each of at least three Member States included for the purpose of point (b), the aggregate turnover of each of at least two of the undertakings concerned is more than ECU 25 million; and

    (d) the aggregate Community-wide turnover of each of at least two of the undertakings concerned is more than ECU 100 million;

    unless each of the undertakings concerned achieves more than two-thirds of its aggregate Community-wide turnover within one and the same Member State.';

    (c) the following paragraphs shall be added:

    '4. Before 1 July 2000 the Commission shall report to the Council on the operation of the thresholds and criteria set out in paragraphs 2 and 3.

    5. Following the report referred to in paragraph 4 and on a proposal from the Commission, the Council, acting by a qualified majority, may revise the thresholds and criteria mentioned in paragraph 3.';

2. in Article 2, the following paragraph shall be added:

'4. To the extent that the creation of a joint venture constituting a concentration pursuant to Article 3 has as its object or effect the coordination of the competitive behaviour of undertakings that remain independent, such coordination shall be appraised in accordance with the criteria of Article 85 (1) and (3) of the Treaty, with a view to establishing whether or not the operation is compatible with the common market.

In making this appraisal, the Commission shall take into account in particular:

– whether two or more parent companies retain to a significant extent activities in the same market as the joint venture or in a market which is downstream or upstream from that of the joint venture or in a neighbouring market closely related to this market,

– whether the coordination which is the direct consequence of the creation of the joint venture affords the undertakings concerned the possibility of eliminating competition in respect of a substantial part of the products or services in question.';

3. in Article 3, paragraph 2 shall be amended as follows:

(a) the first subparagraph shall be deleted;

(b) in the second subparagraph the phrase 'which does not give rise to the coordination of the competitive behaviour of the parties amongst themselves or between them and the joint venture' shall be deleted.

4. in Article 5:

– paragraph 3 shall be replaced by the following:

'3. In place of turnover the following shall be used:

(a) for credit institutions and other financial institutions, as regards Article 1 (2) and (3), the sum of the following income items as defined in Council Directive 86/635/EEC of 8 December 1986 on the annual accounts and consolidated accounts of banks and other financial institutions, after deduction of value added tax and other taxes directly related to those items, where appropriate:

(i) interest income and similar income;

(ii) income from securities:

– income from shares and other variable yield securities,

– income from participating interests,

– income from shares in affiliated undertakings;

(iii) commissions receivable;

(iv) net profit on financial operations;

(v) other operating income.

The turnover of a credit or financial institution in the Community or in a Member State shall comprise the income items, as defined above, which are received by the branch or division of that institution established in the Community or in the Member State in question, as the case may be;

(b) for insurance undertakings, the value of gross premiums written which shall comprise all amounts received and receivable in respect of insurance contracts issued by or on behalf of the insurance undertakings, including also outgoing reinsurance premiums, and after deduction of taxes and parafiscal contributions or levies charged by reference to the amounts of individual premiums or the total volume of premiums; as regards Article 1 (2) (b) and (3) (b), (c) and (d) and the final part of Article 1 (2) and (3), gross premiums received from

Community residents and from residents of one Member State respectively shall be taken into account.

– in paragraph 4, the introductory sentence shall be replaced by the following:

'4. Without prejudice to paragraph 2, the aggregate turnover of an undertaking concerned within the meaning of Article 1 (2) and (3) shall be calculated by adding together the respective turnovers of the following:';

– in paragraph 5, the introductory sentence shall be replaced by the following:

'5. Where undertakings concerned by the concentration jointly have the rights or powers listed in paragraph 4 (b), in calculating the aggregate turnover of the undertakings concerned for the purposes of Article 1 (2) and (3):';

5. in Article 6:

(a) in paragraph 1:

– in point (b) the following subparagraph shall be added:

'The decision declaring the concentration compatible shall also cover restrictions directly related and necessary to the implementation of the concentration.';

– point (c) shall be replaced by the following:

'(c) Without prejudice to paragraph 1 (a), where the Commission finds that the concentration notified falls within the scope of this Regulation and raises serious doubts as to its compatibility with the common market, it shall decide to initiate proceedings.';

(b) the following paragraphs shall be inserted:

'1a. Where the Commission finds that, following modification by the undertakings concerned, a notified concentration no longer raises serious doubts within the meaning of paragraph 1 (c), it may decide to declare the concentration compatible with the common market pursuant to paragraph 1 (b).

The Commission may attach to its decision under paragraph 1(b) conditions and obligations intended to ensure that the undertakings concerned comply with the commitments they have entered into vis-à-vis the Commission with a view to rendering the concentration compatible with the common market.

1b. The Commission may revoke the decision it has taken pursuant to paragraph 1 (a) or (b) where:

(a) the decision is based on incorrect information for which one of the undertakings is responsible or where it has been obtained by deceit,

or

(b) the undertakings concerned commit a breach of an obligation attached to the decision.

1c. In the cases referred to in paragraph 1 (b), the Commission may take a decision under paragraph 1, without being bound by the deadlines referred to in Article 10 (1).';

6. in Article 7:

(a) paragraph 1 shall be replaced by the following:

'1. A concentration as defined in Article 1 shall not be put into effect either before its notification or until it has been declared compatible with the common market pursuant to a decision under Article 6 (1) (b) or Article 8 (2) or on the basis of a presumption according to Article 10 (6).';

(b) paragraph 2 shall be deleted;

(c) paragraph 3 shall be amended as follows:

the words 'paragraphs 1 and 2' at the beginning of the paragraph shall be replaced by the words 'paragraph 1';

(d) paragraph 4 shall be replaced by the following:

'4. The Commission may, on request, grant a derogation from the obligations imposed in paragraphs 1 or 3. The request to grant a derogation must be reasoned. In deciding on the request, the Commission shall take into account inter alia the effects of the suspension on one or more undertakings concerned by a concentration or on a third party and the threat to competition posed by the concentration. That derogation may be made subject to conditions and obligations in order to ensure conditions of effective competition. A derogation may be applied for and granted at any time, even before notification or after the transaction.';

(e) paragraph 5 shall be replaced by the following:

'5. The validity of any transaction carried out in contravention of paragraph 1 shall be dependent on a decision pursuant to Article 6 (1) (b) or Article 8 (2) or (3) or on a presumption pursuant to Article 10 (6).

This Article shall, however, have no effect on the validity of transactions in securities including those convertible into other securities admitted to trading on a market which is regulated and supervised by authorities recognized by public bodies, operates regularly and is accessible directly or indirectly to the public, unless the buyer and seller knew or ought to have known that the transaction was carried out in contravention of paragraph 1.';

7. in Article 8:

(a) paragraph 2 shall be replaced by the following:

'2. Where the Commission finds that, following modification by the undertakings concerned if necessary, a notified concentration fulfils the criterion laid down in Article 2 (2) and, in the cases referred to in Article 2 (4), the criteria laid down in Article 85 (3) of the Treaty, it shall issue a decision declaring the concentration compatible with the common market.

It may attach to its decision conditions and obligations intended to ensure that the undertakings concerned comply with the commitments they have entered into vis-à-vis the Commission with a view to rendering the concentration compatible with the common market. The decision declaring the concentration compatible with the common market shall also cover restrictions directly related and necessary to the implementation of the concentration.';

(b) paragraph 3 shall be replaced by the following:

'3. Where the Commission finds that a concentration fulfils the criterion defined in Article 2 (3) or, in the cases referred to in Article 2 (4), does not fulfil the criteria laid down in Article 85 (3) of the Treaty, it shall issue a decision declaring that the concentration is incompatible with the common market.';

8. in Article 9:

(a) paragraph 2 shall be replaced by the following:

'2. Within three weeks of the date of receipt of the copy of the notification a Member State may inform the Commission, which shall inform the undertakings concerned, that:

(a) a concentration threatens to create or to strengthen a dominant position as a result of which effective competition will be significantly impeded on a market within that Member State, which presents all the characteristics of a distinct market, or

(b) a concentration affects competition on a market within that Member State, which presents all the characteristics of a distinct market and which does not constitute a substantial part of the common market.';

(b) in paragraph 3:

– point (b) shall be replaced by the following:

'(b) it shall refer the whole or part of the case to the competent authorities of the Member State concerned with a view to the application of that State's national competition law.',

– the following subparagraph shall be added:

'In cases where a Member State informs the Commission that a concentration affects competition in a distinct market within its territory that does not form a substantial part of the common market, the Commission shall refer the whole or part of the case relating to the distinct market concerned, if it considers that such a distinct market is affected.';

(c) paragraph 10 shall be replaced by the following:

'10. This Article may be re-examined at the same time as the thresholds referred to in Article 1.';

9. in Article 10:

(a) in paragraph 1, the following text shall be added at the end of the second subparagraph:

'or where, after notification of a concentration, the undertakings concerned submit commitments pursuant to Article 6 (1a), which are intended by the parties to form the basis for a decision pursuant to Article 6 (1) (b).';

(b) at the beginning of paragraph 4 the phrase 'The period set by paragraph 3' shall be replaced by the phrase 'The periods set by paragraphs 1 and 3';

10. in Article 18:

(a) in paragraph 1 the words: 'Article 7 (2) and (4)' shall be replaced by the words 'Article 7 (4)';

(b) paragraph 2 shall be replaced by the following:

'2. By way of derogation from paragraph 1, a decision to grant a derogation from suspension as referred to in Article 7 (4) may be taken provisionally, without the persons, undertakings or associations of undertakings concerned being given the opportunity to make known their views beforehand, provided that the Commission gives them that opportunity as soon as possible after having taken its decision.';

11. in Article 19, the following text shall be added at the end of paragraph 1:

'Such documents shall include commitments which are intended by the parties to form the basis for a decision pursuant to Articles 6 (1) (b) or 8 (2).';

12. in Article 22:

(a) paragraphs 1 and 2 shall be replaced by the following:

'1. This Regulation alone shall apply to concentrations as defined in Article 3, and Regulations No 17 (1), (EEC) No 1017/68 (2), (EEC) No 4056/86 (3) and (EEC) No

3975/87 (4) shall not apply, except in relation to joint ventures that do not have a Community dimension and which have their object or effect the coordination of the competitive behaviour of undertakings that remain independent.';

(b) paragraph 3 shall be amended as follows:

'3. If the Commission finds, at the request of a Member State or at the joint request of two or more Member States, that a concentration as defined in Article 3 that has no Community dimension within the meaning of Article 1 creates or strengthens a dominant position as a result of which effective competition would be significantly impeded within the territory of the Member State or States making the joint request, it may, insofar as that concentration affects trade between Member States, adopt the decisions provided for in Article 8 (2), second subparagraph, (3) and (4).';

(c) paragraph 4 shall be replaced by the following:

'4. Articles 2 (1) (a) and (b), 5, 6, 8 and 10 to 20 shall apply to a request made pursuant to paragraph 3. Article 7 shall apply to the extent that the concentration has not been put into effect on the date on which the Commission informs the parties that a request has been made.

The period within which proceedings may be initiated pursuant to Article 10 (1) shall begin on the day following that of the receipt of the request from the Member State or States concerned. The request must be made within one month at most of the date on which the concentration was made known to the Member State or to all Member States making a joint request or effected. This period shall begin on the date of the first of those events.';

(d) in paragraph 5 the phrase 'or States' shall be inserted after the phrase 'within the territory of the Member State';

(e) paragraph 6 shall be deleted;

13. in Article 23:

(a) the phrase 'time limits pursuant to Article 10' shall be replaced by the phrase 'time limits pursuant to Articles 7, 9, 10 and 22';

(b) the following subparagraph shall be added:

'The Commission shall have the power to lay down the procedure and time limits for the submission of commitments pursuant to Articles 6 (1a) and 8 (2).'

Article 2

This Regulation shall not apply to any concentration which was the subject of an agreement or announcement or where control was acquired within the meaning of Article 4 (1) of Regulation (EEC) No 4064/89, before 1 March 1998 and it shall not in any circumstances apply to any concentration in respect of which proceedings were initiated before 1 March 1998 by a Member State's authority with responsibility for competition.

Article 3

This Regulation shall enter into force on 1 March 1998.

This Regulation shall be binding in its entirety and directly applicable in all Member States.

Done at Luxembourg, 30 June 1997.
For the Council
The President
A. NUIS

APPENDIX 4

Private International Law

JURISDICTION OF COURTS AND ENFORCEMENT OF JUDGMENTS ACT, 1998

Number 52 of 1998

ARRANGEMENT OF SECTIONS

PART I. PRELIMINARY AND GENERAL

PART II. THE 1968 CONVENTION AND THE ACCESSION CONVENTIONS

PART III. THE LUGANO CONVENTION

PART IV. AMENDMENTS AND REPEALS

JURISDICTION OF COURTS AND ENFORCEMENT OF JUDGMENTS ACT, 1998

FIRST SCHEDULE

TEXT (IN THE ENGLISH AND IRISH LANGUAGES) OR THE 1968 CONVENTION AS AMENDED BY THE 1978 ACCESSION CONVENTION, THE 1982 ACCESSION CONVENTION, THE 1989 ACCESSION CONVENTION AND THE 1996 ACCESSION CONVENTION.

SECOND SCHEDULE

TEXT (IN THE ENGLISH AND IRISH LANGUAGES) OF THE 1971 PROTOCOL AS AMENDED BY THE 1978 ACCESSION CONVENTION, THE 1982 ACCESSION CONVENTION, THE 1989 ACCESSION CONVENTION AND THE 1996 ACCESSION CONVENTION.

NINTH SCHEDULE

DOMICILE

AN ACT TO CONSOLIDATE THE JURISDICTION OF COURTS AND ENFORCEMENT OF JUDGMENTS ACTS, 1988 AND 1993, TO GIVE THE FORCE OF LAW TO THE CONVENTION SIGNED AT BRUSSELS ON THE 29TH DAY OF NOVEMBER, 1996 ON THE ACCESSION OF THE REPUBLIC OF AUSTRIA, THE REPUBLIC OF FINLAND AND THE KINGDOM OF SWEDEN TO THE CONVENTION ON JURISDICTION AND THE ENFORCEMENT OF JUDGMENTS IN CIVIL AND COMMERCIAL MATTERS AND TO THE PROTOCOL ON ITS INTERPRETATION BY THE COURT OF JUSTICE OF THE EUROPEAN COMMUNITIES WITH THE ADJUSTMENTS MADE TO THEM BY THE CONVENTION ON THE ACCESSION OF THE KINGDOM OF DENMARK, OF IRELAND AND OF THE UNITED KINGDOM OF GREAT BRITAIN AND NORTHERN IRELAND, BY THE CONVENTION ON THE ACCESSION OF THE HELLENIC REPUBLIC AND BY THE CONVENTION ON THE ACCESSION OF THE KINGDOM OF SPAIN AND THE PORTUGUESE REPUBLIC AND TO PROVIDE FOR RELATED MATTERS.

[*23rd December* 1998]

BE IT ENACTED BY THE OIREACHTAS AS FOLLOWS:

PART I. PRELIMINARY AND GENERAL

1. Short title and commencement

(1) This Act may be cited as the Jurisdiction of Courts and Enforcement of Judgments Act, 1998.

(2) This Act shall come into operation on such day or days as, by order or made by the Minister, may be fixed either generally or with reference to any particular purpose or provision, and different days may be so fixed for different purposes and different provisions.

2. Interpretation

(1) In this Act, unless the context otherwise requires—

'the Accession Conventions' means the 1978 Accession Convention, the 1982 Accession Convention, the 1989 Accession Convention and the 1996 Accession Convention;

'the 1978 Accession Convention' means the Convention on the accession to the 1968 Convention and the 1971 Protocol of the State, Denmark and the United Kingdom, signed at Luxembourg on the 9th day of October, 1978;

'the 1982 Accession Convention' means the Convention on the accession to the 1968 Convention and the 1971 Protocol (as amended in each case by the 1978 Accession Convention) of the Hellenic Republic, signed at Luxembourg on the 25th day of October, 1982;

'the 1989 Accession Convention' means the Convention on the accession to the 1968 Convention and the 1971 Protocol (as amended in each case by the 1978 Accession Convention and the 1982 Accession Convention) of the Kingdom of Spain and the Portuguese Republic, signed at San Sebastian on the 26th day of May, 1989;

'the 1996 Accession Convention' means the Convention on the accession to the 1968 Convention and the 1971 Protocol (as amended in each case by the 1978 Accession Convention, the 1982 Accession Convention and the 1989 Accession Convention) of the Republic of Austria, the Republic of Finland and the Kingdom of Sweden, signed at Brussels on the 29th day of November, 1996;

'the 1968 Convention' means the Convention on jurisdiction and the enforcement of judgments in civil and commercial matters (including the protocol annexed to that Convention), signed at Brussels on the 27th day of September, 1968;

'court' includes a tribunal;

'the European Communities' has the same meaning as in section 1 of the European Communities Act, 1972;

'the European Court' means the Court of Justice of the European Communities;

'the Lugano Convention' means the Convention on jurisdiction and the enforcement of judgments in civil and commercial matters, signed at Lugano on the 16th day of September, 1988, and includes Protocol 1;

'the Minister' means the Minister for Justice, Equality and Law Reform;

'the 1971 Protocol' means the Protocol on the interpretation of the 1968 Convention by the European Court, signed at Luxembourg on the 3rd day of June, 1971;

'Protocol 1' means the protocol on certain questions of jurisdiction, procedure and enforcement, signed at Lugano on the 16th day of September, 1988.

(2) In this Act, unless the context otherwise requires, a reference to, or to any provision of, the 1968 Convention or the 1971 Protocol is to the 1968 Convention, the 1971 Protocol or the provision, as amended by—

(a) the 1978 Accession Convention,

(b) the 1982 Accession Convention,

(c) the 1989 Accession Convention, and

(d) the 1996 Accession Convention in so far as it is in force between the State and a state respecting which it has entered into force in accordance with Article 16 of that Convention.

(3) In this Act—

(a) a reference to a section, a Part or a Schedule is to a section or a Part of, or a Schedule to, this Act unless it is indicated that a reference to some other enactment is intended,

(b) a reference to a subsection or paragraph is to the subsection or paragraph of the provision in which the reference occurs unless it is indicated that a reference to some other provision is intended, and

(c) a reference to an enactment is to that enactment as amended or modified by any other enactment including this Act.

(4) The collective citation 'the Courts (Supplemental Provisions) Acts, 1961 to 1998' shall include *sections* 7 to *10, 13, 14* and *16* of this Act, and those Acts and those sections shall be construed together as one Act.

JURISDICTION OF COURTS AND ENFORCEMENT OF JUDGMENTS ACT, 1998

3. Texts of Conventions and Protocols

(1) For convenience of reference, the following texts are set out in the *Schedules*:

  (a) in the *First Schedule*, the 1968 Convention as amended by—

    (i) Titles II and III of the 1978 Accession Convention,

    (ii) Titles II and III of the 1982 Accession Convention,

    (iii) Titles II and III of, and Annex 1 to, the 1989 Accession Convention, and

    (iv) Titles II and III of the 1996 Accession Convention;

  (b) in the *Second Schedule*, the 1971 Protocol as amended by—

    (i) Title IV of the 1978 Accession Convention,

    (ii) Title IV of the 1982 Accession Convention,

    (iii) Title IV of the 1989 Accession Convention, and

    (iv) Title IV of the 1996 Accession Convention;

  (c) in the *Third Schedule*, Titles V and VI of the 1978 Accession Convention as amended by the 1989 Accession Convention;

  (d) in the *Fourth Schedule*, Titles V and VI of the 1982 Accession Convention;

  (e) in the *Fifth Schedule*, Titles VI and VII of the 1989 Accession Convention;

  (f) in the *Sixth Schedule*, Titles V and VI of the 1996 Accession Convention;

  (g) in the *Seventh Schedule*, the Lugano Convention;

  (h) in the *Eighth Schedule*, Protocol 1.

(2) The texts set out in the *Schedules*, are prepared from—

  (a) in the case of the *First Schedule* and the *Second Schedule*, the authentic texts, in the English and Irish languages, referred to in Articles 37 and 41 of the 1978 Accession Convention, Article 17 of the 1982 Accession Convention, Article 34 of the 1989 Accession Convention and Article 18 of the 1996 Accession Convention, and

  (b) in the case of the remaining *Schedules*, the authentic texts, in the English language, referred to in the Articles mentioned in *paragraph (a)* and in Article 68 of the Lugano Convention.

PART II. THE 1968 CONVENTION AND THE ACCESSION CONVENTIONS

4. Interpretation of this Part

(1) In this Part, unless the context otherwise requires—

'Contracting State' means a state—

  (a) which is—

    (i) one of the original parties to the 1968 Convention (Belgium, the Federal Republic of Germany, France, Italy, Luxembourg and the Netherlands), or

    (ii) one of the parties acceding to the 1968 Convention under any of the Accession Conventions (the State, Denmark, the United Kingdom, the Hellenic Republic, the Kingdom of Spain, the Portuguese Republic, the Republic of Austria, the Republic of Finland and the Kingdom of Sweden), and

  (b) respecting which—

    (i) the 1978 Accession Convention has entered into force in accordance with Article 39 of that Convention,

    (ii) the 1982 Accession Convention has entered into force in accordance with Article 15 of that Convention,

   (iii) the 1989 Accession Convention has entered into force in accordance with Article 32 of that Convention, or

   (iv) the 1996 Accession Convention has entered into force in accordance with Article 16 of that Convention,

as the case may be;

'the Conventions' means the 1968 Convention, the 1971 Protocol and the Accession Conventions;

'enforceable maintenance order' means—

(a) a maintenance order respecting all of which an enforcement order has been made, or

(b) if an enforcement order has been made respecting only part of a maintenance order, the maintenance order to the extent to which it is so ordered to be enforced;

'enforcement order' means an order for the recognition or enforcement of all or part of a judgment where the order—

(a) is made by the Master of the High Court under *section 7*, or

(b) is made or varied on appeal from a decision of the Master of the High Court under *section 7* or from a decision of the High Court relating to the Master's decision;

'judgment' means a judgment or order (by whatever name called) that is a judgment for the purposes of the 1968 Convention, and, except in *sections 10, 12* and *14*, includes—

(a) an instrument or settlement referred to in Title IV of the 1968 Convention, and

(b) an arrangement relating to maintenance obligations concluded with or authenticated by an administrative authority, as referred to in Article 10 of the 1996 Accession Convention;

'maintenance' means maintenance within the meaning of the Conventions;

'maintenance creditor' means, in relation to a maintenance order, the person entitled to the payments for which the order provides;

'maintenance debtor' means, in relation to a maintenance order, the person liable to make payments under the order;

'maintenance order' means a judgment relating to maintenance.

(2) The Minister for Foreign Affairs may, by order, declare—

(a) that any state specified in the order is a Contracting State, or

(b) that a declaration has been made pursuant to Article IV of the 1968 Convention, or a communication has been made pursuant to Article VI of that Convention, to the Secretary General of the Council of the European Communities.

(3) The text of a declaration or communication referred to in *subsection (2) (b)* shall be set out in the order declaring that the declaration or communication has been made.

(4) An order that is in force under *subsection (2)* is—

(a) if made under *subsection (2)(a)*, evidence that any state to which the declaration relates is a Contracting State, and

(b) if made under *subsection (2)(b)*, evidence that the declaration pursuant to Article IV or the communication pursuant to Article VI was made and evidence of its contents.

(5) The Minister for Foreign Affairs may, by order, amend or revoke an order made under *subsection (2)* or this subsection.

5. Conventions to have force of law

The Conventions shall have the force of law in the State and judicial notice shall be taken of them.

6. Interpretation of Conventions

(1) Judicial notice shall be taken of—

    (a) a ruling or decision of, or expression of opinion by, the European Court on any question about the meaning or effect of a provision of the Conventions, and

    (b) the reports listed in *subsection (2)*.

(2) When interpreting a provision of the Conventions, a court may consider the following reports (which are reproduced in the Official Journal of the European Communities) and shall give them the weight that is appropriate in the circumstances:

    (a) the reports by Mr. P. Jenard on the 1968 Convention and the 1971 Protocol;

    (b) the report by Professor Peter Schlosser on the 1978 Accession Convention;

    (c) the report by Professor Demetrios Evrigenis and Professor K. D. Kerameus on the accession of the Hellenic Republic to the 1968 Convention and the 1971 Protocol;

    (d) the report by Mr. Almeida Cruz, Mr. Desantes Real and Mr. P. Jenard on the 1989 Accession Convention.

7. Applications for recognition and enforcement of Community judgments

(1) An application under the Conventions for the recognition or enforcement in the State of a judgment shall—

    (a) be made to the Master of the High Court, and

    (b) be determined by the Master by order in accordance with the Conventions.

(2) An order made by the Master of the High Court under *subsection (1)* may include an order for the recognition or enforcement of only part of a judgment.

8. Enforcement of community judgments by the High Court

(1) Subject to *section 10(4)* and to the restrictions on enforcement contained in Article 39 of the 1968 Convention, if an enforcement order has been made respecting a judgment—

    (a) the judgment shall, to the extent to which its enforcement is authorised by the enforcement order, be of the same force and effect as a judgment of the High Court, and

    (b) the High Court has the same powers respecting enforcement of the judgment, and proceedings may be taken on the judgment, as if it were a judgment of that Court.

(2) Subject to *subsections (3)* and *(6)*, *subsection (1)* shall apply only to a judgment other than a maintenance order.

(3) On application by the maintenance creditor under an enforceable maintenance order, the Master of the High Court may, by order, declare that the following shall be regarded as being payable under a judgment referred to in *subsection (1)*:

    (a) sums which were payable under the maintenance order as periodic payments but were not paid before the relevant enforcement order was made;

    (b) a lump sum (not being a sum referred to in *paragraph (a)*) which is payable under the enforceable maintenance order.

(4) A declaration shall not be made under *subsection (3)* unless the Master of the High Court considers that by doing so the enforceable maintenance order would be more effectively enforced respecting any sums or sum referred to in that subsection.

(5) If a declaration is made under *subsection (3)*, the sums or sum to which the declaration relates shall be deemed, for the purposes of this Part, to be payable under a judgment referred to in *subsection (1)* and not otherwise.

(6) A maintenance order shall be regarded as a judgment referred to in *subsection (1)* if the District Court does not have jurisdiction to enforce the order under *section 9(7)*.

9. Enforcement of Community maintenance orders by the District Court

(1) Subject to *section 10(4)* and to the restrictions on enforcement contained in Article 39 of the 1968 Convention, the District Court shall have jurisdiction to enforce an enforceable maintenance order.

(2) An enforceable maintenance order shall, from the date on which the maintenance order was made, be deemed for the purposes of—

    (a) *subsection (1)*,

    (b) section 98(1) of the Defence Act, 1954, and

    (c) subject to the 1968 Convention, the variation or discharge of that order under section 6 of the Family Law (Maintenance of Spouses and Children) Act, 1976, as amended by the Status of Children Act, 1987,

to be an order made by the District Court under section 5 or section 5A of the Family Law (Maintenance of Spouses and Children) Act, 1976, as may be appropriate.

(3) *Subsections (1)* and *(2)* shall apply even though an amount payable under the enforceable maintenance order exceeds the maximum amount the District Court has jurisdiction to award under the appropriate enactment mentioned in *subsection (2)*.

(4) Where an enforceable maintenance order is varied by a court in a Contracting State other than the State and an enforcement order has been made respecting all or part of the enforceable maintenance order as so varied, or respecting all or part of the order effecting the variation, the enforceable maintenance order shall, from the date on which the variation takes effect, be enforceable in the State only as so varied.

(5) Where an enforceable maintenance order is revoked by a court in a Contracting State other than the State and an enforcement order has been made respecting the order effecting the revocation, the enforceable maintenance order shall, from the date on which the revocation takes effect, cease to be enforceable in the State except in relation to any sums under the order that were payable, but were not paid, on or before that date.

(6) Subject to *section 8(3)* to *(5)* of this Act, the following shall be regarded as being payable pursuant to an order made under section 5 or section 5A of the Family Law (Maintenance of Spouses and Children) Act, 1976:

    (a) any sums that were payable under an enforceable maintenance order but were not paid before the date of the making of the relevant enforcement order;

    (b) any costs of or incidental to the application for the enforcement order that are payable under *section 10(2)* of this Act.

(7) The jurisdiction vested in the District Court by this section may be exercised by the judge of that Court for the time being assigned to—

    (a) if the maintenance debtor under an enforceable maintenance order resides in the State, the district court district in which the debtor resides or carries on any profession, business or occupation, or

(b) if the maintenance debtor under an enforceable maintenance order does not reside in the State but is in the employment of an individual residing or having a place of business in the State or of a corporation or association having its seat in the State, the district court district in which that individual resides or that corporation or association has its seat.

(8) Despite anything to the contrary in an enforceable maintenance order, the maintenance debtor shall pay any sum payable under that order to—

   (a) in the case referred to in *subsection (7)(a)*, the district court clerk for the district court district in which the debtor for the time being resides, or

   (b) in a case referred to in *subsection (7)(b)*, a district court clerk specified by the District Court,

   for transmission to the maintenance creditor under the order or, if a public authority has been authorised by the creditor to receive that sum, to that authority.

(9) If a sum payable under an enforceable maintenance order is not duly paid and if the maintenance creditor under the order so requests in writing, the district court clerk concerned shall make an application respecting that sum under—

   (a) section 10 (which relates to the attachment of certain earnings) of the Family Law (Maintenance of Spouses and Children) Act, 1976, or

   (b) section 8 (which relates to the enforcement of certain maintenance orders) of the Enforcement of Court Orders Act, 1940.

(10) For the purposes of *subsection (9)(b)*, a reference in section 8 of the Enforcement of Court Orders Act, 1940 (other than in subsections (4) and (5) of that section) to an applicant shall be construed as a reference to the district court clerk.

(11) Nothing in this section shall affect the right of a maintenance creditor under an enforceable maintenance order to institute proceedings for the recovery of a sum payable to a district court clerk under *subsection (8)*.

(12) Section 8(7) of the Enforcement of Court Orders Act, 1940, does not apply to proceedings for the enforcement of an enforceable maintenance order.

(13) The maintenance debtor under an enforceable maintenance order shall give notice to the district court clerk for the district court area in which the debtor has been residing of any change of address.

(14) A person who, without reasonable excuse, contravenes *subsection (13)* shall be guilty of an offence and shall be liable on summary conviction to a fine not exceeding £1,000.

(15) If there are two or more district court clerks for a district court area, a reference in this section to a district court clerk shall be construed as a reference to any of those clerks.

(16) For the purposes of this section, the Dublin Metropolitan Area shall be deemed to be a district court area.

10. Provisions in enforcement orders for payment of interest on judgments and payment of costs

(1) Where, on application for an enforcement order respecting a judgment, it is shown—

   (a) that the judgment provides for the payment of a sum of money, and

   (b) that, in accordance with the law of the Contracting State in which the judgment was given, interest on that sum is recoverable under the judgment at a particular rate or rates and from a particular date or time,

   the enforcement order, if made, shall provide that the person liable to pay that sum shall also be liable to pay that interest, apart from any interest on costs recoverable under *subsection (2)*, in accordance with the particulars noted in the order, and the interest shall be recoverable by the applicant as though it were part of that sum.

(2) An enforcement order may, at the discretion of the court concerned or the Master of the High Court, as may be appropriate, provide for the payment to the applicant by the respondent of the reasonable costs of or incidental to the application for the enforcement order.

(3) A person required by an enforcement order to pay costs shall be liable to pay interest on the costs as if they were the subject of an order for the payment of costs made by the High Court on the date the enforcement order was made.

(4) Interest shall be payable on a sum referred to in *subsection (1)* only as provided for in this section.

11. Currency of payments under Community maintenance orders

(1) An amount payable in the State under a maintenance order by virtue of an enforcement order shall be paid in the currency of the State.

(2) If the amount referred to in *subsection (1)* is stated in the maintenance order in a currency other than that of the State, the payment shall be made on the basis of the exchange rate prevailing, on the date the enforcement order is made, between the currency of the State and the other currency.

(3) For the purposes of this section, a certificate purporting to be signed by an officer of an authorised institution and to state the exchange rate prevailing on a specified date between a specified currency and the currency of the State shall be admissible as evidence of the facts stated in the certificate.

(4) In this section, 'authorised institution' means any of the following:

    (a) a body licensed under the Central Bank Acts, 1942 to 1998, or authorised under regulations made under the European Communities Act, 1972, to carry on banking business;

    (b) a building society incorporated or deemed to be incorporated under section 10 of the Building Societies Act, 1989;

    (c) a society licensed under section 10 of the Trustee Savings Banks Act, 1989, to carry on the business of a trustee savings bank;

    (d) An Post;

    (e) ACC Bank public limited company;

    (f) ICC Bank public limited company.

12. Proof and admissibility of certain judgments, documents and related translations

(1) For the purposes of the Conventions—

    (a) a document that is duly authenticated and purports to be a copy of a judgment given by a court of a Contracting State other than the State shall, without further proof, be deemed to be a true copy of the judgment, unless the contrary is shown, and

    (b) the original or any copy of a document mentioned in Article 46.2 or 47 of the 1968 Convention shall be admissible as evidence of any matter to which the document relates.

(2) A document purporting to be a copy of a judgment given by a court of a Contracting State, shall, for the purposes of this Act, be regarded as being duly authenticated if it purports—

    (a) to bear the seal of that court, or

    (b) to be certified by a judge or officer of that court to be a true copy of a judgment given by that court.

(3) A document shall be admissible as evidence of a translation if—

    (a) it purports to be the translation of—

        (i) a judgment given by a court of a Contracting State other than the State,

        (ii) a document mentioned in Article 46.2, 47 or 50 of the 1968 Convention, or

        (iii) a document containing a settlement referred to in Article 51 of the 1968 Convention or containing an arrangement referred to in Article 10 of the 1996 Accession Convention, and

    (b) it is certified as correct by a person competent to do so.

13. Provisional, including protective, measures

(1) On application pursuant to Article 24 of the 1968 Convention, the High Court may grant any provisional, including protective, measures of any kind that the Court has power to grant in proceedings that, apart from this Act, are within its jurisdiction, if—

    (a) proceedings have been or are to be commenced in a Contracting State other than the State, and

    (b) the subject matter of the proceedings is within the scope of the 1968 Convention as determined by Article 1 (whether or not that Convention has effect in relation to the proceedings).

(2) On an application under *subsection (1)*, the High Court may refuse to grant the measures sought if, in its opinion, the fact that, apart from this section, that Court does not have jurisdiction in relation to the subject matter of the proceedings makes it inexpedient for it to grant those measures.

(3) Subject to Article 39 of the 1968 Convention, an application to the Master of the High Court for an enforcement order respecting a judgment may include an application for any protective measures the High Court has power to grant in proceedings that, apart from this Act, are within its jurisdiction.

(4) Where an enforcement order is made, the Master of the High Court shall grant any protective measures referred to in *subsection (3)* that are sought in the application for the enforcement order.

14. Provision of certain documents by courts in the State to interested parties

If a judgment is given by a court in the State, the registrar or clerk of that court shall, at the request of an interested party and subject to any conditions that may be specified by rules of court, give to the interested party—

    (a) a duly authenticated copy of the judgment,

    (b) a certificate signed by the registrar or clerk of the court stating—

        (i) the nature of the proceedings,

        (ii) the grounds, pursuant to the 1968 Convention, on which the court assumed jurisdiction,

        (iii) the date on which the time for lodging an appeal against the judgment will expire or, if it has expired, the date on which it expired,

        (iv) whether notice of appeal against, or, if the judgment was given in default of appearance, notice to set aside, the judgment has been entered,

        (v) if the judgment is for the payment of a sum of money, the rate of interest, if any, payable on the sum and the date from which interest is payable, and

        (vi) any other particulars that may be specified by rules of court, and

(c) if the judgment was given in default of appearance, the original or a copy, certified by the registrar or clerk of the court to be a true copy, of a document establishing that notice of the institution of proceedings was served on the person in default.

15. Domicile for purposes of 1968 Convention and this Part

(1) In order to determine for the purposes of the 1968 Convention and this Part whether an individual is domiciled in the State, in a place in the State or in a state other than a Contracting State, the following provisions shall apply:

(a) *Part I* of the *Ninth Schedule*, in relation to the text in the English language of the 1968 Convention;

(b) *Part II* of the *Ninth Schedule*, in relation to the text in the Irish language of the 1968 Convention.

(2) The seat of a corporation or association shall be treated as its domicile and in order to determine for the purposes of Article 53 of the 1968 Convention and this Part whether a corporation or association has its seat in the State, in a place in the State or in a state other than a Contracting State, the following provisions shall apply:

(a) *Part III* of the *Ninth Schedule*, in relation to the text in the English language of the 1968 Convention;

(b) *Part IV* of the *Ninth Schedule*, in relation to the text in the Irish language of the 1968 Convention.

(3) In order to determine for the purposes of the 1968 Convention and this Part whether a trust is domiciled in the State the following provisions shall apply:

(a) *Part V* of the *Ninth Schedule*, in relation to the text in the English language of the 1968 Convention;

(b) *Part VI* of the *Ninth Schedule*, in relation to the text in the Irish language of the 1968 Convention.

(4) In this section—

'association' means an unincorporated body of persons;
'corporation' means a body corporate.

16. Venue for certain proceedings in Circuit Court or District Court

(1) Subject to Title II of the 1968 Convention, the jurisdiction of the Circuit Court respecting proceedings that may be instituted in the State by virtue of Article 2, 8.1, 11, 14 or 16(1)(b) of that Convention shall be exercised by the judge of that Court for the time being assigned to the circuit where the defendant, or one of the defendants, ordinarily resides or carries on any profession, business or occupation.

(2) *Subsection (1)* shall apply where, apart from that subsection, the Circuit Court's jurisdiction would be determined by reference to the place where the defendant resides or carries on business.

(3) The jurisdiction of the Circuit Court or District Court respecting proceedings that may be instituted in the State by virtue of Article 14 of the 1968 Convention by a plaintiff domiciled in the State may be exercised as follows:

(a) in the case of the Circuit Court, by the judge of the Circuit Court for the time being assigned to the circuit where the plaintiff or one of the plaintiffs ordinarily resides or carries on any profession, business or occupation;

(b) in the case of the District Court, by the judge of the District Court for the time being assigned to the district court district in which the plaintiff or one of the plaintiffs ordinarily resides or carries on any profession, business or occupation.

PART III. THE LUGANO CONVENTION

17. Interpretation of this Part

(1) For the purposes of this Part, unless the context otherwise requires—

'Contracting State' means a state respecting which the Lugano Convention has entered into force in accordance with Article 61 or 62 of that Convention;

'enforceable maintenance order' means—

    (a) a maintenance order respecting all of which an enforcement order has been made, or

    (b) if an enforcement order has been made respecting only part of a maintenance order, the maintenance order to the extent to which it is so ordered to be enforced;

'enforcement order' means an order for the recognition or enforcement of all or part of a judgment where the order—

    (a) is made by the Master of the High Court under *section 7* as applied by this section, or

    (b) is made or varied on appeal from a decision of the Master of the High Court under *section 7* as applied by this Part or from a decision of the High Court relating to the Master's decision;

'judgment' means a judgment or order (by whatever name called) that is a judgment for the purposes of the Lugano Convention, and, except in *sections 10, 12 and 14* as applied by this Part, includes an instrument or settlement referred to in Title IV of that Convention;

'maintenance' means maintenance within the meaning of the Lugano Convention;

'maintenance creditor' means, in relation to a maintenance order, the person entitled to the payments for which the order provides;

'maintenance debtor' means, in relation to a maintenance order, the person liable to make payments under the order;

'maintenance order' means a judgment relating to maintenance.

(2) The Minister for Foreign Affairs may, by order, declare—

    (a) that any state specified in the order is a Contracting State, or

    (b) that—

        (i) a denunciation has been made pursuant to Article 64 of the Lugano Convention,

        (ii) a declaration has been made pursuant to Article Ia, Ib, or IV of Protocol 1, or

        (iii) a communication has been made pursuant to Article 63 of the Lugano Convention or Article VI of Protocol 1.

(3) The text of a denunciation, declaration or communication referred to in *subsection (2) (b)* shall be set out in the order declaring that the denunciation, declaration or communication has been made.

(4) An order that is in force under *subsection (2)* shall be—

    (a) if made under *subsection (2)(a)*, evidence that any state to which the declaration relates is a Contracting State, and

    (b) if made under *subsection (2)(b)*, evidence that the denunciation, declaration or communication, the text of which is set out in the order, was made and evidence of its contents.

(5) The Minister for Foreign Affairs may, by order, amend or revoke an order made under *subsection (2)* or this subsection.

(6) The definition of 'judgment' in *subsection (1)* shall not be construed to limit the effect of Article 54b of the Lugano Convention.

18. Convention to have force of law

The Lugano Convention shall have the force of law in the State and judicial notice shall be taken of it.

19. Interpretation of Convention

(1) Judicial notice shall be taken of relevant decisions delivered by courts of other Contracting States concerning the provisions of the Lugano Convention, and a court shall, when interpreting and applying those provisions, pay due account to the principles laid down in those decisions.

(2) Judicial notice shall be taken of the report prepared by Mr. P. Jenard and Mr. G. Möller on the Lugano Convention, and, when interpreting any provision of that Convention, a court may consider that report and shall give it the weight that is appropriate in the circumstances.

20. Application of certain provisions of Part II

(1) *Sections 7 to 16* apply in relation to the application of the Lugano Convention in the State pursuant to *section 18* as they apply in relation to the application, pursuant to *section 5*, of the convention (as defined in *section 4*) with—

   (a) the modifications set out in *subsection (2)*, and

   (b) any other necessary modifications.

(2) For the purposes of *subsection (1)*,

   (a) a reference in *sections 7 to 16* to a numbered Article or Title of the 1968 Convention shall be construed as a reference to the corresponding Article or Title of the Lugano Convention,

   (b) a reference in *sections 7 to 16* to an instrument or settlement shall be construed as a reference to an instrument or settlement referred to in Title IV of the Lugano Convention, and

   (c) a reference in *sections 7 to 16* to a term defined in *section 17* shall be construed in accordance with that section.

FIRST SCHEDULE

Text of the 1968 Convention as amended by the 1978 Accession Convention, the 1982 Accession Convention, the 1989 Accession Convention and the 1996 Accession Convention

CONVENTION

on jurisdiction and the enforcement of judgments in civil and commercial matters

PREAMBLE

THE HIGH CONTRACTING PARTIES TO THE TREATY ESTABLISHING THE EUROPEAN ECONOMIC COMMUNITY,

DESIRING to implement the provisions of Article 220 of that Treaty by virtue of which they undertook to secure the simplification of formalities governing the reciprocal recognition and enforcement of judgments of courts or tribunals;

JURISDICTION OF COURTS AND ENFORCEMENT OF JUDGMENTS ACT, 1998

ANXIOUS to strengthen in the Community the legal protection of persons therein established;

CONSIDERING that it is necessary for this purpose to determine the international jurisdiction of their courts, to facilitate recognition and to introduce an expeditious procedure for securing the enforcement of judgments, authentic instruments and court settlements;

HAVE DECIDED to conclude this Convention and to this end have designated as their Plenipotentiaries:

[Plenipotentiaries designated by the Member States]

WHO, meeting within the Council, having exchanged their full powers, found in good and due form,

HAVE AGREED AS FOLLOWS:

TITLE I. SCOPE

Article 1

This Convention shall apply in civil and commercial matters whatever the nature of the court or tribunal. It shall not extend, in particular, to revenue, customs or administrative matters.

The Convention shall not apply to:

1. the status or legal capacity of natural persons, rights in property arising out of a matrimonial relationship, wills and succession;

2. bankruptcy, proceedings relating to the winding-up of insolvent companies or other legal persons, judicial arrangements, compositions and analogous proceedings;

3. social security;

4. arbitration.

TITLE II. JURISDICTION

SECTION 1. GENERAL PROVISIONS

Article 2

Subject to the provisions of this Convention, persons domiciled in a Contracting State shall, whatever their nationality, be sued in the courts of that State.

Persons who are not nationals of the State in which they are domiciled shall be governed by the rules of jurisdiction applicable to nationals of that State.

Article 3

Persons domiciled in a Contracting State may be sued in the courts of another Contracting State only by virtue of the rules set out in Sections 2 to 6 of this Title.

In particular the following provisions shall not be applicable as against them:

- in Belgium: Article 15 of the civil code *(Code civil – Burgerlijk Wetboek)* and Article 638 of the judicial code *(Code judiciaire – Gerechtelijk Wetboek)*,

- in Denmark: Article 246 (2) and (3) of the law on civil procedure *(Lov om rettens pleje)*,

258

- in the Federal Republic of Germany: Article 23 of the code of civil procedure *(Zivilprozeßordnung)*,

- in Greece: Article 40 of the code of civil procedure (*Κωδιχαζπολιτιχής σιχονομίαζ*),

- in France: Articles 14 and 15 of the civil code *(Code civil)*,

- in Ireland: the rules which enable jurisdiction to be founded on the document instituting the proceedings having been served on the defendant during his temporary presence in Ireland,

- in Italy: Articles 2 and 4, Nos 1 and 2 of the code of civil procedure *(Codice di procedura civile)*,

- in Luxembourg: Articles 14 and 15 of the civil code *(Code civil)*,

- in Austria: Article 99 of the Law on Court Jurisdiction *(Jurisdiktionsnorm)*,

- in the Netherlands: Articles 126 (3) and 127 of the code of civil procedure *(Wetboek van Burgerlijke Rechtsvordering)*,

- in Portugal: Article 65 (1) (c), Article 65 (2) and Article 65A (c) of the code of civil procedure *(Código de Processo Civil)* and Article 11 of the code of labour procedure *(Código de Processo de Trabalho)*,

- in Finland: the second, third and fourth sentences of the first paragraph of Section 1 of Chapter 10 of the Code of Judicial Procedure *(oikeudenkäymiskaari/rättegångsbalken)*,

- in Sweden: the first sentence of the first paragraph of Section 3 of Chapter 10 of the Code of Judicial Procedure *(rättegångsbalken)*,

- in the United Kingdom: the rules which enable jurisdiction to be founded on:

    (a) the document instituting the proceedings having been served on the defendant during his temporary presence in the United Kingdom; or

    (b) the presence within the United Kingdom of property belonging to the defendant; or

    (c) the seizure by the plaintiff of property situated in the United Kingdom.

Article 4

If the defendant is not domiciled in a Contracting State, the jurisdiction of the courts of each Contracting State shall, subject to the provisions of Article 16, be determined by the law of that State.

As against such a defendant, any person domiciled in a Contracting State may, whatever his nationality, avail himself in that State of the rules of jurisdiction there in force, and in particular those specified in the second paragraph of Article 3, in the same way as the nationals of that State.

SECTION 2. SPECIAL JURISDICTION

Article 5

A person domiciled in a Contracting State may, in another Contracting State, be sued:

1. in matters relating to a contract, in the courts for the place of performance of the obligation in question; in matters relating to individual contracts of employment, this place is that where the employee habitually carries out his work, or if the employee does not habitually carry out his work in any one country, the employer may also be

sued in the courts for the place where the business which engaged the employee was or is now situated;

2. in matters relating to maintenance, in the courts for the place where the maintenance creditor is domiciled or habitually resident or, if the matter is ancillary to proceedings concerning the status of a person, in the court which, according to its own law, has jurisdiction to entertain those proceedings, unless that jurisdiction is based solely on the nationality of one of the parties;

3. in matters relating to tort, delict or quasi-delict, in the courts for the place where the harmful event occurred;

4. as regards a civil claim for damages or restitution which is based on an act giving rise to criminal proceedings, in the court seised of those proceedings, to the extent that that court has jurisdiction under its own law to entertain civil proceedings;

5. as regards a dispute arising out of the operations of a branch, agency or other establishment, in the courts for the place in which the branch, agency or other establishment is situated;

6. as settlor, trustee or beneficiary of a trust created by the operation of a statute, or by a written instrument, or created orally and evidenced in writing, in the courts of the Contracting State in which the trust is domiciled;

7. as regards a dispute concerning the payment of remuneration claimed in respect of the salvage of a cargo or freight, in the court under the authority of which the cargo or freight in question:

(a) has been arrested to secure such payment,

or

(b) could have been so arrested, but bail or other security has been given;

provided that this provision shall apply only if it is claimed that the defendant has an interest in the cargo or freight or had such an interest at the time of salvage.

Article 6

A person domiciled in a Contracting State may also be sued:

1. where he is one of a number of defendants, in the courts for the place where any one of them is domiciled;

2. as a third party in an action on a warranty or guarantee or in any other third party proceedings, in the court seised of the original proceedings, unless these were instituted solely with the object of removing him from the jurisdiction of the court which would be competent in his case;

3. on a counterclaim arising from the same contract or facts on which the original claim was based, in the court in which the original claim is pending;

4. in matters relating to a contract, if the action may be combined with an action against the same defendant in matters relating to rights *in rem* in immovable property, in the court of the Contracting State in which the property is situated.

Article 6a

Where by virtue of this Convention a court of a Contracting State has jurisdiction in actions relating to liability from the use or operation of a ship, that court, or any other court substituted for this purpose by the internal law of that State, shall also have jurisdiction over claims for limitation of such liability.

JURISDICTION OF COURTS AND ENFORCEMENT OF JUDGMENTS ACT, 1998

SECTION 3. JURISDICTION IN MATTERS RELATING TO INSURANCE

Article 7

In matters relating to insurance, jurisdiction shall be determined by this Section, without prejudice to the provisions of Article 4 and 5.5.

Article 8

An insurer domiciled in a Contracting State may be sued:

1. in the courts of the State where he is domiciled, or

2. in another Contracting State, in the courts for the place where the policy-holder is domiciled, or

3. if he is a co-insurer, in the courts of a Contracting State in which proceedings are brought against the leading insurer.

An insurer who is not domiciled in a Contracting State but has a branch, agency or other establishment in one of the Contracting States shall, in disputes arising out of the operations of the branch, agency or establishment, be deemed to be domiciled in that State.

Article 9

In respect of liability insurance or insurance of immovable property, the insurer may in addition be sued in the courts for the place where the harmful event occurred. The same applies if movable and immovable property are covered by the same insurance policy and both are adversely affected by the same contingency.

Article 10

In respect of liability insurance, the insurer may also, if the law of the court permits it, be joined in proceedings which the injured party had brought against the insured.

The provisions of Articles 7, 8 and 9 shall apply to actions brought by the injured party directly against the insurer, where such direct actions are permitted.

If the law governing such direct actions provides that the policy-holder or the insured may be joined as a party to the action, the same court shall have jurisdiction over them.

Article 11

Without prejudice to the provisions of the third paragraph of Article 10, an insurer may bring proceedings only in the courts of the Contracting State in which the defendant is domiciled, irrespective of whether he is the policy-holder, the insured or a beneficiary.

The provisions of this Section shall not affect the right to bring a counterclaim in the court in which, in accordance with this Section, the original claim is pending.

Article 12

The provisions of this Section may be departed from only by an agreement on jurisdiction:

1. which is entered into after the dispute has arisen, or

2. which allows the policy-holder, the insured or a beneficiary to bring proceedings in courts other than those indicated in this Section, or

3. which is concluded between a policy-holder and an insurer, both of whom are domiciled in the same Contracting State, and which has the effect of conferring jurisdiction on the courts of that State even if the harmful event were to occur abroad, provided that such an agreement is not contrary to the law of that State, or

4. which is concluded with a policy-holder who is not domiciled in a Contracting State, except in so far as the insurance is compulsory or relates to immovable property in a Contracting State, or

5. which relates to a contract of insurance in so far as it covers one or more of the risks set out in Article 12a.

Article 12a

The following are the risks referred to in Article 12.5:

1. Any loss of or damage to:

   (a) sea-going ships, installations situated offshore or on the high seas, or aircraft, arising from perils which relate to their use for commercial purposes;

   (b) goods in transit other than passengers' baggage where the transit consists of or includes carriage by such ships or aircraft;

2. Any liability, other than for bodily injury to passengers or loss of or damage to their baggage:

   (a) arising out of the use or operation of ships, installations or aircraft as referred to in 1. (a) above in so far as the law of the Contracting State in which such aircraft are registered does not prohibit agreements on jurisdiction regarding insurance of such risks;

   (b) for loss or damage caused by goods in transit as described in 1.(b) above;

3. Any financial loss connected with the use or operation of ships, installations or aircraft as referred to in 1. (a) above, in particular loss of freight or charter-hire;

4. Any risk or interest connected with any of those referred to in 1. to 3. above.

SECTION 4. JURISDICTION OVER CONSUMER CONTRACTS

Article 13

In proceedings concerning a contract concluded by a person for a purpose which can be regarded as being outside his trade or profession, hereinafter called 'the consumer', jurisdiction shall be determined by this Section, without prejudice to the provisions of Articles 4 and 5.5, if it is:

1. a contract for the sale of goods on instalment credit terms; or

2. a contract for a loan repayable by instalments, or for any other form of credit, made to finance the sale of goods; or

3. any other contract for the supply of goods or a contract for the supply of services, and

   (a) in the State of the consumer's domicile the conclusion of the contract was preceded by a specific invitation addressed to him or by advertising; and

   (b) the consumer took in that State the steps necessary for the conclusion of the contract.

Where a consumer enters into a contract with a party who is not domiciled in a Contracting State but has a branch, agency or other establishment in one of the Contracting States, that party shall, in disputes arising out of the operations of the branch, agency or establishment, be deemed to be domiciled in that State.

This Section shall not apply to contracts of transport.

Article 14

A consumer may bring proceedings against the other party to a contract either in the courts of the Contracting State in which that party is domiciled or in the courts of the Contracting State in which he is himself domiciled.

Proceedings may be brought against a consumer by the other party to the contract only in the courts of the Contracting State in which the consumer is domiciled.

These provisions shall not affect the right to bring a counter-claim in the court in which, in accordance with this Section, the original claim is pending.

Article 15

The provisions of this Section may be departed from only by an agreement:

1. which is entered into after the dispute has arisen; or

2. which allows the consumer to bring proceedings in courts other than those indicated in this Section; or

3. which is entered into by the consumer and the other party to the contract, both of whom are at the time of conclusion of the contract domiciled or habitually resident in the same Contracting State, and which confers jurisdiction on the courts of that State, provided that such an agreement is not contrary to the law of that State.

SECTION 5. EXCLUSIVE JURISDICTION

Article 16

The following courts shall have exclusive jurisdiction, regardless of domicile:

1. (a) in proceedings which have as their object rights *in rem* in immovable property or tenancies of immovable property, the courts of the Contracting State in which the property is situated;

   (b) however, in proceedings which have as their object tenancies of immovable property concluded for temporary private use for a maximum period of six consecutive months, the courts of the Contracting State in which the defendant is domiciled shall also have jurisdiction, provided that the landlord and the tenant are natural persons and are domiciled in the same Contracting State;

2. in proceedings which have as their object the validity of the constitution, the nullity or the dissolution of companies or other legal persons or associations of natural or legal persons, or the decisions of their organs, the courts of the Contracting State in which the company, legal person or association has its seat;

3. in proceedings which have as their object the validity of entries in public registers, the courts of the Contracting State in which the register is kept;

4. in proceedings concerned with the registration or validity of patents, trade marks, designs, or other similar rights required to be deposited or registered, the courts of the Contracting State in which the deposit or registration has been applied for, has taken place or is under the terms of an international convention deemed to have taken place;

5. in proceedings concerned with the enforcement of judgments, the courts of the Contracting State in which the judgment has been or is to be enforced.

JURISDICTION OF COURTS AND ENFORCEMENT OF JUDGMENTS ACT, 1998

SECTION 6. PROROGATION OF JURISDICTION

Article 17

If the parties, one or more of whom is domiciled in a Contracting State, have agreed that a court or the courts of a Contracting State are to have jurisdiction to settle any disputes which have arisen or which may arise in connection with a particular legal relationship, that court or those courts shall have exclusive jurisdiction. Such an agreement conferring jurisdiction shall be either:

(a) in writing or evidenced in writing; or

(b) in a form which accords with practices which the parties have established between themselves; or

(c) in international trade or commerce, in a form which accords with a usage of which the parties are or ought to have been aware and which in such trade or commerce is widely known to, and regularly observed by, parties to contracts of the type involved in the particular trade or commerce concerned.

Where such an agreement is concluded by parties, none of whom is domiciled in a Contracting State, the courts of other Contracting States shall have no jurisdiction over their disputes unless the court or courts chosen have declined jurisdiction.

The court or courts of a Contracting State on which a trust instrument has conferred jurisdiction shall have exclusive jurisdiction in any proceedings brought against a settlor, trustee or beneficiary, if relations between these persons or their rights or obligations under the trust are involved.

Agreements or provisions of a trust instrument conferring jurisdiction shall have no legal force if they are contrary to the provisions of Articles 12 or 15, or if the courts whose jurisdiction they purport to exclude have exclusive jurisdiction by virtue of Article 16.

If an agreement conferring jurisdiction was concluded for the benefit of only one of the parties, that party shall retain the right to bring proceedings in any other court which has jurisdiction by virtue of this Convention.

In matters relating to individual contracts of employment an agreement conferring jurisdiction shall have legal force only if it is entered into after the dispute has arisen or if the employee invokes it to seise courts other than those for the defendant's domicile or those specified in Article 5.1.

Article 18

Apart from jurisdiction derived from other provisions of this Convention, a court of a Contracting State before whom a defendant enters an appearance shall have jurisdiction. This rule shall not apply where appearance was entered solely to contest the jurisdiction, or where another court has exclusive jurisdiction by virtue of Article 16.

SECTION 7. EXAMINATION AS TO JURISDICTION AND ADMISSIBILITY

Article 19

Where a court of a Contracting State is seised of a claim which is principally concerned with a matter over which the courts of another Contracting State have exclusive jurisdiction by virtue of Article 16, it shall declare of its own motion that it has no jurisdiction.

Article 20

Where a defendant domiciled in one Contracting State is sued in a court of another Contracting State and does not enter an appearance, the court shall declare of its own motion that it has no jurisdiction unless its jurisdiction is derived from the provisions of the Convention.

The court shall stay the proceedings so long as it is not shown that the defendant has been able to receive the document instituting the proceedings or an equivalent document in sufficient time to enable him to arrange for his defence, or that all necessary steps have been taken to this end.

The provisions of the foregoing paragraph shall be replaced by those of Article 15 of the Hague Convention of 15 November 1965 on the service abroad of judicial and extra-judicial documents in civil or commercial matters, if the document instituting the proceedings or notice thereof had to be transmitted abroad in accordance with that Convention.

SECTION 8. LIS PENDENS – RELATED ACTIONS

Article 21

Where proceedings involving the same cause of action and between the same parties are brought in the courts of different Contracting States, any court other than the court first seised shall of its own motion stay its proceedings until such time as the jurisdiction of the court first seised is established.

Where the jurisdiction of the court first seised is established, any court other than the court first seised shall decline jurisdiction in favour of that court.

Article 22

Where related actions are brought in the courts of different Contracting States, any court other than the court first seised may, while the actions are pending at first instance, stay its proceedings.

A court other than the court first seised may also, on the application of one of the parties, decline jurisdiction if the law of that court permits the consolidation of related actions and the court first seised has jurisdiction over both actions.

For the purposes of this Article, actions are deemed to be related where they are so closely connected that it is expedient to hear and determine them together to avoid the risk of irreconcilable judgments resulting from separate proceedings.

Article 23

Where actions come within the exclusive jurisdiction of several courts, any court other than the court first seised shall decline jurisdiction in favour of that court.

SECTION 9. PROVISIONAL, INCLUDING PROTECTIVE MEASURES

Article 24

Application may be made to the courts of a Contracting State for such provisional, including protective, measures as may be available under the law of that State, even if, under this Convention, the courts of another Contracting State have jurisdiction as to the substance of the matter.

265

TITLE III. RECOGNITION AND ENFORCEMENT

Article 25

For the purposes of this Convention, 'judgment' means any judgment given by a court or tribunal of a Contracting State, whatever the judgment may be called, including a decree, order, decision or writ of execution, as well as the determination of costs or expenses by an officer of the court.

SECTION 1. RECOGNITION

Article 26

A judgment given in a Contracting State shall be recognized in the other Contracting States without any special procedure being required.

Any interested party who raises the recognition of a judgment as the principal issue in a dispute may, in accordance with the procedures provided for in Sections 2 and 3 of this Title, apply for a decision that the judgment be recognized.

If the outcome of proceedings in a court of a Contracting State depends on the determination of an incidental question of recognition, that court shall have jurisdiction over that question.

Article 27

A judgment shall not be recognized:

1. if such recognition is contrary to public policy in the State in which recognition is sought;

2. where it was given in default of appearance, if the defendant was not duly served with the document which instituted the proceedings or with an equivalent document in sufficient time to enable him to arrange for his defence;

3. if the judgment is irreconcilable with a judgment given in a dispute between the same parties in the State in which recognition is sought;

4. if the court of the State of origin, in order to arrive at its judgment, has decided a preliminary question concerning the status or legal capacity of natural persons, rights in property arising out of a matrimonial relationship, wills or succession in a way that conflicts with a rule of the private international law of the State in which the recognition is sought, unless the same result would have been reached by the application of the rules of private international law of that State;

5. if the judgment is irreconcilable with an earlier judgment given in a non-contracting State involving the same cause of action and between the same parties, provided that this latter judgment fulfils the conditions necessary for its recognition in the State addressed.

Article 28

Moreover, a judgment shall not be recognized if it conflicts with the provisions of Sections 3, 4 or 5 of Title II, or in a case provided for in Article 59.

In its examination of the grounds of jurisdiction referred to in the foregoing paragraph, the court or authority applied to shall be bound by the findings of fact on which the court of the State of origin based its jurisdiction.

Subject to the provisions of the first paragraph, the jurisdiction of the court of the State of origin may not be reviewed; the test of public policy referred to in Article 27.1 may not be applied to the rules relating to jurisdiction.

Article 29

Under no circumstances may a foreign judgment be reviewed as to its substance.

Article 30

A court of a Contracting State in which recognition is sought of a judgment given in another Contracting State may stay the proceedings if an ordinary appeal against the judgment has been lodged.

A court of a Contracting State in which recognition is sought of a judgment given in Ireland or the United Kingdom may stay the proceedings if enforcement is suspended in the State of origin, by reason of an appeal.

SECTION 2. ENFORCEMENT

Article 31

A judgment given in a Contracting State and enforceable in that State shall be enforced in another Contracting State when, on the application of any interested party, it has been declared enforceable there.

However, in the United Kingdom, such a judgment shall be enforced in England and Wales, in Scotland, or in Northern Ireland when, on the application of any interested party, it has been registered for enforcement in that part of the United Kingdom.

Article 32

1. The application shall be submitted:

    –   in Belgium, to the *tribunal de première instance* or *rechtbank van eerste aanleg*,

    –   in Denmark, to the *byret*,

    –   in the Federal Republic of Germany, to the presiding judge of a chamber of the *Landgericht*,

    –   in Greece, to the *Μονομελές Πρωτοδικείο*,

    –   in Spain, to the *Juzgado de Primera Instancia*,

    –   in France, to the presiding judge of the *tribunal de grande instance*,

    –   in Ireland, to the High Court,

    –   in Italy, to the *corte d'appello*,

    –   in Luxembourg, to the presiding judge of the *tribunal d'arrondissement*,

    –   in Austria, to the *Bezirksgericht*,

    –   in the Netherlands, to the presiding judge of the *arrondissementsrechtbank*,

    –   in Portugal, to the *Tribunal Judicial de Círculo*,

    –   in Finland, to the *Käräjäoikeus/tingsrätt*,

> — in Sweden, to the *Svea hovrätt,*
> — in the United Kingdom:
>
> > (a) in England and Wales, to the High Court of Justice, or in the case of a maintenance judgment to the Magistrates' Court on transmission by the Secretary of State;
> >
> > (b) in Scotland, to the Court of Session, or in the case of a maintenance judgment to the Sheriff Court on transmission by the Secretary of State;
> >
> > (c) in Northern Ireland, to the High Court of Justice, or in the case of a maintenance judgment to the Magistrates' Court on transmission by the Secretary of State.

2. The jurisdiction of local courts shall be determined by reference to the place of domicile of the party against whom enforcement is sought. If he is not domiciled in the State in which enforcement is sought, it shall be determined by reference to the place of enforcement.

Article 33

The procedure for making the application shall be governed by the law of the State in which enforcement is sought.

The applicant must give an address for service of process within the area of jurisdiction of the court applied to. However, if the law of the State in which enforcement is sought does not provide for the furnishing of such an address, the applicant shall appoint a representative *ad litem.*

The documents referred to in Articles 46 and 47 shall be attached to the application.

Article 34

The court applied to shall give its decision without delay; the party against whom enforcement is sought shall not at this stage of the proceedings be entitled to make any submissions on the application.

The application may be refused only for one of the reasons specified in Articles 27 and 28.

Under no circumstances may the foreign judgment be reviewed as to its substance.

Article 35

The appropriate officer of the court shall without delay bring the decision given on the application to the notice of the applicant in accordance with the procedure laid down by the law of the State in which enforcement is sought.

Article 36

If enforcement is authorized, the party against whom enforcement is sought may appeal against the decision within one month of service thereof.

If that party is domiciled in a Contracting State other than that in which the decision authorizing enforcement was given, the time for appealing shall be two months and shall run from the date of service, either on him in person or at his residence. No extension of time may be granted on account of distance.

JURISDICTION OF COURTS AND ENFORCEMENT OF JUDGMENTS ACT, 1998

Article 37

1. An appeal against the decision authorizing enforcement shall be lodged in accordance with the rules governing procedure in contentious matters:

   - in Belgium, with the *tribunal de première instance* or *rechtbank van eerste aanleg,*
   - in Denmark, with the *landsret,*
   - in the Federal Republic of Germany, with the *Oberlandesgericht,*
   - in Greece, with the *Εφετείο'*
   - in Spain, with the *Audiencia Provincial,*
   - in France, with the *cour d'appel,*
   - in Ireland, with the High Court,
   - in Italy, with the *corte d'appello,*
   - in Luxembourg, with the *Cour supérieure de justice* sitting as a court of civil appeal,
   - in Austria, with the *Bezirksgericht,*
   - in the Netherlands, with the *arrondissementsrechtbank,*
   - in Portugal, with the *Tribunal da Relação,*
   - in Finland, with the *hovioikeus/hovrätt,*
   - in Sweden, with the *Svea hovrätt,*
   - in the United Kingdom:

     (a) in England and Wales, with the High Court of Justice, or in the case of a maintenance judgment with the Magistrates' Court;

     (b) in Scotland, with the Court of Session, or in the case of a maintenance judgment with the Sheriff Court;

     (c) in Northern Ireland, with the High Court of Justice, or in the case of a maintenance judgment with the Magistrates' Court.

2. The judgment given on the appeal may be contested only:

   - in Belgium, Greece, Spain, France, Italy, Luxembourg and in the Netherlands, by an appeal in cassation,
   - in Denmark, by an appeal to the *højesteret,* with the leave of the Minister of Justice,
   - in the Federal Republic of Germany, by a *Rechtsbeschwerde,*
   - in Austria, in the case of an appeal, by a *Revisionsrekurs* and, in the case of opposition proceedings, by a *Berufung* with the possibility of a revision,
   - in Ireland, by an appeal on a point of law to the Supreme Court,
   - in Portugal, by an appeal on a point of law,
   - in Finland, by an appeal to *korkein oikeus/högsta domstolen,*
   - in Sweden, by an appeal to *Högsta domstolen,*
   - in the United Kingdom, by a single further appeal on a point of law.

Article 38

The court with which the appeal under Article 37 (1) is lodged may, on the application of the appellant, stay the proceedings if an ordinary appeal has been lodged against the judgment in the State of origin or if the time for such an appeal has not yet expired; in the latter case, the court may specify the time within which such an appeal is to be lodged.

Where the judgment was given in Ireland or the United Kingdom, any form of appeal available in the State of origin shall be treated as an ordinary appeal for the purposes of the first paragraph.

The court may also make enforcement conditional on the provision of such security as it shall determine.

Article 39

During the time specified for an appeal pursuant to Article 36 and until any such appeal has been determined, no measures of enforcement may be taken other than protective measures taken against the property of the party against whom enforcement is sought.

The decision authorizing enforcement shall carry with it the power to proceed to any such protective measures.

Article 40

1. If the application for enforcement is refused, the applicant may appeal:

    - in Belgium, to the *cour d'appel* or *hof van beroep*,

    - in Denmark, to the *landsret*,

    - in the Federal Republic of Germany, to the *Oberlandesgericht*,

    - in Greece, to the *Εφετείο'*,

    - in Spain, to the *Audiencia Provincial*,

    - in France, to the *cour d'appel*,

    - in Ireland, to the High Court,

    - in Italy, to the *corte d'appello*,

    - in Luxembourg, to the *Cour supérieure de justice* sitting as a court of civil appeal,

    - in Austria, to the *Bezirksgericht*,

    - in the Netherlands, to the *gerechtshof*,

    - in Portugal, to the *Tribunal da Relação*,

    - in Finland, to *hovioikeus/hovrätten*,

    - in Sweden, to the *Svea hovrätt*,

    - in the United Kingdom:

        (a) in England and Wales, to the High Court of Justice, or in the case of a maintenance judgment to the Magistrates' Court;

        (b) in Scotland, to the Court of Session, or in the case of a maintenance judgment to the Sheriff Court;

        (c) in Northern Ireland, to the High Court of Justice, or in the case of a maintenance judgment to the Magistrates' Court.

2. The party against whom enforcement is sought shall be summoned to appear before the appellate court. If he fails to appear, the provisions of the second and third paragraphs of Article 20 shall apply even where he is not domiciled in any of the Contracting States.

JURISDICTION OF COURTS AND ENFORCEMENT OF JUDGMENTS ACT, 1998

Article 41

A judgment given on an appeal provided for in Article 40 may be contested only:

- in Belgium, Greece, Spain, France, Italy, Luxembourg and in the Netherlands, by an appeal in cassation,

- in Denmark, by an appeal to the *højesteret*, with the leave of the Minister of Justice,

- in the Federal Republic of Germany, by a *Rechtsbeschwerde*,

- in Ireland, by an appeal on a point of law to the Supreme Court,

- in Austria, by a *Revisionsrekurs*,

- in Portugal, by an appeal on a point of law,

- in Finland, by an appeal to *korkein oikeus/högsta domstolen*,

- in Sweden, by an appeal to *Högsta domstolen*,

- in the United Kingdom, by a single further appeal on a point of law.

Article 42

Where a foreign judgment has been given in respect of several matters and enforcement cannot be authorized for all of them, the court shall authorize enforcement for one or more of them.

An applicant may request partial enforcement of a judgment.

Article 43

A foreign judgment which orders a periodic payment by way of a penalty shall be enforceable in the State in which enforcement is sought only if the amount of the payment has been finally determined by the courts of the State of origin.

Article 44

An applicant who, in the State of origin, has benefited from complete or partial legal aid or exemption from costs or expenses, shall be entitled, in the procedures provided for in Articles 32 to 35, to benefit from the most favourable legal aid or the most extensive exemption from costs or expenses provided for by the law of the State addressed.

However, an applicant who requests the enforcement of a decision given by an administrative authority in Denmark in respect of a maintenance order may, in the State addressed, claim the benefits referred to in the first paragraph if he presents a statement from the Danish Ministry of Justice to the effect that he fulfils the economic requirements to qualify for the grant of complete or partial legal aid or exemption from costs or expenses.

Article 45

No security, bond or deposit, however described, shall be required of a party who in one Contracting State applies for enforcement of a judgment given in another Contracting State on the ground that he is a foreign national or that he is not domiciled or resident in the State in which enforcement is sought.

SECTION 3. COMMON PROVISIONS

Article 46

A party seeking recognition or applying for enforcement of a judgment shall produce:

1. a copy of the judgment which satisfies the conditions necessary to establish its authenticity;

2. in the case of a judgment given in default, the original or a certified true copy of the document which establishes that the party in default was served with the document instituting the proceedings or with an equivalent document.

Article 47

A party applying for enforcement shall also produce:

1. documents which establish that, according to the law of the State of origin, the judgment is enforceable and has been served;

2. where appropriate, a document showing that the applicant is in receipt of legal aid in the State of origin.

Article 48

If the documents specified in Articles 46.2 and 47.2 are not produced, the court may specify a time for their production, accept equivalent documents or, if it considers that it has sufficient information before it, dispense with their production.

If the court so requires, a translation of the documents shall be produced; the translation shall be certified by a person qualified to do so in one of the Contracting States.

Article 49

No legalization or other similar formality shall be required in respect of the documents referred to in Articles 46 or 47 or the second paragraph of Article 48, or in respect of a document appointing a representative *ad litem*.

TITLE IV. AUTHENTIC INSTRUMENTS AND COURT SETTLEMENTS

Article 50

A document which has been formally drawn up or registered as an authentic instrument and is enforceable in one Contracting State shall, in another Contracting State, be declared enforceable there, on application made in accordance with the procedures provided for in Article 31 *et seq*. The application may be refused only if enforcement of the instrument is contrary to public policy in the State addressed.

The instrument produced must satisfy the conditions necessary to establish its authenticity in the State of origin.

The provisions of Section 3 of Title III shall apply as appropriate.

Article 51

A settlement which has been approved by a court in the course of proceedings and is enforceable in the State in which it was concluded shall be enforceable in the State addressed under the same conditions as authentic instruments.

JURISDICTION OF COURTS AND ENFORCEMENT OF JUDGMENTS ACT, 1998

TITLE V. GENERAL PROVISIONS

Article 52

In order to determine whether a party is domiciled in the Contracting State whose courts are seised of a matter, the Court shall apply its internal law.

If a party is not domiciled in the State whose courts are seised of the matter, then, in order to determine whether the party is domiciled in another Contracting State, the court shall apply the law of that State.

Article 53

For the purposes of this Convention, the seat of a company or other legal person or association of natural or legal persons shall be treated as its domicile. However, in order to determine that seat, the court shall apply its rules of private international law.

In order to determine whether a trust is domiciled in the Contracting State whose courts are seised of the matter, the court shall apply its rules of private international law.

TITLE VI. TRANSITIONAL PROVISIONS

Article 54

The provisions of this Convention shall apply only to legal proceedings instituted and to documents formally drawn up or registered as authentic instruments after its entry into force in the State of origin and, where recognition or enforcement of a judgment or authentic instrument is sought, in the State addressed.

However, judgments given after the date of entry into force of this Convention between the State of origin and the State addressed in proceedings instituted before that date shall be recognized and enforced in accordance with the provisions of Title III if jurisdiction was founded upon rules which accorded with those provided for either in Title II of this Convention or in a convention concluded between the State of origin and the State addressed which was in force when the proceedings were instituted.

If the parties to a dispute concerning a contract had agreed in writing before 1 June 1988 for Ireland or before 1 January 1987 for the United Kingdom that the contract was to be governed by the law of Ireland or of a part of the United Kingdom, the courts of Ireland or of that part of the United Kingdom shall retain the right to exercise jurisdiction in the dispute.

Article 54a

For a period of three years from 1 November 1986 for Denmark and from 1 June 1988 for Ireland, jurisdiction in maritime matters shall be determined in these States not only in accordance with the provisions of Title II, but also in accordance with the provisions of paragraphs 1 to 6 following. However, upon the entry into force of the International Convention relating to the arrest of sea-going ships, signed at Brussels on 10 May 1952, for one of these States, these provisions shall cease to have effect for that State.

1. A person who is domiciled in a Contracting State may be sued in the courts of one of the States mentioned above in respect of a maritime claim if the ship to which the claim relates or any other ship owned by him has been arrested by judicial process within the

JURISDICTION OF COURTS AND ENFORCEMENT OF JUDGMENTS ACT, 1998

territory of the latter State to secure the claim, or could have been so arrested there but bail or other security has been given, and either:

(a) the claimant is domiciled in the latter State; or

(b) the claim arose in the latter State; or

(c) the claim concerns the voyage during which the arrest was made or could have been made; or

(d) the claim arises out of a collision or out of damage caused by a ship to another ship or to goods or persons on board either ship, either by the execution or non-execution of a manoeuvre or by the non-observance of regulations; or

(e) the claim is for salvage; or

(f) the claim is in respect of a mortgage or hypothecation of the ship arrested.

2. A claimant may arrest either the particular ship to which the maritime claim relates, or any other ship which is owned by the person who was, at the time when the maritime claim arose, the owner of the particular ship. However, only the particular ship to which the maritime claim relates may be arrested in respect of the maritime claims set out in subparagraphs (o), (p) or (q) of paragraph 5 of this Article.

3. Ships shall be deemed to be in the same ownership when all the shares therein are owned by the same person or persons.

4. When in the case of a charter by demise of a ship the charterer alone is liable in respect of a maritime claim relating to that ship, the claimant may arrest that ship or any other ship owned by the charterer, but no other ship owned by the owner may be arrested in respect of such claim. The same shall apply to any case in which a person other than the owner of a ship is liable in respect of a maritime claim relating to that ship.

5. The expression 'maritime claim' means a claim arising out of one or more of the following:

(a) damage caused by any ship either in collision or otherwise;

(b) loss of life or personal injury caused by any ship or occurring in connection with the operation on any ship;

(c) salvage;

(d) agreement relating to the use or hire of any ship whether by charterparty or otherwise;

(e) agreement relating to the carriage of goods in any ship whether by charterparty or otherwise;

(f) loss of or damage to goods including baggage carried in any ship;

(g) general average;

(h) bottomry;

(i) towage;

(j) pilotage;

(k) goods or materials wherever supplied to a ship for her operation or maintenance;

(l) construction, repair or equipment of any ship or dock charges and dues;

(m) wages of masters, officers or crew;

(n) master's disbursements, including disbursements made by shippers, charterers or agents on behalf of a ship or her owner;

274

(o) dispute as to the title to or ownership of any ship;

(p) disputes between co-owners of any ship as to the ownership, possession, employment or earnings of that ship;

(q) the mortgage or hypothecation of any ship.

6. In Denmark, the expression 'arrest' shall be deemed as regards the maritime claims referred to in subparagraphs (o) and (p) of paragraph 5 of this Article, to include a 'forbud', where that is the only procedure allowed in respect of such a claim under Articles 646 to 653 of the law on civil procedure (lov om rettens pleje).

TITLE VII. RELATIONSHIPS TO OTHER CONVENTIONS

Article 55

Subject to the provisions of the second subparagraph of Article 54, and of Article 56, this Convention shall, for the States which are parties to it, supersede the following conventions concluded between two or more of them:

–   the Convention between Belgium and France on jurisdiction and the validity and enforcement of judgments, arbitration awards and authentic instruments, signed at Paris on 8 July 1899,

–   the Convention between Belgium and the Netherlands on jurisdiction, bankruptcy, and the validity and enforcement of judgments, arbitration awards and authentic instruments, signed at Brussels on 28 March 1925,

–   the Convention between France and Italy on the enforcement of judgments in civil and commercial matters, signed at Rome on 3 June 1930,

–   the Convention between the United Kingdom and the French Republic providing for the reciprocal enforcement of judgments in civil and commercial matters, with Protocol, signed at Paris on 18 January 1934,

–   the Convention between the United Kingdom and the Kingdom of Belgium providing for the reciprocal enforcement of judgments in civil and commercial matters, with Protocol, signed at Brussels on 2 May 1934,

–   the Convention between Germany and Italy on the recognition and enforcement of judgments in civil and commercial matters, signed at Rome on 9 March 1936,

–   the Convention between the Kingdom of Belgium and Austria on the reciprocal recognition and enforcement of judgments and authentic instruments relating to maintenance obligations, signed at Vienna on 25 October 1957,

–   the Convention between the Federal Republic of Germany and the Kingdom of Belgium on the mutual recognition and enforcement of judgments, arbitration awards and authentic instruments in civil and commercial matters, signed at Bonn on 30 June 1958,

–   the Convention between the Kingdom of the Netherlands and the Italian Republic on the recognition and enforcement of judgments in civil and commercial matters, signed at Rome on 17 April 1959,

–   the Convention between the Federal Republic of Germany and Austria on the reciprocal recognition and enforcement of judgments, settlements and authentic instruments in civil and commercial matters, signed at Vienna on 6 June 1959,

–   the Convention between the Kingdom of Belgium and Austria on the reciprocal recognition and enforcement of judgments, arbitral awards and authentic instruments in civil and commercial matters, signed at Vienna on 16 June 1959,

- the Convention between the United Kingdom and the Federal Republic of Germany for the reciprocal recognition and enforcement of judgments in civil and commercial matters, signed at Bonn on 14 July 1960,

- the Convention between the United Kingdom and Austria providing for the reciprocal recognition and enforcement of judgments in civil and commercial matters, signed at Vienna on 14 July 1961, with amending Protocol signed at London on 6 March 1970,

- the Convention between the Kingdom of Greece and the Federal Republic of Germany for the reciprocal recognition and enforcement of judgments, settlements and authentic instruments in civil and commercial matters, signed in Athens on 4 November 1961,

- the Convention between the Kingdom of Belgium and the Italian Republic on the recognition and enforcement of judgments and other enforceable instruments in civil and commercial matters, signed at Rome on 6 April 1962,

- the Convention between the Kingdom of the Netherlands and the Federal Republic of Germany on the mutual recognition and enforcement of judgments and other enforceable instruments in civil and commercial matters, signed at The Hague on 30 August 1962,

- the Convention between the Kingdom of the Netherlands and Austria on the reciprocal recognition and enforcement of judgments and authentic instruments in civil and a commercial matters, signed at The Hague on 6 February 1963,

- the Convention between France and Austria on the recognition and enforcement of judgments and authentic instruments in civil and commercial matters, signed at Vienna on 15 July 1966,

- the Convention between the United Kingdom and the Republic of Italy for the reciprocal recognition and enforcement of judgments in civil and commercial matters, signed at Rome on 7 February 1964, with amending Protocol signed at Rome on 14 July 1970,

- the Convention between the United Kingdom and the Kingdom of the Netherlands providing for the reciprocal recognition and enforcement of judgments in civil matters, signed at The Hague on 17 November 1967,

- the Convention between Spain and France on the recognition and enforcement of judgments and arbitration awards in civil and commercial matters, signed at Paris on 28 May 1969,

- the Convention between Luxembourg and Austria on the recognition and enforcement of judgments and authentic instruments in civil and commercial matters, signed at Luxembourg on 29 July 1971,

- the Convention between Italy and Austria on the recognition and enforcement of judgments in civil and commercial matters, of judicial settlements and of authentic instruments, signed at Rome on 16 November 1971,

- the Convention between Spain and Italy regarding legal aid and the recognition and enforcement of judgments in civil and commercial matters, signed at Madrid on 22 May 1973,

- the Convention between Finland, Iceland, Norway, Sweden and Denmark on the recognition and enforcement of judgments in civil matters, signed at Copenhagen on 11 October 1977,

- the Convention between Austria and Sweden on the recognition and enforcement of judgments in civil matters, signed at Stockholm on 16 September 1982,

- the Convention between Spain and the Federal Republic of Germany on the recognition and enforcement of judgments, settlements and enforceable authentic instruments in civil and commercial matters, signed at Bonn on 14 November 1983,

- the Convention between Austria and Spain on the recognition and enforcement of judgments, settlements and enforceable authentic instruments in civil and commercial matters, signed at Vienna on 17 February 1984,

- the Convention between Finland and Austria on the recognition and enforcement of judgments in civil matters, signed at Vienna on 17 November 1986,

and, in so far as it is in force:

- the Treaty between Belgium, the Netherlands and Luxembourg on jurisdiction, bankruptcy, and the validity and enforcement of judgments, arbitration awards and authentic instruments, signed at Brussels on 24 November 1961.

Article 56

The Treaty and the conventions referred to in Article 55 shall continue to have effect in relation to matters to which this Convention does not apply.

They shall continue to have effect in respect of judgments given and documents formally drawn up or registered as authentic instruments before the entry into force of this Convention.

Article 57

1. This Convention shall not affect any conventions to which the Contracting States are or will be parties and which in relation to particular matters, govern jurisdiction or the recognition or enforcement of judgments.

2. With a view to its uniform interpretation, paragraph 1 shall be applied in the following manner:

   (a) this Convention shall not prevent a court of a Contracting State which is a party to a convention on a particular matter from assuming jurisdiction in accordance with that Convention, even where the defendant is domiciled in another Contracting State which is not a party to that Convention. The court hearing the action shall, in any event, apply Article 20 of this Convention;

   (b) judgments given in a Contracting State by a court in the exercise of jurisdiction provided for in a convention on a particular matter shall be recognized and enforced in the other Contracting State in accordance with this Convention.

   Where a convention on a particular matter to which both the State of origin and the State addressed are parties lays down conditions for the recognition or enforcement of judgments, those conditions shall apply. In any event, the provisions of this Convention which concern the procedure for recognition and enforcement of judgments may be applied.

3. This Convention shall not affect the application of provisions which, in relation to particular matters, govern jurisdiction or the recognition or enforcement of judgments and which are or will be contained in acts of the institutions of the European Communities or in national laws harmonized in implementation of such acts.

Article 58

Until such time as the Convention on jurisdiction and the enforcement of judgments in civil and commercial matters, signed at Lugano on 16 September 1988, takes effect with regard to France and the Swiss Confederation, this Convention shall not affect the rights granted to Swiss nationals by the Convention between France and the Swiss Confederation on jurisdiction and enforcement of judgments in civil matters, signed at Paris on 15 June 1869.

Article 59

This Convention shall not prevent a Contracting State from assuming, in a convention on the recognition and enforcement of judgments, an obligation towards a third State not to recognize judgments given in other Contracting States against defendants domiciled or habitually resident in the third State where, in cases provided for in Article 4, the judgment could only be founded on a ground of jurisdiction specified in the second paragraph of Article 3.

However, a Contracting State may not assume an obligation towards a third State not to recognize a judgment given in another Contracting State by a court basing its jurisdiction on the presence within that State of property belonging to the defendant, or the seizure by the plaintiff of property situated there:

1. if the action is brought to assert or declare proprietary or possessory rights in that property, seeks to obtain authority to dispose of it, or arises from another issue relating to such property, or

2. if the property constitutes the security for a debt which is the subject-matter of the action.

TITLE VIII. FINAL PROVISIONS

Article 60

[deleted]

Article 61

This Convention shall be ratified by the signatory States. The instruments of ratification shall be deposited with the Secretary-General of the Council of the European Communities.

Article 62

This Convention shall enter into force on the first day of the third month following the deposit of the instrument of ratification by the last signatory State to take this step.

Article 63

The Contracting States recognize that any State which becomes a member of the European Economic Community shall be required to accept this Convention as a basis for the negotiations between the Contracting States and that State necessary to ensure the implementation of the last paragraph of Article 220 of the Treaty establishing the European Economic Community.

The necessary adjustments may be the subject of a special convention between the Contracting States of the one part and the new Member States of the other part.

Article 64

The Secretary-General of the Council of the European Communities shall notify the signatory States of:

(a) the deposit of each instrument of ratification;

(b) the date of entry into force of this Convention;

(c) [deleted]

(d) any declaration received pursuant to Article IV of the Protocol;

(e) any communication made pursuant to Article VI of the Protocol.

Article 65

The Protocol annexed to this Convention by common accord of the Contracting States shall form an integral part thereof.

Article 66

This Convention is concluded for an unlimited period.

Article 67

Any Contracting State may request the revision of this Convention. In this event, a revision conference shall be convened by the President of the Council of the European Communities.

Article 68

This Convention, drawn up in a single original in the Dutch, French, German and Italian languages, all four texts being equally authentic, shall be deposited in the archives of the Secretariat of the Council of the European Communities. The Secretary-General shall transmit a certified copy to the Government of each signatory State.

[Signatures of the designated plenipotentiaries]

PROTOCOL

The High Contracting Parties have agreed upon the following provisions, which shall be annexed to the Convention:

Article I

Any person domiciled in Luxembourg who is sued in a court of another Contracting State pursuant to Article 5 (1) may refuse to submit to the jurisdiction of that court. If the defendant does not enter an appearance the court shall declare of its own motion that it has no jurisdiction.

An agreement conferring jurisdiction, within the meaning of Article 17, shall be valid with respect to a person domiciled in Luxembourg only if that person has expressly and specifically so agreed.

Article II

Without prejudice to any more favourable provisions of national laws, persons domiciled in a Contracting State who are being prosecuted in the criminal courts of another Contracting

State of which they are not nationals for an offence which was not intentionally committed may be defended by persons qualified to do so, even if they do not appear in person.

However, the court seised of the matter may order appearance in person; in the case of failure to appear, a judgment given in the civil action without the person concerned having had the opportunity to arrange for his defence need not be recognized or enforced in the other Contracting States.

Article III

In proceedings for the issue of an order for enforcement, no charge, duty or fee calculated by reference to the value of the matter in issue may be levied in the State in which enforcement is sought.

Article IV

Judicial and extrajudicial documents drawn up in one Contracting State which have to be served on persons in another Contracting state shall be transmitted in accordance with the procedures laid down in the conventions and agreements concluded between the Contracting States.

Unless the State in which service is to take place objects by declaration to the Secretary-General of the Council of the European Communities, such documents may also be sent by the appropriate public officers of the State in which the document has been drawn up directly to the appropriate public officers of the State in which the addressee is to be found. In this case the officer of the State of origin shall send a copy of the document to the officer of the State applied to who is competent to forward it to the addressee. The document shall be forwarded in the manner specified by the law of the State applied to. The forwarding shall be recorded by a certificate sent directly to the officer of the State of origin.

Article V

The jurisdiction specified in Articles 6 (2) and 10 in actions on a warranty or guarantee or in any other third-party proceedings may not be resorted to in the Federal Republic of Germany or in Austria. Any person domiciled in another Contracting State may be sued in the courts:

– of the Federal Republic of Germany, pursuant to Articles 68, 72, 73 and 74 of the code of civil procedure (*Zivilprozessordnung*) concerning third-party notices,

– of Austria, pursuant to Article 21 of the code of civil procedure (*Zivilprozessordnung*) concerning third-party notices.

Judgments given in the other Contracting States by virtue of Article 6 (2) or 10 shall be recognized and enforced in the Federal Republic of Germany and in Austria in accordance with Title III. Any effects which judgments given in those States may have on third parties by application of the provisions in the preceding paragraph shall also be recognized in the other Contracting States.

Article Va

In matters relating to maintenance, the expression 'court' includes the Danish administrative authorities.

In Sweden in summary proceedings concerning orders to pay (*betalningsföreläggande*) and assistance (*handräckning*), the expression 'court' includes the 'Swedish enforcement service' (*kronofogdemyndighet*).

Article Vb

In proceedings involving a dispute between the master and a member of the crew of a sea-going ship registered in Denmark, in Greece, in Ireland or in Portugal, concerning remuneration or other conditions of service, a court in a Contracting State shall establish whether the diplomatic or consular officer responsible for the ship has been notified of the dispute. It shall stay the proceedings so long as he has not been notified. It shall of its own motion decline jurisdiction if the officer, having been duly notified, has exercised the powers accorded to him in the matter by a consular convention, or in the absence of such a convention has, within the time allowed, raised any objection to the exercise of such jurisdiction.

Article Vc

Articles 52 and 53 of this Convention shall, when applied by Article 69 (5) of the Convention for the European patent for the common market, signed at Luxembourg on 15 December 1975, to the provisions relating to 'residence' in the English text of that Convention, operate as if 'residence' in that text were the same as 'domicile' in Articles 52 and 53.

Article Vd

Without prejudice to the jurisdiction of the European Patent Office under the Convention on the grant of European patents, signed at Munich on 5 October 1973, the courts of each Contracting State shall have exclusive jurisdiction, regardless of domicile, in proceedings concerned with the registration or validity of any European patent granted for that State which is not a Community patent by virtue of the provisions of Article 86 of the Convention for the European patent for the common market, signed at Luxembourg on 15 December 1975.

Article Ve

Arrangements relating to maintenance obligations concluded with administrative authorities or authenticated by them shall also be regarded as authentic instruments within the meaning of the first paragraph of Article 50 of the Convention.

Article VI

The Contracting States shall communicate to the Secretary-General of the Council of the European Communities the text of any provisions of their laws which amend either those articles of their laws mentioned in the Convention or the lists of courts specified in Section 2 of Title III of the Convention.

[Signatures of the designated plenipotentiaries]

SECOND SCHEDULE

Text of the 1971 Protocol as amended by the 1978 Accession Convention, the 1982 Accession Convention, the 1989 Accession Convention and the 1996 Accession Convention 1(7)

PROTOCOL

on the interpretation by the Court of Justice of the Convention of 27 September 1968 on jurisdiction and the enforcement of judgments in civil and commercial matters

281

JURISDICTION OF COURTS AND ENFORCEMENT OF JUDGMENTS ACT, 1998

Article 1

The Court of Justice of the European Communities shall have jurisdiction to give rulings on the interpretation of the Convention on jurisdiction and the enforcement of judgments in civil and commercial matters and of the Protocol annexed to that Convention, signed at Brussels on 27 September 1968, and also on the interpretation of the present Protocol.

The Court of Justice of the European Communities shall also have jurisdiction to give rulings on the interpretation of the Convention on the accession of the Kingdom of Denmark, Ireland and the United Kingdom of Great Britain and Northern Ireland to the Convention of 27 September 1968 and to this Protocol.

The Court of Justice of the European Communities shall also have jurisdiction to give rulings on the interpretation of the Convention on the accession of the Hellenic Republic to the Convention of 27 September 1968 and to this Protocol, as adjusted by the 1978 Convention.

The Court of Justice of the European Communities shall also have jurisdiction to give rulings on the interpretation of the Convention on the accession of the Kingdom of Spain and the Portuguese Republic to the Convention of 27 September 1968 and to this Protocol, as adjusted by the 1978 Convention and the 1982 Convention.

The Court of the Justice of the European Communities shall also have jurisdiction to give rulings on the interpretation of the Convention on the accession of the Republic of Austria, the Republic of Finland and the Kingdom of Sweden to the Convention of 27 September 1968 and to this Protocol, as adjusted by the 1978 Convention, the 1982 Convention and the 1989 Convention.

Article 2

The following courts may request the Court of Justice to give preliminary rulings on questions of interpretation:

1. – in Belgium: *la Cour de Cassation – het Hof van Cassatie* and *le Conseil d'Etat – de Raad van State*,

   – in Denmark: *højesteret*,

   – in the Federal Republic of Germany: *die obersten Gerichtshöfe des Bundes*,

   – in Greece: the *ανώτατα δικαστήαια*,

   – in Spain: *el Tribunal Supremo*,

   – in France: *la Cour de Cassation* and *le Conseil d'État*,

   – in Ireland: the Supreme Court,

   – in Italy: *la Corte Suprema di Cassazione*,

   – in Luxembourg: *la Cour supérieure de Justice* when sitting as Cour de Cassation,

   – in Austria, the *Oberste Gerichtshof*, the *Verwaltungsgerichtshof* and the *Verfassungsgerichtshof*,

   – in the Netherlands: *de Hoge Raad*,

   – in Portugal: *o Supremo Tribunal de Justiça* and *o Supremo Tribunal Administrativo*,

   – in Finland, *korkein oikeus/högsta domstolen* and *korkein hallintooikeus/högsta förvaltningsdomstolen*,

   – in Sweden, *Högsta domstolen, Regeringsrätten, Arbetsdomstolen* and *Marknadsdomstolen*,

282

- in the United Kingdom: the House of Lords and courts to which application has been made under the second paragraph of Article 37 or under Article 41 of the Convention;

2. the courts of the Contracting States when they are sitting in an appellate capacity;

3. in the cases provided for in Article 37 of the Convention, the courts referred to in that Article.

Article 3

1. Where a question of interpretation of the Convention or of one of the other instruments referred to in Article 1 is raised in a case pending before one of the courts listed in Article 2.1, that court shall, if it considers that a decision on the question is necessary to enable it to give judgment, request the Court of Justice to give a ruling thereon.

2. Where such a question is raised before any court referred to in Article 2.2 or 2.3, that court may, under the conditions laid down in paragraph 1, request the Court of Justice to give a ruling thereon.

Article 4

1. The competent authority of a Contracting State may request the Court of Justice to give a ruling on a question of interpretation of the Convention or of one of the other instruments referred to in Article 1 if judgments given by courts of that State conflict with the interpretation given either by the Court of Justice or in a judgment of one of the courts of another Contracting State referred to in Article 2.1 or 2.2. The provisions of this paragraph shall apply only to judgments which have become *res judicata*.

2. The interpretation given by the Court of Justice in response to such a request shall not affect the judgments which gave rise to the request for interpretation.

3. The Procurators-General of the Courts of Cassation of the Contracting States, or any other authority designated by a Contracting State, shall be entitled to request the Court of Justice for a ruling on interpretation in accordance with paragraph 1.

4. The Registrar of the Court of Justice shall give notice of the request to the Contracting States, to the Commission and to the Council of the European Communities; they shall then be entitled within two months of the notification to submit statements of case or written observations to the Court.

5. No fees shall be levied or any costs or expenses awarded in respect of the proceedings provided for in this Article.

Article 5

1. Except where this Protocol otherwise provides, the provisions of the Treaty establishing the European Economic Community and those of the Protocol on the Statute of the Court of Justice annexed thereto, which are applicable when the Court is requested to give a preliminary ruling, shall also apply to any proceedings for the interpretation of the Convention and the other instruments referred to in Article 1.

2. The Rules of Procedure of the Court of Justice shall, if necessary, be adjusted and supplemented in accordance with Article 188 of the Treaty establishing the European Economic Community.

Article 6

[deleted]

Article 7

This Protocol shall be ratified by the signatory States. The instruments of ratification shall be deposited with the Secretary-General of the Council of the European Communities.

Article 8

This Protocol shall enter into force on the first day of the third month following the deposit of the instrument of ratification by the last signatory State to take this step; provided that it shall at the earliest enter into force at the same time as the Convention of 27 September 1968 on jurisdiction and the enforcement of judgments in civil and commercial matters.

Article 9

The Contracting States recognize that any State which becomes a member of the European Economic Community, and to which Article 63 of the Convention on jurisdiction and the enforcement of judgments in civil and commercial matters applies, must accept the provisions of this Protocol, subject to such adjustments as may be required.

Article 10

The Secretary-General of the Council of the European Communities shall notify the signatory States of:

(a) the deposit of each instrument of ratification;

(b) the date of entry into force of this Protocol;

(c) any designation received pursuant to Article 4 (3);

(d) *[deleted]*

Article 11

The Contracting States shall communicate to the Secretary-General of the Council of the European Communities the texts of any provisions of their laws which necessitate an amendment to the list of courts in Article 2.1.

Article 12

This Protocol is concluded for an unlimited period.

Article 13

Any Contracting State may request the revision of this Protocol. In this event, a revision conference shall be convened by the President of the Council of the European Communities.

JURISDICTION OF COURTS AND ENFORCEMENT OF JUDGMENTS ACT, 1998

Article 14

This Protocol, drawn up in a single original in the Dutch, French, German and Italian languages, all four texts being equally authentic, shall be deposited in the archives of the Secretariat of the Council of the European Communities. The Secretary-General shall transmit a certified copy to the Government of each signatory State

[*Signatures of the plenipotentiaries*]

SEVENTH SCHEDULE

Text of the Lugano Convention 1(13)

CONVENTION

on jurisdiction and the enforcement of judgments in civil and commercial matters

PREAMBLE

THE HIGH CONTRACTING PARTIES TO THIS CONVENTION,

ANXIOUS to strengthen in their territories the legal protection of persons therein established,

CONSIDERING that it is necessary for this purpose to determine the international jurisdiction of their courts, to facilitate recognition and to introduce an expeditious procedure for securing the enforcement of judgments, authentic instruments and court settlements,

AWARE of the links between them, which have been sanctioned in the economic field by the free trade agreements concluded between the European Economic Community and the States members of the European Free Trade Association,

TAKING INTO ACCOUNT the Brussels Convention of 27 September 1968 on jurisdiction and the enforcement of judgments in civil and commercial matters, as amended by the Accession Conventions under the successive enlargements of the European Communities,

PERSUADED that the extension of the principles of that Convention to the States parties to this instrument will strengthen legal and economic cooperation in Europe,

DESIRING to ensure as uniform an interpretation as possible of this instrument,

HAVE in this spirit DECIDED to conclude this Convention and

HAVE AGREED AS FOLLOWS:

TITLE I. SCOPE

Article 1

This Convention shall apply in civil and commercial matters whatever the nature of the court or tribunal. It shall not extend, in particular, to revenue, customs or administrative matters.

The Convention shall not apply to:

1. the status or legal capacity of natural persons, rights in property arising out of a matrimonial relationship, wills and succession;

2. bankruptcy, proceedings relating to the winding-up of insolvent companies or other legal persons, judicial arrangements, compositions and analogous proceedings;

3. social security;

4. arbitration.

TITLE II. JURISDICTION

SECTION 1. GENERAL PROVISIONS

Article 2

Subject to the provisions of this Convention, persons domiciled in a Contracting State shall, whatever their nationality, be sued in the courts of that State.

Persons who are not nationals of the State in which they are domiciled shall be governed by the rules of jurisdiction applicable to nationals of that State.

Article 3

Persons domiciled in a Contracting State may be sued in the courts of another Contracting State only by virtue of the rules set out in Sections 2 to 6 of this Title.

In particular the following provisions shall not be applicable as against them:

- in Belgium: Article 15 of the civil code (*Code civil – Burgerlijk Wetboek*) and Article 638 of the judicial code (*Code judiciaire – Gerechtelijk Wetboek*),

- in Denmark: Article 246 (2) and (3) of the law on civil procedure (*Lov om rettens pleje*),

- in the Federal Republic of Germany: Article 23 of the code of civil procedure (*Zivilprozeßordnung*),

- in Greece: Article 40 of the code of civil procedure (*Κώδικας Πολιτικής Δικονομίας*),

- in France: Articles 14 and 15 of the civil code (*Code civil*),

- in Ireland: the rules which enable jurisdiction to be founded on the document instituting the proceedings having been served on the defendant during his temporary presence in Ireland,

- in Iceland: Article 77 of the Civil Proceedings Act (*lög um meðferð einkamála í héraði*),

- in Italy: Articles 2 and 4, Nos 1 and 2 of the code of civil procedure (*Codice di procedura civile*),

- in Luxembourg: Articles 14 and 15 of the civil code (*Code civil*),

- in the Netherlands: Articles 126 (3) and 127 of the code of civil procedure (*Wetboek van Burgerlijke Rechtsvordering*),

- in Norway: Section 32 of the Civil Proceedings Act (*tvistemålsloven*),

- in Austria: Article 99 of the Law on Court Jurisdiction (*Jurisdiktionsnorm*),

- in Portugal: Articles 65 (1) (c), 65 (2) and 65A (c) of the code of civil procedure (*Código de Processo Civil*) and Article 11 of the code of labour procedure (*Código de Processo de Trabalho*),

- in Switzerland: *le for du lieu du séquestre/Gerichtsstand des Arrestortes/foro del luogo del sequestro* within the meaning of Article 4 of the *loi fédérale sur le droit international privé/Bundesgesetz über das internationale Privatrecht/legge federale sul diritto internazionale privato*,

- in Finland: the second, third and fourth sentences of Section 1 of Chapter 10 of the Code of Judicial Procedure (*oikeudenkäymiskaari/rättegångsbalken*),

- in Sweden: the first sentence of Section 3 of Chapter 10 of the Code of Judicial Procedure (*Rättegångsbalken*),

- in the United Kingdom: the rules which enable jurisdiction to be founded on:

  (a) the document instituting the proceedings having been served on the defendant during his temporary presence in the United Kingdom; or

  (b) the presence within the United Kingdom of property belonging to the defendant; or

  (c) the seizure by the plaintiff of property situated in the United Kingdom.

Article 4

If the defendant is not domiciled in a Contracting State, the jurisdiction of the courts of each Contracting State shall, subject to the provisions of Article 16, be determined by the law of that State.

As against such a defendant, any person domiciled in a Contracting State may, whatever his nationality, avail himself in that State of the rules of jurisdiction there in force, and in particular those specified in the second paragraph of Article 3, in the same way as the nationals of that State.

SECTION 2. SPECIAL JURISDICTION

Article 5

A person domiciled in a Contracting State may, in another Contracting State, be sued:

1. in matters relating to a contract, in the courts for the place of performance of the obligation in question; in matters relating to individual contracts of employment, this place is that where the employee habitually carries out his work, or if the employee does not habitually carry out his work in any one country, this place shall be the place of business through which he was engaged;

2. in matters relating to maintenance, in the courts for the place where the maintenance creditor is domiciled or habitually resident or, if the matter is ancillary to proceedings concerning the status of a person, in the court which, according to its own law, has jurisdiction to entertain those proceedings, unless that jurisdiction is based solely on the nationality of one of the parties;

3. in matters relating to tort, delict or quasi-delict, in the courts for the place where the harmful event occurred;

4. as regards a civil claim for damages or restitution which is based on an act giving rise to criminal proceedings, in the court seised of those proceedings, to the extent that that court has jurisdiction under its own law to entertain civil proceedings;

5. as regards a dispute arising out of the operations of a branch, agency or other establishment, in the courts for the place in which the branch, agency or other establishment is situated;

6. in his capacity as settlor, trustee or beneficiary of a trust created by the operation of a statute, or by a written instrument, or created orally and evidenced in writing, in the courts of the Contracting State in which the trust is domiciled;

7. as regards a dispute concerning the payment of remuneration claimed in respect of the salvage of a cargo or freight, in the court under the authority of which the cargo or freight in question:

   (a) has been arrested to secure such payment,

      or

   (b) could have been so arrested, but bail or other security has been given;

   provided that this provision shall apply only if it is claimed that the defendant has an interest in the cargo or freight or had such an interest at the time of salvage.

Article 6

A person domiciled in a Contracting State may also be sued:

1. where he is one of a number of defendants, in the courts for the place where any one of them is domiciled;

2. as a third party in an action on a warranty or guarantee or in any other third party proceedings, in the court seised of the original proceedings, unless these were instituted solely with the object of removing him from the jurisdiction of the court which would be competent in his case;

3. on a counterclaim arising from the same contract or facts on which the original claim was based, in the court in which the original claim is pending;

4. in matters relating to a contract, if the action may be combined with an action against the same defendant in matters relating to rights *in rem* in immovable property, in the court of the Contracting State in which the property is situated.

Article 6a

Where by virtue of this Convention a court of a Contracting State has jurisdiction in actions relating to liability arising from the use or operation of a ship, that court, or any other court substituted for this purpose by the internal law of that State, shall also have jurisdiction over claims for limitation of such liability.

SECTION 3. JURISDICTION IN MATTERS RELATING TO INSURANCE

Article 7

In matters relating to insurance, jurisdiction shall be determined by this Section, without prejudice to the provisions of Articles 4 and 5 (5).

Article 8

An insurer domiciled in a Contracting State may be sued:

1. in the courts of the State where he is domiciled; or

2. in another Contracting State, in the courts for the place where the policy-holder is domiciled; or

3. if he is a co-insurer, in the courts of a Contracting State in which proceedings are brought against the leading insurer.

An insurer who is not domiciled in a Contracting State but has a branch, agency or other establishment in one of the Contracting States shall, in disputes arising out of the operations of the branch, agency or establishment, be deemed to be domiciled in that State.

Article 9

In respect of liability insurance or insurance of immovable property, the insurer may in addition be sued in the courts for the place where the harmful event occurred. The same applies if movable and immovable property are covered by the same insurance policy and both are adversely affected by the same contingency.

Article 10

In respect of liability insurance, the insurer may also, if the law of the court permits it, be joined in proceedings which the injured party has brought against the insured.

The provisions of Articles 7, 8 and 9 shall apply to actions brought by the injured party directly against the insurer, where such direct actions are permitted.

If the law governing such direct actions provides that the policy-holder or the insured may be joined as a party to the action, the same court shall have jurisdiction over them.

Article 11

Without prejudice to the provisions of the third paragraph of Article 10, an insurer may bring proceedings only in the courts of the Contracting State in which the defendant is domiciled, irrespective of whether he is the policy-holder, the insured or a beneficiary.

The provisions of this Section shall not affect the right to bring a counterclaim in the court in which, in accordance with this Section, the original claim is pending.

Article 12

The provisions of this Section may be departed from only by an agreement on jurisdiction:

1. which is entered into after the dispute has arisen; or

2. which allows the policy-holder, the insured or a beneficiary to bring proceedings in courts other than those indicated in this Section; or

3. which is concluded between a policy-holder and an insurer, both of whom are at the time of conclusion of the contract domiciled or habitually resident in the same Contracting State, and which has the effect of conferring jurisdiction on the courts of that State even if the harmful event were to occur abroad, provided that such an agreement is not contrary to the law of that State; or

4. which is concluded with a policy-holder who is not domiciled in a Contracting State, except in so far as the insurance is compulsory or relates to immovable property in a Contracting State; or

5. which relates to a contract of insurance in so far as it covers one or more of the risks set out in Article 12a.

289

Article 12a

The following are the risks referred to in Article 12 (5):

1. any loss of or damage to:

    (a) sea-going ships, installations situated off shore or on the high seas, or aircraft, arising from perils which relate to their use for commercial purposes;

    (b) goods in transit other than passengers' baggage where the transit consists of or includes carriage by such ships or aircraft;

2. any liability, other than for bodily injury to passengers or loss of or damage to their baggage;

    (a) arising out of the use or operation of ships, installations or aircraft as referred to in (1) (a) above in so far as the law of the Contracting State in which such aircraft are registered does not prohibit agreements on jurisdiction regarding insurance of such risks;

    (b) for loss or damage caused by goods in transit as described in (1) (b) above;

3. any financial loss connected with the use or operation of ships, installations or aircraft as referred to in (1) (a) above, in particular loss of freight or charter-hire;

4. any risk or interest connected with any of those referred to in (1) to (3) above.

SECTION 4. JURISDICTION OVER CONSUMER CONTRACTS

Article 13

In proceedings concerning a contract concluded by a person for a purpose which can be regarded as being outside his trade or profession, hereinafter called 'the consumer', jurisdiction shall be determined by this Section, without prejudice to the provisions of Articles 4 and 5 (5), if it is:

1. a contract for the sale of goods on instalment credit terms; or

2. a contract for a loan repayable by instalments, or for any other form of credit, made to finance the sale of goods; or

3. any other contract for the supply of goods or a contract for the supply of services, and

    (a) in the State of the consumer's domicile the conclusion of the contract was preceded by a specific invitation addressed to him or by advertising; and

    (b) the consumer took in that State the steps necessary for the conclusion of the contract.

Where a consumer enters into a contract with a party who is not domiciled in a Contracting State but has a branch, agency or other establishment in one of the Contracting States, that party shall, in disputes arising out of the operations of the branch, agency or establishment, be deemed to be domiciled in that State.

This Section shall not apply to contracts of transport.

Article 14

A consumer may bring proceedings against the other party to a contract either in the courts of the Contracting State in which that party is domiciled or in the courts of the Contracting State in which he is himself domiciled.

Proceedings may be brought against a consumer by the other party to the contract only in the courts of the Contracting State in which the consumer is domiciled.

These provisions shall not affect the right to bring a counterclaim in the court in which, in accordance with this Section, the original claim is pending.

Article 15

The provisions of this Section may be departed from only by an agreement;

1. which is entered into after the dispute has arisen; or

2. which allows the consumer to bring proceedings in courts other than those indicated in this Section; or

3. which is entered into by the consumer and the other party to the contract, both of whom are at the time of conclusion of the contract domiciled or habitually resident in the same Contracting State, and which confers jurisdiction on the courts of that State, provided that such an agreement is not contrary to the law of that State.

SECTION 5. EXCLUSIVE JURISDICTION

Article 16

The following courts shall have exclusive jurisdiction, regardless of domicile:

1. (a) in proceedings which have as their object rights *in rem* in immovable property or tenancies of immovable property, the courts of the Contracting State in which the property is situated;

   (b) however, in proceedings which have as their object tenancies of immovable property concluded for temporary private use for a maximum period of six consecutive months, the courts of the Contracting State in which the defendant is domiciled shall also have jurisdiction, provided that the tenant is a natural person and neither party is domiciled in the Contracting State in which the property is situated;

2. in proceedings which have as their object the validity of the constitution, the nullity or the dissolution of companies or other legal persons or associations of natural or legal persons, or the decisions of their organs, the courts of the Contracting State in which the company, legal person or association has its seat;

3. in proceedings which have as their object the validity of entries in public registers, the courts of the Contracting State in which the register is kept;

4. in proceedings concerned with the registration or validity of patents, trade marks, designs, or other similar rights required to be deposited or registered, the courts of the Contracting State in which the deposit or registration has been applied for, has taken place or is under the terms of an international convention deemed to have taken place;

5. in proceedings concerned with the enforcement of judgments, the courts of the Contracting State in which the judgment has been or is to be enforced.

SECTION 6. PROROGATION OF JURISDICTION

Article 17

1. If the parties, one or more of whom is domiciled in a Contracting State, have agreed that a court or the courts of a Contracting State are to have jurisdiction to settle any disputes which have arisen or which may arise in connection with a particular legal

relationship, that court or those courts shall have exclusive jurisdiction. Such an agreement conferring jurisdiction shall be either:

(a) in writing or evidenced in writing, or

(b) in a form which accords with practices which the parties have established between themselves, or

(c) in international trade or commerce, in a form which accords with a usage of which the parties are or ought to have been aware and which in such trade or commerce is widely known to, and regularly observed by, parties to contracts of the type involved in the particular trade or commerce concerned.

Where such an agreement is concluded by parties, none of whom is domiciled in a Contracting State, the courts of other Contracting States shall have no jurisdiction over their disputes unless the court or courts chosen have declined jurisdiction.

2. The court or courts of a Contracting State on which a trust instrument has conferred jurisdiction shall have exclusive jurisdiction in any proceedings brought against a settlor, trustee or beneficiary, if relations between these persons or their rights or obligations under the trust are involved.

3. Agreements or provisions of a trust instrument conferring jurisdiction shall have no legal force if they are contrary to the provisions of Article 12 or 15, or if the courts whose juridition they purport to exclude have exclusive jurisdiction by virtue of Article 16.

4. If an agreement conferring jurisdiction was concluded for the benefit of only one of the parties, that party shall retain the right to bring proceedings in any other court which has jurisdiction by virtue of this Convention.

5. In matters relating to individual contracts of employment an agreement conferring jurisdiction shall have legal force only if it is entered into after the dispute has arisen.

Article 18

Apart from jurisdiction derived from other provisions of this Convention, a court of a Contracting State before whom a defendant enters an appearance shall have jurisdiction. This rule shall not apply where appearance was entered solely to contest the jurisdiction, or where another court has exclusive jurisdiction by virtue of Article 16.

SECTION 7. EXAMINATION AS TO JURISDICTION AND ADMISSIBILITY

Article 19

Where a court of a Contracting State is seised of a claim which is principally concerned with a matter over which the courts of another Contracting State have exclusive jurisdiction by virtue of Article 16, it shall declare of its own motion that it has no jurisdiction.

Article 20

Where a defendant domiciled in one Contracting State is sued in a court of another Contracting State and does not enter an appearance, the court shall declare of its own motion that it has no jurisdiction unless its jurisdiction is derived from the provisions of this Convention.

The court shall stay the proceedings so long as it is not shown that the defendant has been able to receive the document instituting the proceedings or an equivalent document in sufficient time to enable him to arrange for his defence, or that all necessary steps have been taken to this end.

The provisions of the foregoing paragraph shall be replaced by those of Article 15 of the Hague Convention of 15 November 1965 on the service abroad of judicial and extrajudicial documents in civil or commercial matters, if the document instituting the proceedings or notice thereof had to be transmitted abroad in accordance with that Convention.

SECTION 8. LIS PENDENS – RELATED ACTIONS

Article 21

Where proceedings involving the same cause of action and between the same parties are brought in the courts of different Contracting States, any court other than the court first seised shall of its own motion stay its proceedings until such time as the jurisdiction of the court first seised is established.

Where the jurisdiction of the court first seised is established, any court other than the court first seised shall decline jurisdiction in favour of that court.

Article 22

Where related actions are brought in the courts of different Contracting States, any court other than the court first seised may, while the actions are pending at first instance, stay its proceedings.

A court other than the court first seised may also, on the application of one of the parties, decline jurisdiction if the law of that court permits the consolidation of related actions and the court first seised has jurisdiction over both actions.

For the purposes of this Article, actions are deemed to be related where they are so closely connected that it is expedient to hear and determine them together to avoid the risk of irreconcilable judgments resulting from separate proceedings.

Article 23

Where actions come within the exclusive jurisdiction of several courts, any court other than the court first seised shall decline jurisdiction in favour of that court.

SECTION 9. PROVISIONAL, INCLUDING PROTECTIVE, MEASURES

Article 24

Application may be made to the courts of a Contracting State for such provisional, including protective, measures as may be available under the law of that State, even if, under this Convention, the courts of another Contracting State have jurisdiction as to the substance of the matter.

TITLE III. RECOGNITION AND ENFORCEMENT

Article 25

For the purposes of this Convention, 'judgment' means any judgment given by a court or tribunal of a Contracting State, whatever the judgment may be called, including a decree, order, decision or writ of execution, as well as the determination of costs or expenses by an officer of the court.

JURISDICTION OF COURTS AND ENFORCEMENT OF JUDGMENTS ACT, 1998

SECTION 1. RECOGNITION

Article 26

A judgment given in a Contracting State shall be recognized in the other Contracting States without any special procedure being required.

Any interested party who raises the recognition of a judgment as the principal issue in a dispute may, in accordance with the procedures provided for in Section 2 and 3 of this Title, apply for a decision that the judgment be recognized.

If the outcome of proceedings in a court of a Contracting State depends on the determination of an incidental question of recognition that court shall have jurisdiction over that question.

Article 27

A judgment shall not be recognized:

1. if such recognition is contrary to public policy in the State in which recognition is sought;

2. where it was given in default of appearance, if the defendant was not duly served with the document which instituted the proceedings or with an equivalent document in sufficient time to enable him to arrange for his defence;

3. if the judgment is irreconcilable with a judgment given in a dispute between the same parties in the State in which recognition is sought;

4. if the court of the State of origin, in order to arrive at its judgment, has decided a preliminary question concerning the status or legal capacity of natural persons, rights in property arising out of a matrimonial relationship, wills or succession in a way that conflicts with a rule of the private international law of the State in which the recognition is sought, unless the same result would have been reached by the application of the rules of private international law of that State;

5. if the judgment is irreconcilable with an earlier judgment given in a non-contracting State involving the same cause of action and between the same parties, provided that this latter judgment fulfils the conditions necessary for its recognition in the State addressed.

Article 28

Moreover, a judgment shall not be recognized if it conflicts with the provisions of Sections 3, 4 or 5 of Title II or in a case provided for in Article 59.

A judgment may furthermore be refused recognition in any case provided for in Article 54B (3) or 57 (4).

In its examination of the grounds of jurisdiction referred to in the foregoing paragraphs, the court or authority applied to shall be bound by the findings of fact on which the court of the State of origin based its jurisdiction.

Subject to the provisions of the first and second paragraphs, the jurisdiction of the court of the State of origin may not be reviewed; the test of public policy referred to in Article 27 (1) may not be applied to the rules relating to jurisdiction.

Article 29

Under no circumstances may a foreign judgment be reviewed as to its substance.

Article 30

A court of a Contracting State in which recognition is sought of a judgment given in another Contracting State may stay the proceedings if an ordinary appeal against the judgment has been lodged.

A court of a Contracting State in which recognition is sought of a judgment given in Ireland or the United Kingdom may stay the proceedings if enforcement is suspended in the State of origin by reason of an appeal.

SECTION 2. ENFORCEMENT

Article 31

A judgment given in a Contracting State and enforceable in that State shall be enforced in another Contracting State when, on the application of any interested party, it has been declared enforceable there.

However, in the United Kingdom, such a judgment shall be enforced in England and Wales, in Scotland, or in Northern Ireland when, on the application of any interested party, it has been registered for enforcement in that part of the United Kingdom.

Article 32

1. The application shall be submitted:

   – in Belgium, to the *tribunal de première instance* or *rechtbank van eerste aanleg*,

   – in Denmark, to the *byret*,

   – in the Federal Republic of Germany, to the presiding judge of a chamber of the *Landgericht*,

   – in Greece, to the *Μονομελές Πρωτοδικείο'*

   – in Spain, to the *Juzgado de Primera Instancia*,

   – in France, to the presiding judge of the *tribunal de grande instance*,

   – in Ireland, to the High Court,

   – in Iceland, to the *héraðsdómari*,

   – in Italy, to the *corte d'appello*,

   – in Luxembourg, to the presiding judge of the *tribunal d'arrondissement*,

   – in the Netherlands, to the presiding judge of the *arrondissementsrechtbank*,

   – in Norway, to the *herredsrett* or *byrett as namsrett*,

   – in Austria, to the *Landesgericht* or the *Kreisgericht*,

   – in Portugal, to the *Tribunal Judicial de Círculo*,

   – in Switzerland:

      (a) in respect of judgments ordering the payment of a sum of money, to the *juge de la mainlevée/Rechtsöffnungsrichter/giudice competente a pronunciare sul rigetto dell'opposizione*, within the framework of the procedure governed by Articles 80 and 81 of the *loi fédérale sur la poursuite pour dettes et la faillite/Bundesgesetz über Schuldbetreibung und Konkurs/legge federale sulla esecuzione e sul fallimento*;

      (b) in respect of judgments ordering a performance other than the payment of a sum of money, to the *juge cantonal d'exequatur compétent/zuständiger kantonaler Vollstreckungsrichter/giudice cantonale competente a pronunciare l'exequatur*,

- in Finland, to the *ulosotonhaltija/överexekutor*,

- in Sweden, to the *Svea hovrätt*,

- in the United Kingdom:

   (a) in England and Wales, to the High Court of Justice, or in the case of a maintenance judgment to the Magistrates' Court on transmission by the Secretary of State;

   (b) in Scotland, to the Court of Session, or in the case of a maintenance judgment to the Sheriff Court on transmission by the Secretary of State;

   (b) in Northern Ireland, to the High Court of Justice, or in the case of a maintenance judgment to the Magistrates' Court on transmission by the Secretary of State.

2. The jurisdiction of local courts shall be determined by reference to the place of domicile of the party against whom enforcement is sought. If he is not domiciled in the State in which enforcement is sought, it shall be determined by reference to the place of enforcement.

Article 33

The procedure for making the application shall be governed by the law of the State in which enforcement is sought.

The applicant must give an address for service of process within the area of jurisdiction of the court applied to. However, if the law of the State in which enforcement is sought does not provide for the furnishing of such an address, the applicant shall appoint a representative *ad litem*.

The documents referred to in Articles 46 and 47 shall be attached to the application.

Article 34

The court applied to shall give its decision without delay; the party against whom enforcement is sought shall not at this stage of the proceedings be entitled to make any submissions on the application.

The application may be refused only for one of the reasons specified in Articles 27 and 28. Under no circumstances may the foreign judgment be reviewed as to its substance.

Article 35

The appropriate officer of the court shall without delay bring the decision given on the application to the notice of the applicant in accordance with the procedure laid down by the law of the State in which enforcement is sought.

Article 36

If enforcement is authorized, the party against whom enforcement is sought may appeal against the decision within one month of service thereof.

If that party is domiciled in a Contracting State other than that in which the decision authorizing enforcement was given, the time for appealing shall be two months and shall run from the date of service, either on him in person or at his residence. No extension of time may be granted on account of distance.

JURISDICTION OF COURTS AND ENFORCEMENT OF JUDGMENTS ACT, 1998

Article 37

1. An appeal against the decision authorizing enforcement shall be lodged in accordance with the rules governing procedure in contentious matters:

   - in Belgium, with the *tribunal de première instance* or *rechtsbank van eerste aanleg,*

   - in Denmark, with the *landsret,*

   - in the Federal Republic of Germany, with the *Oberlandesgericht,*

   - in Greece, with the *Εφετείο,*

   - in Spain, with the *Audiencia Provincial,*

   - in France, with the cour *d'appel,*

   - in Ireland, with the High Court,

   - in Iceland, with the *héraðsdómari,*

   - in Italy, with the *corte d'appello,*

   - in Luxembourg, with the *Cour supérieure de justice* sitting as a court of civil appeal,

   - in the Netherlands, with the *arrondissementsrechtsbank,*

   - in Norway, with the *lagmannsrett,*

   - in Austria, with the *Landesgericht* or the *Kreisgericht,*

   - in Portugal, with the *Tribunal da Relação,*

   - in Switzerland, with the *tribunal cantonal/Kantonsgericht/tribunale cantonale,*

   - in Finland, with the *hovioikeus/hovrätt,*

   - in Sweden, with the *Svea hovrätt,*

   - in the United Kingdom:

     (a) in England and Wales, with the High Court of Justice, or in the case of a maintenance judgment with the Magistrates' Court;

     (b) in Scotland, with the Court of Session, or in the case of a maintenance judgment with the Sheriff Court;

     (c) in Northern Ireland, with the High Court of Justice, or in the case of a maintenance judgment with the Magistrates' Court.

2. The judgment given on the appeal may be contested only:

   - in Belgium, Greece, Spain, France, Italy, Luxembourg and in the Netherlands, by an appeal in cassation,

   - in Denmark, by an appeal to the *højesteret,* with the leave of the Minister of Justice,

   - in the Federal Republic of Germany, by a *Rechtsbeschwerde,*

   - in Ireland, by an appeal on a point of law to the Supreme Court,

   - in Iceland, by an appeal to the *Hæstiréttur,*

   - in Norway, by an appeal (*kjæremål* or *anke*) to the *Hoyesteretts Kjæremålsutvalg* or *Hoyesterett,*

   - in Austria, in the case of an appeal, by *a Revisionsrekurs* and, in the case of opposition proceedings, by *a Berufung* with the possibility of a Revision,

   - in Portugal, by an appeal on a point of law,

- in Switzerland, by a *recours de droit public devant le tribunal fédéral/staatsrechtliche Beschwerde beim Bundesgericht/ricorso di diritto pubblico davanti al tribunale federale*,

- in Finland, by an appeal to the *korkein oikeus/högsta domstolen*,

- in Sweden, by an appeal to the *Högsta domstolen*,

- in the United Kingdom, by a single further appeal on a point of law.

Article 38

The court with which the appeal under Article 37 (1) is lodged may, on the application of the appellant, stay the proceedings if an ordinary appeal has been lodged against the judgment in the State of origin or if the time for such an appeal has not yet expired; in the latter case, the court may specify the time within which such an appeal is to be lodged.

Where the judgment was given in Ireland or the United Kingdom, any form of appeal available in the State of origin shall be treated as an ordinary appeal for the purposes of the first paragraph.

The court may also make enforcement conditional on the provision of such security as it shall determine.

Article 39

During the time specified for an appeal pursuant to Article 36 and until any such appeal has been determined, no measures of enforcement may be taken other than protective measures taken against the property of the party against whom enforcement is sought.

The decision authorizing enforcement shall carry with it the power to proceed to any such protective measures.

Article 40

1. If the application for enforcement is refused, the applicant may appeal:

    - in Belgium, to the *cour d'appel* or *hof van beroep*,

    - in Denmark, to the *landsret*,

    - in the Federal Republic of Germany, to the *Oberlandesgericht*,

    - in Greece, to the *Εφετείο*,

    - in Spain, to the *Audiencia Provincial*,

    - in France, to the *cour d'appel*,

    - in Ireland, to the High Court,

    - in Iceland, to the *héraðsdómari*,

    - in Italy, to the *corte d'appello*,

    - in Luxembourg, to the *Cour supérieure de justice* sitting as a court of civil appeal,

    - in the Netherlands, to the *gerechtshof*,

    - in Norway, to the *lagmannsrett*,

    - in Austria, to the *Landesgericht* or the *Kreisgericht*,

    - in Portugal, to the *Tribunal da Relação*,

    - in Switzerland, to the *tribunal cantonal/Kantonsgericht/tribunale cantonale*,

- in Finland, to the *hovioikeus/hovrätt*,

- in Sweden, to the *Svea hovrätt*,

- in the United Kingdom:

  (a) in England and Wales, to the High Court of Justice, or in the case of a maintenance judgment to the Magistrates' Court;

  (b) in Scotland, to the Court of Session, or in the case of a maintenance judgment to the Sheriff Court;

  (c) in Northern Ireland, to the High Court of Justice, or in the case of a maintenance judgment to the Magistrates' Court.

2. The party against whom enforcement is sought shall be summoned to appear before the appellate court. If he fails to appear, the provisions of the second and third paragraphs of Article 20 shall apply even where he is not domiciled in any of the Contracting States.

Article 41

A judgment given on an appeal provided for in Article 40 may be contested only:

- in Belgium, Greece, Spain, France, Italy, Luxembourg and in the Netherlands, by an appeal in cassation,

- in Denmark, by an appeal, to the *højesteret*, with the leave of the Minister of Justice,

- in the Federal Republic of Germany, by *a Rechtsbeschwerde*,

- in Ireland, by an appeal on a point of law to the Supreme Court,

- in Iceland, by an appeal to the *Hæstiréttur*,

- in Norway, by an appeal (*kjæremål* or *anke*) to the *Hoyesteretts kjæremålsutvalg* or *Hoyesterett*,

- in Austria, by *a Revisionsrekurs*,

- in Portugal, by an appeal on a point of law,

- in Switzerland, by a *recours de droit public devant le tribunal fédéral/staatsrechtliche Beschwerde beim Bundesgericht/ricorso di diritto pubblico davanti al tribunale federale*,

- in Finland, by an appeal to the *korkein oikeus/högsta domstolen*,

- in Sweden, by an appeal to the *Högsta domstolen*,

- in the United Kingdom, by a single further appeal on a point of law.

Article 42

Where a foreign judgment has been given in respect of several matters and enforcement cannot be authorized for all of them, the court shall authorize enforcement for one or more of them.

An applicant may request partial enforcement of a judgment.

Article 43

A foreign judgment which orders a periodic payment by way of a penalty shall be enforceable in the State in which enforcement is sought only if the amount of the payment has been finally determined by the courts of the State of origin.

Article 44

An applicant who, in the State of origin, has benefited from complete or partial legal aid or exemption from costs or expenses, shall be entitled, in the procedures provided for in Articles 32 to 35, to benefit from the most favourable legal aid or the most extensive exemption from costs or expenses provided for by the law of the State addressed.

However, an applicant who requests the enforcement of a decision given by an administrative authority in Denmark or in Iceland in respect of a maintenance order may, in the State addressed, claim the benefits referred to in the first paragraph if he presents a statement from, respectively, the Danish Ministry of Justice or the Icelandic Ministry of Justice to the effect that he fulfils the economic requirements to qualify for the grant of complete or partial legal aid or exemption from costs or expenses.

Article 45

No security, bond or deposit, however described, shall be required of a party who in one Contracting State applies for enforcement of a judgment given in another Contracting State on the ground that he is a foreign national or that he is not domiciled or resident in the State in which enforcement is sought.

SECTION 3. COMMON PROVISIONS

Article 46

A party seeking recognition or applying for enforcement of a judgment shall produce:

1. a copy of the judgment which satisfies the conditions necessary to establish its authenticity;

2. in the case of a judgment given in default, the original or a certified true copy of the document which establishes that the party in default was served with the document instituting the proceedings or with an equivalent document.

Article 47

A party applying for enforcement shall also produce:

1. documents which establish that, according to the law of the State of origin, the judgment is enforceable and has been served;

2. where appropriate, a document showing that the applicant is in receipt of legal aid in the State of origin.

Article 48

If the documents specified in Articles 46 (2) and 47 (2) are not produced, the court may specify a time for their production, accept equivalent documents or, if it considers that it has sufficient information before it, dispense with their production.

If the court so requires, a translation of the documents shall be produced; the translation shall be certified by a person qualified to do so in one of the Contracting States.

Article 49

No legalization or other similar formality shall be required in respect of the documents referred to in Articles 46 or 47 or the second paragraph of Article 48, or in respect of a document appointing a representative *ad litem*.

TITLE IV. AUTHENTIC INSTRUMENTS AND COURT SETTLEMENTS

Article 50

A document which has been formally drawn up or registered as an authentic instrument and is enforceable in one Contracting State shall, in another Contracting State, be declared enforceable there, on application made in accordance with the procedures provided for in Article 31 *et seq.* The application may be refused only if enforcement of the instrument is contrary to public policy in the State addressed.

The instrument produced must satisfy the conditions necessary to establish its authenticity in the State of origin.

The provisions of Section 3 of Title III shall apply as appropriate.

Article 51

A settlement which has been approved by a court in the course of proceedings and is enforceable in the State in which it was concluded shall be enforceable in the State addressed under the same conditions as authentic instruments.

TITLE V. GENERAL PROVISIONS

Article 52

In order to determine whether a party is domiciled in the Contracting State whose courts are seised of a matter, the Court shall apply its internal law.

If a party is not domiciled in the State whose courts are seised of the matter, then, in order to determine whether the party is domiciled in another Contracting State, the court shall apply the law of that State.

Article 53

For the purposes of this Convention, the seat of a company or other legal person or association of natural or legal persons shall be treated as its domicile. However, in order to determine the seat, the court shall apply its rules of private international law.

In order to determine whether a trust is domiciled in the Contracting State whose courts are seised of the matter, the court shall apply its rules of private international law.

TITLE VI. TRANSITIONAL PROVISIONS

Article 54

The provisions of this Convention shall apply only to legal proceedings instituted and to documents formally drawn up or registered as authentic instruments after its entry into force in the State of origin and, where recognition or enforcement of a judgment or authentic instrument is sought, in the State addressed.

However, judgments given after the date of entry into force of this Convention between the State of origin and the State addressed in proceedings instituted before that date shall be recognized and enforced in accordance with the provisions of Title III if jurisdiction was founded upon rules which accorded with those provided for either in Title II of this

Convention or in a convention concluded between the State of origin and the State addressed which was in force when the proceedings were instituted.

If the parties to a dispute concerning a contract had agreed in writing before the entry into force of this Convention that the contract was to be governed by the law of Ireland or of a part of the United Kingdom, the courts of Ireland or of that part of the United Kingdom shall retain the right to exercise jurisdiction in the dispute.

Article 54a

For a period of three years from the entry into force of this Convention for Denmark, Greece, Ireland, Iceland, Norway, Finland and Sweden, respectively, jurisdiction in maritime matters shall be determined in these States not only in accordance with the provisions of Title II, but also in accordance with the provisions of paragraphs 1 to 7 following. However, upon the entry into force of the International Convention relating to the arrest of sea-going ships, signed at Brussels on 10 May 1952, for one of these States, these provisions shall cease to have effect for that State.

1. A person who is domiciled in a Contracting State may be sued in the courts of one of the States mentioned above in respect of a maritime claim if the ship to which the claim relates or any other ship owned by him has been arrested by judicial process within the territory of the latter State to secure the claim, or could have been so arrested there but bail or other security has been given, and either:

    (a) the claimant is domiciled in the latter State; or

    (b) the claim arose in the latter State; or

    (c) the claim concerns the voyage during which the arrest was made or could have been made; or

    (d) the claim arises out of a collision or out of damage caused by a ship to another ship or to goods or persons on board either ship, either by the execution or non-execution of a manoeuvre or by the non-observance of regulations; or

    (e) the claim is for salvage; or

    (f) the claim is in respect of a mortgage or hypothecation of the ship arrested.

2. A claimant may arrest either the particular ship to which the maritime claim relates, or any other ship which is owned by the person who was, at the time when the maritime claim arose, the owner of the particular ship. However, only the particular ship to which the maritime claim relates may be arrested in respect of the maritime claims set out under 5. (o), (p) or (q) of this Article.

3. Ships shall be deemed to be in the same ownership when all the shares therein are owned by the same person or persons.

4. When in the case of a charter by demise of a ship the charterer alone is liable in respect of a maritime claim relating to that ship, the claimant may arrest that ship or any other ship owned by the charterer, but no other ship owned by the owner may be arrested in respect of such claim. The same shall apply to any case in which a person other than the owner of a ship is liable in respect of a maritime claim relating to that ship.

5. The expression 'maritime claim' means a claim arising out of one or more of the following:

    (a) damage caused by any ship either in collision or otherwise;

    (b) loss of life or personal injury caused by any ship or occurring in connection with the operation on any ship;

    (c) salvage;

(d) agreement relating to the use or hire of any ship whether by charterparty or otherwise;

(e) agreement relating to the carriage of goods in any ship whether by charterparty or otherwise;

(f) loss of or damage to goods including baggage carried in any ship;

(g) general average;

(h) bottomry;

(i) towage;

(j) pilotage;

(k) goods or materials wherever supplied to a ship for her operation or maintenance;

(l) construction, repair or equipment of any ship or dock charges and dues;

(m) wages of masters, officers or crew;

(n) master's disbursements, including disbursements made by shippers, charterers or agents on behalf of a ship or her owner;

(o) dispute as to the title to or ownership of any ship;

(p) disputes between co-owners of any ship as to the ownership, possession, employment or earnings of that ship;

(q) the mortgage or hypothecation of any ship.

6. In Denmark, the expression 'arrest' shall be deemed as regards the maritime claims referred to under 5. (o) and (p) of this Article, to include a *'forbud'*, where that is the only procedure allowed in respect of such a claim under Articles 646 to 653 of the law on civil procedure (*lov om rettens pleje*).

7. In Iceland, the expression 'arrest' shall be deemed, as regards the maritime claims referred to under 5. (o) and (p) of this Article, to include a *'lögbann'*, where that is the only procedure allowed in respect of such a claim under Chapter III of the law on arrest and injunction (*lög um kyrrsetningu og lögbann*).

RELATIONSHIP TO THE BRUSSELS CONVENTION AND TO OTHER CONVENTIONS

Article 54b

1. This Convention shall not prejudice the application by the Member States of the European Communities of the Convention on Jurisdiction and the Enforcement of Judgments in Civil and Commercial Matters, signed at Brussels on 27 September 1968 and of the Protocol on interpretation of that Convention by the Court of Justice, signed at Luxembourg on 3 June 1971, as amended by the Conventions of Accession to the said Convention and the said Protocol by the States acceding to the European Communities, all of these Conventions and the Protocol being hereinafter referred to as the 'Brussels Convention'.

2. However, this Convention shall in any event be applied:

(a) in matters of jurisdiction, where the defendant is domiciled in the territory of a Contracting State which is not a member of the European Communities, or where Article 16 or 17 of this Convention confer a jurisdiction on the courts of such a Contracting State;

(b) in relation to a *lis pendens* or to related actions as provided for in Articles 21 and 22, when proceedings are instituted in a Contracting State which is not a member of

303

the European Communities and in a Contracting State which is a member of the European Communities;

(c) in matters of recognition and enforcement, where either the State of origin or the State addressed is not a member of the European Communities.

3. In addition to the grounds provided for in Title III recognition or enforcement may be refused if the ground of jurisdiction on which the judgment has been based differs from that resulting from this Convention and recognition or enforcement is sought against a party who is domiciled in a Contracting State which is not a member of the European Communities, unless the judgment may otherwise be recognized or enforced under any rule of law in the State addressed.

Article 55

Subject to the provisions of Articles 54 (2) and 56, this Convention shall, for the States which are parties to it, supersede the following conventions concluded between two or more of them:

- the Convention between the Swiss Confederation and France on jurisdiction and enforcement of judgments in civil matters, signed at Paris on 15 June 1869,

- the Treaty between the Swiss Confederation and Spain on the mutual enforcement of judgments in civil or commercial matters, signed at Madrid on 19 November 1896,

- the Convention between the Swiss Confederation and the German Reich on the recognition and enforcement of judgments and arbitration awards, signed at Berne on 2 November 1929,

- the Convention between Denmark, Finland, Iceland, Norway and Sweden on the recognition and enforcement of judgments, signed at Copenhagen on 16 March 1932,

- the Convention between the Swiss Confederation and Italy on the recognition and enforcement of judgments, signed at Rome on 3 January 1933,

- the Convention between Sweden and the Swiss Confederation on the recognition and enforcement of judgments and arbitral awards signed at Stockholm on 15 January 1936,

- the Convention between the Kingdom of Belgium and Austria on the reciprocal recognition and enforcement of judgments and authentic instruments relating to maintenance obligations, signed at Vienna on 25 October 1957,

- the Convention between the Swiss Confederation and Belgium on the recognition and enforcement of judgments and arbitration awards, signed at Berne on 29 April 1959,

- the Convention between the Federal Republic of Germany and Austria on the reciprocal recognition and enforcement of judgments, settlements and authentic instruments in civil and commercial matters, signed at Vienna on 6 June 1959,

- the Convention between the Kingdom of Belgium and Austria on the reciprocal recognition and enforcement of judgments, arbitral awards and authentic instruments in civil and commercial matters, signed at Vienna on 16 June 1959,

- the Convention between Austria and the Swiss Confederation on the recognition and enforcement of judgments, signed at Berne on 16 December 1960,

- the Convention between Norway and the United Kingdom providing for the reciprocal recognition and enforcement of judgments in civil matters, signed at London on 12 June 1961,

- the Convention between the United Kingdom and Austria providing for the reciprocal recognition and enforcement of judgments in civil and commercial matters, signed at Vienna on 14 July 1961, with amending Protocol signed at London on 6 March 1970,

- the Convention between the Kingdom of the Netherlands and Austria on the reciprocal recognition and enforcement of judgments and authentic instruments in civil and commercial matters, signed at The Hague on 6 February 1963,

- the Convention between France and Austria on the recognition and enforcement of judgments and authentic instruments in civil and commercial matters, signed at Vienna on 15 July 1966,

- the Convention between Luxembourg and Austria on the recognition and enforcement of judgments and authentic instruments in civil and commercial matters, signed at Luxembourg on 29 July 1971,

- the Convention between Italy and Austria on the recognition and enforcement of judgments in civil and commercial matters, of judicial settlements and of authentic instruments, signed at Rome on 16 November 1971,

- the Convention between Norway and the Federal Republic of Germany on the recognition and enforcement of judgments and enforceable documents, in civil and commercial matters, signed at Oslo on 17 June 1977,

- the Convention between Denmark, Finland, Iceland, Norway and Sweden on the recognition and enforcement of judgments in civil matters, signed at Copenhagen on 11 October 1977,

- the Convention between Austria and Sweden on the recognition and enforcement of judgments in civil matters, signed at Stockholm on 16 September 1982,

- the Convention between Austria and Spain on the recognition and enforcement of judgments, settlements and enforceable authentic instruments in civil and commercial matters, signed at Vienna on 17 February 1984,

- the Convention between Norway and Austria on the recognition and enforcement of judgments in civil matters, signed at Vienna on 21 May 1984, and

- the Convention between Finland and Austria on the recognition and enforcement of judgments in civil matters, signed at Vienna on 17 November 1986.

Article 56

The Treaty and the conventions referred to in Article 55 shall continue to have effect in relation to matters to which this Convention does not apply.

They shall continue to have effect in respect of judgments given and documents formally drawn up or registered as authentic instruments before the entry into force of this Convention.

Article 57

1. This Convention shall not affect any conventions to which the Contracting States are or will be parties and which in relation to particular matters, govern jurisdiction or the recognition or enforcement of judgments.

2. This Convention shall not prevent a court of a Contracting State which is party to a convention referred to in the first paragraph from assuming jurisdiction in accordance with that convention, even where the defendant is domiciled in a Contracting State which is not a party to that convention. The court hearing the action shall, in any event, apply Article 20 of this Convention.

3. Judgments given in a Contracting State by a court in the exercise of jurisdiction provided for in a convention referred to in the first paragraph shall be recognized and enforced in the other Contracting States in accordance with Title III of this Convention.

4. In addition to the grounds provided for in Title III, recognition or enforcement may be refused if the State addressed is not a contracting party to a convention referred to in the first paragraph and the person against whom recognition or enforcement is sought is domiciled in that State, unless the judgment may otherwise be recognized or enforced under any rule of law in the State addressed.

5. Where a convention referred to in the first paragraph to which both the State of origin and the State addressed are parties lays down conditions for the recognition or enforcement of judgments, those conditions shall apply. In any event, the provisions of this Convention which concern the procedures for recognition and enforcement of judgments may be applied.

Article 58

[None]

Article 59

This Convention shall not prevent a Contracting State from assuming, in a convention on the recognition and enforcement of judgments, an obligation towards a third State not to recognize judgments given in other Contracting States against defendants domiciled or habitually resident in the third State where, in cases provided for in Article 4, the judgment could only be founded on a ground of jurisdiction specified in the second paragraph of Article 3.

However, a Contracting State may not assume an obligation towards a third State not to recognize a judgment given in another Contracting State by a court basing its jurisdiction on the presence within that State of property belonging to the defendant, or the seizure by the plaintiff of property situated there:

1. if the action is brought to assert or declare proprietary or possessory rights in that property, seeks to obtain authority to dispose of it, or arises from another issue relating to such property, or

2. if the property constitutes the security for a debt which is the subject-matter of the action.

TITLE VIII. FINAL PROVISIONS

Article 60

The following may be parties to this Convention:

  (a) States which, at the time of the opening of this Convention for signature, are members of the European Communities or of the European Free Trade Association;

  (b) States which, after the opening of this Convention for signature, become members of the European Communities or of the European Free Trade Association;

  (c) States invited to accede in accordance with Article 62 (1) (b).

Article 61

1. This Convention shall be opened for signature by the States members of the European Communities or of the European Free Trade Association.

2. The Convention shall be submitted for ratification by the signatory States. The instruments of ratification shall be deposited with the Swiss Federal Council.

3. The Convention shall enter into force on the first day of the third month following the date on which two States, of which one is a member of the European Communities and the other a member of the European Free Trade Association, deposit their instruments of ratification.

4. The Convention shall take effect in relation to any other signatory State on the first day of the third month following the deposit of its instrument of ratification.

Article 62

1. After entering into force this Convention shall be open to accession by:

   (a) the States referred to in Article 60 (b);

   (b) other States which have been invited to accede upon a request made by one of the Contracting States to the depository State. The depository State shall invite the State concerned to accede only if, after having communicated the contents of the communications that this State intends to make in accordance with Article 63, it has obtained the unanimous agreement of the signatory States and the Contracting States referred to in Article 60 (a) and (b).

2. If an acceding State wishes to furnish details for the purposes of Protocol 1, negotiations shall be entered into to that end. A negotiating conference shall be convened by the Swiss Federal Council.

3. In respect of an acceding State, the Convention shall take effect on the first day of the third month following the deposit of its instrument of accession.

4. However, in respect of an acceding State referred to in paragraph 1 (a) or (b), the Convention shall take effect only in relations between the acceding State and the Contracting States which have not made any objections to the accession before the first day of the third month following the deposit of the instrument of accession.

Article 63

Each acceding State shall, when depositing its instrument of accession, communicate the information required for the application of Articles 3, 32, 37, 40, 41 and 55 of this Convention and furnish, if needs be, the details prescribed during the negotiations for the purposes of Protocol 1.

Article 64

1. This Convention is concluded for an initial period of five years from the date of its entry into force in accordance with Article 61 (3), even in the case of States which ratify it or accede to it after that date.

2. At the end of the initial five-year period, the Convention shall be automatically renewed from year to year.

3. Upon the expiry of the initial five-year period, any contracting State may, at any time, denounce the Convention by sending a notification to the Swiss Federal Council.

4. The denunciation shall take effect at the end of the calendar year following the expiry of a period of six months from the date of receipt by the Swiss Federal Council of the notification of denunciation.

Article 65

The following are annexed to this Convention:

–   a Protocol 1, on certain questions of jurisdiction, procedure and enforcement,

–   a Protocol 2, on the uniform interpretation of the Convention,

–   a Protocol 3, on the application of Article 57.

These Protocols shall form an integral part of the Convention.

Article 66

Any Contracting State may request the revision of this Convention. To that end, the Swiss Federal Council shall issue invitations to a revision conference within a period of six months from the date of the request for revision.

Article 67

The Swiss Federal Council shall notify the States represented at the Diplomatic Conference of Lugano and the States who have later acceded to the Convention of:

(a) the deposit of each instrument of ratification or accession;

(b) the dates of entry into force of this Convention in respect of the Contracting States;

(c) any denunciation received pursuant to Article 64;

(d) any declaration received pursuant to Article Ia of Protocol 1;

(e) any declaration received pursuant to Article Ib of Protocol 1;

(f) any declaration received pursuant to Article IV of Protocol 1;

(g) any communication made pursuant to Article VI of Protocol 1.

Article 68

This Convention, drawn up in a single original in the Danish, Dutch, English, Finnish, French, German, Greek, Icelandic, Irish, Italian, Norwegian, Portuguese, Spanish and Swedish languages, all fourteen texts being equally authentic, shall be deposited in the archives of the Swiss Federal Council. The Swiss Federal Council shall transmit a certified copy to the Government of each State represented at the Diplomatic Conference of Lugano and to the Government of each acceding State.

]*Signatures of Plenipotentiaries of the fourteen Contracting States.*]

NINTH SCHEDULE

Domicile

PART 1

1. An individual is domiciled in the State, or in a state other than a Contracting State if, but only if, he is ordinarily resident in the State or in that other state.

2. An individual is domiciled in a place in the State if, but only if, he is domiciled in the State and is ordinarily resident or carries on any profession, business or occupation in that place.

PART III

1. A corporation or association has its seat in the State if, but only if—

    (a) it was incorporated or formed under the law of the State, or

    (b) its central management and control is exercised in the State.

2. A corporation or association has its seat in a particular place in the State if, but only if, it has its seat in the State and—

    (a) it has its registered office or some other official address at that place, or

    (b) its central management and control is exercised in that place or it is carrying on business in that place.

3. Subject to *paragraph 4* of this Part, a corporation or association has its seat in a state other than the State if, but only if—

    (a) it was incorporated or formed under the law of that state, or

    (b) its central management and control is exercised in that state.

4. A corporation or association shall not be regarded as having its seat in a Contracting State other than the State if—

    (a) it has its seat in the State by virtue of *paragraph 1 (a)* of this Part, or

    (b) it is shown that the courts of that other state would not regard it for the purposes of Article 16.2 as having its seat there.

5. In this Part—

    'association' means an unincorporated body of persons;

    'business' includes any activity carried on by a corporation or association;

    'corporation' means a body corporate;

    'official address' means, in relation to a corporation or association, an address which it is required by law to register, notify or maintain for the purpose of receiving notices or other communications.

PART V

A trust is domiciled in the State if, but only if, the law of the State is the system of law with which the trust has its closest and most real connection.

CONTRACTUAL OBLIGATIONS (APPLICABLE LAW) ACT 1991

Number 8 of 1991

ARRANGEMENT OF SECTIONS

Section
1. Definitions.
2. Conventions to have force of law.
3. Interpretation of Conventions.
4. Short title and commencement.

CONTRACTUAL OBLIGATIONS (APPLICABLE LAW) ACT 1991

FIRST SCHEDULE

The text in the English language of the 1980 Convention

AN ACT TO GIVE THE FORCE OF LAW TO THE CONVENTION ON THE LAW APPLIC-
ABLE TO CONTRACTUAL OBLIGATIONS SIGNED AT ROME ON BEHALF OF THE
STATE ON THE 19th DAY OF JUNE, 1980, AND THE CONVENTION ON THE ACCES-
SION OF THE HELLENIC REPUBLIC TO THE AFORESAID CONVENTION SIGNED AT
LUXEMBOURG ON THE 10th DAY OF APRIL, 1984, AND TO PROVIDE FOR CON-
NECTED MATTERS.

[*8th May* 1991]

BE IT ENACTED BY THE OIREACHTAS AS FOLLOWS:

1. Definitions

In this Act—

'the 1980 Convention' means the Convention on the law applicable to contractual
obligations signed at Rome on behalf of the State on the 19th day of June, 1980;

'the 1984 Accession Convention' means the Convention on the accession of the
Hellenic Republic to the 1980 Convention signed at Luxembourg on the 10th day
of April, 1984;

'the Conventions' means the 1980 Convention and the 1984 Accession Convention;

'the European Communities' has the same meaning as in section 1 of the European
Communities Act, 1972;

'the European Court' means the Court of Justice of the European Communities;

'the Minister' means the Minister for Justice.

2. Conventions to have force of law

(1) Subject to *subsection (2)* of this section, the Conventions shall have the force of law in
the State and judicial notice shall be taken of them.

(2) Article 7 (1) of the 1980 Convention shall not have the force of law in the State.

(3) For convenience of reference there are set out in the *First, Second, Third* and *Fourth
Schedules*, respectively, to this Act—

   (a) the text in the English language of the 1980 Convention,

   (b) the text in the English language of the 1984 Accession Convention,

   (c) the text in the Irish language of the 1980 Convention, and

   (d) the text in the Irish language of the 1984 Accession Convention.

3. Interpretation of Conventions

(1) Judicial notice shall be taken of—

   (a) any ruling or decision of, or expression of opinion by, the European Court on any
        question as to the meaning or effect of any provision of the Conventions, and

   (b) the report referred to in *subsection (2)* of this section.

(2) The report by Professor Mario Giuliano and Professor Paul Lagarde on the 1980
Convention (which is reproduced in the Official Journal of the European Commu-
nities) may be considered by any court when interpreting any provision of that
Convention and shall be given such weight as is appropriate in the circumstances.

CONTRACTUAL OBLIGATIONS (APPLICABLE LAW) ACT 1991

4. Short title and commencement

(1) This Act may be cited as the Contractual Obligations (Applicable Law) Act, 1991.

(2) (a) This Act, other than *section 2* in so far as it relates to the 1984 Accession Convention, shall come into operation on such day or days as the Minister shall fix by order or orders either generally or with reference to any particular purpose or provision and different days may be so fixed for different purposes and for different provisions.

(b) *Section 2* of this Act shall, in so far as it relates to the 1984 Accession Convention, come into operation on such day or days as the Minister shall fix by order or orders either generally or with reference to any particular purpose or provision and different days may be so fixed for different purposes and different provisions and any day so fixed may be the same day as a day fixed under *paragraph (a)* of this subsection or a different day.

Section 2

FIRST SCHEDULE

THE TEXT IN THE ENGLISH LANGUAGE OF THE 1980 CONVENTION
CONVENTION ON THE LAW APPLICABLE TO CONTRACTUAL OBLIGATIONS

PREAMBLE

THE HIGH CONTRACTING PARTIES to the Treaty establishing the European Economic Community, anxious to continue in the field of private international law the work of unification of law which has already been done within the Community, in particular in the field of jurisdiction and enforcement of judgments,

WISHING to establish uniform rules concerning the law applicable to contractual obligations,

HAVE AGREED AS FOLLOWS:

TITLE I. SCOPE OF THE CONVENTION

Article 1. Scope of the Convention

1. The rules of this Convention shall apply to contractual obligations in any situation involving a choice between the laws of different countries.

2. They shall not apply to:

   (a) questions involving the status or legal capacity of natural persons, without prejudice to Article 11;

   (b) contractual obligations relating to:

   – wills and succession,

   – rights in property arising out of a matrimonial relationship,

   – rights and duties arising out of a family relationship, parentage, marriage or affinity, including maintenance obligations in respect of children who are not legitimate;

   (c) obligations arising under bills of exchange, cheques and promissory notes and other negotiable instruments to the extent that the obligations under such other negotiable instruments arise out of their negotiable character;

(d) arbitration agreements and agreements on the choice of court;

(e) questions governed by the law of companies and other bodies corporate or unincorporate such as the creation, by registration or otherwise, legal capacity, internal organization or winding up of companies and other bodies corporate or unincorporate and the personal liability of officers and members as such for the obligations of the company or body;

(f) the question whether an agent is able to bind a principal, or an organ to bind a company or body corporate or unincorporate, to a third party;

(g) the constitution of trusts and the relationship between settlors, trustees and beneficiaries;

(h) evidence and procedure, without prejudice to Article 14.

3. The rules of this Convention do not apply to contracts of insurance which cover risks situated in the territories of the Member States of the European Economic Community. In order to determine whether a risk is situated in these territories the court shall apply its internal law.

4. The preceding paragraph does not apply to contracts of reinsurance.

Article 2. Application of law of non-contracting States

Any law specified by this Convention shall be applied whether or not it is the law of a Contracting State.

TITLE II. UNIFORM RULES

Article 3. Freedom of choice

1. A contract shall be governed by the law chosen by the parties. The choice must be expressed or demonstrated with reasonable certainty by the terms of the contract or the circumstances of the case. By their choice the parties can select the law applicable to the whole or a part only of the contract.

2. The parties may at any time agree to subject the contract to a law other than that which previously governed it, whether as a result of an earlier choice under this Article or of other provisions of this Convention. Any variation by the parties of the law to be applied made after the conclusion of the contract shall not prejudice its formal validity under Article 9 or adversely affect the rights of third parties.

3. The fact that the parties have chosen a foreign law, whether or not accompanied by the choice of a foreign tribunal, shall not, where all the other elements relevant to the situation at the time of the choice are connected with one country only, prejudice the application of rules of the law of that country which cannot be derogated from by contract, hereinafter called 'mandatory rules'.

4. The existence and validity of the consent of the parties as to the choice of the applicable law shall be determined in accordance with the provisions of Articles 8, 9 and 11.

Article 4. Applicable law in the absence of choice

1. To the extent that the law applicable to the contract has not been chosen in accordance with Article 3, the contract shall be governed by the law of the country with which it is most closely connected. Nevertheless, a severable part of the contract which has a closer connection with another country may by way of exception be governed by the law of that other country.

2. Subject to the provisions of paragraph 5 of this Article, it shall be presumed that the contract is most closely connected with the country where the party who is to effect the performance which is characteristic of the contract has, at the time of conclusion of the contract, his habitual residence, or, in the case of a body corporate or unincorporate, its central administration. However, if the contract is entered into in the course of that party's trade or profession, that country shall be the country in which the principal place of business is situated or, where under the terms of the contract the performance is to be effected through a place of business other than the principal place of business, the country in which that other place of business is situated.

3. Notwithstanding the provisions of paragraph 2 of this Article, to the extent that the subject matter of the contract is a right in immovable property or a right to use immovable property it shall be presumed that the contract is most closely connected with the country where the immovable property is situated.

4. A contract for the carriage of goods shall not be subject to the presumption in paragraph 2. In such a contract if the country in which, at the time the contract is concluded, the carrier has his principal place of business is also the country in which the place of loading or the place of discharge or the principal place of business of the consignor is situated, it shall be presumed that the contract is most closely connected with that country. In applying this paragraph single voyage charter-parties and other contracts the main purpose of which is the carriage of goods shall be treated as contracts for the carriage of goods.

5. Paragraph 2 shall not apply if the characteristic performance cannot be determined, and the presumptions in paragraphs 2, 3, and 4 shall be disregarded if it appears from the circumstances as a whole that the contract is more closely connected with another country.

Article 5. Certain consumer contracts

1. This Article applies to a contract the object of which is the supply of goods or services to a person ('the consumer') for a purpose which can be regarded as being outside his trade or profession, or a contract for the provision of credit for that object.

2. Notwithstanding the provisions of Article 3, a choice of law made by the parties shall not have the result of depriving the consumer of the protection afforded to him by the mandatory rules of the law of the country in which he has his habitual residence:

   – if in that country the conclusion of the contract was preceded by a specific invitation addressed to him or by advertising, and he had taken in that country all the steps necessary on his part for the conclusion of the contract, or

   – if the other party or his agent received the consumer's order in that country, or

   – if the contract is for the sale of goods and the consumer travelled from that country to another country and there gave his order, provided that the consumer's journey was arranged by the seller for the purpose of inducing the consumer to buy.

3. Notwithstanding the provisions of Article 4, a contract to which this Article applies shall, in the absence of choice in accordance with Article 3, be governed by the law of the country in which the consumer has his habitual residence if it is entered into in the circumstances described in paragraph 2 of this Article.

4. This Article shall not apply to:

   (a) a contract of carriage;

   (b) a contract for the supply of services where the services are to be supplied to the consumer exclusively in a country other than that in which he has his habitual residence.

5. Notwithstanding the provisions of paragraph 4, this Article shall apply to a contract which, for an inclusive price, provides for a combination of travel and accommodation.

Article 6. Individual employment contracts

1. Notwithstanding the provisions of Article 3, in a contract of employment a choice of law made by the parties shall not have the result of depriving the employee of the protection afforded to him by the mandatory rules of the law which would be applicable under paragraph 2 in the absence of choice.

2. Notwithstanding the provisions of Article 4, a contract of employment shall, in the absence of choice in accordance with Article 3, be governed:

   (a) by the law of the country in which the employee habitually carries out his work in performance of the contract, even if he is temporarily employed in another country; or

   (b) if the employee does not habitually carry out his work in any one country, by the law of the country in which the place of business through which he was engaged is situated;

   unless it appears from the circumstances as a whole that the contract is more closely connected with another country, in which case the contract shall be governed by the law of that country.

Article 7. Mandatory rules

1. When applying under this Convention the law of a country, effect may be given to the mandatory rules of the law of another country with which the situation has a close connection, if and in so far as, under the law of the latter country, those rules must be applied whatever the law applicable to the contract. In considering whether to give effect to these mandatory rules, regard shall be had to their nature and purpose and to the consequences of their application or non-application.

2. Nothing in this Convention shall restrict the application of the rules of the law of the forum in a situation where they are mandatory irrespective of the law otherwise applicable to the contract.

Article 8. Material validity

1. The existence and validity of a contract, or of any term of a contract, shall be determined by the law which would govern it under this Convention if the contract or term were valid.

2. Nevertheless a party may rely upon the law of the country in which he has his habitual residence to establish that he did not consent if it appears from the circumstances that it would not be reasonable to determine the effect of his conduct in accordance with the law specified in the preceding paragraph.

Article 9. Formal validity

1. A contract concluded between persons who are in the same country is formally valid if it satisfies the formal requirements of the law which governs it under this Convention or of the law of the country where it is concluded.

2. A contract concluded between persons who are in different countries is formally valid if it satisfies the formal requirements of the law of one of those countries.

3. Where a contract is concluded by an agent, the country in which the agent acts is the relevant country for the purposes of paragraphs 1 and 2.

4. An act intended to have legal effect relating to an existing or contemplated contract is formally valid if it satisfies the formal requirements of the law which under this Convention governs or would govern the contract or of the law of the country where the act was done.

5. The provisions of the preceding paragraphs shall not apply to a contract to which Article 5 applies, concluded in the circumstances described in paragraph 2 of Article 5. The formal validity of such a contract is governed by the law of the country in which the consumer has his habitual residence.

6. Notwithstanding paragraphs 1 to 4 of this Article, a contract the subject matter of which is a right in immovable property or a right to use immovable property shall be subject to the mandatory requirements of form of the law of the country where the property is situated if by that law those requirements are imposed irrespective of the country where the contract is concluded and irrespective of the law governing the contract.

Article 10. Scope of the applicable law

1. The laws applicable to a contract by virtue of Articles 3 to 6 and 12 of this Convention shall govern in particular:

   (a) interpretation;

   (b) performance;

   (c) within the limits of the powers conferred on the court by its procedural law, the consequences of breach, including the assessment of damages in so far as it is governed by rules of law;

   (d) the various ways of extinguishing obligations, and prescription and limitation of actions;

   (e) the consequences of nullity of the contract.

2. In relation to the manner of performance and the steps to be taken in the event of defective performance regard shall be had to the law of the country in which performance takes place.

Article 11. Incapacity

In a contract concluded between persons who are in the same country, a natural person who would have capacity under the law of that country may invoke his incapacity resulting from another law only if the other party to the contract was aware of this incapacity at the time of the conclusion of the contract or was not aware thereof as a result of negligence.

Article 12. Voluntary assignment

1. The mutual obligations of assignor and assignee under a voluntary assignment of a right against another person ('the debtor') shall be governed by the law which under this Convention applies to the contract between the assignor and assignee.

2. The law governing the right to which the assignment relates shall determine its assignability, the relationship between the assignee and the debtor, the conditions under which the assignment can be invoked against the debtor and any question whether the debtor's obligations have been discharged.

Article 13. Subrogation

1. Where a person ('the creditor') has a contractual claim upon another ('the debtor'), and a third person has a duty to satisfy the creditor, or has in fact satisfied the creditor in discharge of that duty, the law which governs the third person's duty to satisfy the creditor shall determine whether the third person is entitled to exercise against the debtor the rights which the creditor had against the debtor under the law governing their relationship and, if so, whether he may do so in full or only to a limited extent.

2. The same rule applies where several persons are subject to the same contractual claim and one of them has satisfied the creditor.

Article 14. Burden of proof, etc.

1. The law governing the contract under this Convention applies to the extent that it contains, in the law of contract, rules which raise presumptions of law or determine the burden of proof.

2. A contract or an act intended to have legal effect may be proved by any mode of proof recognized by the law of the forum or by any of the laws referred to in Article 9 under which that contract or act is formally valid, provided that such mode of proof can be administered by the forum.

Article 15. Exclusion of renvoi

The application of the law of any country specified by this Convention means the application of the rules of law in force in that country other than its rules of private international law.

Article 16. 'Ordre public'

The application of a rule of the law of any country specified by this Convention may be refused only if such application is manifestly incompatible with the public policy ('ordre public') of the forum.

Article 17. No retrospective effect

This Convention shall apply in a Contracting State to contracts made after the date on which this Convention has entered into force with respect to that State.

Article 18. Uniform interpretation

In the interpretation and application of the preceding uniform rules, regard shall be had to their international character and to the desirability of achieving uniformity in their interpretation and application.

Article 19. States with more than one legal system

1. Where a State comprises several territorial units each of which has its own rules of law in respect of contractual obligations, each territorial unit shall be considered as a country for the purposes of identifying the law applicable under this Convention.

2. A State within which different territorial units have their own rules of law in respect of contractual obligations shall not be bound to apply this Convention to conflicts solely between the laws of such units.

Article 20. Precedence of Community law

This Convention shall not affect the application of provisions which, in relation to particular matters, lay down choice of law rules relating to contractual obligations and which are or will be contained in acts of the institutions of the European Communities or in national laws harmonized in implementation of such acts.

Article 21. Relationship with other conventions

This Convention shall not prejudice the application of international conventions to which a Contracting State is, or becomes, a party.

Article 22. Reservations

1. Any Contracting State may, at the time of signature, ratification, acceptance or approval, reserve the right not to apply:

   (a) the provisions of Article 7 (1);

   (b) the provisions of Article 10 (1) (e).

2. Any Contracting State may also, when notifying an extension of the Convention in accordance with Article 27 (2), make one or more of these reservations, with its effect limited to all or some of the territories mentioned in the extension.

3. Any Contracting State may at any time withdraw a reservation which it has made; the reservation shall cease to have effect on the first day of the third calendar month after notification of the withdrawal.

TITLE III. FINAL PROVISIONS

Article 23

1. If, after the date on which this Convention has entered into force for a Contracting State, that State wishes to adopt any new choice of law rule in regard to any particular category of contract within the scope of this Convention, it shall communicate its intention to the other signatory States through the Secretary-General of the Council of the European Communities.

2. Any signatory State may, within six months from the date of the communication made to the Secretary-General, request him to arrange consultations between signatory States in order to reach agreement.

3. If no signatory State has requested consultations within this period or if within two years following the communication made to the Secretary-General no agreement is reached in the course of consultations, the Contracting State concerned may amend its law in the manner indicated. The measures taken by that State shall be brought to the knowledge of the other signatory States through the Secretary-General of the Council of the European Communities.

Article 24

1. If, after the date on which this Convention has entered into force with respect to a Contracting State, that State wishes to become a party to a multilateral convention whose principal aim or one of whose principal aims is to lay down rules of private international law concerning any of the matters governed by this Convention, the procedure set out in Article 23 shall apply. However, the period of two years, referred to in paragraph 3 of that Article, shall be reduced to one year.

2. The procedure referred to in the preceding paragraph need not be followed if a Contracting State or one of the European Communities is already a party to the multilateral convention, or if its object is to revise a convention to which the State concerned is already a party, or if it is a convention concluded within the framework of the Treaties establishing the European Communities.

Article 25

If a Contracting State considers that the unification achieved by this Convention is prejudiced by the conclusion of agreements not covered by Article 24 (1), that State may request the Secretary-General of the Council of the European Communities to arrange consultations between the signatory States of this Convention.

Article 26

Any Contracting State may request the revision of this Convention. In this event a revision conference shall be convened by the President of the Council of the European Communities.

Article 27

1. This Convention shall apply to the European territories of the Contracting States, including Greenland, and to the entire territory of the French Republic.

2. Notwithstanding paragraph 1:

    (a) this Convention shall not apply to the Faroe Islands, unless the Kingdom of Denmark makes a declaration to the contrary;

    (b) this Convention shall not apply to any European territory situated outside the United Kingdom for the international relations of which the United Kingdom is responsible, unless the United Kingdom makes a declaration to the contrary in respect of any such territory;

    (c) this Convention shall apply to the Netherlands Antilles, if the Kingdom of the Netherlands makes a declaration to that effect.

3. Such declarations may be made at any time by notifying the Secretary-General of the Council of the European Communities.

4. Proceedings brought in the United Kingdom on appeal from courts in one of the territories referred to in paragraph 2 (b) shall be deemed to be proceedings taking place in those courts.

Article 28

1. This Convention shall be open from 19 June 1980 for signature by the States party to the Treaty establishing the European Economic Community.

2. This Convention shall be subject to ratification, acceptance or approval by the signatory States. The instruments of ratification, acceptance or approval shall be deposited with the Secretary-General of the Council of the European Communities.

Article 29

1. This Convention shall enter into force on the first day of the third month following the deposit of the seventh instrument of ratification, acceptance or approval.

2. This Convention shall enter into force for each signatory State ratifying, accepting or approving at a later date on the first day of the third month following the deposit of its instrument of ratification, acceptance or approval.

Article 30

1. This Convention shall remain in force for 10 years from the date of its entry into force in accordance with Article 29 (1), even for States for which it enters into force at a later date.

2. If there has been no denunciation it shall be renewed tacitly every five years.

3. A Contracting State which wishes to denounce shall, not less than six months before the expiration of the period of 10 or five years, as the case may be, give notice to the Secretary-General of the Council of the European Communities. Denunciation may be limited to any territory to which the Convention has been extended by a declaration under Article 27 (2).

4. The denunciation shall have effect only in relation to the State which has notified it. The Convention will remain in force as between all other Contracting States.

Article 31

The Secretary-General of the Council of the European Communities shall notify the States party to the Treaty establishing the European Economic Community of:

(a) the signatures;

(b) the deposit of each instrument of ratification, acceptance or approval;

(c) the date of entry into force of this Convention;

(d) communications made in pursuance of Articles 23, 24, 25, 26, 27 and 30;

(e) the reservations and withdrawals of reservations referred to in Article 22.

Article 32

The Protocol annexed to this Convention shall form an integral part thereof.

Article 33

This Convention, drawn up in a single original in the Danish, Dutch, English, French, German, Irish and Italian languages, these texts being equally authentic, shall be deposited in the archives of the Secretariat of the Council of the European Communities. The Secretary-General shall transmit a certified copy thereof to the Government of each signatory State.

PROTOCOL

The High Contracting Parties have agreed upon the following provision which shall be annexed to the Convention:

Notwithstanding the provisions of the Convention, Denmark may retain the rules contained in Søloven (Statute on Maritime Law) paragraph 169 concerning the applicable law in matters relating to carriage of goods by sea and may revise these rules without following the procedure prescribed in Article 23 of the Convention.

INDEX

INDEX

INDEX

324

INDEX